Medieval Crime
and Social Control

NC

1

MEDIEVAL CULTURES

SERIES EDITORS
Rita Copeland
Barbara A. Hanawalt
David Wallace

*Sponsored by the Center for Medieval Studies
at the University of Minnesota*

Volumes in the series study the diversity of medieval cultural histories and practices, including such interrelated issues as gender, class, and social hierarchies; race and ethnicity; geographical relations; definitions of political space; discourses of authority and dissent; educational institutions; canonical and non-canonical literatures; and technologies of textual and visual literacies.

For other books in the series, see p. 260

Medieval Crime and Social Control

❖

Barbara A. Hanawalt and David Wallace, editors

Medieval Cultures
Volume 16

University of Minnesota Press

Minneapolis

London

The University of Minnesota Press gratefully acknowledges permission to reprint the following essays. Chapter 1 originally appeared as chapter 5 in "De grâce especial": Crime, état et société en France à la fin du Moyen Age, copyright 1991, Publications de la Sorbonne, Paris. Chapter 9 originally appeared as chapter 7 in "Of Good and Ill Repute": Gender and Social Control in Medieval England, copyright 1998, Oxford University Press.

Published by the University of Minnesota Press
111 Third Avenue South, Suite 290
Minneapolis, MN 55401-2520
http://www.upress.umn.edu

Library of Congress Cataloging-in-Publication Data
Medieval crime and social control / Barbara A. Hanawalt
   and David Wallace, editors.
      p.   cm. — (Medieval cultures ; v. 16)
   Includes index.
   ISBN 0-8166-3168-9 (hardcover : alk. paper). — ISBN
   0-8166-3169-7 (pbk. : alk. paper)
      1. Crime—Europe—History.   2. Social control—
   Europe—History.   3. Social history—Medieval,
   500–1500.   I. Hanawalt, Barbara.   II. Wallace, David,
   1937–   .   III. Series.
   HV6937.M43   1999
   364.94'09'02—dc21   98-29192

Printed in the United States of America on acid-free paper

The University of Minnesota is an equal-opportunity educator and employer.

10 09 08 07 06 05 04 03 02 01 00 99 98   10 9 8 7 6 5 4 3 2 1

Contents

⁘

Contents

Preface

✛

Bringing a volume to press requires the help of many people. Jeffrey Brunner and Amy Brown did the editorial work on the volume to put it into the required form for the University of Minnesota Press and to check footnote references. Jonathan Good did the final proofreading and index. Kathryn Reyerson was kind enough to bring her expert knowledge of French legal history to the project by checking the translation of Claude Gauvard's essay. The collection of essays grew out of a conference held by the Center for Medieval Studies at the University of Minnesota in 1995. Funding for the conference came from the College of Liberal Arts and the Frenzel Chair. The editors, Barbara Hanawalt and David Wallace, are grateful for the help they have received in making this volume possible. It is the authors, of course, who did the most work to make the volume a success.

✥

Introduction

Barbara A. Hanawalt and David Wallace

*C*rime, a term that enters Middle English from Old French, derives ultimately from the Latin *cernere* (to decide, discern, pass judgment). It is hence always bound up with matters of interpretation; such matters always subtend the most basic procedures for tracking down, trying, and punishing those who commit the basic felonies of larceny, burglary, robbery, arson, homicide, rape, and receiving of unknown felons. Medieval societies were continually redefining the actions that constituted these felonies; their legal definitions shifted markedly with variations of place and time. Many people took a role in formulating such definitions: officials administering the law, victims of criminous actions, and the accused all refined arguments for their self-interested positions. Victims demanded satisfaction, the accused sought exculpation, and the officers of social control sought to regulate things in such a way that their idea of good lordship or communal order in the emerging states could be maintained. Crime also encompassed behaviors that fell outside standard framings of felonious acts. Societies define deviance differently, proscribing certain sorts of behavior but tolerating others. In many medieval communities, for instance, levels of violent self-help in solving disputes far exceeded what we would consider desirable norms. And yet, at the same time, medieval society was gradually moving—through the repetitive definition, regulation, and punishment of behaviors considered antisocial—toward broader empowerment of the kind of state apparatus that suggests itself as normative, even indispensable, today.

If medieval communities were generally more accepting of personal vendetta, it is because it was a ready and often justifiable solution to perceived wrongs. Other recourses to justice could be too remote to guarantee satisfaction. Furthermore, the eye-for-eye, tooth-for-tooth principles could be reconciled with both biblical and Germanic law. Even when written law codes and the establishment of monarchies and feudal states meant that legal responsibility was in the hands of these authorities or of those to whom they delegated them, enforcement was sporadic. Set standards for social control officers varied from place to place, so that processes of arrest, trial, and punishment were as experimental and subject to change as were the very definitions of criminal behavior. Authorities competed. Lay, noble, and royal jurisdictions overlapped; towns had their own laws, courts, and gallows; and church courts intruded into a wide variety of cases. Individuals involved in the judicial systems sought to manipulate them for their own ends.

In the experimental defining of criminous acts and in evolving mechanisms for social control, numerous and heterogeneous forces in society interacted and competed. Since the literate men who were formulating laws and administering justice were reading and hearing imaginative literature as well as studying legal cases, literature and law were subject to strong, reciprocal influences. The jurist Philippe de Beaumanoire grew up in a household in which his father wrote romances; the legal pleader or *causidicus* Albertano da Brescia was keen to spread knowledge of rhetorical principles (and to dramatize rhetorical interchange through imaginary dialogues). Geoffrey Chaucer absorbed Albertano's account of Prudence and Melibee into his *Canterbury Tales* (and has his own fictions listed by a Man of Law); William Langland puts Lady Meed on trial at Westminster. References to law courts and legal practices permeated all levels of society. Thus, rape stories in literary fiction could influence the thinking of counts and kings in issuing pardons to convicted offenders or of judges in granting acquittals; and the forms of narration that a clever convicted criminal might adopt in telling his or her tale when seeking a pardon could borrow from the everyday culture of storytelling.

One outstanding development recorded by the essays gathered here is the role played by rape and homicide in provoking and defining increased powers for the state over retributions formerly assigned to the family and the victim. While societies gradually accepted, even demanded, that the state intervene in regulating violence and transgressions against people and property, violence against women and the taking of life had remained a family matter involving honor and negotiation. The replacement of the family by the state as agent of justice in matters of honor forms a landmark in the evolution of state power. Such a shift also speaks to the change in the types of rape or homicide that occurred, or were said to occur. During times of war in France, for example, accusations of murder and rape became increasingly politicized.

State regulation of violence, however, could give the parties yet another tool to play with as they sought revenge for crimes. One could pursue a case in court while also pursuing an alleged perpetrator by stealth or ambush. The law was viewed as a tool of vendetta and revenge, not necessarily as a final arbitrator, and societies and their law enforcement officials permitted a certain fluidity in settlements (so long as at least minimal appearances of maintenance of order could be sustained).

The first three essays in this book speak of the problems that medieval societies—in France, Iceland, and England—faced in defining crime and its relationship to politics, state formation, individual honor, and considerations of property and poverty. Claude Gauvard's essay begins the volume by addressing what seems to us an issue of pressing contemporary relevance: fear of crime. She notes that in late-fourteenth-century France crime was not a common topic for inclusion in chronicles, journals, and registers of communes. It was only in the later fifteenth century that crimes became a noteworthy topic to record. And when writers began to tell their audiences about crimes, all sorts of other issues became entwined with their narratives. The depredations of the civil war between the Burgundians and the Armagnacs, as well as those of the English in the renewed Hundred Years' War, had much to do with the combining of political crimes, theft, homicides, and rape. So common was this form of recital that it sounds like a litany: after an attack on a city the immediate results of the sack were murder, arson, looting, and rape of married women and young girls. For instance, when the Bourgeois de Paris chronicles the sack of Soissons in 1414, he provides accurate details of the person who led the assault; once the assault is over, however, he reverts to the usual stereotypical accusations. But fear of crime was no less powerful for being expressed in such formulaic terms. As Gauvard points out, modern sociologists have noted that in discourses about crime, real acts and established narratives become intertwined. So powerful was the stereotypical narrative in fifteenth-century France that it was employed by political theorists and jurists to attack a weak monarchy that would not or could not effect reform of the judicial system. Fear of crime finally did bring about judicial reform, including capital punishment for offenders who committed the stereotypical crimes.

In England, as Louise Fradenburg notes in chapter 2, the judicial system was already firmly in place. The English thoroughly enjoyed playing with a court system that allowed them their day in court; they were reputed to be the most litigious of Europeans. English writers, such as Langland in *Piers Plowman*, are to be seen worrying away at the subtle interrelationships connecting poverty, crime, and law. How, Fradenburg asks in her essay, "Needful Things," do distinctions between need and desire become established; how do formulations of the law uphold such a distinction? What happens when need slides into excess, when Need (in Langland's poem) yields to the figure of Rechelessnesse? How might the benefits and pleasures of charity protect themselves from the deceptions of "sturdy beggars"? And if a material object is needful, can it be acceptable to steal such an object? Crime goes beyond the acquiring or appropriating of that which is needful for elementary food and shelter by extending to acts that take forbidden objects that are passionately desired (but not strictly necessary). The connection between poverty and crime is not a necessary one, since those who offer charity may also be the thieves.

William Ian Miller, like Fradenburg in the later part of her essay, explicitly invites us in chapter 3 to consider medieval dilemmas in addressing our own behaviors. Miller considers the possibilities of employing violent revenge as a viable and acceptable means of dispute resolution. Turn-

ing to Old Icelandic texts, Miller reads the saga world against modern revenge films such as *Dirty Harry*. Saga revenge, he argues, formed part of
the public, personal, and moral order of society; failure to seek revenge
was a sign of shame and personal weakness. In our world, the taking of
revenge entails flouting the law and can appear to be "adolescent." The
Icelandic upper classes, encouraged by the church and reliant on their
own dominant position, learned to "walk away from violence," while
the lower classes could only rely on vengeance to be sure of "justice,"
that is, "honor and revenge." Miller shows how Icelandic saga heroes
manipulated the increasingly intrusive prominence of the state judicial
system to extract their own satisfactions. For instance, the practice of
outlawry—declaring the price of the wolf's head on the outlaw—permitted legal killing. And the delaying of revenge could lend a hero an appearance of forbearance while adding to the anxiety of the potential victim. This society presumed that if a gift created a debt, so too did a crime
create the need for vengeance. Not to respond to either situation with appropriate action was construed as a cause of shame for the hero who did
not act. For the modern "avenger film" hero, however, generalized anger
against societal enemies replaces a sense of personal shame; this renders
his character, his patterns of motivation and action, less compelling than
that of his saga counterpart.

The legal theorist who spoke most thoughtfully to both the continental
and the English models of government was the mid-fifteenth-century jurist, Sir John Fortescue. As chief justice of King's Bench to Henry VI and
then as chancellor-in-exile for Prince Edward (son of Henry VI) in France
and Flanders, Fortescue knew at first hand the practices of the English
and French judicial systems. As James Landman points out in chapter 4,
this pioneering scholar of comparative law had much to contemplate from
his experiences on both sides of the Channel. His condemnation of torture—a practice that, as Gauvard notes in her essay, was well established
in fifteenth-century France—suggests his preference for the jury system
of England, and yet Fortescue saw problems in the jury system. If the
jury were to act as a group of neighbors who have informed themselves
about a crime and have formed their opinions by the time they are to
render their verdicts before the judges, what is to keep these ordinary
laymen from being corrupted by bribes? Fortescue makes an early argument for property qualifications in selecting those who will serve as jurors (so that they will be more impartial, less susceptible to bribes). His
anxiety would not have troubled a fourteenth-century jurist, since it was
assumed that the jurors were as much witnesses as assessors of guilt and
innocence.

Fortescue seeks a new role for justice, but finds trouble with the form
and direction that justice should take. *Justitia* is a feminine noun; representations of Justice in the Middle Ages were always gendered female (the
same figure with sword and scales that we use today). What are the im-

plications of this female gendering of justice? Here Fortescue experiences a conflict. As chancellor, petitions would be addressed to him seeking equity judgments. Petitioners would tell tales of woe, stupidity, gullibility, and abuse, of broken hearts and broken contracts. As a genre of special pleading, such narratives are not unlike the pardon tales of the continent that Gauvard relates or those of Flanders and Burgundy analyzed by Walter Prevenier in chapter 8. Both types of narrative ask that the petitioned official (the chancellor in England, the duke in Burgundy, or the king in France) respond with equity rather than by applying the letter of the law. A "feminine" response is clearly required; Fortescue is plainly troubled by the addition of such gendered considerations to legal interpretation. Simple fact, to him, is feminine, but the analysis of a case (jurisprudence) is a masculine act, and yet, "the quality of mercy" is also to be seen (and acted out) as a feminine attribute.

As Landman points out, Fortescue's contemporary, Bishop Reginald Pecock, was struggling with similar problems of evidence and the layperson's ability to interpret it. Law may be a reasonable province for the laity, but what of Scripture: who should control the sacred text? Pecock, even while wishing to convince lay people that clergy should exercise such control, felt bound to insist upon the fallibility of all human reasonings. Since such human fallibilities necessarily extend to clerical interpretations of Scripture, Pecock found himself situated perilously close to Lollard positions. Judged heretical, Pecock was forced to see his written works burn or be burned himself.

Elizabeth Fowler, in chapter 5, "Chaucer's Hard Cases," continues such exploration of coercive hermeneutics by addressing a question of vexing urgency for late medieval commentators: what is the nature of *dominium*, or lordship? The issue of dominion caused consternation in the late Middle Ages because of the instability of major monarchies. England underwent the deposition of Richard II by Henry Bolingbroke (Henry IV); France suffered the interruption of monarchy by, first, a failure in direct succession and, second, the madness of its king. In such erratic times for rulers and subjects, anxieties and puzzles over the extent of kingly power and privilege became burning issues. Scholars have wondered why Chaucer avoided more direct confrontation with major political events such as the Peasants' Revolt of 1381, the attacks of nobles against the autocratic excesses of Richard II, or the victory of Henry IV. Fowler approaches Chaucer's relationship to structures of power by considering three kinds of jurisprudential issue: the topos of Eden (and the origins of sexual and political dominion), dominion by conquest (and its triumphal forms), and the role of consent in sovereignty (specifically, the admixture of political and sexual vows). Such issues are closely explored through a reading of the *Knight's Tale* that concentrates on Theseus as *dominus* by conquest (a role, Fowler suggests, inimical to the English political settlement) and on the problematic status of the conquered Amazon queen, Ypolita.

Fowler, Gauvard, and Landman are all concerned with the extent of the law's control, manipulation, and protection of women. Women, denied a role in the magisterial power of the state, occupy an ambiguous place as victims and as the accused. On the one hand, ecclesiastical and lay laws tend to regard women as dangerous temptresses; on the other, they tend to treat women on trial with more consideration than they do men. The ratio of women indicted for crimes has hardly changed in Europe over the centuries (one woman to eight men); the rate of actual conviction is even lower. But what might the legal rhetoric, court statistics, and literature mean to the historical women who were undergoing the rigors of late medieval law? And how might their experiences be accessed? Such issues are taken up by Louise Mirrer, Christopher Cannon, and Walter Prevenier.

In chapter 6, "The 'Unfaithful Wife' in Medieval Spanish Literature and Law," Louise Mirrer considers and challenges the ruthless attitude supposedly taken by Spanish law toward the adulterous wife (as portrayed in fictional and in popular historical accounts). Invariably, the adulterous wife, even if provoked to adultery by a husband who has never cohabited with her or has not himself been faithful, will be judged deserving of corporal punishment. But Mirrer detects in both the law and the literature a flexibility that is missing from the "official" position. Casebooks indicate that a man can forgive his wife and a wife can forgive her husband for unfaithfulness (while publicly acknowledging that the law requires more than simple acceptance of past spousal faults). She suggests that the literature may also be read, through its constitutive gaps and silences, as providing openings for forgiveness. Even the famous *La bella malmaridada* does not provide a conclusion to the confrontation of husband and suitor. And in Spanish equivalents of the fabliaux, a reader may discern strategies for feminine resistance when wifely deceptions come coupled with alternative explanations (the lump in the bed is a cat, not a man). The poor husband, still bothered that the cat is wearing trousers and boots, nonetheless lets his wife's explanation suffice.

While Mirrer suggests that women in medieval Spain were able to negotiate degrees of freedom from tightly circumscribed official positions, Christopher Cannon, in chapter 7, emphasizes that the voices of English women in legal forums prove very difficult to trace. English legal theory allowed women a voice only as married women; through their husbands, women who had clear title to property through inheritance and through the right of dower—the husband's grant of a third of his property for his widow's life use—could plead their case in court. Similarly, a woman could plead her husband's murder and her own rape. But the law, Cannon argues, offered a very limited range of expression for women's voices. Everything had to be recited through a legal formula according to which the woman's English speech was translated by scribes into Latin. Women's legal voices, therefore, were translated from oral and vernacular language to literate and learned discourse. Deviations from the required formula, such as an appeal of murder of a son rather than of a husband, silenced the woman's voice entirely. Considering the *Revelations* of Julian of Norwich and the *Book of Margery Kempe,* along with legal theory and court cases, Cannon suggests that women's narratives were told within highly restricted spaces; their "lived lives" were likewise circumscribed.

Walter Prevenier also takes up the issue of men's play with women's voices in chapter 8, "Violence against Women in Fifteenth-Century France and the Burgundian State." In examining the legal systems that evolved in the late medieval Netherlands and in Burgundy (now partly in France), Prevenier focuses on the ecclesiastical laws and state laws that outlined areas of vulnerability for women. Prostitution, seduction, abduction, and rape were all potential areas in which these laws were applied. The rape and abduction cases, at first reading, appear to be filled with different voices trying to dominate the narrative—those of the accused, the victim, and the legal authorities. Some cases even show that the parties changed their narratives within a short space of time. While there could be particular, idiosyncratic explanations for such narrative shifts, Prevenier finds that such changes often represented a move toward resolution of the case. Sometimes marriage brought about reconciliation between the victim and the accused. Sometimes shifting power relationships within the duchy of Burgundy exerted subtle but palpable influences on a particular case; negotiations within and between the powerful clans often secured pardons for the accused, satisfaction for the victim, and a general maintenance of social order.

Gender considerations also play a large role in the contributions of Barbara Hanawalt and William Perry Marvin. In chapter 9, "The Host, the Law, and the Ambiguous Space of Medieval London Taverns," Hanawalt describes the contested space of taverns in the Middle Ages. On the one hand, they were associated with women because women did most of the brewing and the space where ale and beer were sold was an extension of female, domestic space. On the other hand, all women associated with taverns had a bad reputation in literature and in law. Policing inns and taverns and the strangers who congregated there was a major concern for English and civic laws. The taverner became a peacekeeper with responsibilities to control his clientele and inform them of the city laws. But he was also responsible to his clients in that he had to protect them and their goods from harm. The role of taverner required a combination of a dominating character and an ability to keep an affable good order. The Host of the Tabard Inn in *The Canterbury Tales* proves to be a good example of the type of person needed for the position. But his confession of his own marital troubles with his wife indicates that he, too, succumbs to the ambiguities of the gendered space of the tavern; his wife dominates him within this disputed space.

In chapter 10, "Slaughter and Romance," Marvin carries the account of medieval crime and social control to issues of masculine identity and the violence of the hunt. Control over hunting was an issue first raised when William the Conqueror imposed royal forests on the land. The resentment of the population, fierce in every century, found memorable expression in the revolt of 1381. But it was the forest law of 1390 that, Marvin shows, divided those who could hunt from those who could not along lines of property ownership. In this respect, the law anticipated Fortescue's ideas about property qualification for jurors: gentlemen could hunt, but laborers could not. Marvin's account moves between the Yorkshire rebellion of the Beckwith gang and the romance of Sir Degrevant. In the Beckwith revolt against Duke John of Gaunt and his foresters, modes of killing animals, attacking officers, and stealing the manly symbols of the forester's office — bow, arrows, and hunting horn — form part of the meditated theatrics of revolt. When the noble masculine protagonists in the romance raid each other's hunting preserves, the narrative assumes that this is to be interpreted not as part of a criminal action, but as part of the "disport of gentlemen." In the romance feud, the rituals of the hunt are preserved in the laying out of the game rather than in vindictive slaughter. Furthermore, the romance extends the metaphor of the hunt into the winning of the opponent's daughter as a bride for the hero. Romance and revolt, therefore, articulate distinct identities, issuing from two distinct hunting communities, that the law of 1390 strove to establish: gentlemanly hunter and criminous poacher.

In formulating their accounts of medieval crime and social control, the authors of these essays drew upon combinations of legal treatises, statutes, court cases, court poems, romances, canonical texts, and comic tales. Earlier conferences at the University of Minnesota that have generated volumes for this Medieval Cultures series witnessed both genuine collaboration between historians and literary scholars and moments of methodological impasse (moments that provided ample scope for commentary in the volume published as *Bodies and Disciplines*). The "Medieval Crime" conference, however, came very much closer to achieving a common currency of discourse than did any of its predecessors. We like to think that this reflects both the progress such interdisciplinary conferences have made and the nature of the subject itself, for "medieval crime" and its attendant discourses of social control recognize no hard-and-fast distinctions between theory and practice, the "fictional" and the "real," the literary and the historical. Medieval crime must be recovered from its textual traces; texts require interpretation; interpretation demands recourse to jurisprudence, politics, and economics. It follows that on this topic, at least, interdisciplinary approaches must be regarded not as experimental, but as axiomatic.

CHAPTER 1

❖

Fear of Crime in
Late Medieval France

Claude Gauvard

The fear of crime permeated French society in the late Middle Ages.
The protracted disorder resulting from the Hundred Years' War, the
civil war between the Burgundians and the Armagnacs, and the
increased mobility of the population as a result of war, plague, and widen-
ing economic networks induced a perception that heinous crimes were
on the increase. The population believed that crimes such as murder, arson, rape, highway robbery, incest, and sodomy struck at the very heart
of society and threatened to tear apart the social fabric. The clergy saw
these stereotypical crimes as God's punishment for the sins of his people, but blamed the king for not doing more to protect his subjects. Humanists joined in the discussion of crime and urged judicial reform on
the king. The fear of crime, therefore, played a major role in the emergence
of the French state at the end of the Middle Ages. Pursuit and punishment of criminals became a mandate for the French monarch and, in
turn, strengthened the control of the monarchy over the countryside.

In late medieval judicial practice, solving a crime required the truth,
not so much for the sake of making a case that morally and intellectu-
ally satisfied the judges and the opposing party, but rather for finding a
guilty party whose arrest could atone for the offense committed against
society. The more heinous the crime, the more essential it was to find
the criminal and punish him. The nature of the crime, therefore, began
to determine the ordinary or extraordinary judicial procedures used. At
the end of the fourteenth century, Jean Bouteiller clarified the principles
for allowing the seriousness of the crime to determine treatment of the
offender: "Thus, you can and must know that there are several cases
that are not to receive forgiveness, such as murderers, arsonists, rapists,
highway robbers (whom the clerics call plunderers of the people [de-
praedatores populorum]), traitors, heretics, sodomites. Such ones as these
are not to receive pardon legally." Aleaume Cachemarée's itemization
of cases at Châtelet during the same period points to the same conclusion.[1] Justice, however, limited itself to experimentation, and it was not
before the ordinance of 1498 that two distinct procedures were defined.[2]
In practice, however, a hierarchy among the crimes was sketched out
that irreversibly dictated the type of proceedings by which the suspect
was tried, sentenced, and punished. Fear aroused by these stereotypical

1

accounts of heinous crimes increasingly led authorities to employ torture to find suspects and use capital punishment to allay public fears. By what criteria did they choose the crimes for which extraordinary proceedings were employed? What impact did the crimes singled out have on political and social life?

Crime and Reporting

Written documents in the late fourteenth and early fifteenth centuries demonstrated a certain uneasiness with regard to recounting crime: crime was not a common topic in chronicles, journals, and registers of the commune.[3] From this perspective, the perception of crime in this era seems different from what it became a century later. Indeed, Natalie Zemon Davis thinks that from the sixteenth century onward and maybe even as early as the middle of the fifteenth century, everyone could recount a crime story that they had heard.[4] Already at the beginning of the sixteenth century Philippe de Vigneulles's *Cent nouvelles nouvelles* stands out clearly as an example of this, as does the Burgundian equivalent of 1460. They begin with a description of a murder as a "marvelous adventure" (*merveilleuse aventure*).[5] After the *Cent nouvelles nouvelles*, the outrageous crimes make up an effective vulgarization of the crime narrative.[6] It is also possible that letters of remission, linked to the customs of confession, contributed to making these narratives commonplace.

To view the increasing importance of crimes as news items, we must consider the types of crime recounted, the connections that they had with current events, and the extent of information provided about them. The few criminal cases that J. P. Seguin cites for the reigns of Louis XII to Henri II can only be qualified with difficulty as crime reporting. While printed documents enjoyed spectacular distribution as early as the Italian wars, especially after 1529, their circulation owed more to their supernatural elements than to their descriptive and picturesque qualities. And therein is a reason for the historian to proceed with caution when analyzing them. It was said, for example, that a butcher found upon opening a cow's body an image of a monster that had the deformed head of a big man, with a large crown verging on white, and a body in the shape of a bull, almost like that of a pig.[7] The meaning of this case, which occurred during the Italian wars and the reign of François I, was not simply picturesque or sensational but, rather, reflected political imagery.[8] The depiction of other crimes reflected the same political concerns, whether they be the matter of the Swiss treason in 1524 or the judgment given in the governor of Touraine's criminal trial in 1526.[9] Just as in the Middle Ages, crime and sin were closely linked; they were connected to the most spectacular manifestations of life, whether natural phenomena, miracles, or visions. Earthquakes represented a punishment and warning from God, "the hand of God on his disobedient people" (*main de Dieu sur son peuple a luy desobeissant*).[10] Crime was only an epiphenomenon of a moral situation; its description contributed to the metaphysical understanding of the world.

The crimes reported in the Burgundian *Cent nouvelles nouvelles* (c. 1460) invite the same caution. These texts tell stories of adultery, abduction, and amorous adventures with servants. Their description and their outcome were supposed to strike the reader with their novelty, as in the story of the gentleman who surprises his sister in the romantic company of a shepherd and accepts their marriage, "because he was and had always been a very gracious, modern, and agreeable gentleman."[11] I will come back to the incongruity of this decision, but it was exactly in its unexpectedness that the appeal of the "nouvelle" resided; the term was understood in its literal sense to designate an event that goes against custom. Similarly, the husband forgives the adulterous wife caught in the act while the lover consents to pay twelve sheaves of grain for his offense—on the condition that he finish what he started![12] Was this not simply a means of ridiculing the pardon in matters of adultery that the church advocated, because in reality it conflicted with noble honor?[13] The tales contain no moral precepts to regulate behavior, as was true of moralizing literature of the beginning of the fifteenth century; instead, their light-hearted humor (*légèreté*) had the same social impact. The irony in these narratives' denouement underlined the importance of the laws that governed marriage. These are the same laws that the duke of Burgundy, to whom the collection was dedicated, pledged himself to support in his lands. The novelty resided clearly in the pirouette of the writer describing impossible solutions and searching, as Roger Dubuis has shown, to anchor his narrative in "the chance adventure" (*aventure occasionnelle*).[14] But, as far as the context goes, the painting of the social and moral order prevailed, and the laws of marriage emerged as strict as those depicted in a painting of Van Eyck.

The only threshold crossed in the second half of the fifteenth century was that of the vulgarization of crime narratives, which, presented in this derisory way, lost a part of their sinister content—already a sign of secularization. A further shift lay in an attraction to a modernity that had become common in writing: the author was looking for recent and especially novel crimes. The description of crime, like the content of historical events that chroniclers reported during the same period, followed the latest fashion, moving in the direction of that which was new, or "moderne."[15] But a deeper interpretation of these stories proves necessary. Even if they reveal an evolution of the perception of crime, which could be henceforth spoken of more freely, they still carry meaning borrowed largely from medieval moral traditions.

In order to determine how this vulgarization took effect I will consider the crimes reported by the *Chronique scandaleuse* between 1460 and 1475, approximately contemporary with the *Cent nouvelles nouvelles*, and compare them with the way in which its predecessors described crime in the first half of the fifteenth century.[16] The authors chosen, Nicolas de Baye, Clément de Fauquembergue, and the Bourgeois de Paris, all give a Parisian testimony in the vernacular, similar to Jean de Roye's accounts about the Châtelet. The testimony of such chroniclers as Enguerrand de Monstrelet, who were very involved in the pro-Burgundian party, has been put aside, even though their perspective on the information is in other respects interesting.

In each case, the crimes described are first and foremost of a sexual and political nature. Thefts are rarer than suicides. Murders virtually do not appear.[17] The crimes are told through a narrative filter. They are also distorted by the overlappings and the accumulations that associate different crimes (murders, thefts, and rapes) with the guilty party, with the result that no quantitative study can be done regarding the crimes inventoried in the chronicles.

Nevertheless, is it possible to see a chronological evolution in these crime narratives? A clear opposition appears between the narration of the two clerks of Parlement, Nicolas de Baye and Clément de Fauquembergue, and the narration of Jean de Roye, even though their authors could be considered professionally comparable. Baye and Fauquembergue were concerned first and foremost with the jurisdictions that should judge the guilty parties.[18] Jean de Roye, the notary of the Châtelet, preferred to describe the crime, with the places and the concrete circumstances narrated in order to integrate it into everyday life. He added to the story his eloquence and his expertise. The woman guilty of adultery is described without fail as "a beautiful young woman" (*une belle jeune femme*).[19] But the literary methods used are not limited to these considerations. Action verbs and the use of the active voice shape the movements of the criminal, thereby creating plausibility. The criminal "cuts the throat," "shares the booty," and "picks locks."[20] Crime was, in part, secularized because a narrative could translate it into an act. It should be said at the outset, however, that the crimes that were depicted were not commonplace. If Nicolas de Baye recounts as a jurist the scene of a "normal" murder during the ordinary unfolding of the crime in which insult precedes injury, Jean de Roye, on the contrary, does not choose just any crime story: a man kills his wife, a clergyman of the Temple in Paris murders "his brother and companion" (*frere et compaignon*).[21] The motives that were put forth, simple "quarrels" between the parties, only emphasized the incongruity and the enormity of the acts, which called into question the most sacred ties of the relationships between men. Jean de Roye does not relate just any sexual crime. The husband held up to ridicule is a "powerful" man; the "beautiful young woman" is from the social milieu of the Châtelet notaries.[22] The example was striking because it came from the upper echelons of society. Another case with the same kind of significance involved a young girl, already engaged, who was abducted by an archer who subsequently received royal authorization despite the complaint of the parents. Abduction and reneging on one's given word were thus validated in the service of the will of the prince and his servants. The example was exceptional, and any power of seduction that the crime might have vis-à-vis the reader was only of secondary importance in the end. All these elements contributed to marking the offense's significance, affirming the hierarchy of social and cultural values that the society recognized in itself or that the king imposed on it. It was not exactly a question of news items destined to provide the most complete information possible, but rather of supplying the kinds of examples whose function was to strike the imagination, or even better, to lead to a moral lesson. Jehannette Du Bois, after having disappeared from her household and having gone to "wherever she saw fit to go" (*ou bon lui sembla*), ended up returning to her husband, who, "well counseled by his closest friends, took her back, and she was well content and honest from that time forward with her said husband."[23] At the end of the fifteenth century, adultery had to end in forgiveness.[24] Crimes whose content was hard to believe did happen; it was society's role to draw the consequences from them.

A comparison between the Bourgeois de Paris and Jean de Roye allows us, nonetheless, to measure the distance covered over about fifty years in the formulation of the crime narratives. Like Jean de Roye, the Bourgeois de Paris was concerned with inserting crime into the everyday environment, and, from this perspective, the domestic rape scene that he sketches is particularly significant.[25] Narratives borrowed from letters of remission recount similar scenes.[26] One should not be fooled, however; the recourse of the Bourgeois de Paris to the concrete description was in the service of credibility destined to provoke everyone's conscience. The rape scene comes at the height of a torrent of interwoven crimes of both a political and a sexual nature.[27] The concrete description was not a starting point, but rather an end point, a last argument destined to deepen the truth and to make the depth of the disturbances known. In the Bourgeois de Paris's texts, the crime is part of a double narrative process whose elements are complementary; on the one hand, he uses a mechanical and stereotypic description of the criminal act; on the other hand, he uses the crime as a tool of propaganda. This is why it is so difficult to isolate a criminal act in these narratives. Thefts committed by thieves (*larrons*) could be those committed by the Armagnacs or by the "common," wild Parisian.[28] Rape was added to theft and to murder in order to better accuse the guilty party.

Despite an apparent similarity in the narrative, there is, however, a perceptible difference between the Bourgeois de Paris and Jean de Roye. At the end of the fifteenth century, stereotyped criminal descriptions had probably lost their impact. The description of the ravages caused by soldiers are convincing enough. Stereotypes are present in the *Chronique scandaleuse,* but the author rarely needs to turn to them. In 1472 the Burgundians were described specifically as "setting the fires in the wheat fields and in the villages, everywhere they passed."[29] The main theme of the narrative was concrete criminal action. In contrast, in the texts of the Bourgeois de Paris, it is impossible to grasp the crimes in any other way than through stereotyped formulas, whatever the time or the place. In 1410 armed men "pillaged, stole, and killed both inside and outside the church"; in 1419 they "killed, pillaged, set fire everywhere against women and men and in the fields and did worse things than the Saracens"; in 1423 they "killed, set fires, raped women and girls, and hanged men if they didn't pay the ransom they wanted."[30] These litanies were useful in describing the ravages of men-at-arms, and a few details borrowed from concrete descriptions enabled the author to render them plausible. A study of the content and the impact of such formulations, their possible affiliations and their persistence over the course of the fifteenth century, permits us to determine whether or not the Bourgeois de Paris was an isolated author in his use of stereotypes; it allows us to measure the degree of entrenchment of the fantasies about crime.

Stereotypes of Serious Crime

Stereotypes of serious crime were organized around simple components: the setting of fires, sacrilege committed in churches, rape, abduction, theft, and sometimes murder. These themes could be embellished, a point I will come back to, but throughout the whole period they were used to solidify the horror of crime.

Stereotypes were independent of a social and cultural milieu. The clerks of Parlement, Nicolas de Baye and Clément de Fauquembergue, both use such clichés to describe the ravages of soldiers.[31] The Bourgeois de Paris, who was probably a member of the chapter of Notre-Dame, uses them to evoke the Armagnacs' repeated crimes.[32] The narrative of the *Chronographia,* describing the pillaging of Courtrai that followed the battle of Roosebecque in 1382, modeled itself on the classic schema: "After all had been plundered, and the slaughter and rape of maidens and women had been completed by the French, they burned down the city along with most of the other rural towns of Flanders."[33] Finally, Jean Petit did not hesitate to return to these stereotypes when, in the justification that he delivered on behalf of the duke of Burgundy, he evoked the ravages of the soldiers who came "to pillage, to steal, to kidnap, to slay, to kill, and to take women by force."[34] Theologians and jurists alike manipulated the same language. Those who spoke from a humanist perspective also knew how to use these references, even if the litany lost some of its dryness in their style of writing. From the pen of the Religieux de Saint-Denis, it became biblical poetry: "The widow and the foreigner they slew, and they cut down the young, both man and maid, the nursing mother and the old gentleman."[35] In a letter to Jean Gerson, Nicolas de Clamanges describes for him the horrible crimes soldiers committed and the necessity of imposing moral discipline in order to reform the kingdom. These "criminals" "are of the sort who do not fear raiding the beds of matrons, scattering the feathers to the wind, not to mention their sacrileges, rapes, adulteries, secret violations of virgins, or their looting of monasteries, churches and shrines, or their blasphemies and unholy desecrations."[36] In 1405, in the *Vivat Rex*, Gerson gives the same version to designate the paralysis into which the country had fallen and of which the university took note: "Alas, what does she see upon examination? She sees turbulation everywhere, misfortune everywhere . . . the rape of young girls, the prostitution of wives, fires set at certain holy places, desecration of holy places, the assassination of many."[37] The humanists had no qualms about answering with interposed topoi.

The letters of remission took up this litany of crimes as well, whether they were granted in the langue d'oïl, the language spoken in the north of France, or the langue d'oc, the language of the south. In 1390 members of the king's council, sent as reformers to the Languedoc region, demanded that crimes that the inhabitants of Montagnac committed be curtailed.[38] The reformers drew their vocabulary for designating crime from a palette of reproachful words. They begin by listing them: "various crimes, abuses, and offenses resulting from fraud, malice, trickery, collusions, price fixing, deception, false oaths, conspiracy, solicitation, bribing witnesses, . . . corruption of the royal officers, . . . dishonest exchange, usurious contracts of time, of annuities, of food taxes in the said city, . . . monopolies and fraudulent alliances in the matter of these taxes and payment of counterfeit monies and other transgressions." These offenses correspond well to those which reflect bad city management, whether it be fiscal or political. But, finally, the list disassociates itself from real, even plausible charges, to conclude that "as elsewhere there was theft, plundering, adultery, the rape of young girls, and fornication." Recourse to this kind of reference served to demonstrate that political crimes were, in reality, capital crimes. It did not differentiate the officers from the soldiers, and it served to designate all as serious criminals, at least until the mid–fifteenth century. In 1448 this was still the litany of crimes in a list delivered to Robert de Flocques, at that time bailiff of Evreux, whose burdensome past the king forgives: "all murders, sacrilege, setting of fires, rape of women, pillage, robberies, kidnapping, and whatever other evils, crimes, abuses and offenses . . ."[39] These stereotypes of all the most serious crimes made up the common bases of theoretical and practical political thought of the fourteenth and fifteenth centuries.

In order to understand their power, it is necessary to analyze where authors inserted these obligatory descriptions into their narratives. The example of the sacking of Soissons on May 21, 1414, is significant. The Bourgeois de Paris begins his narrative with an extremely precise description; he focuses first on the character of Enguerran de Bournonville, then continues with the revolt against him, and finishes with the repression that followed the taking of the city.[40] In the conclusion, as if a pause from the depicted violence, the stereotype arrives: "and the women of religion and other wise women and good girls were raped and all the men and little children were kidnapped and the churches and relics and books and vestments were pillaged; and before ten days were over after the city was taken, it was so cleanly pillaged that there was nothing left to be taken away."[41] Enguerrand de Monstrelet used an identical method to describe the same event.[42] At a given moment in the narrative, the description of the facts slips into the litanies. The discourse on crime replaces reality such that the relationship between the real act and the narrative no longer has any importance. This process, specific to discourse on public safety, has been described by sociologists. As H. P. Jeudy has shown, the discourse became, through this transformation of the narrative, "a *de facto* identity."[43]

From this perspective, there is a certain similarity between the arguments in Parlement and the chronicle narratives. In Parlement the lawyers' speeches, constructed on simplified themes, break with the argument, which is teeming with concrete details. We have already noted this difference with regard to portraits drawn of the criminal; the same is true for the content of the crime.[44] What is more, the portrait of the criminal was mixed up with references to the crime. A 1404 trial opposed the king's prosecutor, who was appealing against the seneschal of Ponthieu, to the bishop of Amiens and to Jehannequin d'Avesnes. The king's prosecutor began by specifying a concrete crime: "Jehannequin assaulted Pierre François, prosecutor, representative of the king in Ponthieu." Then the speech slips into grievances that fall into the domain of general categories that define the criminal and the crime: Jehannequin killed a sergeant and abducted several women. What follows is the undifferentiated portrait of the great criminal just as other examples have defined him; he is "a murderer from the forest and a highwayman, quarreler, fighter, and rioter." To prove the legitimacy of his speech, the prosecutor adds, "of which the specific cases are in the reports of the accusation."[45] The definition of the crime, like that of the criminal, contains generalities whose content had very little to do with the reality of the case. The essential point was to insert the crime into the list of stereotypes of serious crime. References to concrete events played a minor role in authenticating the speech. This hiatus between the evidence and the arguments, between the event and the narrative, filled a need or function that is worth investigating.

The repetition of clichés relative to crime paradoxically filled an informative function, even if the content of this information had only a distant relationship with the real sequence of events. In recounting the famous case of the sacking of Soissons, Nicolas de Baye hints at the crimes committed, but he does so by conforming with trends in current opinion since he notes, "And numberless were the crimes there committed, as it is said."[46] His comment is an implicit reference to the commonplace descriptions, even if the clerk was still skeptical about the true facts.

These stereotypes also fed into political propaganda, leading us to speculate about their impact on public opinion. The Bourgeois de Paris shows how Parisian public opinion could be sensitized to such themes, particularly when they are spread as rumors. He probably gathered such themes himself before transcribing them, but he also indicates the crowd's reaction to them. Such was the case in May 1418 in Paris, which he describes as "falsely" governed by the Armagnacs. The rumor was spread that the Armagnacs would kill without mercy and would drown the wives and the children of those who did not support them.[47] This propaganda was not limited to Paris; it nurtured an official correspondence that fed the civil war. On October 3, 1411, a particularly tense moment of the war following Jean sans Peur's entry into the campaign, the king of France repudiated the dukes of Orléans, Bourbon, and others as rebels against him. The declaration has the solemnity appropriate to a political decision made at the council, but the letter's style is not solely theoretical. The action of the Armagnacs' mercenaries includes concrete charges; they "pillaged and ravaged, and continue to ravage, rob, and pillage our said kingdom and our good and loyal subjects; they took and continue to attempt to take our cities and fortresses and our vassals and subjects; they have killed, kidnapped, set fires, raped married women and others, raped girls to be married, robbed churches and monasteries, and still commit and attempt to commit the inhumanities that our enemies and enemies of our said kingdom can and could do."[48]

Charles VI uses these same stereotypes in a letter of October 14, 1411, addressed to the provost of Paris informing him that these same figures, to whom the duke of Berry is added, were attempting to "dismiss" (*debouter*) royal authority and "to destroy everything in their power" (*destruire du tout a leur povoir*). The stereotypical charges come after a speech of a slightly different tone centered on events directly concerning the provostship of Paris. The letter describes the occupation of Saint-Denis, "where there are several relics and holy bodies, our crown, our oriflamme, and many other precious and rich jewels."[49] One could surmise that such a sacrilege, added to the anguish caused by the taking of Saint-Cloud Bridge, would have been enough to stir a response.[50] But the scenario that this letter presents does not end here, although it would in itself have sufficed to justify the Armagnacs' desire to "make a new king in France" (*faire nouvel roi en France*). The author imposes onto the already stark political narrative the ravages of the Armagnacs' mercenaries: they "set fires, ransacked churches, kidnapped, killed, mutilated, raped married women and young girls and did all the evil anyone could do." The list of crimes rehearsed the letter of October 3 with only slight variations that adapted it to the public for which it was destined. The second version suggested police detections rather than politics. These two missives were widely circulated.[51] Moreover, the propaganda had the desired effect. Enguerrand de Monstrelet, who kept only a small part of the October 3, 1411, letter in his narrative, chose precisely to report the stereotypes of serious crime, abandoning the rest of the content, which, one could suppose, was politically original and innovative.[52] In the texts of the propagandists, the clichés of crime prevailed over the actual events. They constituted a slogan.

A similar example can be taken from the opposing camp. In May 1417 the Armagnacs, writing to the city of Reims to list their grievances against Jean sans Peur and to forbid any succor for him, drew up the list of misdeeds of the Burgundian companies in the kingdom, where they "have done and still continue to do each day all the evils that enemies can do, by taking castles and walled cities, by killing, raping married women and others, setting fires, seeking ransom from people, pillaging churches everywhere and in every country where they have been and where they are."[53] Both the Armagnacs and the Burgundians used the same theme indiscriminately. Surprisingly, in August 1412, the stereotypical depiction of the ravages resulting from civil war helped to reinforce a reconciliation between the two parties at the Peace of Auxerre. In 1422, after the death of Henry V of England, when it was feared that the city of Reims would pass into the hands of the dauphin's party, a letter from the royal chancery denounced "those who notoriously converted the sacrifice of peace into murders and homicides and other innumerable crimes."[54]

The use of serious-crime stereotypes in political propaganda reveals the strength of their entrenchment and appeal. With the Armagnacs back in power, when Charles VI prohibited them in writing from making a "new king in France" (*nouvel roi en France*), he was careful to restore the princes to favor, even to the point of rehabilitating them from the violent acts of which their soldiers were accused.[55] Honor, which Jean sans Peur held up to ridicule, demanded this kind of atonement. Serious crime could be manipulated, but its depiction called for a counterattack because its content endangered the honor of those it targeted, just as it was dangerous for community cohesion in the realm. Crime contrasted well with peace.

The mold of sharp repetitive angles in which information and propaganda was formed facilitated the encounter between historical fact and collective memory. Contemporary magistrates could be impugned with a reference to the coded stereotype. If Henri de Taperel lingered on in memory, it was because, as provost of Paris, he was in "many embarrassing predicaments" (*maint encombrement*) whose content was not at all political: "he took away from a young girl of noble lineage her virginity and an abundance of money."[56] The popularity of Jourdain de l'Isle drew partly from the same sources because the crimes that were attributed to him could conform to the usual litanies: "this Jourdain was known for violence against virgins, for robberies, for murders, and for rebellions against the king."[57] The system was still working well in 1435 when the *Petite chronique de Guyenne* reported the misdeeds of Rodrigue de Villandrando.[58]

As a general rule, the enumeration of these crimes accompanied the description of the death sentence reserved for the guilty. The common scenes of the crime were justification for a society that, for diverse reasons, had chosen to expel one of its members. Their political function united with their legal one; these were charges that would result inexorably in the death penalty. The connection between the death penalty and the stereotypes of serious crimes is evident in two domains that can be compared, that of political defamation and that of oral arguments in Parlement. The aim was identical: to demonstrate that the accused ought to be banned from the community. In the case of political defamation, the depiction of a capital crime sufficed as an argument to proceed to the adversary's destruction. For instance, the accusation of "terrible things" (*terribles choses*) drawn up against Robert Le Coq, the bishop of Laon, contained all his alleged means of slandering the king's officers and the king himself. Arguing for a change in dynasty, Robert Le Coq allegedly said "that the king was of very bad and rotten blood; that he was worth nothing; that he governed very poorly; that he was not worthy of being king; that he had no right to the kingdom; that he did not merit living; and that he had had his wife killed."[59] Burgundians and Armagnacs utilized the same procedure when they insinuated poisoning fomented by their adversary. Capital crime was the supreme argument in political defamation.

The denunciation was an extension of the one used between feuding neighbors. In January 1406, a trial opposed the Tourants and the Le Triches, neighbors between whom a deep hatred had developed. The Tourants were rich, with the result that Le Triche and his children "came often to eat and drink, take milk and cheese and other gifts from Tourant and his wife." These invitations were never returned, and the Tourants "talked about it" (*en parlerent*). In order to get back at them, the Le Triches made up a defamatory scenario: their daughter, Macée, was allegedly raped and abducted by the son of the Tourants with the knowledge and consent of his mother. The Le Triches told Macée "that she had to say and maintain that the mother (la Tourande) took her aside and had her violently raped and that the mother (la Tourande) took from their garden 350 ecus." An accusation of rape would have created an irreversible situation for the honor of the opposing party; theft was a secondary issue. On the other hand, the Le Triches had nothing to lose as far as honor was concerned because Macée was reputed to "do it for all men" (*faire pour les compaignons*). Because she refused to enter into the family scenario, she was condemned to an atrocious punishment whose sexual significance corresponded to the stakes of the rivalry between the two families. Her father and her brothers "undress her, tie her to a pillory and beat her and then make her sit in the coals of the hearth."[60]

The stereotypes of serious crime played a similar role even if unfounded in fact. Jean Petit did not hesitate to associate them with a vassal's lèse-majesté in allowing his soldiers to commit such crimes, requiring that the vassal "must be punished as a false and disloyal traitor to the said king and as a criminal of lèse-majesté to the kingdom."[61] Rape, the setting of fires, and abduction were definitive arguments against those one wished to exclude from society, justifying the death sentence.

Reading the confessions extorted from criminals before Parlement or the Châtelet, one sees that crimes are easily organized according to defined categories. Jourdain de l'Isle, for instance, was dragged to the gallows in Paris. While confessing to precise murders, he also categorized his crimes in general terms, admitting that his people murdered women and children, committed arson, and pillaged churches and monasteries.[62] Several Parisian chronicles reported his confession: at the moment of death, the last reflex of this war chief consisted of confessing to all crimes generally attributed to men-at-arms. By evoking the greatest number of accusations, he could hope to qualify for eternal forgiveness. Not all the confessions of men-at-arms were modeled on his; some stayed closer to real offenses, even when tortured.[63] The distance seems great between the reality of the crimes and the juridical categories in which the soldiers were placed. Whatever the facts, when the verdict was delivered, soldiers were executed according to these categories in a list read at execution.

Men-at-arms and their commanders were not alone in suffering from being tarred with this broad brush. Willemot Briart of the *bailliage* of Vermandois was accused before the Parlement in November 1407 of stereotypical sex crimes, among others. But these crimes only appeared in the final analysis. Originally, Willemot Briart was accused of several "murders or offenses" (*meurtres ou malefices*) by Bernard Dany, a man condemned to death and executed at Péronne. The accusation was a classic example of a condemned man naming accomplices at the foot of the gallows. The procedure led to the discovery of a long quarrel between two families that had been played out through successive rapes. Confronting Willemot, the opposing party "accused him of an old murder, the rape of a girl, and the beating of the mother of the said girl."[64] It is unclear what relation these charges had to the first accusation that the king's prosecutor made. Similarly, in the same *bailliage* in 1410, Jean Dausale, a cloth manufacturer of Reims, claimed that false accusations had been fabricated against him. They consisted of various offenses leading up to the one that surely led to conviction: he abducted and raped a young girl. It was immediately published that Dausale would be hanged, and the reaction of the crowd was swift: "On account of this a great crowd of people had gathered before the jail where the said Dausale was being detained."[65] Sex crimes

worked well as the most rigorous proof of guilt and were useful in justifying the death sentence.

A stereotypical account of crime was systematically used when the
guilty parties were tortured and when they claimed clerical status. It was
imperative that these criminals not escape the king's justice, so extraordinary proceedings were justified. The dossiers of several cases in the Parlement's criminal archives in the early fifteenth century reveal the power
accorded to criminal portraits, just as to the capital crimes. Grievances
centered on sexual behavior, on thefts or murders committed on the roads,
and, secondarily, on sacrilege committed in churches. The expression
"highwayman" (*espieur de chemins*) summed up the portrait. Recourse
to these general categories justified the extraordinary juridical procedure
and the death penalty. In 1402 Jacotin de Neauville became the victim
of a crazy, vengeful inquisition punctuated with inhuman torture, which
the provost of Saint-Riquier organized. The officers of Amiens's bailiff
apparently complied with the provost in trying to get Jacotin to repeat
the confessions in order to justify the torture and the death sentence. Jacotin's defenders argued that the rape of the girl, the robbing of pilgrims,
and the arson charges were "general terms" that had been extorted "by
the force of torture" (*par force de gehine*). The official response was simple: the description of the crimes corresponded to the portrait of the criminal, who was declared "a murderer, a thief, a rapist, and a highwayman,
and he confessed this."[66] The indictment made the criminal.

Cases in the Parlement also reflected the stereotypes, and they were
influential in formulating royal jurisdiction that was being defined at
this time.[67] In 1401, for instance, Jean Jouvenel collected in a speech for
the defense various grievances, among which he made distinctions such
as "infraction of guaranteed peace given in the king's court and fire set
in the king's jurisdiction and the raping of a woman."[68] In 1411 a letter
of commission similarly defined the offenses of which Robert de La Ma-
bilière and his accomplices were accused: "or on account of abduction,
rape, violation and defloration, transporting of arms and the detention
far away of Johanne de la Fleche." Inserting charges of sex offenses into an
ensemble of political ones such as broken safeguard, illegal transporting
of arms, and assault on a public road strengthened royal jurisdiction.[69]

The goal was not only to demonstrate the king's power, but also to
impose royal power over ecclesiastical jurisdictions that had claimed
authority over all sexual offenses. The king's officers did not fail to use
arguments of royal supremacy over all aspects of his subjects' sexual lives.
One criminal is described as "living a debauched life with a woman"
(*marié et gouliart*); another is "a public thief, married, dressed like a cleric"
(*larron public, marié, en habit de clerc*). The criminal for whom Jouvenel
launched his formula for sentencing was "accused of theft and of keeping the wife of the said Denis, against the will of the husband and everyone else,"[70] and he was seen "setting fire to a baby's cradle" (*bouter le*

feu en un barsel a enfant).[71] Significantly, the argument was addressed to
the cathedral chapter of Thérouanne which detained the guilty prisoner.
By the end of the fifteenth century the sergeants of the Châtelet of Paris
brought many prisoners in on sex offenses, because the king's justice
succeeded in extending its scope into private life and marriage laws.[72]

The royal jurisdiction's appropriation of all stereotypical crimes absolved the bailiff or the provost who too readily applied torture or gave an
order for a suspect's execution without taking into account clerical privileges. These stereotypes were used as a justification for the nascent state
to define and to extend the cases under royal jurisdiction. This conquest
not only took place horizontally in opposition to rival jurisdictions, but
also vertically, carving out a hierarchy of those crimes for which extraordinary proceedings proved to be necessary. This move is important,
because by referring to this kind of crime, the authorities mobilized public opinion. The decision to proceed in an extraordinary way and carry out
a death sentence could be presented to the public as a necessary measure, rather than a coercive one. The implication was that acceptance of
torture and the death sentence was difficult to impose on society in the
fourteenth and fifteenth centuries. Only by appealing to a common fear
of serious crime could the state form a consensus for its actions.

The Sensitivity of Public Opinion to Crime

That society shared an abhorrence to certain heinous crimes has been
demonstrated, but it is necessary to assess the scope of this public opinion and the extent to which it entered the general imagination. As we
have seen, the real crime was often relegated to a secondary rank in order
to free up its position in favor of a commonplace stereotype capable of
gaining a consensus between judges and the public alike. But even if a
theme was derived from propaganda, it had to resonate with the public.
How and by what channels did the fear of crime spread?

The stereotypes of serious crime have a long history whose first written manifestations go back to eleventh-century peace movements: the
peace of God and the truce of God. The sermon on the Peace of 1023 that
Warin, bishop of Beauvais, submitted to Robert le Pieux gives an idea of
the most feared crimes and the reasons they were defined as heinous and
blasphemous.[73] The bishop's list is more concrete than that of the four-
teenth- and fifteenth-century texts. The peasant worries about his livestock, while the merchant and the pilgrim fear travel on the road. The
vulnerability of houses awaiting fire, the horses and the mules in the field
with their young, the slowly growing vines that must not be uprooted,
and the mills whose earnings and price are recited all are sources of anxiety. As the peace movement spread, the themes became more abstract
and more dense.

The themes expressed in the early peace movement, paradoxically, did not reappear until the first French humanists, particularly Nicolas de Clamanges, wrote comparable texts illustrating infracted peace. Early commentators were influenced by canon law and Virgil, to whom Nicolas de Clamanges himself made reference in citing the *Georgics*. Thus, in his writings, *villanus* (villein) becomes *agricola* (farmer), *clericus* (cleric) becomes *vir ecclesiasticus* (churchman), and the ravages are portrayed in this way: "But is it lawful for thieves and robbers to steal indiscriminately gold, silver, clothing, goods, horses, cattle, asses, mules, and anything else they want, from farmers and merchants or churchmen if they happen to go forth from town or city? In fact, most soldiers have no wages other than the freedom to steal."[74]

From the eleventh century onward these considerations, which generally condemned the abduction of men as well as women, grew richer in deploring sexual violence to women. Raoul Glaber mixed the preservation of peace with obedience to the laws of marriage: "For who had ever before heard of so many cases of incest and adultery, so many forbidden inbreedings, so many affairs with concubines, so much rivalry in matters of wickedness?"[75] Peace was not only insured by the laying down of arms; it rested also on strict laws that must regulate the exchange of women. It was, indissoluably, both private and public.

It is impossible to measure the extent to which these themes circulated. They were probably a part of the prayers widely repeated as the parish became synonymous with community.[76] Their impact was stronger from the twelfth century onward when the truce of God became the "king's peace."[77] As early as 1114 Ivo of Chartres was speaking of the "pact of peace" whose scope of application had probably gone beyond the simple limits of the royal domain. In 1155 Louis VII made the barons and the prelates swear to a peace whose content, in defining violence on the highways, established premises for royal jurisdiction. But he retained the traditional themes of peace concerning protection of peasants and livestock.[78] During the same period, Abbot Suger of Saint-Denis similarly described the evils committed by Hugues du Puiset, and, in a purely clerical tradition, he associated them with forbidden relationships.[79]

Saint Louis's edicts (mid–thirteenth century) revived these descriptions of crimes while associating them closely with a condemnation of unrestrained behavior and the ravages of the private wars.[80] Philip IV le Bel and his successors issued edicts against private wars, which perpetuated the stereotypical vision of serious crimes committed by soldiers.[81] At the same time, canon law also used this theme. From the twelfth century the conciliar canons took up Ivo of Chartres's terms: "We order that priests, clerks, monks, pilgrims, merchants who are coming and going, as well as peasants with their work animals, seed, and sheep be always safe."[82]

Political practice and religious reflection, theoretical reflection and canon law—all used these commonplaces to denounce soldiers' disruption of the lives of the lay population. Such crimes were a sacrilege that made their perpetrators pillagers and scoundrels. From the eleventh century onward the social goal of such condemnations was to define and limit the field of warfare until it was reserved in the mid–fifteenth century for a handful of professionals whose ethic was, in theory, clearly set.[83] The principles of canon law joined with the political directives to guarantee peace in the kingdom and contributed to the formatting of stereotypes of serious crime. The notion of *nephandum* (the unspeakable) summarizes their scope and the disturbance they cause.[84]

Sensibilities over crime differed from one region to the next and over time. In langue d'oc during the Inquisition, homoscxuality was added to the sex crimes. Homosexuality was usually not mentioned as a capital crime in langue d'oïl, where rape and offenses against kinship laws were priorities. The edicts of Saint Louis were more concerned with prostitutes and gamblers than with sodomites. But the royal chancery, through edicts or letters of remission, adapted itself to the different circumstances and could identify heinous crimes in both the north and the south of the kingdom.[85] Theorists of humanist culture, perhaps influenced by Roman law, were also more sensitive than others to crimes against nature. The Religieux de Saint-Denis did not fail to report the accusation of homosexuality of which a royal officer in Languedoc, Jean de Betizac, was accused and which was closely tied to his political crimes.[86] Nicolas de Clamanges likewise linked capital crimes to sodomy, Babylon being the prime example.[87] Literary and biblical references supported the fear of crimes against nature, but on the whole, this kind of reference was extremely rare in the north. Homosexuality was not one of the commonplaces of confession extracted under torture, nor did lawyers use it to discredit an opponent. At the Châtelet, admission of homosexuality was rare, even rarer than confessions of bestiality and, for all the more reason, rape.[88] Rather than representing reality, these crimes reflected a different type of sexual fantasy.[89]

As the formulation of serious crime evolved over the course of the fourteenth century, rape was almost systematically implicated, indicating the legal importance of virginity and marriage laws. Murders committed against children were also more frequent, although they were completely absent in the earliest provisions of the peace of God. From the mid–fourteenth century onward child murder indicated the horror of a crime made more fearful when linked to the awful fantasy of roasting and eating innocent children. The criminal literally "devours" the crime, but he devours also the innocence and future of the society whose reproduction he compromises. The theme develops in the mid–fourteenth century, appearing in a report of the knight of the *Songe du vergier*, around 1375. Having described the "usual" crimes committed by the king of England and the Black Prince, "murder, abduction, sacrilege, by setting fires and by doing all other war acts," he adds, "and among the other inhumane things, it must not be forgotten how they roasted the children and several elderly persons."[90] The harmonious distribution by age, the leitmotiv of evil society, was thus compromised. At the beginning of the fifteenth century, the Armagnacs were accused of killing children and eating them, as was Rodrigue de Villandrando. The image was not only popular; it was also scholarly. Christine de Pizan and even Jean de Montreuil, who was an avid supporter of celibacy, inserted child murder into the bloody horror of the civil war.[91] The vital forces of society were affected.

What role did collective anxiety play in the composition of this topos? Tense from the long-lasting war, the Parisian crowd in 1448 began to make its anger heard while at the same time looking for a scapegoat. Beggars were forced under torture to admit to kidnapping children that they subsequently massacred.[92] Child murder became one of the most feared crimes, probably threatening the social fabric more clearly than homosexuality, whose implications were more clerical and scholarly than popular. Up until the French Revolution the theme of kidnapped and devoured children was one in a long series of collective fears that blended together fact and rumor.[93] Wolves were the final element linking fantasy to crime. Likened to the legendary ogre, wolves were feared for their sexual and aggressive natures. Their image spread from the learned humanists to the people, from Nicolas de Clamanges to the Bourgeois de Paris, who reported the ordinary people's fears.[94] Wolves eat men, women, and children without distinction. The flock is made up of the lambs of innocence. Justice has fled and society no longer has any point of reference. Crime slogans were not imposed from above by a judge or a constraining power; they fed off of the imagination of a terrified crowd.

This volatile mixture of fantasies about crime was grafted on to fantasies about uncontrollable social phenomena that heightened generalized anxiety. Stereotypes of serious crime were not limited to judicial argument or a chronicler's foil, but became generalized through the rumors that coalesced around unexplained crimes or unknown assassins. The legal process dealing with these cases was caught in an environment of collective psychosis. Starting with the reality of one or several unsolved crimes, a rumor would generalize itself until it paralyzed active life. With a rumor it is very difficult, as Jean-Noël Kapferer has shown, "to define with precision where the phenomenon begins and where it ends" and, we could add, to know who manipulates it.[95]

The word *rumor* exists in both chronicles and in the texts of legal practice. The Bourgeois de Paris, for instance, uses it in its etymological sense of "noise" (*bruit*). The medieval use of *rumor*, in which the peddling of the event is foremost, is stronger than simple gossip or even "they say"; it implied the *consensus* that unites the crowd.

Examples borrowed from Parlement's criminal archives help define this broader meaning. In Carcassonne in March 1403 the curate had four criminals caught and hanged by exploiting the atmosphere of anxiety prevalent in the city. He said that "at this time there were several complaints of pillaging, robberies, and murders" and that he had found at the entrance to Carcassonne "several persons who were complaining about the four above mentioned and about the evils they were doing."[96] They were then taken to the "brothel" (*bordel*) and made prisoner. Their case having been brought up in a council assembled to consider the affair of the lord of Olonzac,[97] an animated discussion followed: "and at the end of the council, murders, thefts and other evils that were being done in the country were talked about, and it was asked whether the accomplices of the said [Olonzac], who were caught, had anything to say about it or had confessed and the seneschal answered no, and people marveled at this situation." Then came the pursuit of scapegoats: "the one who was speaking said that he had four prisoners against whom he had accusations and that one would do well to interrogate them."[98] A series of notorious crimes could not be left unpunished because the heightened popular anxiety required satisfaction and closure.

A rumor could have a more precise point of departure. Crimes occurring on July 22, 1408, the feast of Mary Magdelene, at Château-Thierry were never solved. Several years later (1411) the city's provost described before Parlement the rumor's paralyzing effects: "A great multitude of highwaymen, thieves, robbers, and other malefactors was at large, and because of this a scandalous rumor arose everywhere in the said district and in the surrounding regions with such effect that good folk neither dared nor were able to leave their homes and attend to their business unless banded together."[99] At the same time an identical rumor shook the region of Laon, in the same bailliage and the same bishopric. The narration is similar: "The said advocates declared moreover that around the beginning of June in the aforesaid year, a great and notorious rumor of numerous thieves and murderers in the region of Laon and environs had arisen, to such effect that the good folk of the district did not dare attend to their business unless well banded together."[100] While resisting the assumption of new stereotypes again related to peace and the common good, it should not surprise us that rumors linked to crimes left unpunished could create a kind of panic that the authorities used to their advantage.

A veritable system developed for designating appropriate scapegoats to restore order. The Carcassonne incident suggests the tactic: the authorities attempted to use confessions obtained from the lord of Olonzac's accomplices at the foot of the gallows. The provost of Paris in 1389–90 used this very method to break up gangs, since everyone believed that a criminal association was stirring up a plot.[101] Common words for these criminal conspiracies were *alliance* or *societas*. Plots were said to resemble *uniones*, *conspirationes*, *monopolia*, *consilia*, *conventicula*; in other words, crime and rebellion used an identical vocabulary.[102] A sense of public danger arose when criminals "have taken counsel together" (*pris leur conseil ensamble*),[103] so that the crime was "premeditated" (*aguet apensé*). Numerous accomplices, often more than four, heightened anxiety. In Laon, Gaulcher Lamy gave evidence during his confession of a *rotulus* that sealed the *complicium societas* of which he was a member and that held in secrecy a magic formula that empowered its members: "To his gang of accomplices he had brought a certain roll on which was written the formula for a certain potion of such power that if anyone drank of it, he would instantly be rendered crazy, covetous, and willing to kill people. The said Gaulcher along with his accomplices or co-conspirators had drunk of or tasted this potion."[104] Oaths sometimes sealed the alliance and, in the public mind, made the criminals an "evil intrigue" or cabal (*diablerie*).[105] Crime was scarcely separated from subversion. Jacotin de Neauville, who was tortured and hanged by the provost of Saint-Riquier, had "an inventory of enemies written on a roll including gentlemen and peasants against whom he waged war and he spied, one after the other to beat and kill them."[106] The rumor surrounding him suggested a social war ill distinguished from personal hatreds.

So we move from actual fact—the crime or crimes—to rumor. Certain circumstances may have favored this transition. The coincidence of rumors in 1408 is startling. Should these be linked to the civil war in the north? Jean sans Peur was still in Paris and would not leave for Liège until July. We do not know the channels, official or not, by which the rumors spread or what role propaganda played in spreading them. The sources can only be guessed until the intended victim is identified.

When rumor became an official, legal complaint, it became *clamor*. The bailiff of Amiens often received complaints from the population about the murders and offenses that Jacotin was committing "in the country" (*sur le pays*). The same was true for the *viguier* of Carcassonne. The culprits were those whom the society had excluded from its institutions: vagabonds and strangers, the unemployed, former criminals, bastards, and sexual deviants, men as well as women, who made up the horde of "pimps, brothel clients, libertines, and gluttons" (*houlliers, bordeliers, rufiens, et gouliars*). This diverse group did not inhabit the same space as ordinary people but, instead, swore mutual oaths secretly and frequented brothels and the highways. They dwelt on the outskirts of a disquieting wilderness. The house of one of Laon's condemned was built in this way: "adjoining the woods of Rest and situated in a dangerous area or pass where many bad things were wont to happen, because it was widely reputed to be a refuge for thieves."[107] It was itself "a cave of thieves" (*une caverne de voleurs*). These people and places evoked such fear that the Latin texts used for *fear* the word *metus*, drawn from legal vocabulary.

Crime provoked disorder as well as fear. All death was contagious, beginning with unnatural death. The anthropologists James George Frazer and Bronislaw Malinowski speak of the "stain" that crime left in primitive societies.[108] Medieval texts show that at the beginning of the fourteenth century the "quarantine" still existed, probably a remnant left from a time when purification rituals followed a crime. The remonstrances of 1315 assured the nobility of their "ancient" privilege of staying "in quarantine" with their lord if they were suspected of committing a crime.[109] The will of God was necessary to reverse the contagion of crime. Wanting to show the legitimacy of the Burgundians and of the 1418 massacres, the Bourgeois de Paris claimed that it was divine grace that sent torrents of rain to wash the corpses without staining the city with the victims' blood: the crime against the Armagnacs did not "pollute," since it was clean.[110] Crime was even more contagious when the victim's body was not found and his death could not be ritualized. The obsessive fear was even greater if it was known that the corpse was rotting in a pond or pool of water.[111] Death by drowning, as certain jurisdictions saw it, was considered to be the most ignominious because it was putrefying.

The best theorist of crime's contagion was, without question, Nicolas de Clamanges. For him, crime was not only the companion of vice, but also of sickness. He speaks of pestilential crime (*crimen pestiferum*), of the *contagio*, words that he associates in his little treatises as well as in his letters with the verbs *polluere, infectare, corrumpere.*[112] The effects of crime appeared immediately, and the earth promised to become a wilderness empty of people. Taking up the words of the prophets, Nicolas de Clamanges announces, "until the city is stripped of inhabitants, and the house is left unpeopled and the land deserted."[113] He clearly associated crime with contemporary misfortune. The encounter between erudition and the interpolation of current crises, between theoretical discourse and the concerns of public opinion, was thus sealed.

Purifying the Kingdom

The Great Plague and other epidemics, the war with the English, the civil wars between Charles le Mauvais and the king and then between the Armagnacs and the Burgundians were played out against the background of the Great Schism and Charles VI's madness. These calamities manifested God's anger with his people's sins and crimes. The most heinous crimes, from which the stereotypes of classic criminals were invented — thieves, highwaymen, and rapists — were both the cause and the consequence of impurities contaminating the kingdom. The *Chronique de Richard Lescot*'s successor assimilated in his narrative the new crimes and misfortunes befalling the population, and Jean de Venette claimed that crime doubled after the Plague. A new commonplace developed. We do not know the degree of its popularization, but its formulation is similar in the two chronicles: "For people were thereafter more greedy and grasping, since they possessed many more things than before; thus they were even more covetous and prone to stir themselves up with lawsuits, feuds, quarrels, and court dates."[114]

The connection between the contagion of crime and that of disease was close, and the congruence of the two threatened the entire society's future. Jean Gerson's and Nicolas de Clamanges's descriptions of devastated fields are only the external image of a still more serious sterility that 3 touched the normal rules of human reproduction. Births were uncertain, unpredictable, or monstrous by nature, jeopardized by the horrible crimes that targeted both women's honor and pregnant women. Youth were cheated by death as they were by the blindness of soldiers. Chance did not dictate Jean de Venette's insertion of fear of shameful births and sterile women into accounts of the ravages of the companies in 1360 and of the hordes of ruffians and thieves in 1365.[115] The contaminated society had become incapable of reproducing itself at the normal rhythm regulated by honored marriage laws.

This obsessive fear was latent in the collective unconscious; the repetition of societal ills exacerbated it, and it reemerged with each new epidemic. A century later Jean de Roye's writings recaptured the fear intact. With the resurgence of plague during the summer of 1466, thieves and picklocks invaded Paris, and a "big Norman" was finally caught who was considered the author of the most abominable crime for the future of society: incest accompanied by infanticide.[116] Under these conditions the attention that Parisians gave to extraordinary births, whether it be of man or animal, is less a proof of a spirit of curiosity than a sign of their anxiety in a world that they perceived as perverted.[117]

The degree of social upheaval was measured by those sex crimes that transgressed reproductive laws. The fratricidal belligerence between the Armagnacs and the Burgundians was against nature in that it spilled common blood, but this atrocious crime led to even more serious ones. Nicolas de Clamanges denounced the civil war, describing such inadmissible crimes as parricides plunging swords into the breast of the nurturing motherland and her own sons raping her. The calls became more urgent: "O sons, cease to violate your mother, if any fiber of piety remains in you. Who among you, pray, would not shudder to strike the mother of his own flesh, if she threw herself between you as you fought?"[118]

Chroniclers' reports of these horrible crimes reflected astrologers' predictions and the books of prophecies. The attention given to external manifestations of these crimes doubled. Comets, eclipses of the moon or of the sun, or unusual frost or heat accompanied dissoluteness and paved the way to crime, which contemporaries associated with madness.[119] The presumption was that the internal and external world were united. The darkness of crime was an extension of the darkness of the sky; crime's contagion was an extension of the plague epidemic; and crime's spiritual causes were an extension of the mud that invaded the streets and of the pustules of the lepers whom the authorities forced out of the city. For the judges of the Châtelet in 1389 neither "the low estate" of Gervaise Caussois nor the sacrileges he committed by stealing from churches justified recourse to extraordinary proceedings; it was necessary also to add that he had "scabies."[120] As a just reward for the crime, a cart and mud accompanied the prisoner to his execution.[121] Disease and filth were one with criminal behavior. Saint Louis used this vocabulary in the edicts of reform, and in the fourteenth century those who charged the provost of Paris with the task of "cleaning" the capital, indeed the kingdom, also invoked these words. Such regulations confirm a complementarity that foresaw a general purification, both physical and spiritual.[122]

What societal needs did generalized reports of crime, filth, and disease fill? The reference to Saint Louis indicates that an awareness of crime and evil was not entirely restricted to the fourteenth-century crises. Penitential literature also moved the discourse from a simple conception of criminality toward an element in state formation. Latin and biblical cultures reinforced these manifestations. Lucan, denouncing the ravages of the civil war, pointed to the accompanying heavenly signs; biblical prophets announced the perils of Babylon and Israel in a similar fashion.[123] But at the end of the fourteenth century, it was the Revelation of Saint John that dominated the expression of political, literary, and artistic thought.[124] Specific facts can be directly related to it. Desirous that the Peace of Auxerre in August 1412 be fruitful, Christine de Pizan saw a miracle in the union of two dukes named John (Jean de Berry and Jean sans Peur), which she associated with the cult of Saint John.[125] Peace distanced for some time the knight of the Apocalypse. Nurtured by both the Old and the New Testaments, apocalyptical thinking was probably not reserved to theorists. The widespread rumor that the wells were poisoned, which ran through the kingdom in 1321, 1350, and 1390, can be interpreted in the same way.[126] The contamination of evil, in this case lepers, Jews, and criminals, was physical. The usually nurturing water carried poison to the deepest parts where it was hidden to man—the well, the spring, and the rivers. But such a crime also announced the end of the world: the Revelation of Saint John predicted that tainted water was one of the seven scourges of the seven cups of the anger of God![127]

The generalized evil contained tangible evils that contemporaries attempted to decipher in their specificity. Theorists looked for explanatory elements in current events. Jean Gerson found them in the torments of civil war that started in 1400 but took shape in 1405 with the dauphin's kidnapping. He associated them with the continuation of the Great Schism.[128] Finally, as Françoise Autrand has shown, the king's madness played an essential role.[129] None of these components can, in fact, be disassociated. They all converge to show how in this society, closed in as it was in its points of reference, disorder delivered up its secrets little by little.

Contemporaries were correct: even though their explanation was contingent, it was presented as globally as were the remedies they recommended. The theorists inquired about all these ills while people formed processions to ward off the causes of dissension, to stop the chaos, and to return to order. Signs of evil, ritual, and reflection on sin intermingled. Nicolas de Baye and Clément de Fauquembergue were perfect witnesses. To describe the procession of July 1404 during which Charles de Savoisy's men attacked the students of the University of Paris, the clerk of Parlement intertwined the cold weather, the incessant rains, and the king's sickness with peace in the church and in the kingdom, so many evils making the people suffer: "but our sins deserved it" (*sed peccata nostra meruerunt*).[130] Some years later, in October 1418, the procession, the prayers to the Virgin, and the sermons that Clément de Fauquembergue described had exactly the same meaning.[131] Recourse to rituals juxtapose the growing struggle against the epidemic, the peace between the princes, and the spreading crimes that threatened to undermine Parisian moral order. Confessions of infamies followed rituals of purification. Crime and sin elbowed each other in an urgent need to confess.

The remedy was not only religious but political. Civilization, as political theorists and public opinion understood it, was not simply measured in terms of reproduction. The kingdom was the body of civilization, the king was its head, and the royal roads were its nerves. This image, which served the well-being and "common good" of society, appeared in the theorists' metaphors. In a traditional society in which wealth was measured by reproduction of the population, civilization was regressing. In order to measure the fear that depopulation generated, one only has to follow the emergence of another commonplace: to preserve their numbers, communities turned in on themselves because of the intense fear that one of their members might be attacked on the road. Community paralysis began with the fear of crime.

Both chroniclers and lawyers of Parlement evoked the theme of crime-infested roads, while at the same time the theme was used to justify coercive measures first instituted in the early fourteenth century. From whence did this theme emerge? Chronologically it first appeared in legislative texts. On March 20, 1316, the king addressed a letter to the bailiff of Meaux directing him to protect the safety of the roads and guard against thieves, because "we strongly desire the peace and safety of our subjects and of the people who come each day into our realm to sell and buy merchandise, because without this commerce it would not be possible to govern our said realm nor any other."[132] By the mid–fourteenth century, the successor of the *Chronique de Richard Lescot* and Jean de Venette used this theme in describing the perverse effects of crime. Merchants no longer circulated because the roads and the woods were given over to despoilers.[133] In 1413, Christine de Pizan, in the *Livre de la paix*, took up this theme to show the disastrous effects of widespread crime.[134]

During exactly that period, Parlement used the same formula. To exculpate himself, Jean Drouin, the *viguier* of Carcassonne, who had allegedly hanged four innocent clerks, advanced the argument that he had reacted to widespread fear and rumor. He said that rumors of robbery and murder arose because the city was near the realm of Aragon and was surrounded by woods so that merchants were afraid to come there.[135] This argument incontestably justified his recourse to severe peacekeeping measures. However, arbitrary judicial brutality was not routine. The royal order to the Meaux bailiff in 1316 was in response to the "great noise" or disturbing rumors that had reached the king's ears. This decision paralleled measures adopted by Philip V in response to representatives of those cities that came to Paris demanding the appointment of captains capable of guarding their safety. The imminence of war in Flanders was not the cause for the establishment of military defenses but rather a contributing factor to the generalized fear sweeping the country. The *viguier* of Carcassonne, the provost of Château-Thierry, and the provost of Laon were responding to widespread rumors among a troubled population; the communities wanted peace and order through legal measures. As early as 1274, the abbot of Saint-Maur-des-Fossés held up the specter of criminals who were armed with hauberks, steel-tipped pitchforks, and knives and who threatened daily life.[136] When the powers-that-be confessed their impotence in stamping out crime through force, fear was a necessary defense, and it was essential to find a guilty party at any price.

A consensus prevailed, a least in theory, in bringing about coercive measures. It welded itself together in a common ideal evoked in each text: a peace capable of mitigating crime. The content of this peace was both religious and political, representing a reinstatement of an order that mankind's crimes had disturbed. The charge to dispensers of justice was to identify the guilty parties and to expose them to popular condemnation.

Reformatting the Kingdom and Defining Crime

Political theorists' understanding of events and of civilization was not limited to seeing them as epiphenomena manifesting the hidden will of God. Engaged in active intellectual inquiry, they went in search of guilty parties. This quest began with the head of the body politic, with the king and the crimes that he committed. Before the king of France, the kings in the Bible loomed large: Solomon, master of wisdom; David, responsible for the death of his people because of his sins; and Job, sufferer in the flesh for the evils of injustice.[137]

Political theorists pointed to a double principle: that crime is contagious and that the king should serve as an example. If the king is a criminal, then his people suffer the effects of the crime doubly, an idea that was widespread during Charles VI's reign. Guillaume de Tignonville expressed it in the *Ditz moraulx*: "The bad king is like a vulture that brings to the earth a foul stench all around him; the good king is like a clean running river that brings benefit to everyone."[138] Nicolas de Clamanges used a theoretical but practical approach in listing the weaknesses that he saw in the house of Valois, which contributed to fostering evil and resulted in the kingdom's decline. From the English captivity and death of John the Good to the madness of Charles VI, with the intervening physical weakness of Charles V, the signs of evil were apparent.[139] The kings did not check the crimes, epidemics, and wars that were spreading throughout the kingdom but, on the contrary, encouraged them.

Theorists posited a definition of the good prince, characterizing him in opposition to a tyrant. While defining the ideal prince as opposed to the tyrant in late medieval political theory is beyond the scope of this study, the relationship between politics and criminality elucidates one aspect that is often overlooked.[140] Tyranny is associated with illness and crime. Pierre Salmon compares earthly tyranny to Purgatory. The pride and envy of tyrants forces the good and just into physical and moral suffering.[141] Christine de Pizan associates tyranny with a hell that "began in this world" (*commencent en cestui monde*).[142] Scriptural examples and those taken from antiquity reinforce her argument. In her *Livre de la paix*, she describes a large number of tyrants, their principle crimes, and the shameful deaths that they suffer.[143] The author of the *Chronographia* enriched this portrait gallery with a description of Tamerlan, whom he defines as "a certain powerful tyrant of the region of Tartary" (*quemdam potentissimum tirannum Tartarie regionis*) and with whom he associates crimes, "thefts and robberies" (*furtis et latrociniis*), typical of the criminal horde that formed his entourage.[144]

The tyrant was above all cruel.[145] In the theoretical texts as well as in legal practice, the words *cruel* and *cruauté* only rarely had a moral and affective sense. They were, for instance, unusual in letters of remission, because their meaning was specifically political, being closely associated with tyranny.[146] Jean Gerson speaks of "the merciless oppression" (*l'oppression crueuse*) that the people suffer because of "deceivers and merciless pillagers" (*sodoiers et cruelx pillars*) who act like tyrants.[147] Christine de Pizan systematically links cruelty to tyranny and pillaging.[148] The tyrant, bursting with blood, "full of venom and of cruelty" (*plain de venim et de cruaulté*), commits crimes and visits crime on his people. Christine de Pizan and Jean Gerson equate crime with poison: "Just as venom or poison kills the human body, tyranny likewise is the venom and the poison and the disease that puts to death all political and royal life."[149] Evoking the proverbs of Solomon, Christine de Pizan elaborates: "You have despised counsel and you did not want to be blamed; so I will laugh at your destruction and I will not take you into account when misery comes to you suddenly and thus will the bad prince be merciless in all things; God keep us from such ones, full of blood and of vengeance. For having put into effect such horrible things, endless woes will arise and continue against him [the tyrant] and his country."[150]

Finally, the theorists suggest that the tyrant indiscriminately devours men, women, and children, thus raising again the theme of the criminal eating his victim and the terrible association with the anthropophagi who represented the total death of humanity—anticivilization. In this vein, theorists singled out Herod as the most perfect and hence most cruel of the tyrants because he commanded the slaughter of innocent children.[151] Through these associations reflections on power were connected to stereotypes of serious crime. Once more the troubling image, both biblical and popular, of the wolf devouring innocent lambs completed the portrait: "and the tyrant is like the violent wolf amongst the lambs."[152]

Committed to the struggle against the criminal threat troubling society, the theorists embraced political reform as a part of the solution. Given their intellectual backgrounds, they looked for remedies that combined the religious and political. Ritual, strictly performed, was the first remedial action suggested. Processions and prayers of those opposed to disorder might check the contagion of evil. On November 1, 1408, Pierre Salmon wrote to the king from Avignon suggesting "remedies" for his well-being and that of the kingdom. Among the "remedies" he prescribed were processions and prayers "in your kingdom, commanding all the prelates of this your kingdom to have the same done in their dioceses, inciting their subjects to pray continually to God for the union of our mother the Holy Church, for the good health of your person and for peace and reconciliation of your said kingdom, which presently is in great confusion and on the path of desolation."[153]

Such ritual demonstrations were a prelude to reforms for which political theorists longed. The call for such spectacles was nothing more than an admission that the rising state had fostered crime through its officers and ordinances from the middle of the thirteenth century onward (especially from 1303).[154] Incited by the *clamor,* each "reformation" presented itself as a legal inquiry in which the guilty parties were punished and the reformers, at least in the trials, could practice a witchhunt.[155]

This admission found its justification in the general principles of judicial practice. These judged a person according to his faults and distributed justice equally among the different classes. The works of both theorists and practitioners of justice reflected these principles.[156] The stakes were high, demanding peace throughout the kingdom. In the enthusiasm for perfectibility characterizing the first French humanism, the idea prevailed that well-governed men would make amends to a wronged society. Christine de Pizan expressed this ideal by putting complete faith in mankind. Two reasons were cited: "First, the evil men will not dare to persecute the good men because they will know well that your legitimate justice will punish them, and second, no one will want to become evil when everyone will know that you are their punisher. Thus they will have cause to make amends, and in this way there will necessarily be peace among your people, which is the glory and dignity of every kingdom."[157]

The reformers were not satisfied in limiting themselves to theoretical principles. From the mid-century onward, the greatest among them, such as Guillaume de Machaut and Philippe de Vitry, gave practical advice and became reformers in practice. Nicolas de Clamanges, Christine de Pizan, and Jean Gerson all dreamed of an intense judicial undertaking based on the idea that crimes were not sufficiently punished and that criminals who ran free contributed to criminal contagion. They admitted that the king could not be everywhere in his kingdom and that the power of the royal judge must be recognized as derived from that of the king. As Christine de Pizan writes, it is proper for the king to put "various ministers and lieutenants in all the widespread jurisdictions."[158] Nicolas de Clamanges informs Jean Gerson of the same concern and suggests, among the *medicamenta* necessary in the reformation of the kingdom, that the military powers of the bailiffs be increased. The *bailliage* had to become a fortress where violence was enclosed and quelled in such a way that the evil contained therein could not escape.[159] Judicial efficacy was at hand.

The use of the death penalty was an important part of the reformers' original thought. Gerson saw in it a guarantee of the rule of law enabling a distinction between good and evil people and preventing the contamination of the good by the evil.[160] But this analysis posed a basic problem: how does one reconcile this necessity with the immutable divine law that stated: "Thou shalt not kill" (*non occides*)? In the *Diligite justiciam* Gerson reviewed this point as jurists presented it at the beginning of the fifteenth century. Unfortunately, this speech cannot be easily dated. He might have given it in 1408, following the "affair" of Guillaume de Tignonville, or in 1405–6 following an earlier affair that opposed the provost of Paris to the bishop's justice over clerks hanged as thieves.[161] Gerson demonstrated that next to divine law there existed the sovereign's civil law. This law defined the principles of justice to which men were subjected; the death penalty figured as a punishment for certain crimes. But Gerson could only justify the death penalty in civil law drawn from divine law, which provided that a certain number of criminals "such as murderers, adulterers, heretics, witches" be executed. He carefully exempts highway theft, which the provost of Paris claimed as a capital crime.[162] The fundamental difference in abhorrence accorded to theft in the canonists' and theologians' texts was in large part the raison d'être of Gerson's *Diligite justiciam* and a point of contention between the provost of Paris and the clerks.

To exercise and administer civil justice, the sovereign had judges at his disposal. Gerson argues that the death penalty as exercised by royal officers in accordance with the king's law was not homicide. Given the difficulty of passing legislation in France at the end of the Middle Ages, Gerson's demonstration indicated the degree of maturity in his thinking about justice. The judges owed it to themselves to be honest. Gerson was close in reasoning to Nicolas de Clamanges when the latter, addressing Gérard Machet, deplored the financial pressures that silenced the judges: "We rarely see thieves and murderers or others convicted of the gravest crimes sentenced to death, except because of poverty. Therefore, in the case of the parricide or other evildoers, being poor is their weightier offense. And so, if some rich and sinful man is condemned to death, his money discharges the obligation instead, no matter what his crimes."[163] The state as dispenser of justice was thus defined in its principles, in its coercive apparatus, and in its sanctions.[164]

These statements were not only political theorists' declamations, they appeared as arguments at Parlement. The Moret affair of 1405, in which the father of Pierre Moret opposed Antoine Garnier, former magistrate of Montpellier, serves as an example. Arguing for the necessity of the death penalty, the king's prosecutor said "that when a person is condemned for a heinous crime which is against the public good, he must be executed."[165] To reinforce his argument, he finished by evoking the favors from which the inhabitants of Montpellier benefited, in particular the richest members of the population, by saying "that the people of Montpellier are remarkable and that it has been more than one hundred years since they have served justice to powerful people because they always negotiate with money and always have the habit of threatening the judge and of putting him on trial if he carries out justice."[166] Theorists and practitioners of justice denounced the abuses of a lax justice. The greatest reformers, therefore, called for the death penalty. The union of church and state was so strong on this point that Jean Gerson could demand in 1396 that the king grant that convicts receive confession and communion.[167] The measure was a charitable one, but it marked the recognition that the decisions made in civil law implied acquiescence in divine law. It brought the death sentence into the bosom of the church.

The reformers laid out both the power of the institutions and punishment of guilty parties. Contemporary texts administering the law mirrored their wishes. On January 31, 1355, royal letters established Pierre de Lieuvilliers as the commissioner charged with putting the criminals who were overrunning the kingdom on trial: "We have heard that there are several people, men and women, banished from our kingdom for murder, theft, and other offenses that they committed in our said kingdom who are traveling and staying in our kingdom." At the head of the list of scapegoats are the *roigneurs de monnaie*, people who depreciate the value of money by clipping coins. The political situation in this period of social and ideological conflict explains why currency was a strong player in political thought and reality. Measures taken for "purging" the kingdom suggest the progress of judicial centralization and extraordinary procedure. Criminals had to be brought to the Châtelet where they could undergo "questioning and torture" (*question et gehine*) "until the truth is known and they be taken care of accordingly."[168]

During the reign of Charles VI, the organization and institution of these judicial principles were centralized. The provost of Paris's position continued to grow while the Châtelet was being organized. The evolution can be dated to 1320. In that moment of intense state formation which marked the last Capetian's reign, the inadequacy of the Châtelet was denounced. The absence of archives facilitated neither the continuity of justice nor the publicity that must be made for it; "the provosts who for the moment were each in their right, brought in the accounts in which the king had lost many fines and in which many acts were left unpunished."[169] The distinctions between the public and the private that should exist had been implicitly noted in regard to a provost's responsibility. Charles V's decisions consequently facilitated the increased autonomy of the provosts in regard to Parlement and the princes of blood.[170] Hugues Aubriot, although not widely known, knew how to finesse this concentration of powers.[171] But the Marmousets brought about the real change. The legislative decisions of 1389 made of the Châtelet a center where "there is a great harvest of good and wise advice and where we have our council and other officers to help to protect our rights and the good of justice."[172] From this date through the ordinance of November 29, 1407, the provosts' powers were repeated and increased. The personality of Parisian provosts, Jean de Folleville and Guillaume de Tignonville, and the pugnacity of their clerks, beginning with Aleaume Cachemarée, reinforced their judicial power with a theory of justice and capital punishment.[173] The civil war apparently marked a break in this evolution because of Burgundian propaganda. Guillaume de Tignonville's deposition on May 5, 1408, of Armagnac allegiance, the fine imposed on him on May 16, 1408, the restitution of the powers of the provost of merchants on January 20, 1412, and the silence of the *Ordonnance cabochienne* concerning the powers of the provost of Paris were all signs of a final blow to the Burgundian program of theory and practice of justice concerning Parisian "liberties."[174] This retreat was far from being complete, and public opinion was perhaps not entirely favorable to it. In May 1425 Henry VI's regulations entrusted the Châtelet and the provost of Paris with difficult tasks, including if necessary "secrecy for the good of justice" (*[le] secret pour le bien de la justice*).[175] It was not before the reign of Charles VII and the ordinance of October 6, 1447, however, that the provost of Paris's judicial role was linked again with the Marmousets' reforming tradition.[176]

Two stereotypes or myths were again used in this progression: that of serious crime and that of origins. The stereotype of origins belongs to history. It made Etienne Boileau a model provost and permitted the reformers to go back, once more, to the time of the good king, Saint Louis.[177] A legal exemplum reports how the provost, "a good and legitimate judge" (*bon justicier et droiturrier*), did not hesitate to hang his godson, "whom he loved greatly" *(qu'il aymoit fort)* but who "was caught stealing" (*fut reprins de larrecin*).[178] As a result of this evenhanded justice, no criminals remained in the city and people left other lordships to "live in the king's territory"(*demourer en la terre de roy*).[179] The exemplum contributed to justifying the death penalty for theft. A negative example that the anonymous chronicles conveyed, and that perhaps the Parisians' memory conserved, was that of Taperel, the provost whose lax enforcement brought disorder and made the gallows that he had constructed ridiculous.[180]

Recourse to stereotypes of serious crime was constantly evoked in the acts that enunciated provosts' power during Charles VI's reign. The ordinance of May 1389 used the double argument of crime and criminal associations to justify stringent enforcement.[181] Borrowing rhetoric from the previous reign, Charles VII delegated to Robert d'Estouteville in 1447 the power to "inform against thieves, beggars, highwaymen, abductors of women, violators of churches, poachers, dishonest gamblers, cheaters, counterfeiters, criminals and others associated with them, receivers and accomplices."[182] Stereotypes of serious crime, unexplained crime, and gangs of criminals accompanied the birth of the state.

Even though the Châtelet privileged the argument of serious crime, it was not reserved exclusively for use there. In order to justify the execution of Gaulcher Lamy, Colard Le Cuisinier, country provost of Laon, took refuge behind the instructions that he received at the *bailliage* of Vermandois and that he swore to apply: "The said provost, and the other servants named in the said *bailliage*, swore to observe unswervingly their orders and instructions written down and enrolled in the hall of the court of the bailiff of Vermandois at Laon." He confirmed that among his instructions was the authorization to use torture. He made specific reference to "my letter from the said court sent on April 28, 1408, in which authority was mandated for the capture and punishment of any criminals or evildoers in the *bailliage* of Vermandois and the prefecture of Laon and even other jurisdictions and their adjoining territories."[183] For the bailiff of Amiens in 1406 the king's prosecutor used the same arguments, connecting the bailiff's police responsibilities to the orders that he received: "The bailiff of Amiens was given order and the commission by this Court to take and punish the criminals and those banished, etc., and by giving the said bailiff the said order the Court takes on the responsibility of moving quickly against these criminals who work against the public good each day."[184] The order became an inherent part of the job. Another provost in Laon in 1414 affirmed "that his job is to ride the borders of the said jurisdiction and catch and interrogate criminals."[185] The lesson was understood. Influenced by justifications that impregnate political thought and that came from the central organs of justice, pursuit of crime, in practice, became a duty.

Because crimes, especially the most heinous, did not enter the ranks of routine news at the end of the Middle Ages, they remained the originators of the most destructive fantasies. Depiction of stereotypes was capable of destroying all points of reference in the cultural order. Murders undermined the hierarchy of sexes and ages, rape and incestuous relations abolished the normal laws of reproduction, pillaging hindered the beneficial network of exchange. The persecuting crowd shifted blame for general misery and discord onto a small percentage of the population, while the nascent state was charged with tracking down the suspects who were scapegoats sacrificed to popular vengeance and to the progress of legal institutions.

Conclusion

The words one uses to talk about crime are not without effect. The difference between crime defined by practitioners of law and that by political theorists leads us from descriptive neutrality to moral connotation, from the criminal act to evil. This shift occurred because the king's justice had to calm people's fears and silence the extreme uneasiness that crime provoked in the bosom of society. The vocabulary of evil allowed for coercive judicial practices but could also be expressed as being purifying and "useful." Crime was not interesting in and of itself and its proofs were not yet autonomous; rather the criminal was at the heart of the debate. The pursuit of the guilty party was essential, and, after he was apprehended, it was clear that the crime would be punished and that social order would be protected. By way of conclusion I would like to try to envision what these reactions meant.

Crime is disturbing. This reaction was so deeply felt in fourteenth- and fifteenth-century society that it led to two antithetical aspirations: to know the truth and to find a guilty party. In a local context, identifying a guilty party posed no problem. The community quickly tracked down the unknown murderer or the clever thief. Reputation spread even to the ears of justice, relayed sometimes by accusation and, in the most spectacular cases, by the miracle of blood that spilled on contact with the murderer. A kind of complicity developed with the legal authorities. While the population did not fear obvious crimes, it was afraid of accidents that were not easily attributable to natural death. A little anecdote, occurring at Mireval, confirms this observation. In January 1353 a woman was looking after her daughter who was about to give birth. When the mother left her daughter to look for a lantern, she fell down the stairs and died.[186] A woman, whose age and physical state did not predispose her to such an accident, had died. The community suspected the son-in-law of murder.

To defend himself the son-in-law pointed out that he was absent at the time and that the door was still locked. He finally found the accused: "It's God who did it" (*La mort, c'est Dieu qui l'a faite*). The crime found its guilty party.

Whether it used its own devices or entrusted prosecution to the king's justice, the community had to know. A community's frenzy could push it to a forced confession. Such was the case in Mirande in 1389 when all the inhabitants were obliged to ask forgiveness for abuses they had committed against a criminal who died in the prison in which they had confined him.[187] The satisfaction of the family and, in the case of murder, the victim's family was paramount. Death and the relationship between men and death were central to their concern. A man from the bailliage of Vermandois, for instance, knew to say to his attacker, "Rotten scoundrel, I was taken by death through you, by God you will die for this."[188] The preoccupation with murder reveals the extent to which this society still needed to tame death.

The fear of crime increased with uncertainty. The expansion of communication networks and repeated crises increased the number of crimes whose authors were not native to the village or urban environment and thus escaped detection. Because communities needed to find someone responsible for deeds that they perceived as threatening the survival of the social body, they focused on scapegoats: Jews, vagabonds, thieves, arsonists, and rapists. At the same time, the nascent state was becoming aware of its role in the country's security, a role that it defined from the start in terms of salvation. Legal institutions and procedural forms went together. The reform of the kingdom that accompanied the birth of the state presented itself as purifying in the sense that, through an ordained repetition, evil would be exorcised.

Translated by Mary Skemp and Barbara Hanawalt

Notes

This chapter has been translated and adapted from Claude Gauvard, "The Fear of Crime," chap. 5 in *"De grace especial": Crime, état et société en France à la fin de Moyen Age*, 2 vols. (Paris: Publications de la Sorbonne, 1991), 191–236. The editors thank the publisher and author for permission to reproduce this essay.

1. Jean Bouteiller, *Le Grand Coutumier et Practique du droict civil et canon observé en France . . . cy-devant imprimé soubs le nom de la Somme rural*, ed. Louis Charondas Le Caron (Paris: Bvon, 1621), book 1, title 13, pp. 386–87: "si peux et dois savoir qu'ils sont plusieurs cas qui ne sont a recevoir en purge, si comme meurtres, arsins de maison, enforceurs de femmes, derobeurs de gens en chemin que les clercs appellent depraedatores populorum, traitre, herese, bougre: tel ne sont pas a recevoir a loi de purge." For Cachemarée's itemization, see *Registre criminel du Châtelet de Paris du 6 septembre 1389 au 18 mai 1392*, ed. Henri Duplès-Agier, 2 vols. (Paris, 1861 and 1864). Aleaume Cachemarée was the clerk of Châtelet's court. On this court's role, see Claude Gauvard, "Les sources judiciaires de la fin de Moyen Age peuvent-elles permettre une approche statistique du crime?" in *Commerce, finances et societé (XIe-XVIe siècles)*, ed. Philippe Contamine, Thierry Dutour, and Bertrand Schnerb (Paris: Presses de l'Université de Paris-Sorbonne, 1993), 469–88.

2. René Laingui and Arlette Lebigre, *Histoire du droit pénal* (Paris: Cujas, n.d.), 2:64.

3. Gauvard, *"De grace especial,"* chap. 1, 50 ff.

4. Natalie Zemon Davis, *Fiction in the Archives: Pardon Tales and Their Tellers in Sixteenth-Century France* (Stanford, Calif.: Stanford University Press, 1987), 61 ff.

5. Philippe de Vigneulles, *Les cent nouvelles nouvelles,* ed. Charles H. Livingston, Francis R. Livingston, and Robert H. Ivy (Geneva: Droz, 1972), 8.

6. Jean-Pierre Seguin records 517 hoaxes printed between 1529 and 1631 where the authors responded to the sense of detail and the readers to a thirst for news; *L'information en France de Louis, XII à Henri II* (Paris: Droz, 1961), 30.

7. See in particular Jean-Pierre Seguin, "Fait divers sensationnels dans seize bulletins imprimés en France pendant le règne de François Ier," in *Mélanges Frantz Calot* (Paris: Librairie d'Argences, 1960), 65 ff.: "lequel avoit la teste d'un grand homme, mal formee, avec couronne large en la teste, laquelle tiroit sur le blanc et le reste du corps en forme de beuf approchoit a la forme d'un pourceau."

8. Ibid., 66–67.

9. Seguin, *L'information en France,* 83 and 85.

10. Seguin, "Faits divers sensationnels," 73.

11. *Les cent nouvelles nouvelles,* ed. Pierre Champion (Paris: Droz, 1928), tale 57: "car il estoit et a esté toujours tres gracieux et nouveau et bien plaisant gentil homme."

12. Ibid., tale 43. For other cases of adultery, see tales 33 and 68.

13. On the resolution of adultery by a pardon, see examples cited in Gauvard, *"De grace especial,"* chap. 18, nn. 115–28.

14. Roger Dubuis, *Les "Cent nouvelles nouvelles" et la tradition de la nouvelle en France au Moyen Age* (Grenoble: Presses universitaires de Grenoble, 1973), 13 ff.

15. On the taste for modernity in the narrative of historical events, see Claude Gauvard and Gilette Labory, *Une chronique rimée parisienne écrit en 1409: "Les aventures depuis deux cents ans,"* in *Le métier d'historien au Moyen Age: Etudes sur l'historiographie médiévale,* ed. Bernard Guenée (Paris: Université de Paris I Panthéon-Sorbonne, Centre de recherches sur l'histoire de l'Occident médiéval, 1977), 189–92.

16. These dates correspond to the first part of the *Journal de Jean de Roye, dit Chronique Scandaleuse,* ed. Bernard de Mandrot, 2 vols. (Paris: Renouard, 1894).

17. See the remarks outlined in Gauvard, *"De grace especial,"* chap. 1, 50–52.

18. *Journal de Nicolas de Baye,* ed. Alexandre Tuetey (Paris: Renouard, 1885 and 1888), 1:213–14, and 2:238, 253–54; and *Journal de Clément de Fauquembergue,* ed. Alexandre Teutey (Paris: Renouard, 1903–15), 3:65.

19. *Journal de Jean de Roye,* 1:33. The author can also give evidence of juridical preoccupations and can give an account of criminal deeds, all the while worrying about the fate reserved for the guilty, as is the case with lèse-majesté; ibid., 70.

20. For other examples of this recourse to concrete actions see ibid., 156, 166, where the thieves are *"crocheteurs"* (picklocks), "in the night to pick doors, windows, wine cellars, and storerooms."

21. Ibid., 175, to describe the murder of Thomas Louette, receiver of the Temple who "had his throat cut in said Temple by one of his brothers and companions named brother Henry, for some quarrels he had picked with the said brother Henry."

22. Ibid., 156. The "belle jeune femme" belonged also to the Parisian milieux in question since Jeanne Du Bois was "wife of a notary of the Châtelet in the said place of Paris," cited above, n. 20.

23. Ibid., 111: "bien conseillé de ses principaulx amis, la reprint et (elle) se contint de la en avant avecques sondit mary bien et honnestement."

24. See Gauvard, *"De grace especial,"* chap. 18, 819.

25. *Journal d'un bourgeois de Paris, 1405–1449,* ed. Alexandre Tuetey (Paris: Champion, 1881), 186.

26. For example, a young girl, a seamstress in Paris, is a victim of a go-between who, several times, made her ascend to the room of her neighbor, Oudart. Two times he "was

Claude Gauvard

in the carnal company of the said girl on a bench," then the next day "on the trunk" placing "the robe of Jehan Regnard under the two of them"; cited by Louis-Claude Douët-d'Arcq, "Un procès pour outrage aux moeurs en 1470," *Bibliothèque de l'Ecole des Chartes*, ser. 2, 4 (1847–48):507.

27. See the succession of events after 1417, in *Journal d'un bourgeois de Paris*, 79 ff.; for the appeal to the strongest sacrilegious crimes, in particular those relative to children, see Gauvard, *"De grace especial,"* chap. 18, 823.

28. *Journal d'un bourgeois de Paris*, 186, 277, with respect to theft committed in the palace during the dinner for the consecration of Henry VI. A theft in these places is sacrilegious; Ernest Perrot, *Les cas royaux: Origine et développement de la théorie au XIIIe et XIVe siècles* (Paris: Rousseau, 1910), 244 ff.

29. *Journal de Jean de Roye*, 1:281: "boutans les feux es blez et es villages partout ou ilz passoient." On the totality of armed crimes committed by the Bourguignons, see ibid., 286 ff.

30. *Journal d'un bourgeois de Paris*, 7, 124, 191: "pilloient, roboient, tuoient en eglise et hors eglise"; "tuoient, pilloient, boutoient feu partout sur femmes, sur hommes et sur grains et faisoient pis que Sarrazins"; "tuoient, boutoient feux, efforçoient femmes et filles, pendoient hommes, s'ilz ne paioient rançon a leur guise."

31. Nicolas de Baye assimilates armed people with thieves when the court finds itself embarrassed in performing justice and when the violence of deeds surpasses the witnesses of the story. See, for example, in November 1410, *Journal de Nicolas de Baye*, 1:338–39. The expression "pillars" or "pillars et banniz" reappears frequently in the writing of Fauquembergue, Archives Nationales, Série X Parlement de Paris, Conseil (1400–1457) (hereafter cited as X 1a 1480), fol. 65, August 1416; fol. 78, January 1417, and *Journal de Nicolas de Baye*, 1:14–15.

32. *Journal d'un bourgeois de Paris*; see n. 30 above.

33. *Chronographia regum Francorum (1270–1405)*, ed. Henri Moranvillé (Paris: Renouard, 1891–97), 3:46, December 1, 1382: "ubi protinus omnibus predatis, cedibusque et violationibus virginum ac mulierum a Francis exactis, ipsi totaliter eam cum pluribus aliis villis campestribus in Flandria igne combusserunt."

34. Jean Petit, quoted in Enguerrand de Monstrelet, *Chronique*, ed. Louis-Claude Douët-d'Arcq (Paris: Renouard, 1857–62), 1:241: "piller, rober, raençonner, occire, tuer et prendre femmes a force."

35. *Chronique du religieux de Saint-Denys contenant le règne de Charles VI de 1380 à 1422*, ed. and trans. Louis-François Bellaguet (Paris: Crapelet, 1839–52), 1:366: "viduam et advenam interfecerunt et pupillos occiderunt juvenem simul ac virginem, lacatantem cum homine sene." This citation conjoins two passages from the Old Testament, Psalm 93:6, "Viduam et advenam interfecerunt et pupillos occiderunt," and Deuteronomy 32:25, "juvenum simul ac virginem lactantem cum homine sene."

36. Nicolas de Clamanges, *Ad Johannem de Gersonio..., Epistola LIX*, in *Opera omnia*, ed. J. M. Lydius (Lyons: Elzeuirij & Laurencij, 1613), 161–62: "sunt qui matronarum lectos discerpere non vereantur, plumamque in ventos spargere, praeterea sacrilegia, raptus, adulteria, clandestinas virginum stuprationes, praeterea: monasteriorum atque ecclesiarum, sacrorumque locorum spolia, violationes, impias prophanationes..."

37. Jean Gerson, *Vivat Rex*, in *Œuvres complètes*, ed. Mgr. Palémon Glorieux (Paris: Desclee, 1968), 7:1138: "Las que voit-elle en consideracion? Elle voit turbacion partout, meschief partout, ... violacion de pucelles, prostitution de marieez, boutemens de feu en aucun saintz lieux, prophanacion de sainctes places, murtrissemens de plusieurs..."

38. Dom Claude de Vic and Dom Joseph Vaissette, *Histoire général de Languedoc avec des notes et les pièces justificatives*, vol. 10 (Toulouse: Privat, 1885), no. 728, columns 1809–11.

39. Archives Nationales, Série JJ Registres du Trésor des chartes (hereafter cited as JJ), 179, 149, August 1448 (*prévôté* of Paris), cited by André Plaisse, *Un chef de guerre du XVe siècle, Robert de Flocques, bailli royal d'Evreux* (Evreux: Société libre de l'Eure, 1984), 256–

57: "divers crimes, exces et deliz a cause des fraudes, malices, engins, collations, monopoles, decepcions, faulx seremens, conspiracions, mauvaiz conseilz, subornacions de tesmoigns... corrupcions des officiers royaulx...mauvaiz achas, contraux usuraires de chevances, de rentes, d'imposicions sur vivres en ladite ville...monopoles et collusions sur le fait d'icelles aides et paiement de fausses monnoies et transgressions d'icelles"; "comme d'autre part furs, rapines, adulteres, violemment de pucelles, furnicacions"; "tous meurtres, sacrileges, boutemens de feux, forcemens de femmes, pilleries, roberies, raençonnemens et aultres maulx, crimes, exces et deliz quelzconques." The difference between this formula and the reality of the exactions results in their comparison with the information cited by Plaisse, *Un chef de guerre*, 253–56. On this enumeration of the crimes of soldiers by contemporary theoreticians, see Jean Juvénal des Ursins, *Tres chretien, tres hault, tres puissant roy*, in *Ecrits politiques*, ed. Peter S. Lewis (Paris: Klincksieck, 1978), 116. The treatise is dated 1446 but it describes the crimes committed by Edward III between 1347 and 1350 "as he took, burned, destroyed cities, villages, and countries, castles, fortresses, killed people, stole, ransomed, destroyed churches, raped women" ("comme de prendre, ardoir, destruire citez, villes et pays, chasteulx, forteresses, tuer gens, rober, rançonner, destruire eglises, violer femmes"). I thank Françoise Autrand for having drawn my attention to this text.

40. *Journal d'un bourgeois de Paris*, 51–53.

41. Ibid., 53: "et les femmes de religion et autres prudes femmes et bonnes pucelles efforcees, et tous les hommes rançonnez et les petiz enffans, et les eglises et reliques pillees, et livres et vestemens; et avant qu'il fut dix jours apres la prinse de la ville, elle fu si pillee au net qu'il n'y demoura chose que on peust emporter."

42. Monstrelet, *Chronique*, 3:9; see also *Chronique du religieux de Saint-Denys*, 5:323.

43. Werner Ackermann, Renaud Dulong, and Henri-Pierre Jeudy, *Imaginaires de l'insécurité* (Paris: Meridiens, 1983), 25.

44. Contemporaries perceived this difference between the information and the contents of the argument very well; *Journal de Nicolas de Baye*, 1:246. The same discontinuity accompanies the motives given for the remission and the crime; see n. 39.

45. Archives Nationales, Série X Parlement de Paris, Parlement Criminel, Procès-verbaux des séances (1400–1408) (hereafter cited as X 2a 14), fol. 204v., August 1404: "Jehannequin a batu autrefois Pierre François, procureur, substitut du roi en Ponthieu"; "meurtrier de bois et espieur publique de chemins, noiseur, bateur, et rioteur"; "dont les cas particuliers sont es informacions."

46. *Journal de Nicolas de Baye*, 1:186. Moreover, in order to celebrate the event, the Armagnacs organized a solemn procession to Saint-Magloire on May 22, 1414; ibid., and X 1a 1479, fol. 296: "et ibi infinita facta sunt crimina, ut dicitur." The execution of Raoul Du Plessis, who was decapitated and whose head was sent to his birthplace, sustained the report of crimes committed at Soissons; see the letter of remission granted to his widow, giving her authorization to bury him in holy ground and restoring to her his goods, which had been confiscated: "at the request and entreaty of some of our blood and lineage" ("a la requeste et priere d'aucuns de nostre sanc et lignaige"); JJ 168, July 1415 (*bailliage* of Rouen). With respect to this sack, the chronology inserted into the formulary of Odart Morchesne expressed one of these rare value judgments: "and the town of Soissons was taken by assault and it was a pitious thing" ("et fut prise la ville de Soissons d'assault et fut piteuse chose"); Bibliothèque Nationale de France (hereafter cited as BNF), fr. 2024, fol. 201. Finally, this event compelled the Religieux-de-Saint-Denis to resort to the stereotypes of criminality, even if these were diluted in the narration; *Chronique du religieux de Saint-Denys*, 5:325–27.

47. *Journal d'un bourgeois de Paris*, 87, 97.

48. BNF, fr. 4768, fol. 27, and *Ordonnances des rois de France de la troisième race* (Paris: Impr. Royale, 1723–1849), 11:635. On the context, Jacques d'Avout, *La querelle des Armagnacs et des Bourguignons* (Paris: Gallimard, 1943), 145 ff.: "ont pillé et gasté, gastent, robbent et pillent de jour en jour nostredit royaume et nos bons et loyaux subgets,

ont prins et de jour en jour s'efforcent de prendre nos villes et forteresses et de nos vassaux et subgetz ont tué gens, rançonné, bouté feux, efforcié femmes mariees et autres, violé filles a marier, robé eglises et monasteres et encore sont et s'efforcent de faire toutes autres inumanités que ennemis de nous et de notredit royaume pevent et pourroient faire."

49. BNF, fr. 4768, fol. 31v., and fr. 23 364, fol. 26r-v: "en laquelle sont plusieurs reliques et corps saincts, nostre couronne, nostre oriflamme et plusieurs autres precieulx et riches joyaulx."

50. The event, and it alone, was effectively retained by a small abbreviated note that listed the "principal deeds that occurred in the kingdom from 1302 to 1417" ("principaux faits advenus dans le royaume de 1302 a 1417") and that record laconically: "1411: Monseigneur d'Orleans a Saint-Denis"; BNF, fr. 19 186, fol. 146. A comparable note is the formulary of Odart Morchesne; BNF, fr. 5024, fol. 201: "then they returned to Saint-Denis and to Saint-Cloud near Paris and there was the battle of Saint-Cloud" ("puis s'en retournerent a Saint-Denis et a Saint-Cloud pres Paris et fut bataille de Saint-Cloud"); "ont boutez feux, desrobés esglises, rançonné, tué, mutillé, efforcié femmes mariees, violé pucelles et faict tous maux que aucuns pouvoient faire."

51. The letter of October 14, 1411, was addressed to the consuls of Albi; *Histoire générale de Languedoc,* vol. 10, no. 793, columns 1946–48. A later text, not dated, but undoubtedly from September 1413, indicates that these letters had been "sent through all our kingdom and outside to diverse lordships and kingdoms, even to our saintly Father, the pope, and his college and other great princes and lords" ("envoyees par tout notre royaume et dehors en diverses seigneuries et royaumes mesmement a notre sainct Pere le pape et son college et autres grans princes et seigneurs"); BNF, fr. 2699, fol. 206.

52. Monstrelet, *Chronique,* 2:195.

53. Léon Mirot, "Lettres closes de Charles VI conservées aux Archives de Reims et de Tournai," *Le Moyen Age* 29 (1917–18): 320. The letter was addressed to the town of Reims May 14, 1417: "y ont fait et font encores continuelment chascun jour tous les maulx que ennemis pevent faire, en prenant chasteaulx et villes fermees, en tuant gens, violans femmes mariees et autres, boutans feux, raençonnant gens, pillant eglises en tous lieux et païs ou ilz ont esté et sont."

54. BNF, fr. 4768, fol. 40, and Mirot, "Letters closes," *Le Moyen Age* 30 (1919): 20: "ceulx qui notoiremment ont converti le sacrifice de paix en murdres et homicides et autres innumerables crimes."

55. BNF, fr. 2699, fols. 206–207v.

56. Gauvard and Labory, *Une chronique rimée parisienne,* 207: "car a une pucelle qui fut de haulte gent / Toly son pucellaige et grant planté d'argent." Perhaps an oral tradition is the key.

57. Joseph-Daniel Guigniault and Natalis de Wailly, eds., "Fragment d'une chronique anonyme finissant en 1328, et continué jusqu'en 1340, puis jusqu'en 1383," *Recueil des Historiens des Gaules et de la France* (Paris, 1855), 21:154: "lequel Jourdain estoit renommez de maintes oppressions de vierges et de roberies, de meurtres et de rebellions contre le roy." See also Guillaume de Nangis, *Chronique latine:... Deuxième continuation...,* ed. Hercule Géraud (Paris: Renouard, 1843), 2:46, and Amédée Hellot, ed., "Chronique parisienne anonyme de 1316 à 1339, précédée d'additions à la chronique française dite de Guillaume de Nangis," *Mémoires de la Société de l'histoire de Paris et de l'Ile de France* 11 (1884): 88. Not all chronicles of this kind give the same version of the grievances, however. The discrepancy probably corresponds to other channels and other traditions of information. Certain chroniclers are closer to reality or at least to the confession that this person made at the moment of his torture. For example, Gauvard and Labory, *Une chronique rimée parisienne,* 208: "for they say that many honest men were put to death by him" (car on dist que par lui fut maint proudomme occis). Other chronicles deal with homosexuality; see *Recueil des Historiens des Gaules et de la France,* 21:426.

58. "In 1435 Rodrigo came to Guienne and waged war against the French and the English and they said that he hit children and cut off the breasts of women taken and hit hard with other crimes"; "Petite chronique de Guyenne jusqu'à l'an 1442," ed. Georges Lefèvre-Pontalis, *Bibliothèque de l'Ecole des Chartes* 47 (1886): 65.

59. Louis-Claude Douët-d'Arcq, "Acte d'accusation contre Robert le Coq," *Bibliothèque de l'Ecole des Chartes*, ser. 1, 2 (1841): 367: "que le roy estoit de tres malvais sang et pourry; -et que il ne valoit riens; -et que il gouvernoit tres mal; -et que il n'estoit dignes d'estre roys; -et que il n'avoit droit au royaume; -et que il n'estoit digne de vivre; -et que il fait murdrir sa femme." The same method was used by the Burgundians and the Armagnacs when they insinuated that death by poison was planned by the enemy. On the place accorded to noncontaminated royal blood, see below, n. 138.

60. X 2a 14, fol. 297, January 1406: "vient souvent manger et boire, prendre lait et fromage et autres avantages sur Tourant et sa femme"; "qu'il faloit qu'elle deist et mainstenist que la Tourande l'eust soustraite et fait cognoistre violamment et que la Tourande a pris dans leur jardin trois CL ecus"; "(la) depouillent et la lient a une estache et la battent puis la font asseoir dans la braise de l'atre."

61. It is a question here of the accusation of lèse-majesté to the fourth degree. Monstrelet, *Chronique*, 1:222: "doit estre puny comme traistre, faulx et desloyal audit roy et au royaumes comme criminel de leze-majesté." The accusation is rejected by the abbot of Cerisy; Monstrelet, *Chronique*, 1:332.

62. Monique Langlois and Yvonne Lanhers, *Confessions et jugements de criminels au Parlement de Paris (1319–1350)* (Paris: S.E.V.P.E.N., 1971), 38–39.

63. See the confession of Guillaime de Bruc, which was made under identical circumstances in 1389. Numerous detailed thefts are mentioned in it; *Registre criminel du Châtelet*, 1:26 ff. A comparison with the confession of Mérigot Marchès, which was extremely detailed, shows that the reality of crimes committed by men-at-arms has only a distant connection to the stereotypes; *Registre criminel du Châtelet*, 2:185 ff. The crimes of the famous highwayman are mentioned in detail in Auvergne, JJ 141, 34, July 1391 (*bailliages* of the Mountains of Auvergnes, of Saint-Pierre-le-Moûtier, of Velay). Nonetheless the judges of Châtelet brought this case around to the capital crimes contained in the stereotypes and condemned him to death as "a very strong thief, murderer, and arsonist" ("tres fort larron, murdrier et bouteur de feux"); *Registre criminel du Châtelet*, 1:207.

64. X 2a 14, fol. 404, November 1407: "lui met sus un vieux meurtre, l'efforcement d'une fille et la bature de la mere de ladicte fille."

65. Archives Nationales, Série X Parlement de Paris, Parlement Criminel, Lettres et arrêts (1409–25) (hereafter cited as X 2a 16), fol. 89, September 1410: "magna populorum multitudo ante carceres ubi dictus Dausale detinebatur fuerat propter hoc pluries congregata."

66. X 2a 14, fols. 60v.-67, March 1402: "murtrier, larron et efforceur de femmes et espieur de chemins et l'a confessé."

67. In particular, those which concern the offenses committed on the highways; Perrot, *Les cas royaux*, 206.

68. X 2a 14, fol. 46v., December 1401: "enfreinte d'asseurement donné en la Court du roy et feu bouté dont la cognoissance appartient au roy et efforcement de femme."

69. X 2a 16, fol. 148, January 1411: "seu occasione captionis, raptus, violationis et deflorationis, transportationis et longe detentionis Johanne de la Fleche."

70. X 2a 14, fol. 33 and 34v. July 1401. See the cases cited by Robert Génestal, *Le Privilegium fori en France du décret de Gratien à la fin du XIVe siècle* (Paris: El Leroux, 1921–24), 2nd part, 84 ff.: "accusé de larrecins et maintenoit la femme dudit Denis, maugré mary et tous aultres."

71. Case cited above, n. 68.

72. For example, Archives Nationales, Série Y Châtelet de Paris, Registres des prisonniers entrés au Châtelet (14 juin 1488–31 janvier 1489) (hereafter cited as Y 5266), fol. 3v, June 1488: Jeanne, wife of Jean Soyer, was brought in by the guard at eleven o'clock in the

evening "because she was not behaving properly." See Y 5266, fol. 92v., September 1488, for a couple who were forbidden to see each other. In the same case Y 5266, fol. 132, September 1488, the guard intervened at the request of the spouse, who complained that "for about one year or so the said Gillet and Cassine formed a household together instigated by the said Cassine" and who demanded "that this Gillet be forced to return to his wife and for this reason presented himself before the judge" ("il y a ung an ou environ que lesdiz Gillet et Cassine sont ensemble a pain et pot par l'ennortement de ladicte Cassine...que ycellui Gillet soit contrainct de revenir avecques sa dites femme et pout ce ester a droit").

73. See the text cited by Ludwig Huberti, *Studien zur Rechtsgeschichte der Gottesfrieden und Landsfrieden.* I, *Die Friedensordnungen in Frankreich* (Ansbach: Brugel, 1892), 165–67. Moreover, the truce of 1054 readdressed the same themes; Huberti, *Studien*, 319–20. On the permanence of the vocabulary, Elisabeth Magnou-Nortier, "The Enemies of the Peace: Reflections on a Vocabulary, 500–1000," in *The Peace of God: Social Violence and Religious Response in France around the Year 1000*, ed. Thomas Head and Richard Landes (Ithaca, N.Y.: Cornell University Press, 1992), 58–79.

74. "Sed latronibus quibuslibet ac praedatoribus, licet passim ab agricolis et mercatoribus atque viris ecclesiasticis si extra urbes atque oppida exierint, aurum, argentum, vestem, merces, equos, boves, asinos, jumenta, et bona quaelibet eripere? In qua non alia stipendia quam libertatem rapiendi plerumque militantes habent"; Clamanges, *De lapsu...*, in *Opera omnia*, 44. This "humanist" form of stereotypes also appears in the criminal archives but it is rare; for example, X 2a 14, fol. 290, November 1405, where the criminal is presented as a *depopulator agrorum*. In fact, rather than borrowing from humanism, the defense was inspired by the vocabulary of the clerks mentioned by Jean Bouteiller; see n. 1.

75. Raoul Glaber, *Les cinq livres des histoires*, cited by Huberti, *Studien*, 231–32. And, as early as 1027, Oliva added this clause to the oath of peace that must be taken "ut nullus homo vel femina, de supresscriptis aliquid voluntarie temerare vel infringere praesumat nec invadat res sanctus, neque aliquis se sciente in incestu usque ad sextum gradum permaneat, neque aliquis uxorem propriam dimittat, nec alteram feminam habeat." Huberti, *Studien*, 240–41: "Quis enim umquam antea tantos incestus, tanta adulteria, tantas consanguinitatis illicitas permixtiones, tot concubinarum ludibria, tot malorum aemulationes audiverat."

76. On the means of diffusion of these peace movements, see Roger Bonnaud-Delamare, "Les institutions de paix en Aquitaine au XIe siècle: La paix," *Recueils de la Société Jean Bodin*, (Brussells, 1962), 14–15:421 ff., which insists on a vision of peace in the preamble, in the miracle narratives, and in the content of the oaths. See also Jean-Baptiste Molin, "L'Oratio communis fidelium au Moyen Age en Occident du Xe au XVe siècle," *Miscellanea liturgica in honore cardinale G. Lercaro* 2 (Rome, 1967): 313 ff.

77. Aryeh Grabois, "De la trêve de Dieu à la paix du roi: Etude sur la transformation du mouvement de paix au XIIe siècle," in *Mélanges offerts à René Crozet* (Poitiers: Société d'études médiévales, 1966), 1:585 ff.

78. Ibid., 594 n. 63.

79. Suger, *Vie de Louis VI le Gros*, ed. Henri Waquet (Paris: Champion, 1964), 134–35, 172–73.

80. *Ordonnances des rois de France de la troisième race*, 1:65 ff.

81. Ibid., 390, January 1303; 701 ff., November 1319.

82. Grabois, "De la trêve de Dieu," 586: "Nous prescrivons que les prêtres, les clercs, les moines, les pèlerins, les marchands allant et revenant, ainsi que les paysans avec leur animaux de labourage, les semences et les moutons soient toujours en sûreté."

83. On the consequences of this evolution, see Georges Duby, "Les laïcs et la paix de Dieu," *Hommes et structures du Moyen Age* (Paris: Mouton, 1973), 227–40, and Philippe Contamine, *La guerre au Moyen Age* (Paris: Presses universitaires de France, 1980), 438.

84. On the word *nephandum*, see Jacques Chiffoleau, "Dire l'indicible: Remarques sur la catégorie du *nefandum* du XIIe au XVe siècle," *Annales (Economies, Sociétés, Civilisations)* 45 (1990): 304. Even in the south, the palette of crimes of the *nephandum* is not

reduced to homosexuality. The crimes committed by the rioters of Clermont-en-Lodève are characterized as "perpetratis homicidiis et aliis nephandissimis criminibus"; *Histoire générale de Languedoc,* vol. 10, columns 1632, 1634: it is essentially a question of a prohibition of carrying arms. In the texts of the scholarly clerks, the *nephandum* is not exclusively associated with sodomy; for example, Jean de Venette, *Continuationis Chronici Guillelmi de Nangiaco pars tertia (1340–1368),* ed. Hercule Géraud (Paris: Renouard, 1843), 2:249, 264, designates the murder of the marshals as a crime of *nephandum,* as well as the excesses committed by the Jacques who were associated with the murders and rape. Clamanges, *De lapsu,* 46, uses it in the same way when he assimilates civil war with the rape of the Church, bride of Christ, and concludes that this sacrilege is part of the *nephanda.* Nevertheless, in the texts of this author, the *nephandum* can also be associated with sodomy; see examples cited in n. 87 below. There is the same content of the *nephandum* in the texts of Guillaume de Tignonville; Robert Eder, "*Tignonvillana inedita,*" *Romanische Forschungen* 23 (1915): 919. On the other hand, Jean Gerson does not include homosexuality in his texts; see below, nn. 161, 162. The references of these scholars on this point is probably indicative of the extent to which they are influenced by Roman law, which was very careful to stigmatize homosexuality.

85. In the South, the laws made allusions to heresy and sodomy; see the examples in Gauvard, "*De grace especial,*" 597–98.

86. He was finally burned at the stake for them; *Chronique du religieux de Saint-Denys,* 1:631. See the report of Jean Froissart, *Chroniques,* ed. Siméon Luce, Gaston Raynaud, Léon and Albert Mirot (Paris: Renouard, 1869–1975), book 4, chap. 7.

87. Clamanges, *Epistola LXXVII,* in *Opera omnia,* 231, and *De praesulibus.* in *Opera omnia,* 165.

88. *Registre criminel du Châtelet,* 1:112, 230, 565–66, and 2:273–74. On the importance of rape, see Gauvard, "*De grace especial,*" 332, 814.

89. For example, this remark of the author of the *Chronographia,* who is surprised by the action of Tamerlan against Christian sodomites, is difficult to interpret: "Fide Sarracenus est iste Temurlanus et dure pugnat ac castigat illos qui non tenent regulam Sarracenorum, et maxime acriter corrigit Christianos propter peccatum sodomie quod mirabiler odit super omnia peccata"; *Chronographia regum Francorum,* 3:216 (see n. 33). Is this a model for the king of France to follow?

90. *Le Songe du vergier,* ed. Marion Schnerb-Lièvre, vol. 1 (Paris: Centre national de la recherche scientifique, 1982), 282: "Murtres, ravissemens, sacrileges, en boutant feus et en faisant tout autre fais de guerre"; "et entre les aultres inhumaités, ce ne fait pas a oblier comment ilz rotissoient lez enffans et plusieurs personnez aagees." At the same moment, Venette, *Continuationis,* 2:264–65, describes the carnage of the blind destruction with the same stereotypes in which rape and the massacre of children and pregnant women are mixed together. On the attention given to crimes committed by children, see Gauvard, "*De grace especial,*" 822–27. On the necessary balance between age groups in a civil society, see Gauvard, "*De grace especial,*" 378 ff.

91. For example, Christine de Pizan, "Une épître à Isabeau de Bavière et Lamentation sur les maux de la guerre civile," ed. Raimond Thomassy, in *Essai sur les écrits politiques de Christine de Pisan, suivi d'une notice littéraire et de pièces inédites* (Paris: Debecourt, 1838), 138, and Jean de Montreuil, *Epistolario,* in *Opera,* ed. Ezio Ornato, Nicole Grévy-Pons, and Gilbert Ouy (Turin: Giapichelli, 1963), *epistola* 162, lines 65–77.

92. *Journal d'un bourgeois de Paris,* 389. This accusation is in complete contradiction with the attention that the beggars gave to their own children.

93. See Arlette Farge and Jacques Revel, *Logiques de la foule: L'affaire des enlèvements d'enfants, Paris, 1750* (Paris: Hachette, 1988), 87 ff.

94. Clamanges, *Ad Johannem de Gersonio . . . , Epistola LIX,* 161; and *Journal d'un bourgeois de Paris,* 348, in which the writer paints a portrait of Courtaut, the "terrible and horrible" (*terrible et horrible*) wolf who "had no tail" (*n'avoit point de queue*) when he was captured.

95. Jean-Noël Kapferer, *Rumeurs: Le plus vieux média du monde* (Paris: Seuil, 1987), 10.

96. X 2a 14, fol. 111 ff., March 1403: "que en ce temps estoient plusieurs plaintes de pilleries et roberies et murtres"; "plusieurs personnes qui se plaignirent des IIII dessus diz et des maulx qu'ilz faisoient."

97. On the context of this affair and the people in question, see Eugène Martin-Chabot, "L'affaire des quatre clercs pendus et dépendus à Carcassonne," *Recueil des travaux offerts à Clovis Brunel* (Paris: Société de l'Ecole de Chartes, 1955), 238–52. The confrontation was political. Simon de Cramaud finally won the case in August 1408, and the vicar of Carcassonne, Jean Drouin, was condemned to take down the bodies of the four clerks. Notice that the resolution of the affair followed closely the one concerning Guillaume de Tignonville; see below, n. 161.

98. X 2a 14 (cited above, n. 96), and fol. 133, July 1403: "et sur le fin du conseil fu parlé des murtres, larrecins et autres maulx qui se faisoient au païs et fu demandé se les complices dudit de Louzac qui estoient prins en avoient riens dit ne confessé et le senechal respondi que non et pour se s'esmerveilloit qui povoit ce fere"; "il qui parle dist qu'il avoit IIII prisonniers dont il avoit informacion et qu'il seroit bon qu'on les examinast."

99. "[G]randis multitudo itinerum aggressorum, latronum, disrobatorum et aliorum malefactorum exiterat et ex hoc rumor scandalosus ubicumque in dicta prepositura et locis circumvicinis insurrexerat adeo quod bone gentes nisi sociate se congregate ac dubitanter suas domos exire et ad sua negotia accedere non poterant nec audebant"; X 2a 16, fol. 136v, May 1411.

100. "[D]icebant ulterius dicti defensores quod circa principium mensis junii, anno predicto, grandis et famosus rumor plurimorum latronum et murtrariorum in patria Laudunensi et circumcirca insurrexerat adeo quod bone gentes patrie ad sua negotia nisi congregate et bene associate accedere non audebant"; X 2a 16, fol. 166v. The deeds reported are dated June 1408. See also Archives Nationales, Série X Parlement de Paris, Lettres de arrêts (1404–9) (hereafter cited as X 2a 15), fol. 237, August 1408.

101. *Registre criminel du Châtelet,* 1:69.

102. See Claude Gauvard, "Les révoltes du règne de Charles VI: Tentative pour expliquer un échec," *Révolte et Société: Actes du IVe Colloque d'Histoire au Présent* 1 (1988): 53–55.

103. JJ 137, 108 January 1390 (sénéchaussée de Beaucaire), letter cited in *Histoire générale de Languedoc,* vol. 10, column 1792.

104. "[I]n ipsorum complicium societate quemdam rotulum gesserat in quo recepta confectionis certi poculi tante vigoris quod si quis ex eo biberet statim totus rabidus, invidus et voluntarius gentes occidendi efficeretur, scripta fuerat ex quo poculo dictus Galcherius cum sociis seu complicibus suis supradictis biberat seu gustaverat"; X 2a 16, fol. 168, April 1412.

105. See examples cited in Gauvard, "Les révoltes," 60 n. 7.

106. X 2a 14, fol. 65v. (case cited above, n. 66): "un role ou il avoit en un costé les gentils hommes et d'autre costé les vilains a qui il avoit guerre et les espioit tous, l'un apres l'autre pour les batre et tuer."

107. "[N]emoribus de Rest contiguo ac in periculo districtu sive passagio ubi plura mala fieri consueverant situato quod latronibus fore refugium notorie reputabatur"; X 2a 16, fol. 168 (cited above, n. 100).

108. James George Frazer, *La crainte des morts dans la religion primitive,* 3 vols. (Paris: Nourry, 1934–37), 182–83, 221; and Bronislaw Malinowski, *Trois essais sur la vie sociale des primitifs* (Paris: Payot, 1975), 83–86. Frazer's work was originally published in English as *The Fear of the Dead in Primitive Religion,* 3 vols. (London: Macmillan, 1933–36).

109. "And if in this period of time no one is accused of the crime, he would be freed on bail and through participation they must have their defense through a challenge"; *Ordonnances des rois de France de la troisième race,* 1:558–60, para. 1, April 1315. The extent of this privilege can be measured, but this one is probably supported by an old custom of disparity that corresponds to the time necessary for purification before the resolution of the conflict that caused the crime.

110. *Journal d'un bourgeois de Paris*, 91, May 1418: "and it rained so hard that night that no one smelled any bad odor, and their wounds were washed by the force of the rain, so that in the morning there was no dirty blood or waste on their wounds" ("et plut tant fort celle nuyt que oncques ne sentirent nulle malle odeur, et furent lavez par force de la pluie leurs plaies, que au matin n'y avoit que sang bete, ne ordure sur leur plaies").

111. See Gauvard, *"De grace especial,"* 179 ff.

112. Clamanges, *Opera omnia*, 42, 46, 96, 98, 161, 174–78.

113. "[D]onec desoletur civitas absque habitatore, et domus sine homine et terra relinguatur deserta"; Clamanges, *Epistola XXVII* in *Opera omnia*, 98. These words are a summary of Isaiah as well as Jeremiah and Ezekiel. They follow the description of the crimes committed by the people of Israel or by Babylon when blood was spilled and the women dishonored. Nicolas de Clamanges feeds off three sources concerning the effects of the crime—the Old Testament, the Apocalypse, and Virgil—and by extension the example of Babylon, Jerusalem, and Rome.

114. "Nam homines fuerunt postea magis avari et tenaces, cum multo plura bone quam antea possiderunt; magis etiam cupidi et per lites, brigas et rixas atque per placita seipsos conturbantes"; Venette, *Continuationis*, 2:215; compare with *Continuation de la chronique de Richard Lescot (1344–1364)*, ed. Jean Lemoine (Paris: Renouard, 1896), 84: "Et proh dolor ex hac renovatione non est mundus mutatus in melius nam postea homines fuerunt magis indisciplinati, magis etiam tenaces et cupidi et per lites atque rixas amplius se ipsos perturbantes."

115. Venette, *Continuationis*, 316–17, 331–32.

116. *Journal de Jean de Roye*, 1:166, June 1466: "In the said time a big Norman, native of Coustantin in Normandy, was hanged and strangled on the said gallows of Paris because he had kept his daughter for a long time and had several children with her that he and his said daughter killed as soon as she delivered them; and he was hanged for this case, as it is said, and his daughter was burned in Maigny near Pontoise, where they had come to live from the said country of Normandy" ("oudit temps fut pendu et estranglé oudit gibet de Paris ung gros Normant natif de Coustantin en Normandie pour ce qu'il avoit longuement maintenu une sienne fille et en avoit eu plusiers enfans que lui et sadicte fulle, incontinent qu'elle en estoit delivree, murdrissoient; et pout ledit cas fut pendu, comme dit est, et sadicte fille fut arse a Maigny pres Pontoise ou ilz estoient venus demourer dudit pays de Normandie").

117. *Journal d'un bourgeois de Paris*, 238–39; X 1a 1481, fol. 13, June 1429. For comparable examples at the beginning of the sixteenth century, see nn. 7 and 8. This connection between the fantasies of reproduction and violence is apparent at least as early as the twelfth century; Guillaume de Nangis, *Chronique*, 9, 15, recounts monstrous births in France, Spain, and Brabant in 1115 and 1125. The narratives take a place next to the tyrany of Thomas de Marle and the murder of the Count of Flanders.

118. "Parcite o filii parcite, si qua viscera pietatis in vobis restant, matrem violare. Quis oro vestrum, carnalem matrem si inter bellantes se mediam objiceret, non ferire perhorresceret"; Clamanges, *Epistola LXIII*, in *Opera omnia*, 182. The vision of an unpopulated kingdom takes shape in the end in the powerful description Nicolas de Clamanges paints for the duke of Guyenne; *De lapsu*, 47.

119. For example, Guillaume de Nangis, *Chronique . . . : Deuxième continuation*, 2:156; Venette, *Continuationis*, 2:214, 236 (prophecies of 1348 and 1356). There are numerous examples in the Bourgeois de Paris and in the chronicle of Jean de Roye (see *Journal de Jean de Roye*, 1:160–61), who, because the beans blossomed in June 1466, cites the proverb "The beans are in bloom, the mad are in force."

120. That is to say that he was mangy; *Registre criminel du Châtelet*, 1:38.

121. For example, *Journal de Jean de Roye*, 1:82, cites the case of a sergeant (police officer) beaten in the crossroads "in a dirty, vile, and coarse cart in which there had just been mud and trash" ("dedens ung ort, vilain et paillart tombereau dont on venoit de porter la boe en la voierie"). The cart in and of itself is a sign of infamy.

Claude Gauvard

122. This double purification is translated by the word *expurger* used by Saint Louis, Lettres d'Aigues-Mortes, June 1269, in *Ordonnances des rois de France de la troisième race*, 1:104–6. From this point of view, the first purifier of the kingdom is probably Phillipe Auguste when he decided to pave the roads of Paris. For the fourteenth century, see Archives Nationales, Série Y Châtelet de Paris, Livre rouge vieil (hereafter cited as Y 2), fol. 98, 1388. The cries ordered by the provost of Paris concern the obligation "to keep the streets clean," to take away the rubble, to not throw anything into the Seine, to get rid of pigs, to chase away the "lepers" (*meseaulx*); comparable content in 1404 Y 2, fol. 236. Another cry, during the reign of Charles V, associated mud with the English; Y 2, fol. 111.

123. On the importance of scriptural influences, in particular the Old Testament, in texts of theorists of the reign of Charles VI, see the example of Jean de Terrevermeille studied by Jean Barbey, *La fonction royale: Essence et légitimité, d'après les Tractatus de Jean de Terrevermeille* (Paris: Nouvelles Editions Latines, 1983), 132–51. Nicolas de Clamanges and Jean Gerson borrow from them a thinking and a sensibility that applies perfectly to the hardships of the times and to the hoped-for appearance of the Majestas proper to the Old Testament; see above, n. 113. Pierre d'Ailly uses a comparable step in his *Discours de 1406 devant l'Université de Paris*, cited by Noël Valois, *La France et le Grand Schisme d'Occident* (Paris: Picard, 1896–1902), 2:457 n. 4.

124. On the manifestations of apocalyptic thought in the learned culture of the fourteenth century, see Jean Delumeau, *La peur en Occident: XIVe-XVIIIe siècles* (Paris: Fayard, 1978), 278–80. A close connection existed between the predicators and the political theorists; see the remarks of Etienne Delaruelle, "L'antéchrist chez saint Vincent Ferrier, saint Bernardin de Sienne et autour de Jeanne d'Arc," in *La piété populaire au Moyen Age* (Turin: Bottega d'Erasmo, 1975), 329–54. On the political theorists' vision of the Antichrist, see the example in Pierre Salmon, *Les demandes faites par le roi Charles VI touchant son état et le gouvernement de sa personne, avec les réponses de Pierre Salmon, son secrétaire et familier*, ed. Georges-Adrien Crapelet (Paris: Crapelet, 1823); BN, fr. 9610, fol. 56r-v.

125. Christine de Pizan, *Le livre de la paix*, ed. Charity Cannon Willard (The Hague: Mouton, 1958), 61.

126. For example, for the contaminations of the wells attributed to lepers in 1321, see Guillaume de Nangis, *Chronique...: Deuxième continuation*, 2:31; texts abound for those which, toward 1350, are attributed to Jews; see in particular Guillaume de Machaut, *Œuvres de Guillaume de Machaut*, ed. Ernest Hoepffner, 3 vols. (Paris: Firmin-Didot, 1908–21), 1:144–45. Finally, on the contaminations of 1390, which allowed the provost of Paris to move to make numerous arrests of criminals subjected to extraordinary procedure, see *Registre criminel du Châtelet*, 1:311–22, 419–80, and 2:1–6. In total a dozen people were arrested in this way and condemned to death by Châtelet. On this episode and the interpretations of it given by contemporaries, see *Chronique du religieux de saint-Denys*, 1:682–85.

127. Revelation of Saint John 16:4. The contamination of wells is also severely punished by Roman law and is considered an extraordinary crime; *Digest*, 47.11, in *Corpus Juris Civilis*, ed. Paul Krueger and Theodor Mommsen, 2 vols. (Berlin: Weidmann, 1888–89).

128. These are the circumstances of the *Vivat Rex*. On the agitation surrounding the taking of political positions that follows the agitation surrounding the facts, see Claude Gauvard, "Christine de Pisan a-t-elle eu une pensée politique?" *Revue Historique* 250 (1973): 426. On the effects of the schism in 1408, see, for example, Jean Gerson, *Discours sur la réconciliation*, in *Œuvres complètes*, 7:1105: "It is a very holy task to arrive at bringing back the much desired spiritual peace to the bosom of the Holy Church; may temporal peace be made and be maintained between the lords and especially may peace be restored through this obedience and more especially of this noble kingdom of France" ("C'est tres sainte besongne pour parvenir a ramener paix espirituelle tant desiree au giron de Saincte Eglise, que paix temporelle se face ou se maintiengne entre les seigneurs et par especial de ceste obeissance, et plus especialement de ce noble royaume de France...reviengne paix").

129. Françoise Autrand, *Charles VI: La folie du roi* (Paris: Fayard, 1986), 324–28. Contemporaries are very clear on the connections between the illness of the king and the crimes that are spreading throughout the kingdom. For example, *Journal de Nicolas de Baye*, 1:137–38, August 19, 1405. The court clerk starts by evoking the illness of the king — "This said day, the king being sick in his home of Saint Pol in Paris of the illness of alienation of his mental faculties, which has lasted from the year 1393 with several intervals of remission," ("Cedit jour, le roy estant malade en son hostel de Saint Pol a Paris de la maladie de l'alienation de son entendement, laquelle a duré des l'an 1393, hors aucuns intervalles de resipiscence") — and then listing the crimes committed by the men at war.

130. *Journal de Nicolas de Baye*, 1:93.

131. *Journal de Clément de Fauquembergue*, 1:183–92. There is mention made here of the rhetorical intervention of Jean Courtecuisse and of Pierre aux Boeufs, chaplains of the king and queen. On the specific role that the chaplain plays in the purification of the kingdom, see Pierre Salmon, *Les demandes...*, BNF, fr. 9610, fol. 8v.

132. *Ordonnances des rois de France de la troisième race*, 1:636–37: "nous desirons de plus grant affeccion la pais et seurté de nos subiez et dou peuple qui en nostre reaume vient chacun jour pour vendre et acheter leurs marcheandises car senz marchandises ne se porroit nostre diz reaumes ne nul autre gouverner."

133. Venette, *Continuationis*, 2:311–12, 314, 319.

134. Pizan, *Le livre de la paix*, 96–97.

135. "[I]n dicta villa Carcassone quae multum notabilis fuerat et erat ac prope regnum Arragonie circumdata montaniis et nemoribus quod plurimis situabatur, de die in diem perpetrari dicebant metu quorum multi mercatores et alii ad dictam villam pro suis mercaturis et aliis negotiis venire formidabant rumorem magnum audivisset"; X 2a 15, fol. 237, August 1408. For identical remarks accompanying the famous rumors of the *bailliage* of Vermandois in 1408, see above, n. 100.

136. "Precepit omnibus hominibus dicte ville Fossatensis, ut quilibet ipsorum, infra XL dies, propter defensionem ville predicte contra vires malignantium seu delinquentium, haberet arma sufficienter, secundum quantitatem facultatum suarum"; cited by Louis Tanon, *Histoire des justices des anciennes églises et communautés monastiques de Paris* (Paris: Larose et Forcel, 1883), 323.

137. On this relation between the sin of the king and wars and "pestilence," see *Le Songe du vergier*, book 1, chap. 139, p. 239: "Sir Knight, several times you have tried to exalt the king of France, who is here present, over all other Christian kings; according to what you say, he is not corrupted from any great sin or great vice. I beg you, how can you excuse wars, pestilence, famine, and divisions and mortalities that have happened in his time? Certainly, we must assume that it is because of the sin of the king that the people have such wars and such pestilence. For, because of the sin of King David, eighty thousand people perished" ("Sire Chevalier, vous estes plusieurs foys efforcié d'essaucer le roy de France, qui a present est, sur touz aultres roys crestians, et a vostre dit, il n'est conme de nul grant pechié ou grant vice entechié. Je vous prie, conment le pourrés vous excuser dez guerres, dez pestilences, famines et divisions et mortalités, lesquelles sont avenues de son temps? Certes, nous devons presumer que ce soit pour le pechié du roy David, quatre vinz mille du pueple si perirent"). The knight's answer clarifies the sin of David, who had dared to count his people, but, without denying the contagion of the crime through the "head," he adds the contagion through the limbs. See *Le Songe du vergier*, chap. 140. On Job as a royal and human model, see Clamanges, *Opera omnia*, 192, 216.

138. Eder, "*Tignonvillana inedita*," 1018: "le mauvais roy est comme un charogne qui fait puir la terre en tout de lui; et le bon roy est semblable a la bonne riviere courant qui porte proffit a chascun." This maxim could be compared with another: "A king resembles a great river giving birth to smaller waters; this is why if he is of fresh water, the smaller rivers will be of fresh water, if he is salt, they will be salt"; "*Tignonvillana inedita*," 953.

139. Clamanges, *De lapsu*, 51.

140. A general, synthetic study of the tyranny of the time that interests us has never been done; see Peter S. Lewis, "Jean Juvenal des Ursins and the Common Literary Attitude towards Tyranny in Fifteenth Century France," *Medium Aevum* 34 (1965): 103 ff. On the contribution of the *Policraticus* of Jean de Salisbury, the Aristotelian influences, and theories of Saint Thomas and of Gilles de Rome, see Bernard Guenée, *L'Occident aux XIVe et XVe siècles: Les Etats* (Paris: Presses universitaires de France, 1971), 155–57, and Walter Ullman, "John of Salisbury's *Policraticus* in the Later Middle Ages," in *Jurisprudence in the Middle Ages* (London: Variorum Reprints, 1980), 519–45. On the ideal prince, see Jacques Krynen, *Idéal du prince et pouvoir royal en France à la fin du Moyen Age (1380–1440): Etude sur la littérature politique du temps* (Paris: Picard, 1981), 155–99, and Krynen, *L'empire du roi: Idées et croyances politiques en France XIIIe-XVe siècles* (Paris: Gallimard, 1993).

141. Salmon, *Les demandes*, BN, fr. 9610, fol. 49v.

142. Pizan, *Le Livre de la paix*, 94.

143. Ibid., 121–23.

144. *Chronographia*, 3:200–207.

145. This aspect is treated by Krynen, *Idéal du prince*, 124.

146. They appear rarely; the word *cruauté* is cited only once in the corpus of three hundred letters treated in full text. It is associated with the idea that the adversary is formidable.

147. Gerson, *Vivat Rex*, 7:1138, 1150. Nevertheless, in his texts these words can have a moral sense when they are associated with *horrible,* and also *hideux,* to distinguish the imagined dismemberment of the human and mystic body under the effect of the divisions, Gerson *Vivat Rex,* 1156.

148. Pizan, *Le Livre de la paix*, 82, 96, 93–99. Cruelty is also connected to fiscal exactions: the tyrant exploits and fleeces the innocent, who soon become martyrs. On this form of violence, see Nicolas Oresme, *Traité des monnaies, et autres écrits monétaires du XIVe siècle* (Jean Buridan, Bartole de Sassoferrato), ed. Claude Dupuy and trans. Frédéric Chartrain (Lyons: La Manufacture, 1989), 75, where the author takes the example of Rehoboam, and 85–89.

149. Gerson, *Vivat Rex,* 1158: "Comme venin ou poison occit le corps humain, pareillement tirannie est le venin ou le poison et la maladie qui met a mort toute vie politique et royale."

150. Pizan, *Le Livre de la paix*, 121: "Vous avez desprisié conseil et n'avez voulu estre repris; si me riray de vostre destruccion et ne tendray compte de vous quant soubdaine misere vous vendra et ainsi sera cruel en toutes choses le mauvais prince, dont de telz Dieu nous gart, plain de sang et de vengence, pour lesqueles orribles taches mectre a effect sourdront et courront maulx infinis a lui et a sa contree." See also 93: "Cruelty of the royalty increases and multiplies the number of enemies by putting certain people to death."

151. Such is the image Clamanges gives (*Opera omnia,* 176) concerning the flight to Egypt, "a facie Herodis crudelissimi, suumque sanguinem sitientis"; the same vision appears in Gerson's text where he reinforces it with paintings of representations of the massacre of the Innocents; Gerson, *Œuvres complètes,* 7:331.

152. Pizan, *Le Livre de la paix,* 143: "et le tirant est comme le loup ravissable entre les brebis." This theme comes up in the texts of all the theorists of the reign of Charles VI and beyond, particularly in the texts of Jean Juvénal des Ursins, where it concerns criticizing the tax system.

153. Salmon, *Les demandes*, BNF, fr. 9610, fols. 74v.-75: "parmi vostre royaume, mandant a tous les prelats d'icellui votre royaume que aincy facent faire parmy leurs dioceses, excitant leurs subgiez a prier Dieu continuellement pour l'union de notre mere Sainte Eglise, pour la bonne sancté de vostre personne et pour la paix et concorde de votre dit royaume qui de present est en grant perplexité et en voye de desolation." The Burgundian character of obedience is familiar, but the attitude of the reformers who called themselves Armagnacs is no different. Everyone admits the necessity of processions; Froissart, *Chroniques*, 13:189. On the application of this advice see above, n. 130. Christine de Pizan gives

this same advice of recourse to processions to Isabeau of Bavaria; see "La Lamentacion sur les maux de la France," in *Mélanges de langue et littérature française du Moyen Age et de la Renaissance offerts à Charles Foulon,* ed. Angus J. Kennedy (Rennes: Institut Française de l'Université de Haute-Bretagne, 1980), 144: "Why not have processions with devout prayer?" ("pourquoy ne faiz processions par devotes prieres?").

154. Claude Gauvard, "Ordonnance de réforme et pouvoir législatif en France au XIVe siècle (1303–1413)," in *Renaissance du pouvoir législatif et genèse de l'Etat,* ed. André Gouron and Albert Rigaudière (Montpellier: Socapress, 1988), 94–96.

155. On the action of the reformers, see the case cited in Gauvard, *"De grace especial,"* chap. 4, n. 23.

156. See the examples cited by Krynen, *Idéal du prince,* 93–94, 184–99. From this point of view, the best theorist of the king-dispenser of justice is Gerson, in particular when he defines the natural sources of justices, "virtue by which the person who has it is inclined to render to each person that which is his right by nature" ("vertus par laquelle celui qui l'a est enclin rendre a chascun ce qui est sien par le droit de nature"), and then the political sources of justice, "who is inclined to render to each person that which is his according to the laws and goal of the policy which is either temporal or spiritual" ("qui incline rendre a un chascun ce qui est sien selon les ordonnances et la fin de la policie ou il est soit temporelle soit spirituelle"); Gerson, *Œuvres complètes,* 7:608.

157. Pizan, *Le Livre de la paix,* 95: "l'une car les mauvais n'oseront persecuter les bons pour ce qu'ilz saront bien que ta droituriere justice les pugniroit, l'autre que nul n'ara envie de devenir mauvais quant chascun sara que tu soies le pugnisseur d'iceulx. Si auront cause d'eulx amender et par ainsi convendra estre paix entre les tiens, laquelle chose est la gloire et augmentacion de toute royaume."

158. Pizan, *Le Livre de la paix,* 96: "divers ministres et lieuxtenans en toutes les juridiccions espandus."

159. Clamanges, *Ad Johannem de Gersonio..., Epistola LIX,* 164: "Quod praeterea illis Regiis magistratibus, quos vulgo Bavilos appellant, cura mandata sit, ut quoties per fines quos administrant, exercitum duci continget, ipsi cum via exercitu donec fines suos exeat adequitent, villas custodiant, praedas inhibeant, damni et injuriarum quaerelas audiant, et pro delictorum modo poena noxios afficiant." On the efficacy of such justice, see *De lapsu,* 56.

160. Gerson, *Vivat Rex,* 1173–74; he illustrates this consideration with a certain number of examples where, in order to protect the law, the princes did justice against themselves and their own children.

161. Mgr. Glorieux links the writing of the *Diligite justiciam* by Jean Gerson to the Guillaume de Tignonville affair, which brought about the deposition of the provost. It dates from the lecture of May 5 or 12, 1408; Gerson, *Œuvres complètes,* 7:viii, 598–615. Remember that the provost had two "clerks" hanged, Leger Du Moncel, a Norman, and Olivier Bougeois, a Breton, on October 26, 1406, and over the course of 1407 the king underwent pressures to condemn the provost to an honorable fine. The defense relative to this affair took place November 27–28, 1407, at the council and it was only registered in the civil registers of the Parlement and not in the criminal registers; X 1a 4788, fols. 1v-4. The provost was repudiated only after the purge that followed Jean sans Peur's entry into Paris in the spring of 1408. Guillaume de Tignonville was replaced by Pierre Des Essarts, and he was subjected to an honorable fine on May 16, 1408. On this episode, see *Chronique du religieux de Saint-Denys,* 3:722. This is a political affair since the provost had allegiances with Orleans *Journal de Nicolas de Baye,* 1:229 n. 1), but it also inscribed against a theoretical background that puts into question the relation between the church and state. In this context, it is important to determine the date of the *Diligite justiciam* in order to evaluate the position of Jean Gerson vis-à-vis Jean sans Peur. G. H. M. Posthumus Meyjes, *Jean Gerson et l'Assemblée de Vincennes (1329)* (Leiden: Brill, 1978), 33–53, gives excellent reasons borrowed from the religious politics to date the *Diligite justiciam* at November 12, 1405, which would place it just after the *Vivat Rex* of November 6, 1405. But

other reasons exist to push the date of the *Diligite justiciam* to the winter of 1405–6, in particular the similarities between the themes treated in the two sermons, whether it concerns justice or the death penalty; see above, n. 158. In both cases, this problem is not evoked according to tyrranicide, which refutes absolutely the suggestion of May 1408 as its date. Gerson would not have passed over in silence the murder of the duke of Orleans, and especially the justification of Jean Petit of March 8, 1408, in which the *Non occides* is evoked to justify the suppression of the tyrant. In fact, the *Diligite justiciam* should be connected to another trial, which put Guillaume de Tignonville in question on January 18, 1406, and which up until now has been virtually ignored by historians; X 2a 14, fols. 298v–300v. The provost was defender at the sides of counsel Jean Larcheveque, examiner of the Châtelet, and counsel Robert Carlier, the king's prosecutor at the Treasury, against the bishop of Paris, plaintiff. The provost is accused of having two wrongdoers hanged who called themselves "clerks," Jaquet Blondel from the county of Montcornet and Cardin Cabre of Rouen. Both of them belonged to a gang of petty criminals that Guillaume de Tignonville had succeeded in dismantling. The trial gave rise to a discussion of the rapport between the two justices and their reciprocal efficiency. Unfortunately the trial does not give the date on which the two clerks, incarcerated at the Châtelet November 17, 1405, were hanged. Is there a connection between this affair and the *Diligite justiciam*? The themes of the oath and the arguments of the provost in the defense intersect. Guillaume de Tignonville's argument aims at making the clerks *publici larrones* and at evoking the crimes that they committed and to which they confessed at the foot of the gallows, crimes that, in the eyes of the provost, consequently deserve the death penalty because these men are incorrigible. Is there a connection between this action of the provost and the university strike, which only ended at the end of January 1406? The elements converge. They show, in any case, that the second affair is known, that is to say that the hanging of the two clerks decided on October 26, 1407, is a recurrent offense in a concerted politic in which the provost of Paris has complete support of the Counsel dominated by the partisans of the duke of Orleans. At the trial of January 1406, he has the support of the king's prosecutor, and in November 1407, the trial took place in the civil, not the criminal, courts. The decision made May 5, 1408, against Guillaume de Tignonville is anti-Orleanist. But behind the men there are also the ideas. The stakes concern the freedom of the clergy and on the degree of concentration of police powers at the disposition of the provost. See below, n. 173. The text of the trial is now published; see Claude Gauvard, "Les humanistes et la justice sous le regne de Charles VI," in *Pratiques de la culture écrite en France au XVe siècle*, ed. Monique Ornato et Nicole Pons (Louvain-la-Neuve: FIDEM, 1995), 217–66.

162. In his argument, Jean Gerson does not deny the necessity of the death penalty, but he refutes it in the case of theft. The goal of the bishop of Paris, like that of Gerson, is to show, among other arguments, that these clerks are not thieves. Theft acquired its place in the hierarchy of major crimes with difficulty, "comme des meurtriers, des adulteres, des herites, des sorciers." See Gauvard, *"De grace especial,"* 827. The theoretical ground that opposes divine law to civil law is already questioned by Gilles Couvreur, *Les pauvres ont-ils des droits? Recherches sur le vol en cas d'extrême nécessité depuis la Concordia de Gratien (1140) jusqu'à Guillaume d'Auxerre (mort en 1231)* (Rome: Libreria editrice dell'Università gregoria, 1961), 172–77.

163. "[R]aros latrones et homicidas aut quorumlibet gravissimorum reos criminum videmus nisi propter inopiam capitis supplicio affici. Est itaque parricidia, et quibuslibet facinoribus aliis crimen gravius esse pauperem. Quoniam propter illud capite quis plectitur, dives autem facinorosus, si quaelibet mala commiserit, pecunia militat"; Clamanges, *Ad Gerardum Macheti . . . , Epistola LXVII*, in *Opera omnia*, 192.

164. On this difficult emergence of legislation, see Jacques Krynen, " 'De nostre certaine science . . .': Remarques sur l'absolutisme législatif de la monarchie médiévale française," in *Renaissance du pouvoir législatif*, 131–44. In the *Diligite justiciam*, the influence of Jean de Salisbury is probably important, but one must take into account the teaching of the civilists and the *Digest*, which, as early as the twelfth century, formulated a veritable

doctrine of equity. For them, the human law flows from the law of God. The law is only the goodwill of the prince if he conforms to equity. The Ciceronian influence that fed the defenders of Jean de Salisbury on tyrannicide and on the law was probably appealing to Jean Gerson; see Jean de Salisbury, *Policraticus*, book 3, chaps. 15 and 17.

165. X 2a 14, fols. 267–275v, August 11, 1405, cited in Gauvard, *"De grace especial,"* chap. 4, n. 126. In this affair, Jean de Terrevermeille would have shown the judge that he had acted wrongly; X 2a 14, fol. 273: "que quant une personne est condempnee pour un crime enorme et qui est contre chose publique, il doit estre executé."

166. X 2a 14, fol. 275v: "que les gens de Montpellier sont merveilleux et y a plus de cent ans que on ne fist justice de personne qui eust puissance car il composent toujours a argent et ont toujours a coustume de mencier le juge et de le mectre au proces se il fait justice."

167. *Ordonnances des rois de France de la troisième race*, 8:122; Gerson, *Œuvres complètes*, 7:341–43. See the examples cited by Mireille Vincent-Cassy, "Prison et châtiments à la fin du Moyen Age," in *Les marginaux et les exclus dans l'histoire*, Cahiers Jussieu n. 5 (Paris: Union Générale, 1979), 274 n. 39.

168. "Nous avons entendu que parmi nostre royaume sont et vont et conversent plusieurs personnes, hommes et fammes, banniz et bannies de nostredit royaume pour meurtres, larrecins et autres malefaçons que ils ont fait et commis en nostredit royaume"; "jusques à ce que la verité soit scüe et qu'il en soit ordonné et a ce fait"; *Ordonnances des rois de France de la troisième race*, 4:158–59.

169. *Ordonnances des rois de France de la troisième race*, 1:743, December 1320: "car les prevosts qui pour le temps ont esté, chascun en droit loy, en apporte les registres dont ly roys a perdu moult de amendes et moult de fais sont demourés impunis."

170. Y 2, fol. 55–55v, February 1368 and May 1369: Only the provost has the seal of Châtelet, and he must have been suspicious of the "princes of blood and lineage and high dispensers of justice" for the dismissals and remissions, in particular concerning the people of the Hôtel of the king. Y 2, fol. 47, November 16, 1370: the dismissals in front of the Parlement operated by the bailiffs, sergeants, and officers are condemned. On the other hand, the statutes of the jail of Châtelet enacted in the first half of the fourteenth century are put back in order by Hugues Aubriot on June 28, 1372; *Registre criminel du Châtelet*, 1:246, 351. On the putting into place of extraordinary procedure in Paris during his tenure, see Gauvard, *"De grace especial,"* chap. 4, n. 21.

171. On the originality of this person and his decisive role in the events that oppose him to the university at the beginning of Charles VI's reign, sign of a long restraint imposed on the clerks, see Autrand, *Charles VI*, 76–78. Numerous acts passed by the provost are cataloged by Antoine-Jean-Victor Le Roux de Lincy, "Hugues Aubriot, prévôt de Paris sous Charles V," *Bibliothèque de l'Ecole des Chartes*, ser. 5, 3 (1862):173 ff.

172. *Ordonnances des rois de France de la troisième race*, 7:227, February 1389: "il a grant foison de bon conseil et saige et ou nous avons nostre conseil et autres officiers pour aidier a garder noz droiz et le bien de justice." This text criticizes the judicial action of Jean Truquam against the Jews whose crimes are unpunished. In June 1389, the provost, Jean de Folleville, proceeds to a reformation of the Châtelet, *Ordonnances des rois de France de la troisième race*, 7:283.

173. On the ordinances relative to the power of the provost, see Y 2, piece 184, fol. 134, May 20, 1389; *Ordonnances des rois de France de la troisième race*, 8:364, March 2, 1399; 8:443, June 21, 1401; 12:578, April 20, 1402; 9:261, November 29, 1407. The king calls the provost of Paris "steward and general reformer of the police of our good city and workers of Paris," as early as 1368 ("commissaire et general reformateur sur le fait de la police de nostre bonne ville et mestier de Paris"); Nicolas de La Mare, *Traité de la police* (Paris: Brunet, 1729), vol. 4, book 6, 663, and *Ordonnances des rois de France de la troisième race*, 9:172, April 1399. The Parlement recognizes this title at the beginning of the fifteenth century; Archives Nationales, Série X Parlement de Paris, Procès-verbaux de séances (1411–17) (hereafter cited as X 2a 17), fol. 2v, February 1411.

174. Alfred Coville, *Les Cabochiens et l'ordonnance de 1413* (Paris: Hachette, 1888), 145–46.

175. Cited by Charles Desmaze, *Le Châtelet de Paris, son organisation, ses privilèges,* 2nd ed. (Paris: Didier, 1863), 133.

176. *Ordonnances des rois de France de la troisième race,* 12:509, October 6, 1447.

177. On the meaning of this backward-looking theme in political reform, see Raymond Cazelles, "Une exigence de l'opinion depuis Saint Louis: La réformation de royaume," *Annuaire Bulletin de la Société historique de France,* 1962–63, 91 ff., and Colette Beaune, *Naissance de la nation France* (Paris: Gallimard, 1985), 126 ff.

178. "Extraits d'une chronique anonyme finissant en 1380," *Recueil des Historiens des Gaules et de la France,* 21:141.

179. "Extraits des chroniques de Saint-Denis," *Recueil des Historiens des Gaules et de la France,* 21:118.

180. There are numerous examples of the case of Taperel in the little chronicles, for example, "Extraits des chroniques de Saint-Denis," *Recueil des Historiens des Gaules et de la France* 21:140. See above, n. 56.

181. Y 2, fol. 134, May 20, 1389.

182. See above, n. 176: "informer contre plusieurs larrons, mendiants, espieurs de chemins, ravisseurs de femmes, violeurs d'eglises, tireurs a l'oye, joueurs de faulx dez, trompeurs, faulx monnoyeurs, malfaicteurs et autres associez, recepteurs et complices."

183. X 2a 16, fols. 162–169v, April 1412: "ordinationes et instructiones factas et in auditorio curie baillivi Viromandensis apud Laudunensem scriptas et registras suas dictus prepositus et alii servientes nominati in dicta baillivia inviolabiliter observare juraverant"; "littere nostre a dicta nostra curia emanate sub data XXVIII diei aprilis anno predicto millio CCCC octavo per quas quoscumque criminosos et malefactores ubicumque in dictis baillivia Viromandensi et prepositura Laudunensi ac etiam aliis juridicionibus et locis eisdem contiguis . . . capiendi et puniendi auctoritatem mandatum."

184. X 2a 14, fol. 308v, March 1406: "que par la Court de ceans a esté donné mandement et commission au bailli d'Amiens pour prendre et punir les malfaiteurs et bannis etc. et audit bailli en donnant ledit mandement en chargea la Court faire bonne diligence contre cez malfaiteurs qui chacun jour labeurent contre la chose publique."

185. X 2a 17, fol. 127v, January 1414: "que son office est chevaucher par les mettes de laditte prevosté et de prendre et enquerir les malfaiteurs."

186. Merriam Sherwood, "Un registre de la cour criminelle de Mireval," *Annales du Midi* 53 (1941): 174.

187. JJ 135, 267, April 1389, Mirande (*sénéchaussée* of Agen).

188. JJ 118, 82, November 1380, Reims (*bailliage* of Vermandois): "Ribaud mauvais, j'ay esté par toy pris par la mort Dieu tu y mourras."

CHAPTER 2

✧

Needful Things

Louise O. Fradenburg

There is nothing that permits one to define what is useful to man.
— Georges Bataille, *Visions of Excess,* 116

He lives in justice and sanctity who is an unprejudiced assessor of the intrinsic value of things.
— Saint Augustine, *On Christian Doctrine*

We would rather have a gay time than work and still have nothing.
— Jean Gerson, citing one of the working poor of Paris

This essay explores the relevance of the concept of need to some of the questions that historians of medieval crime have posed for themselves. I will be interested in how the concept of need has structured thinking about the relation of crime to poverty, and about the relationship of crime and poverty, in turn, to discourses of charity. In considering the notion of the "needful thing," I will also be addressing some issues about subjectivity in relation to the law: how the law both emanates from and structures desire, on the level of the subject and on the level of what Slavoj Žižek calls "communal enjoyment."[1]

My theoretical starting point is a psychoanalytic one: law structures and is structured by desire.[2] However, the concealment or management of this intimacy between law and desire is fundamental to what Žižek calls the "ideological operation," including that of traditional ethics, which often posits the law (reason, natural law, divine law, *ius gentium*) as forming a different order from desire, hence as that which disciplines or purifies, rather than emanates from, concupiscence.[3] The English jurist Henry de Bracton treats legal judgment as an activity resonant with long-established ethical concerns about prematurity and maturity, reason and passion, presumption and humility, care of the self and carelessness of the self, and proper and improper "gain": even if "one is fit to judge and to be made a judge, let each one take care for himself lest, by judging perversely and against the laws, because of prayer or price, for the advantage of a temporary and insignificant gain, he dare to bring upon himself sorrow and lamentation everlasting."[4] The severance of desire from the law, such that the law becomes that to which our desire must submit itself for review, has some obvious benefits: it persuades us that we are indeed disciplining or purifying our passions when we obey the law, rather than enjoying ourselves just as passionally in a roundabout way, and it persuades us that the law to which we submit takes its origins beyond, rather than from, the arbitrariness and changefulness of desire.

The concept of need does much of its ideological work in the context of the severance of the law from desire. The distinction between need and desire permits the association of desire with superfluity and the law with necessity. The link between law and necessity is clearly attested in the semantic range of "need" in Middle English.[5] It is also attested in a fearful passage in Proverbs (30:8–9): "'beggerie and richessis ne ȝiue thou [God] to me; ȝif onli to my liflode nedeful thingus; lest par auenture I fulfild, be drawen to denyen, and seie, Who is the Lord? and thurȝ nede constreyned, stele, and forswere the name of my God.'"[6] In this formulation, needful things are the warranty of a life free of crime, the warranty of belief, of the devotional subject's very ability to recognize, and be recognized by, his God.

Moreover, need not only underwrites the law; the distinction between need and desire enables the calculation of the sacrifice of the broken heart, which is also to say, the "good" superfluity of charity. That Christ need not have lived under the law but willed his submission to it—that he "chose this most powerful way to destroy the devil's work"—is for Bracton the "analogy" that justifies the king's submission to the law.[7] And as Michel Mollat notes, in medieval writing about charity the rich man was to give "whatever he held in excess, beyond his needs." But Mollat notes further that "this [measure] was difficult to pinpoint precisely, because it depended on so many things."[8] As we shall see, need can slide very easily into excess, precisely because the one cannot be thought—or deployed—without the other, and because the permeability of the borderline between them is as ideologically useful as is its power of demarcation. The ease with which need can slide into excess is both fundamental and dangerous to the ideological power of the concept of need.

Law in Piers Plowman

Passus I of *Piers Plowman* begins with the dreamer petitioning Holy Church to know the meaning of the landscape in which he finds himself: "Mercy, madame, what may this be to mene?"[9] Her response is that "Truth" is inside "the tour vppon þe tofte" (C.I.12). The passage brings out the trauma of signification characteristic of medieval dreamvision: the sense of awakening into an Other scene, into an indecipherable symbolic order whose relation to the desire of the dreamer is oblique, and whose desires with respect to the dreamer are similarly oblique. For Langland, the problem of Truth is the problem of acting according to words that seek, mysteriously, to design us, of living according to a law

50

that seems to precede the subject and about which the subject knows nothing: "wolde þat ȝe wroghton as his word techeth," says Holy Church, "For he is fader of fayth and formor of alle" (C.I.13–14).

By bringing out the strange disjunction, the disjunctive strangeness, between the believer and the author of his belief, the "fader of fayth," this passage reveals to us how the subject is bound to the law through the law's very strangeness, through the way that strangeness propels us into the very undecideability that is the vertiginous ground of the most rigorous conceptions of belief.[10] But the passage also brings out the extent to which the making of meaning (Žižek's "jouis-sense," the "enjoyment-in-sense" proper to ideology) seeks to close the gap constitutive of faith, to fill the unknowability of Truth or of the words one should work by with endless positive precepts.[11] The productivity of the unknowability of absolute law also emerges in medieval legal discourse; respect for the very remoteness of Truth, a remoteness figured in Bracton as God's distant throne, the "seat of judgment," is what propels the subject into a life of lawfulness and humility and the learning of mundane custom.[12]

The series of precepts on which Holy Church now embarks centers on the body's need for "mesure" (C.I.19); the first of many truths that the dreamer does not know but ought to work by is that there are three needful things.[13] Holy Church explains that Truth has

> comaundede of his cortesye in comune thre thynges;
> Aren non nidefole but tho thre, and nemne hem y thenke
> And rekene hem by rewe—reherse hem wher þe liketh.
> The firste is fode, and vesture þe seconde,
> And drynke þat doth the good—and drynke nat out of tyme.
> (C.I.20–24)

Food, clothing, and good and timely drink are, according to Holy Church and Ecclesiastes 29:28 and 39:31, the *only* needful things. In this moment of the subject's confrontation with the commandments one should live by, the establishment of such a baseline directly links Langland's evocation of the strangeness of the law to the discourses on poverty that fill his poem. The mysteriousness of the law—the arbitrariness and exteriority of commandment—is mitigated through the concept of necessity, through the figure of an obligation *to* necessity. Only by establishing what is needful can one's obligations to one's own body and life and to the bodies and lives of others be calculated and acted upon.

The emergence of the economics of charity at this moment of the subject's radical uncertainty, moreover, suggests the role such a baseline can play precisely when the subject is in question. To know what is owed to the poor *is* to know what one owes to Truth. Later on in the poem, Hunger argues that society's obligations to the poor have their limits:

no one should starve, but on the other hand the lives of the poor need not be maintained, as Pearsall puts it, "beyond the meanest level."[14] And yet were this baseline so clear it would not be necessary to worry endlessly, as Langland's poem does, over what should be given and how and under what circumstances.[15]

Both the ethical force and the restless form of *Piers Plowman* derive from Langland's inscription into the poem of how the law, through its very attempts to discipline desire, propels desire; the law defines need, but creates thereby an unstable borderline whereby what is defined as need can slip into desire. The dreamer dreams of tutelage as to what he must do; his desire is *for* instruction, for meaning, for "enjoyment-insense." And yet this desire is also posited as a vagrant desire for strangeness; the dreamer who will shortly find Holy Church sets out for "wondres to here" (C.Prol.4). The alterity of the law that he will confront in his dream is precisely the "scene" to which his mobility and desire draw him—as is further attested when Holy Church will relocate Truth within the dreamer's own strange "heart."[16]

Lacan on Law and Desire

The fact that desire leads us to the law, and the law to desire, is fundamental also to Jacques Lacan's understanding of the process whereby the subject comes into being, through its attempts to identify with certain signifiers of the symbolic order—names, kinship terms, and so on. Lacan worked out this logic in his famous essay "The Mirror Stage," where he argued that before the subject's later negotiations with the signifiers of the open-ended symbolic order, the infantile being will attempt to identify with its own mirror image—an image marked by its formal symmetry as against the turbulent life of the being and its *"jouissance,"* and therefore by the capacity of the image to represent an ideal that could seem either persecutory or grand, as well as by the emptiness of the image and its distance from the being.[17] The anxieties and satisfactions of the subject in this "imaginary" relation to its own image would resurface in the subject's attempt to identify and possess the protean signifiers of the symbolic order. These notions of subject formation can help us to understand the melancholic economy of sacrifice.

Two fundamental points of Lacanian theory provide a starting point: the notion that desire is always desire of the other, the desire to be recognized by the other (the mirror image, the symbolic order); and the notion of the "fundamental dimension of the unknown in desire, of something that doesn't resemble me," a dimension that has been variously named *jouissance,* the unconscious, the *Nebenmensch* (neighbor), *das Ding* (the Thing), or, in one of Žižek's favorite formulations, that which is in the subject more than itself, the "'something in it more than itself,'" the stranger to myself who is also my closest neighbor, and who structures my relations with all my other neighbors.[18] As that portion of *jouissance,* of enjoyment, made inaccessible to the subject when the subject identifies with, "assumes," or is "interpellated by" the signifier, *das Ding* is "extimate," both interior and exterior to the subject, inhabiting the subject but also strange, unconscious, unknowable. Lacan remarks that *"Das Ding* presents itself at the level of unconscious experience as that which already makes the law. . . . It is a capricious and arbitrary law, the law of the oracle, the law of signs *in which the subject receives no guarantee from anywhere."*[19] Because the Thing emerges as a consequence of the restructuring of the subject's *jouissance* by the signifier, the Thing is inseparable from the subject's assumption of the signifier, but is also, by definition, where the signifier *is not.* The Thing "presents itself at the level of unconscious experience as that which already makes the law," because the laws that govern signification—laws that are structural and empty of "positive" meaning, whose "messages" are therefore perplexing, "oracular"—constitute the subject and its relation to the Thing, and because the Thing, although not present in the signifier, nevertheless does not cease to mobilize it, to put it through its paces.

There are two consequences of this logic that are particularly significant to this essay: one, that submission to the law always points the subject in the direction of the Thing, of lost *jouissance* (discipline and sacrifice are "next to" desire, as the opening of *Piers Plowman* indicates); two, that the objects that come to acquire value for the subject do so insofar as they participate in the symbolic order and insofar as they also point the subject in the direction of the Thing. From the point of view of Lacanian psychoanalysis, the circumstances in which objects acquire meaning for the subject make it difficult indeed to define some objects as needful and others as luxurious. And the ethical dimension of the subject's sacrifice of such objects must be analyzed in terms of the patterning of the subject's (lost) *jouissance* by the signifier, of the production of what Žižek calls "surplus enjoyment" or the *"plus-de-jouir,"* that portion of *jouissance* left over, and structured through, the designs of the signifier.[20]

Need in Piers Plowman

We now have the beginnings of a basis for understanding the emergence of the figure of Need toward the end of *Piers Plowman*. Robert Adams, in "The Nature of Need in *Piers Plowman,*" contends that the personification of Need in *Piers Plowman* is not meant to be a sympathetic figure but a disquieting warning of last things. Medieval apocalyptic literature associated need with Satan and with the Antichrist, and with the last age of the church as a time of dearth and universal deception. Thus Will dreams of the Antichrist as one who made "fals sprynge and sprede and spede mennes nedes," so that men would misinterpret their sinful desires as legitimate needs (following Job 41:13, "nede shal go befom his [Leviathan's] face" [Wycliffe]); and the figure of Need is followed by Rechelessnesse, in Adams's view, because "nede haþ no lawe."[21]

I share David Aers's reservations about Adams's reading of the import of Need; Aers argues that the figure of Need reaffirms the rights of those in need to "the necessities for physical survival disciplined by temperance" and that the purpose of Need is to reassure the poet that he has "some justification for his own peculiar life," his vagrancy and vagrant art, "so long as he takes no more than he needs for survival."[22] Indeed it is significant that, at the end as well as at the beginning of *Piers Plowman*, the question of the poet's vagrancy and desire for strangeness should emerge so powerfully in connection with need, as potential ethical justification for the poet's "mode of enjoyment." While I think Need is on the whole a sympathetic figure, however, I think Need should not be altogether shorn of ambiguity. The ambiguity of Need has produced such markedly different readings of these passages in part because need is so terribly useful in legitimating various (critical) desires and not others; Need will be read variously because the concept Need embodies is impossible to stabilize. *Piers Plowman* is remarkable, in my view at least, not so much because it knows that the search for ethical certainty is endless, but because it knows that that search is inspired by the endlessness of desire.

This knowledge is, however, far from comforting, and the strangeness sought by desire, "that which is in us more than ourselves," the remote Truth within our hearts, is also feared and defended against in *Piers Plowman*. The fact that the proliferation of needs immediately precedes the Antichrist's coming in the apocalyptic literature of the Middle Ages forcefully suggests the terror that need's potential for deception could inspire. We might at any time believe that we are calculating properly, obeying necessity, observing the law, respecting property; but all the while we might instead be tipping over into excess, into a vile enjoyment, into crime — an anxiety embodied in the figure of Rechelessnesse and not resolved, because unresolvable, at the end of *Piers Plowman*.[23] This is why discourses of charity were (and remain) so calculating; they are propelled by an anxious concern to detect excess, to "know" that moment when the needful has passed into the luxurious or enjoyable, indeed to "know" that moment when mere survival passes into something more ambitious.

Communal Enjoyment: Theft, Things, and the Pauper

Thus the needful thing, in discourses of charity, becomes a measure that enables the calculation of a life that exceeds or transcends necessity. The life lived by the poor is a means of producing economic value through its very privation of value. The needful thing operates similarly to an economic index; it is, in Gilles Deleuze and Félix Guattari's terms, a "limit-object" enabling the calculations that make profit possible.[24] It is how the almsgiver knows she is spending the minimum necessary to ensure salvation; it is also how the almsgiver structures the difference between her life and the life lived by the poor, between mere survival and more honorable, because ethically riskier (in the ideological fantasy of the almsgiver), modes of living.

But such an index is not absolute, and the fear that the subject can deceive itself as to its needs is closely related to the fear, expressed in the rigorist discourses of charity in the later Middle Ages, that the subject can be deceived as to the needs of others, that the subject might find itself wrongfully dispossessed, emptied out, by the tricks of "sturdy beggars" (beggars who can work but refuse to do so). The close relation of these two anxieties is one more indication that the problem of "need" names something central to the economy of the subject's relation to the other, just as the apocalyptic proportions these anxieties could attain indicate the potential of need to shatter that economy, to derange fatally the subject's relation to community and to providential order: in *Piers Plowman* the poet's desire for strangeness, even his desire to *be* strange, to wander, is in question because the strangeness of vagrancy has put the community's mode of enjoyment in question.[25]

The problematic status of need points to our fear of excessive enjoyment, the strangely other Thing that inhabits us and makes us fear the enjoyment of the strange Other outside of us. It thus points to our finitude, to the limits of our knowledge of ourselves and of the other, and, paradoxically, to the limits of our enjoyment, insofar as to approach our *jouissance* is to lose ourselves as we know ourselves. This is why, when we approach too closely the *jouissance* that is within us and within the other, both our image and the image of the other threaten to fall apart, to fragment. The concepts of need and of the needful thing protect us from the enjoyment we fear within as well as outside of ourselves. They are how we attempt to measure what we give to the other and what the other takes from us; they are also how we measure the pleasure of such exchanges. Modes of renunciation are also and inevitably modes of enjoyment.

It is this irreducible partiality of the subject's enjoyment that emerges in the figure of what Žižek calls the "theft of enjoyment," whereby we explain to ourselves that we are not completely happy, that we mourn some lost piece of ourselves, that we feel like strangers to ourselves, because the other, the stranger, outside us, has stolen it from us.[26] That other, that stranger, can seem to possess an excessive enjoyment, a surplus vitality, because that other has stolen ours from us; and paradoxically that other might also seem to be empty, avid, avaricious, envious, because of its designs on our inner substance. The ease with which we make the assumption that poverty passes easily into crime exemplifies the ease with which the dispossessed other comes to mean the dispossessing other, the inverted figure of the abundance and superlative vitality of the sovereign.[27]

The figure of the "sturdy beggar," often also a "strong robber," haunts the labor legislation of the fourteenth-century monarchies, as well as *Piers Plowman* and many other poems: the able-bodied beggar produces nothing but takes deceptively, often disfiguring his or her own image in an attempt to appeal to the giving subject's "charitable" wish to sustain the integrity of the image on which his or her own being as subject is founded.[28] Aers notes Gower's "outrage" at the reluctance of the poor "to live on the margins of subsistence": the poor man "demands things for his belly like a lord"; the peasant lacks charity, there is "bitterness in his hateful heart."[29] In *Piers Plowman* the wayward poor are also associated with concupiscence: truculent laborers only work as "a means to immediate enjoyments"; beggars

> lyue in no loue ne no lawe holde.
> [Thei] wedde [no] womman þat þei wiþ deele
> But as wilde bestes with wehee worþen vppe and werchyn,
> And bryngen forþ barnes þat bastardes men calleþ.[30]
> (B.VII.90–93)

And the poor join sodomites in the list of candidates for well-poisoning accusations in the later Middle Ages.

The sturdy beggar, both stranger and thief, is a melancholic ideological fantasy whose purpose is to explain why we feel dispossessed, at risk, incompletely happy, incomplete: that missing but crucial part of ourselves is in the hands of a thief of enjoyment, a thief who does not deserve his (our) enjoyment. Hence the rage with which the mode of enjoyment of the poor is so often greeted, and hence the passion with which "need" will be deployed as an index against which to measure the enjoyment to which the poor are not entitled—not entitled because that enjoyment is, or should be, our own.[31] Discriminatory charity, which is to say, charity, is one of the most discouraging social realities produced by the melancholic fantasy of the dispossessing poor; and it is, once again, a mode of enjoyment as well as of mourning, insofar as it is aimed at the question of the subject's, and/or the community's, *jouissance*. Through sacrifice the charitable subject repetitively produces the experience of surplus enjoyment; sacrifice puts into play the inaccessibility of *jouissance* while promising its safe return in the form of the sublime capital of heaven, through the giving, the return, enjoined on the subject by the law.

The pauper is thus a version of Žižek's "sublime object," the kind of object that acquires its uncanny value by pointing to and screening the place of the Thing, of our dreaded and mourned *jouissance*.[32] More specifically, the deserving pauper is a sublime object *in the making,* an artful production, and to minister to him or her is to foreground both the artfulness of the subject's construction of its objects and the liminal zone in which that construction takes place—a zone that occupies the limit between the alterity and the recognizability of the human image. The deserving pauper subject to charitable reshaping thus maintains the function of the sublime object as a screen that hides the Thing through the fantasy of the subject's reparative power; the undeserving pauper, on the other hand, is an abject or monstrous object because the Thing, in its fearful aspect, is detected *within* the malicious and hard heart of the sturdy beggar. The testing, disciplining, and managing of the poor becomes a way to test, discipline, and manage the structuring of the subject's and the community's relation to its *jouissance,* its "inner antagonism": is a way, in short, to *endure,* to surmount loss, to attain the fantasy of superexistence.[33] Through the figure of the pauper, the image or signifier on which the identity of the subject and the community is founded may be perpetually reshaped, thus providing to the charitable community the enjoyment of what Jacques Derrida calls the "triumph over death," in the form of the ethical power of self/other fashioning, of rescuing the image.[34]

Thus the artfulness of the figure of poverty, its representational status, is inseparable from the social meaning of poverty. Writing on poverty often makes a distinction between images of the poor that emanate from social elites and the lives of "actual" poor people; this position needs to be amended, so as to register not only the fact that the actual lives of poor people will always involve a negotiation of diverse cultural images of themselves, but also the fact that representation—the signifier—is intrinsic to the practices of exchange that produce culturally variable definitions of "wealth" and "poverty."[35] To fail to register this fact is to risk replicating the economic imaginaries that establish poverty as a baseline, an index, of relative wealth, as a "reality" against which things and their modes of production and possession might be measured.

Recent work by anthropologists of economic life has accordingly insisted on the impossibility of distinguishing, in a positivistic way, "luxuries"—"incarnated signs"—from "necessities"; necessities and luxuries are culturally variable categories, not positive objects, so that what is a luxury in one culture will be a necessity in another, what is a luxury at one moment in the life of a culture or of an individual subject will be a necessity at another.[36] This perspective owes much to Jean Baudrillard's critique of the notions of need and utility in economic theory.[37] But despite the ironically "theological" character of Marx's notions of need and of the unproblematic status of "use value" (wherein, for Marx, use value, the utility of the object, is self-evident in a way that exchange value is not), the notions of need and utility are unstable for Marx, too, and not just inexplicitly so.

Louise O. Fradenburg

In a passage in *The German Ideology* that might almost be called Lang-landian for its association of necessity with the entrance into the symbolic order, Marx famously writes:

> the first premiss of all human existence and, therefore, of all history, [is] the premiss . . . that men must be in a position to live in order to be able to "make history." But life involves before everything else eating and drinking, a habitation, clothing, and many other things. The first historical act is thus the production of the means to satisfy these needs, the production of material life itself.[38]

In this highly compressed logical chain, those things necessary to life function as indexes. Marx's rhetoric takes us back to first things, and they are needful things. But the very compression of Marx's logic insists that the production of material life *is* historical, is indeed history-making; to produce material life is not merely to survive, because it is always also the making of this thing called history. To produce the needful thing is at the same time to produce history.

Marx's insistence that the making of history does not follow upon the securing of necessities, but is rather coincident with them, is further clarified in his next premise:

> The second point is that the satisfaction of the first need (the action of satisfying, and the instrument of satisfaction which has been acquired) leads to new needs; and this production of new needs is the first historical act.[39]

Acting historically means producing needs *from* needs—as happens, for Marx, also in the way capitalist production fills out lack only to produce more lack in need of filling. To historicize need is thus to embed excess in need itself, and is truly to transform the cultural significance of the work of survival, of the living of those people subjected to lives of "mere" survival.

When Georges Bataille contends that "there is nothing that permits one to define what is useful to man," he, like Baudrillard, does so in the context of a critique of the discourse of utility, its preoccupation with the acquisition, production, and conservation of goods.[40] For Bataille such explanatory procedures are incapable of taking into account the passional violence, the transgressive, indeed destructive enjoyment that so strongly marks our economic behavior. Our desire to expend, waste, lose without the calculation of return—our "*interest* in considerable losses, in catastrophes, . . . in . . . a certain orgiastic state"—is what makes it impossible for us to define "what is useful to man."[41] We might say that sacrifice loves arithmetic, but it counts in part because of its desire to measure the dimensions of the unaccountable Thing.

58

As Rebecca Comay points out, however, Bataille also recognized the impossibility of separating calculation from the incalculable.[42] If there is always something of excess in the needful, there is also always something of the needful in excess, because the two concepts construct each other. Thus while Bataille sought to locate passional expenditure in the violent production of aristocratic glory or the sacrificial production of the sacred, battlefield heroics were compromised by "conformism and servility," the dying god by the economics of atonement.[43] Noble expenditure for Bataille ultimately had the function of producing abjection, of continually producing a phantasmatically fundamental division between noble and ignoble persons, between the life of "mere" survival and the life of honor. Bataille reads the class struggle as an attempt on the part of the powerful to reduce people to the level of "mud" and "baseness," in order that *the end of the workers' activity is to produce in order to live, but the bosses' activity is to produce in order to condemn the working producers to a hideous degradation.*[44]

In this Bataille stands with Marx, who notes that, in the process of the production of surplus population, "Accumulation of wealth at one pole is ... at the same time accumulation of misery, the torment of labour, slavery, ignorance, brutalization and moral degradation at the opposite pole, i.e. on the side of the class that produces its own product as capital."[45] To which Marx adds, "Everything therefore depends on making hunger permanent among the working class."[46] This gives a further edge, not that one is needed, to Langland's use of Hunger as a mouthpiece for the virtues of giving only "benes" to "Bolde beggares" who will not work: "And yf þe gromes gruche bide hem go and swynke / And he shal soupe swettere when he hit hath deserued" (VIII.227–28).

For all their differences, Marx, Bataille, and Baudrillard point us toward the recognition that "need" is never a pure experience because it is caught up in production and destruction, in the making and unmaking of objects and of their value. The aesthetic implications of this recognition are pursued most insistently by Baudrillard, but also emerge with clarity in Lacan's thought. Lacan writes that "the first thing that poor, defenseless man can do when he is tortured by need is to begin to hallucinate his satisfaction."[47] Need is always inseparable from a hallucinatory rerepresentation, from a "scene" of deprivation and satisfaction; in short, from art. Where need arises, the law of the signifier will also be found, and may be foregrounded, as in the case of the elaborate codes and calculations of courtly love, as well as those of charity. In both cases the intrication of need with signification issues in preoccupations with deception (the insincere speech of the *finamen*, the lying tongue or deliberately disfigured body of the sturdy beggar) and with the slide of need into excess (will the *finamen*/sturdy beggar really die without the *don de merci*?). What must then inevitably emerge in the vicinity of need is *ascesis*, the "pleasure of desiring, the pleasure of unpleasure"; ethics is a luxurious discourse whose mastery of excess emerges from the way need must always exceed itself in signification, from the way need is always something the subject must signify for itself. Another way, then, of thinking about how and why *Piers Plowman* is remarkable is that it thematizes so insistently the centrality of need to poetic production itself. And this is an ethical matter; what is of the utmost political and ethical significance, to *Piers Plowman* and to all other writing on poverty, is, again, whether or not *ascesis* and the law are to be recognized as modes of enjoyment that support communal belief.

For Žižek, the "Thing" is a community matter. The bond linking members of a community always, Žižek argues, implies a shared relationship toward the Thing, toward "enjoyment incarnated."[48] Our Thing, the "unique way a community organizes its enjoyment," is "the real thing," it's "it" ("Coke is It")—it's the Thing that organizes the ontological consistency, the believability, of the things that the community enjoys. How things are enacts the ideological fantasies of the community; people may know perfectly well, for example, that "there are relations between people behind the relations between things," but they act as if there were not.[49] In fact things *believe in the place of* subjects, believe instead of subjects; they in effect have our feelings for us, or operate in such a way that we can feel our feelings are being had for us. "Needful things," and the "mesure" grounded upon them, arise in Langland's poem at the very moment of the dreamer's first uncomprehending take on the desire of the "fader of fayth" because, as Žižek writes, it is belief "which is radically exterior, embodied in the practical, effective procedure of people"—and in the extimacy of the unconscious.[50]

If the social life of things enacts both the subject's and the community's modes of enjoyment and renunciation, the law in its ideological form must therefore take care to define adjudicable things, lest it come to seem too obvious that things are perfectly capable of adjudicating the law. Bracton offers a complex typology of things, including those things that belong to no one and therefore cannot be stolen, like wild beasts.[51] For a thing to come within the sphere of the law means that it is not a wild thing; it must be a thing that has a relationship to a person, that has a social history. Conversely, it is also true that for a person to have full rights within the law, he or she has to have a relationship to things. As the Friend notes of the poor in the *Romance of the Rose*, "They are even refused as witnesses by those who observe the proper canons, for in law they are said to be equivalent to those who have lost their reputation."[52]

In *On Christian Doctrine* Saint Augustine conflates the ethical importance of the treatment of things and people by using the paradoxical rhetoric of the high and the low, the great and the small, identified by Peter Brown as central to late antique Christianity's deployment of the "love of the poor" in its struggles for community power. Augustine writes:

In legal questions those things are called "small" which are concerned in cases involving money; they are called "great" when they
have to do with human welfare or life.... Among our orators, however, everything we say... must be referred, not to the temporal welfare of man, but to his eternal welfare and to the avoidance of eternal punishment, so that everything we say is of great importance,
even to the extent that pecuniary matters, whether they concern
loss or gain, or large or small amounts of money, should not be considered "small" when they are discussed by the Christian teacher.
For neither is justice small.... Therefore, what is least is least, but
to be faithful in what is least is great.[53]

For Saint Augustine the adjudication of "worldly cases (and which of them
is not concerned with money?)" is embedded in the hypereconomy of
charity; no object is so small that its donor "shall...lose his reward."[54]
And no temporal good is so insignificant as not to be worthy of judgment.
Precisely *because* the temporal good is subjected in medieval Christianity
to a rigorous critique of value, then, the least temporal good becomes
the means by which the high stakes of Christian judgment, the stakes
of eternal reward and punishment, of superexistence and absolute death,
are revealed. It is not surprising, then, that theft was so important a crime
in the Middle Ages; Bronislaw Geremek calls it the "supreme crime,"
and cites the following passage, worthy of comparison with Saint Augustine's economy of thing-enjoyment for what it reveals about the hyste-
ria at stake in the image of the dispossessing poor:

These sorts of miserable person say that God only made things for
the pleasure of friends, and they declare and conclude that they will
do with them whatever pleases their senses. And what is worse, they
say that this is God's will, and it is for this that he made them....
They also say that God did not distinguish goods nor order what
each should have, but everyone should take what he can get.[55]

Burglary and larceny were two of the most common crimes in fourteenth-century England; robbery was less common but had high conviction rates. All counties except Surrey and Yorkshire ranked robbery as
the crime, after treason and counterfeiting, that should be punished most
frequently. Barbara Hanawalt remarks that "from these figures one might
conclude that medieval jurors put a low value on life and a high value
on property."[56] We might, however, reformulate this characterization by
suggesting that these figures reveal the extent to which the community
lived its life through its things, practiced its relation to enjoyment—to
pleasure and privation—through its ways of enjoying and losing and
stealing and recovering things. The frequency of property disputes within
families, as well as the prominent roles played by apparently petty ob-

jects—half pennies, candles—in some homicides, indicate that the very "otherness" of things, an otherness that might seem to disqualify candles and halfpennies from the realm of serious insult, is what they share with the otherness of other people and of ourselves, and is what enables the saturation of the thing with the value of life.[57] It is, in short, a complete misunderstanding of the social and subjective agency of things to regard the medieval preoccupation with theft as barbarism; indeed theft might well join homicide in helping us to understand the scene of group subjectivity.

The way a community practices enjoyment means the way it breaks as well as makes its laws, and crime, theft included, plays its part in the discourse of the nation. Violence and litigiousness are now part of the U.S. national Thing; our troublesome ways are often laid at the door of a certain American resistance to authority—a resistance that helps us, in current nationalist talk, *not* to be too much like the Japanese, whose supposedly obsessive work habits and obedience to authority have been menacing our Thing pretty seriously, or at least were until the Kobe quake.[58] So Americans identify the American thing as being, paradoxically, *not* altogether communal; we believe in the existence of "us" insofar as our beliefs do not altogether oblige us. That we are equally obsessed with "law and order," with not being "soft on crime," merely indicates once again the role of the law in producing the surplus enjoyment that can fantasize itself as freedom.

And so it was, apparently, in late medieval England, according to the historians of crime. Hanawalt notes that "England in the Middle Ages had the reputation of being the most violent country in Europe and also the one where people most enjoyed protracted lawsuits."[59] This national crime profile is also remarked by John Bellamy, in *Crime and Public Order in England in the Later Middle Ages*: "Late medieval England was known throughout Europe for its high rate of crime."[60] Hanawalt speaks of similarities between medieval English and contemporary American notions of "self-help." Bellamy cites Sir John Fortescue's speculations in the *De laudibus legem Angliae* (1476) "that England's many robberies indicated a rather praiseworthy determination not to be overawed by the law, an independence of spirit which gave and took hard knocks in good part."[61] And despite Fortescue's praise of the English custom of trial by jury, Fortescue was, according to Bellamy, "aware that trial by jury failed to produce as many convictions as the methods used in continental Europe. He defended the English practice by saying it was better for twenty guilty to escape than a single innocent to be condemned."[62]

This pride in the shortness of the arm of the English law is expressed in Fortescue's comments on the reluctance of English law to torture: " 'An innocent man cannot suffer in body or members' and he 'will not fear the calumny of his enemies because he will not be tortured at their pleasure. Under this law, therefore, life is quiet and secure,' " despite the lawlessness of those who live under this law, or despite the gaps in the execution of the law, or the law's own occasional lawlessness.[63] Bellamy recapitulates this pride in the power of English law to restrain *and* deliver enjoyment: "by the mid–thirteenth century the old Norman punishments of mutilation had become neglected."[64] The English law restrains the pleasures of enemies but touches lightly the body of the accused, and its criminals refuse to be overawed by the law, supposedly enjoying "many robberies." A light-fingered nation indeed.

We might suggest here that the "constitutively senseless character of the Law" is being repressed, as Žižek puts it, "through the ideological, imaginary experience of the 'meaning' of the Law," but this time in the form of a nationalist discourse about how justice is best served when the law doesn't serve everyone right, when things as well as people are allowed to circulate with a certain degree of lawless freedom.[65] So belief in the English law is affirmed most movingly in Bellamy's book at the moments when the arbitrariness of that law is most visible.

At least in Bellamy's account of Fortescue, theft is construed as an aspect of the national character. To what extent was theft understood as motivated by need? According to Bellamy, "Medieval man had little curiosity about causation of crime," excepting preachers; "there is very little in medieval writings to suggest that Englishmen thought that economic and social grievances caused criminal acts."[66] This is an odd remark given the interest in need in theoretical discussions of crime, and so influential a piece of medieval writing as the *Romance of the Rose* explains that poverty "is worse than death, for she torments and gnaws at soul and body, . . . and brings them not only to condemnation but also to larceny and perjury and many other difficulties which hit them very hard."[67] Medieval historical literature also explicitly discusses need and poverty in relation to crime. In the *Description of Wales*, poverty itself is a national Thing; Gerald of Wales explains that poverty has corrupted the "natural propensities" of the Welsh and encouraged them in "wrongdoing."[68] Mollat mentions one twelfth-century northern French chronicler who wrote that "many people, reduced to . . . cruel necessity, chose to live contrary to custom, became thieves, and ended up in a noose."[69]

For the learned theorists of charity and social justice, "the problem of theft by the needy was a difficult one to resolve," writes Mollat.[70] Opinion varied. Some rigorists argued that the excuse of need could, at best, only mitigate punishment.[71] Others were persuaded that a starving man could be absolved of guilt for a theft he had committed.[72] As noted earlier, rigorist thinking tended to predominate in the statutory law of the fourteenth century, which repeatedly linked poverty to crime; the rolls of Parliament for 1377 complained of able-bodied beggars who "become strong robbers, and their robberies and felonies increase from one day to another on all sides."[73] In fact the Middle Ages was passionate about making sense of "the poor," in part because the passions of the community were at stake in so doing, hence the fascination with detecting and calculating and managing the enjoyment of the poor. We find in the Middle Ages not a disinterest in the motivations of crime, but the passionate belief that crime was linked to poverty through necessity, and the link appears also in contemporary historiography on medieval crime.

Hanawalt's *Crime and Conflict in English Communities* oscillates between the notion, on the one hand, that "all levels of society used crime and the judicial system as weapons in social conflicts to further their own power over others," and the notion, on the other hand, that economic necessity was a significant factor in crime.[74] Hanawalt comments that during the "trying years" of the early fourteenth century, "the populace did not hesitate to steal and commit acts of violence in order to survive or simply to maintain the standard of living to which they had become accustomed." She also suggests that, later on in the century, war "may also have reduced many of the peasantry to a level of poverty and anger that would lead them to make up their losses through criminal means." And Hanawalt presents evidence for a link between increases in the crime rate and in the price of wheat.[75]

Yet there is no evidence to show that, at moments of famine, rising food prices, or war, the poorest of peasants turned to crime in greater numbers than the more prosperous in society. "Anger," too, is a passional motive for crime, and Hanawalt's invocation of it should point us to the way in which theft, as Arjun Appadurai puts it, is—and was in the Middle Ages—a significant means of diversion of commodities from preordained paths, and could in fact be a form of dissent; diversion, Appadurai notes, is "frequently a function of irregular desires and novel demands."[76] Moreover, the distinction between stealing "in order to survive" and "to maintain [a]...standard of living" is both a significant one and one difficult, if not impossible, to sustain analytically. Finally, Hanawalt's comparison of crime county by county shows that "wealth did not attract criminals nor did poverty in a county create a greater need to make a living through criminal means."[77]

The evidence of Hanawalt's book thus, in fact, indicates that the relation between poverty and crime is impossible to substantiate through the concept of necessity. Geremek, in *The Margins of Society in Late Medieval Paris*, regards economic necessity as a highly problematic way of accounting either for vagrancy or for crime; his period does *not*, in his view, support François Simiand's argument that "the largest number of beggars and vagabonds are found in periods of low or stagnant wages."[78] When people take needful things, they do so, quite simply, at all levels of society; that they do so at some times more than others is something that cannot be adequately analyzed unless and until the complexity of the needful thing, of the passional and constitutive relations between things and subjectivity, including communal subjectivity, is taken into account.

Conclusion

I believe the most important implications of my argument to be as follows. First, liberalism's attempt to assert that poor people commit crimes because they are needy will, however well meaning, never prove adequate to the task of achieving social justice, because such attempts finally work to legitimate the very discourse of necessity and the refusal of excess on which the production and management of the poor have historically depended.

Neither will a materialist politics predicated on the possibility of categorical distinction between needful and luxurious things prove any more successful in the work of social emancipation. This is because, as is decipherable in Marx's own discourse, things are always already passional. Insofar as we proceed with the distinction between necessity and excess, we will remain caught up in the melancholic economies of sacrifice that have worked to ensure the production of the difference between noble and ignoble persons, and we will thereby continue to perpetuate the myth that there is such a person who lives or can live a life of "mere" survival, as well as that myth's corresponding reality—a life of struggle. The distinction between luxuries and necessities will always be a prelude to the withholding of things in general and of the social agency attendant upon their possession.

And what is our stake in this as medievalists, not simply as cultural workers living and thinking in times dreadful for the poor? We devote our work to a period that has for centuries been associated with, on the one hand, the rule of law and harmonious community, and on the other, lawless violence and poverty—precisely the conceptual poles around which the discourses of poverty we have been examining tend to oscillate.[79] Until we do a deeper thinking about needful things, we will not understand our period as well as we might, nor the ways in which the definitive imputation to the Middle Ages of a simultaneous capacity and incapacity to discipline enjoyment functions to authorize some of the most lethal ideological fantasies of modern capitalism.

Notes

1. Slavoj Žižek, "Eastern Europe's Republics of Gilead," *New Left Review* 183 (1990): 50–62.

2. Freud, as Lacan points out, locates "the genesis of the moral dimension...nowhere else than in desire itself"; Jacques Lacan, *The Seminar of Jacques Lacan: Book VII: The Ethics of Psychoanalysis, 1959–1960*, ed. Jacques-Alain Miller, trans. Dennis Porter (New York: Norton, 1992), 3.

3. Slavoj Žižek, *The Sublime Object of Ideology* (London: Verso, 1989), 37–38, 43.

4. George Woodbine, ed., *Bracton de legibus et consuetudinibus Angliae*, and Henry de Bracton, *On the Laws and Customs of England*, trans. Samuel E. Thorne (Cambridge, Mass.: Harvard University Press, 1968), 2:21. Bracton introduces this point as follows: "Let no one, unwise and unlearned, presume to ascend the seat of judgment, which is like unto

the throne of God, lest for light he bring darkness and for darkness light, and, with un-skillful hand, even as a madman, he put the innocent to the sword and set free the guilty, and lest he fall from on high, as from the throne of God, in attempting to fly before he has wings."

5. One of the definitions of "need" given in the *MED* is "[a] necessary act; required work or duty; business, pressing affairs or urgent matters; . . . also, a legal case . . . or the decision in a legal case" (s.v. "ned(e)"). "Needful" can also refer to something "compelling, necessitating obedience" (*MED*, s.v. "ned(e)ful").

6. *The Holy Bible by John Wycliffe and His Followers*, ed. Josiah Forshall and Sir Frederic Madden (Oxford, 1850), 3:49; cited by Robert Adams, "The Nature of Need in *Piers Plowman* XX," *Traditio* 34 (1978): 287–88.

7. *Bracton on the Laws of England*, 33; the Virgin Mary is also instanced here as "an example of humility" who "did not refuse to be subjected to established laws."

8. Michel Mollat, *The Poor in the Middle Ages: An Essay in Social History*, trans. Arthur Goldhammer (New Haven, Conn.: Yale University Press, 1986), 110.

9. Derek Pearsall, ed., *Piers Plowman by William Langland: An Edition of the C-Text* (Berkeley: University of California Press, 1978), passus I, line 11. All subsequent citations to the C-text are taken from this edition and are cited in the text.

10. On the strangeness of the law, see Žižek, *Sublime Object of Ideology*, 37, 82; and Jacques Derrida, *The Gift of Death*, trans. David Wills (Chicago: University of Chicago Press, 1995), on the figures of secrecy and noncommunication in relation to absolute belief.

11. Žižek, *Sublime Object of Ideology*, 43.

12. Bracton, *On the Laws of England*, 21.

13. See Jacques Le Goff's discussion of "the ideal of *measure* that, from the twelfth to the thirteenth century, imposed itself upon morals and theology," in *Your Money or Your Life: Economy and Religion in the Middle Ages* (New York: Zone, 1988), 72–73.

14. Pearsall, *Piers Plowman*, 154 n. 210.

15. Even the history of *Piers Plowman*'s revisions suggest an accelerating focus on questions of poverty and charity. Pearsall notes that "an exceptionally large proportion of the new material in C has to do with questions of poverty"; Derek Pearsall, "Poverty and Poor People in *Piers Plowman*," in *Medieval English Studies Presented to George Kane*, ed. Edward Donald Kennedy et al. (Woodbridge, England: Brewer, 1988), 167.

16. The association of vagrancy with crime and poverty in the fourteenth century is well documented and is part of the tendency, in the later Middle Ages, toward a more rigorist position on charity and the poor, which may in part have been the outcome of the greater mobility of population and new concentrations in urban centers. The classic text is Mollat, *The Poor in the Middle Ages*. Bronislaw Geremek, in *The Margins of Society in Late Medieval Paris*, trans. Jean Birrell (Cambridge: Cambridge University Press, 1987), one of the most important recent works on late medieval poverty, discusses demographic shifts and the new hostility toward vagrancy (29–40) and the association of the wandering minstrel with criminality and the refusal to work (163). See also David Aers, "Piers Plowman: Poverty, Work, and Community," *Community, Gender, and Individual Identity: English Writing, 1360–1430* (New York: Routledge, 1988), 20–72. See also Pearsall, "Poverty and Poor People in *Piers Plowman*," 170–73.

17. Jacques Lacan, "The Mirror Stage as Formative of the Function of the I as Revealed in Psychoanalytic Experience," in *Ecrits: A Selection*, trans. Alan Sheridan (New York: Norton, 1977), 1–7.

18. Lacan, *Ethics of Psychoanalysis*, 52, 134. On that which is in the subject more than the subject, which both exceeds the boundaries of the subject and forms an empti-ness within it, see Žižek, *Sublime Object of Ideology*, 94, 180.

19. Lacan, *Ethics of Psychoanalysis*, 73 (emphasis added).

20. Žižek, *Sublime Object of Ideology*, 43, 52, 82.

21. See Adams, "The Nature of Need in *Piers Plowman*," 279; citing George Kane and E. Talbot Donaldson, ed., *Piers Plowman: The B Version* (London: University of London/

Athlone Press, 1975), XX.55. All citations to the B-text are from this edition and hereafter appear in the text. The idea that need has no law is a scholastic commonplace frequently cited by Aquinas (Adams, "Nature of Need," 283 n. 13; cf. Aers, "Poverty, Work, and Community," 64, citing the use of this commonplace also in *Dives and Pauper,* 2 vols., EETS 275, 280 [Oxford: Oxford University Press, n.d.], 2:141). Adams describes Langland's views on need as follows: "Because need is impossible to judge objectively, it always tempts a man to act immorally, to exaggerate his needs and make his begging either perpetual or an expression of his merely selfish desires" (289 n. 30). The justification of theft by need was much discussed in medieval writing on poverty and is frequently, although not often successfully, invoked in legal cases; see Geremek, *Margins of Society,* 18, 52, 63.

22. Aers, "Poverty, Work, and Community," 63–64. Geoffrey Shepherd, "Poverty in *Piers Plowman,*" in *Social Relations and Ideas: Essays in Honour of R. H. Hilton,* ed. T. H. Aston et al. (Cambridge: Cambridge University Press, 1983), 169–89, links Recklessness to the philosophy behind the "Great Revolt," and argues that Langland presents him with a sympathy that shades into wariness (182). Pearsall also argues that Need reasserts "the primacy of the claim of the indigent upon society" ("Poverty and Poor People in *Piers Plowman,*" 185; see 185 n. 61 and Pearsall, *Piers Plowman,* n. to XXII.15, on the right of the poor in extreme need to seize what is needed to maintain life).

23. The ease of this track is theorized by Saint Augustine in *On Christian Doctrine,* where crime and vice are interlinked as violations of charity; crime is a violation of charity toward the other, whereas vice is a violation of charity toward oneself; trans. D. W. Robertson Jr. (New York: Bobbs-Merrill, 1958), 88–89.

24. Gilles Deleuze and Félix Guattari, "The Apparatus of Capture," in *A Thousand Plateaus: Capitalism and Schizophrenia,* trans. Brian Massumi (Minneapolis: University of Minnesota Press, 1987), 438–39.

25. See Aers's discussion of the problem of "fraternity" and exclusivity in fourteenth-century England, and of the poet's vagrancy as indicating a "*lack* of fraternal bonds" ("Poverty, Work, and Community," 67–69, 71). Derek Pearsall also argues that, for Langland, the "sufferings of poor people" constituted a "rebuke" "to himself, to his fellow human beings, and to the notion of good government" ("Poverty and Poor People in *Piers Plowman,*" 167).

26. Žižek, "Republics of Gilead," 54–57. As is usual in Lacanian discourse, I try, in the preceding discussion, to reserve the capitalized "Other" for the symbolic order and the unconscious.

27. See Derek Pearsall's discussion of Mollat's remark that the "passage from poverty to criminality is an easy one" ("Poverty and Poor People in *Piers Plowman,*" 171). The association of vagrancy and social marginality with crime was almost automatic in the later Middle Ages; Barbara Hanawalt, *Crime and Conflict in English Communities: 1300–1348* (Cambridge, Mass.: Harvard University Press, 1979), notes that "*vagabundus* often meant a person fleeing from a crime" (26). Geremek, *Margins of Society,* insists that "we will not . . . confuse people on the margins and criminals, because the marginal fringe of society embraced elements who were vilified, but who did not commit crimes" (3).

On the figure of the condemned criminal as the obverse of the superabundant vitality, the good excess, of sovereign value, Foucault's discussion of the symmetrical contrast enacted by spectacular punishment between the monarch and the least body of the condemned criminal is relevant (*Discipline and Punish,* trans. Alan Sheridan [New York: Pantheon, 1977]); and see Jean-Joseph Goux on the "general equivalent," that commodity embodying vital surplus that "enables accounts to be settled" (31), for example, God, "the place where all things are evaluated in common" (11) (*Symbolic Economies: After Marx and Freud* [Ithaca, N.Y.: Cornell University Press, 1990]). Goux notes, interestingly, that only commodities *not* socially defined as necessities can assume the form of the general equivalent (27).

28. The pauper's characteristic of "producing little" appears in the etymology of the Latin "pauper"; Charlton T. Lewis and Charles Short, *A Latin Dictionary Founded on Andrews Edition* (1879; reprint, Oxford: Clarendon Press, 1966), s.v. "pauper."

Louise O. Fradenburg

29. Aers, "Poverty, Work, and Community," 32–33, citing John Gower, *Vox Claman-tis,* in *The Major Latin Works of John Gower,* trans. and ed. Eric W. Stockton (Seattle: University of Washington Press, 1962), V.9–10, pp. 208–10, and I, pp. 94–95.

30. Aers cites B.VI.302–11 on waste and enjoyment; "Poverty, Work, and Community," 47, and 51 on the sexuality of the poor.

31. Arjun Appadurai, "Introduction: Commodities and the Politics of Value," in *The Social Life of Things: Commodities in Cultural Perspective* (Cambridge: Cambridge University Press, 1986), 26–27, 29.

32. Žižek, "From the Courtly Game to *The Crying Game,*" re:*Post* 1 (1993): 5, and *Sublime Object of Ideology,* 94; Lacan, *Ethics of Psychoanalysis,* 150.

33. Žižek, "Republics of Gilead," 60.

34. Derrida, *Gift of Death,* 16.

35. The distinction between representations of the poor and "the realities of poverty" is insistent in Pearsall's "Poverty and Poor People in *Piers Plowman,*" 167–69.

36. Moreover, there is evidence to suggest that the production of prestige items drives technological innovation and the development of markets as much as, or more than, the production of "useful" or "necessary" items; see Appadurai, "Introduction," 16–17, 36–38; and Colin Renfrew, "Varna and the Emergence of Wealth in Prehistoric Europe," in *The Social Life of Things,* ed. Appadurai, 146.

37. Baudrillard argues that "there is nothing clear and natural in the fact of 'transforming nature according to one's needs' or in 'rendering oneself useful' as well as things"; also that *"the structure of the sign is at the very heart of the commodity form";* The Political Economy of the Sign, in *Jean Baudrillard: Selected Writings,* ed. Mark Poster (Stanford, Calif.: Stanford University Press; Cambridge: Polity Press, 1988), 75, 79.

38. Karl Marx and Friedrich Engels, *The German Ideology,* in *Karl Marx: Selected Writings,* ed. David McLellan (Oxford: Oxford University Press, 1977), 165.

39. Ibid., 166.

40. Georges Bataille, "The Notion of Expenditure," in *Visions of Excess: Selected Writings, 1927–1939,* ed. Allan Stoekl, trans. Allan Stoekl et al. (Minneapolis: University of Minnesota Press, 1985), 116.

41. Ibid., 117.

42. Rebecca Comay, "Gifts without Presents: Economies of 'Experience' in Bataille and Heidegger," in *On Bataille,* ed. Allan Stoekl, *Yale French Studies* 78 (1990): 66–89, at 81–83.

43. Ibid., 84 n. 14; emphasis in original.

44. Bataille, "Expenditure," 125–26.

45. Karl Marx, *Capital: Volume One,* intro. Ernest Mandel, trans. Ben Fowkes (New York: Vintage, 1977), 799.

46. Ibid., 800.

47. Lacan, *Ethics of Psychoanalysis,* 138. Baudrillard links the importance of form, "the object form," to his critique of Marx's handling of use-value in "The Political Economy of the Sign," 80.

48. Žižek, "Republics of Gilead," 51.

49. Žižek, *Sublime Object of Ideology,* 31.

50. Ibid., 34.

51. Bracton, *On the Laws of England,* 41.

52. *The Romance of the Rose/Guillaume de Lorris and Jean de Meun,* trans. and ed. Frances Horgan (Oxford: Oxford University Press, 1994), 126.

53. Saint Augustine, *On Christian Doctrine,* 143–44.

54. Ibid., 144–45.

55. Geremek, *Margins of Society,* 304, citing what he describes as "a treatise on social morals from the end of the Middle Ages"; the treatise is in Bibliothèque Nationale, MS. fr. 1148 (16 c.), fol. 64v.

56. Hanawalt, *Crime and Conflict,* 61.

57. Ibid., 66, 173.

58. Žižek, "Republics of Gilead," 54.

59. Hanawalt, *Crime and Conflict*, 45.

60. John G. Bellamy, *Crime and Public Order in England in the Later Middle Ages* (London: Routledge and Kegan Paul, 1973), 3.

61. Sir John Fortescue, *The Governance of England*, ed. C. Plummer (Oxford: Oxford University Press, 1926), 141–42; cited by Bellamy, *Crime and Public Order*, 31.

62. Bellamy, *Crime and Public Order*, 156.

63. Sir John Fortescue, *De laudibus legum Anglie*, ed. and trans. S. B. Chrimes (Cambridge: Cambridge University Press, 1942), 65; cited by Bellamy, *Crime and Public Order*, 139. Bellamy notes that "by the sixteenth century at least, English criminals had a great reputation for going to their executions with great composure. Holinshed held that 'our condemned persons doo go so cheerefullie to their deths for our nation is free, stout, hautie, prodigall of life and bloud'" (189). This would have been around the time that physical cruelty began to play a more spectacular role in English punition, so that we have now a nation of feisty Socrateses, enacting the vigil over death not philosophically but by acceding with insouciance to the new exactions of the law.

64. Bellamy, *Crime and Public Order*, 181.

65. Žižek, *Sublime Object of Ideology*, 37–38, 82.

66. Bellamy, *Crime and Public Order*, 30, 32.

67. *Romance of the Rose*, ed. Horgan, 125. At lines 9511ff. the Friend relates an allegory in which "Drear Poverty brought her son, Larceny, who runs to the gibbet to help his mother and sometimes gets himself hanged there" (146).

68. Gerald of Wales, *The Journey through Wales; and, The Description of Wales*, trans. Lewis Thorpe (Harmondsworth, England: Penguin, 1978), 255.

69. Mollat, *The Poor in the Middle Ages*, 68.

70. Ibid., 111.

71. Gerhoh of Reichersberg "tolerated no justification for theft and condemned the intention to appropriate another person's property. At most he was willing to make allowance for extenuating circumstances, which might reduce the gravity of the sin and justify a reduction in punishment. The law shared this viewpoint" (ibid.).

72. At the end of the twelfth century "Richard the Englishman was persuaded by the theory of need to invoke the *Lex Rhodia* in order to absolve a starving man of guilt for the theft he had committed"; "by the beginning of the thirteenth century it was generally accepted that the starving thief was innocent of any crime"; "the bishop of Paris, William of Auxerre [d. 1231], dealt with alms in the opening chapter of his treatise on justice, in which he states...that a pauper in need and in a situation where all property is deemed to be held in common may without sin appropriate the bread he needs in order to survive" (ibid.).

73. Hanawalt, *Crime and Conflict*, 199.

74. Ibid., 2.

75. Ibid., 164, 266, 238.

76. Appadurai, "Introduction," 26, 29. See also Igor Kopytoff, "The Cultural Biography of Things: Commoditization as Process," in *The Social Life of Things*, ed. Appadurai, 64–91, on "how one breaks the rules by moving between spheres [of value] that are supposed to be insulated from each other, how one converts what is formally unconvertible, how one masks these actions and with whose connivance" (88); and Patrick Geary's discussion of thefts of relics as a means of escaping from patronage systems, in "Sacred Commodities: The Circulation of Medieval Relics," in *The Social Life of Things*, ed. Appadurai, 185–86.

77. Hanawalt, *Crime and Conflict*, 258.

78. Geremek, *Margins of Society*, 42, citing François Simiand, *Le salaire, l'evolution sociale et la monnaie* (Paris, 1932), 2:31ff., and 3: diagram 2.

79. Pearsall, "Poverty and Poor People in *Piers Plowman*," 169, takes issue with the tendency of some historians of fourteenth-century England to minimize poverty during that period and emphasize instead the harmonious functioning of society.

CHAPTER 3

✛

In Defense of Revenge

William Ian Miller

One of the risks of studying the Icelandic sagas and loving them is, precisely, loving them. And what is one loving when one loves them? The wit, the entertainment provided by perfectly told tales? And just how are these entertaining tales and this wit separable from their substance: honor, revenge, individual assertion, and yes, some softer values, too, like peacefulness and prudence? Yet one suspects, and quite rightly, that the softer values are secondary and utterly dependent on being responsive to the problems engendered by the rougher values of honor and vengeance. Is it possible to study the sagas and not be attracted to the nobility, the dignity, the heroism of an ethic of "face," not to thrill to revenge and the open admission that it is the most satisfying way to reestablish the moral, if not the social, order after a wrong has been done? The risk, it so happens, is in coming to love their way as well as their way of talking about it.

Revenge, for us, is not a publicly admissible motive for individual action.[1] Church, state, and reason all counsel against it; as sin, as crime, or as an irrationally backward-looking obsession with sunk costs. Officially revenge is a bad thing, although collectivities are given greater leeway than individuals in asserting it as a justification for action. The very polity that will not allow its citizens to claim revenge as justification in its courts of law sees nothing strange about telling its people that revenge and honor are good reasons for invading another state. In sports, the desire to pay back for past humiliations is thought to add to and not merely to reproduce the motive of winning for the present and future. The big difference between us and the denizens of the saga world is that revenge was constitutive of much of their public, personal, and moral order. The person who did not want to take it had to feel shame for not wanting to, or at least had to come up with a plausible account as to why it was not shameful for him not to seek revenge; this marks an obvious contrast with us.

By the twelfth century in Iceland, Christianity helped provide a discourse for vengeance avoidance and helped legitimate a politics of forgiveness.[2] But even Christianity could not tolerate too much forgiveness. It allowed revenge to God and kings in the same proportion that it insisted on denying it to average mortals.[3] A practical and somewhat legalistic priest intent on revenge could finesse the matter by making use of God's delight in revenge. Thus Gudmund Arason, concerned not to lose his ordination should he kill the man he outlawed, but stricken with anxiety at the prospect of dishonor for not killing him, offered God the property he stood to gain from the case if God could contrive to get him out of the dilemma that honor in its collision with honoring clerical vows produced. God was obliging. He intervened to have the outlaw killed in a general brawl in which Gudmund was in no way complicit.[4] There were ways of honorably avoiding the demand for revenge without invoking Christianity. But these were only generally available to the honorable, that is, to those who gave every impression of being willing and able to take revenge the next time around.[5] True, those who urged peace were honored and appreciated, but most peacemakers were positioned as third parties, not as people who were supposed to take revenge.[6] The point, however, is not that viable alternatives to revenge did not exist; it is that the implementation of those options required work, a practical sense of when and how to back off and back down, before others would believe that forgoing revenge was an act of courageous self-denial rather than cowardice.

Not so with us, at least as an official matter. Revenge has been removed from the center of our practical lives and has been relocated to the fantastic marches. Revenge is there, to be sure, via fantasy in movie and via fantasy in foreign affairs. It has little legitimate public life in the normal domain. Instead, among one repressed segment of us, revenges go on inside as fantasies of getting even, of dominating, of discomfiting those we envy, fantasies that are what Nietzsche supposed were the substance of *ressentiment*. And in another less repressed segment revenge still thrives, but it is understood that that very thriving is the determinative element in the ineffable vulgarity of young lower-class males.[7] In our world revenge becomes either small-minded or vulgarly loud and adolescent.

Officially we subscribe at some level to the evolutionary legal historical account of the nineteenth century that supposed that natural selection preferred compensation payment to blood revenge and then state bureaucratic law to compensation. By this account revenge died simply because it was obsolete and nonadaptive. We are also heirs to a competing account generated by contractarian political theory. Like the legal-historical one, it supposes a vengeful world in times long past, but it departs from the legal-historical model in seeing revenge not as disappearing by some inevitable force of human progress, but rather as something that must be continually overcome by acts of will, conscious political commitment, and wise social planning. If for the legal historian the order-threatening nature of honor and revenge doomed them by natural selection to extinction, then for Hobbes honor and revenge doomed humanity unless one worked to devise institutions to suppress them; Hobbes knew that honor and glory are as much a temptation to us as they are a terror. Both accounts agree, however, that it is better for civil society and the rule of law that honor (and thus revenge) die a death.

So it did after a fashion. That is, the ruling elites officially gave up on it, substituting reason and cost-benefit analysis instead. But if the upper classes learned to walk away from fights with each other, the lower classes, the medieval "meek," who by aristocratic ideology were denied the very capacity for honor, kept it alive in barrooms and in back alleys; even the children of the elite still cared about these things on the playground. Unofficially, of course, the upper classes still cared to get even, held grudges, and behaved like normally vengeful human beings, but their revenges were transmuted and took place in economic arenas and muted social activities like gossip and slighting rather than in face-to-face confrontation. Honor and revenge did not so much disappear as become vulgar and unfashionable, a source of embarrassment to the refined and civilized that needed to be glossed over and carried out in disguise, if carried out at all.

At one level, the contrast between us and saga society is the difference between a society in which revenge is a publicly professable motive for action and one in which it is not. But the contrast, although in some broad way defensible, ends by being subverted by the thinness of the notion of revenge that is put on the table, either to be condemned by moralists, rationalists, and political theorists or, with a somewhat self-conscious sense of perversity, to be welcomed by romantics as the substance of gothic fantasy. Romantics tend to underestimate the degree of rationality, pragmatics, and cold calculation that motivated a lot of honorable and vengeful action. One always suspects that many romantics, for all their fascination with violence, are rather often strangers to blood, pain, and the smells of death. The sagas, as any reader of them knows, are only occasionally romantic in sensibility. They share with the best heroic literature the ability to articulate and sustain powerful critiques of feud, revenge, and honor. The heroic world is not simply one of joy at the recovery of honor and *Schadenfreude* for the shame of one's adversary. That world is also painfully aware of the costs, social and individual, of honorable self-assertion. In our world the story is not just one of the triumph of reason, law, and gentle socialization, either. Despite the antihonor discourse and pretense that revenge is inimical to a just legal order, we still feel at some visceral level that the world of honor and revenge is nobler than ours, and it still remains for us grand and frightfully alluring. We might suspect that when God claimed vengeance to himself—"Vengeance is mine, saith the Lord"—he was not taking upon himself a burden but rather selfishly reserving to himself a pleasure too good to share with mere mortals. It was because revenge was so alluring that barriers of sinfulness, criminality, and other forms of taxing it were felt to be necessary. When, after all, was the last time someone decided to make sin and crime out of something that has no allure at all?

Adherents to the ideology of the rule of law cannot disguise their horror and contempt at the rudeness and physicality of honor-based action (and their pleasure in a social order that allows people like themselves to occupy positions of prestige). And in revenge they connive to construct a notion of revenge that trivializes it. Revenge is thus distinguished from retribution by moral, legal, and political philosophers. Retribution can still be mentioned in polite company and only with minor apology offered as a respectable reason for punishment of wrongs, administered as it must be by the state in a controlled, proportional fashion. Revenge, in contrast, is portrayed as crazed, uncontrolled, subjective, individual, admitting no reason, no rule of limitation. It is conceived of not only as lawless, but as unruled and ruleless. Revenge, so understood, is anathema to the rule of law, but a source of fascination for the romantic. Criminal law books quote passages like this: "Vengeance is self-serving since it is arbitrarily (by its own authority) taken by anyone who feels injured and wishes to retaliate. Vengeance is not defined by preexisting rules nor proportioned to the injury avenged." These observations come from a dedicated proponent of capital punishment anxious to deny that capital punishment is merely revenge.[8] Consider how Robert Nozick distinguishes revenge from retribution, turning revenge by definitional fiat into a pathology rather than a behavior upon which many societies we still think of as rather glorious based their moral and social order. (I take his distinction here as representative of the general antirevenge tradition of political, moral, and legal philosophy):

1. Revenge is for an injury; retribution for a wrong.
2. Retribution sets an internal limit to the amount of the punishment according to the seriousness of the wrong; revenge need not.
3. Revenge is personal; the agent of retribution need have no special or personal tie to the victim of the wrong for which he exacts retribution.
4. Revenge involves a particular emotional tone, pleasure in the suffering of another, while retribution need involve no emotional tone.
5. There need be no generality in revenge. Not only is the avenger not committed to revenging any similar act done to anyone, he is not committed to avenging all done to himself.[9]

Some might wonder whether we only gain by preferring retribution to revenge, even with revenge so unfavorably defined. We might wonder whether a serious commitment to restoring the victim's dignity, rather than worrying only about how the victimizer might not be deprived of his, might lead us to prefer revenge to retribution in point 3. As to point 4, what do we suppose retribution without the accompaniment of emotions, such as a sense of duty, indignation, disapproval, or outrage, would look like? How could retribution possibly be justified without an emotional accompaniment? Unemotional bureaucratic implementation of punishment looks much like law according to Kafka. Nozick's problem more correctly must not be with emotions in general as with particular emotions, namely *Schadenfreude*. (One might reasonably wonder whether *Schadenfreude* is in some real sense a necessary feature of corrective justice). Point 5 prefers generality in the application of sanction; there is much to recommend this position, but it comes at a cost: it rejects mercy in favor of dreary bureaucratic uniformity. Let's put all this aside as raising issues both too complex and too divisive for quick disposition. What is clear is that revenge in the eyes of this tradition is merely a stand-in for anarchy and anomie. It is an uninteresting straw man. Of course no one wants to live around people carrying out revenge without measure for any imagined slight. Honor-based vengeance cultures found such people no less troublesome than bureaucratized societies fear them likely to be. And honor cultures knew how to handle such misfits with more than a slap on the wrist. The Norse called them berserks or *ójafnaðar-menn* (men of no measure) and usually found ways of disposing of them.

We might certainly want to historicize the notion of revenge; we would want to see if it means one thing in a culture in which it is valued, a culture openly committed to the norms of honor and "face," and another when it is consciously relegated to the status of "that which must be suppressed and overcome." In an honor-based culture we might suspect that revenge will be richly embedded in a complex normative structure that regulates it, cabins and constrains it, so that any meaningful distinction between retribution and revenge disappears.

The Icelandic legal order had an intimate relation with revenge.[10] Icelandic law understood itself as providing an arena in which a modified form of revenge could take place. Iceland had no state authority, no real lordship; the responsibility for righting wrongs was the wronged person's. He sued and he enforced the judgment unless he assigned his action, in which case the responsibility devolved upon the assignee. The law did not issue money judgments in disputes involving injuries or killing. The penalty was outlawry, which allowed anyone to kill the outlaw with impunity and obliged the judgment holder to do so. This was very close to revenge pure and simple. But it was a constraint on pure feud, a rather big one. One could only sue someone who had engaged in culpable conduct, whereas in feud, one could kill the kin of the actual wrongdoer. The law limited the range of possible revenge targets, and it compensated for this restriction in a strange way. Suppose Thorgrim and six others attack and kill Bjorn. Bjorn's brother can outlaw all seven of the assailants, who can then be killed as outlaws. If Bjorn simply takes revenge, he will be thought to be acting without measure if he takes more than a life or two, depending finally on how worthy his vengeance targets turn out to be: the more worthy your victims the fewer you need to kill to complete your vengeance.[11] The law, in other words, contemplated more corpses than feuding norms. In some respects feuding norms, in fact, supplied restraint to the law. Seldom do we see all those who engaged in conduct making them liable for outlawry actually get outlawed, or if outlawed actually get hunted down and killed.[12] Compromises and arbitrated settlements were usually worked out. Those who went to law recognized the more limiting constraints of feuding norms by rarely going after everyone they had a claim against to the full extent of the law.

If outlawry looked not all that different from revenge killing, what was the inducement to go to law? In either case one courted the danger of hunting down dangerous men. The law, it seems, conferred practical advantage by conferring moral advantage. Even in this stateless setting, with enforcement up to the plaintiff, people cared about the law, held it in reverence, and thought it mattered. Law accorded legitimacy to actions whose legitimacy might otherwise be uncertain. Legitimacy had the advantage of inducing others to assist you in your endeavor and to desist in aiding or abetting your outlaw. The law punished assisting an outlaw with lesser outlawry (three years' exile and loss of property), and the sagas show that the threat of prosecution was not a negligible deterrent.[13] Having the law with you, interestingly enough, also altered or even suspended the rules of fair play. The law not only induced others to join your posse, it made a posse look like the right thing to do. It was considered dishonorable for three to attack one in revenge, but foolish for a man to hunt down his outlaw alone and not take advantage of numbers.[14] And finally, by going to law you made a public decision to limit your response to the actual wrongdoers. No doubt this came as a nice relief to those innocent kin of the wrongdoer who still might have been appropriate vengeance targets had you decided to pursue that course. Such people might now have a self-interested reason not to oppose you too aggressively in your legal action against their kinsman. They surely had no great interest in getting you to change your strategy from legal recourse to blood revenge. By going to law you have let them off the hook.

If outlawry wasn't a sufficient concession to the blood urge, the law allowed a limited right to kill as a kind of summary judgment. Simply put, a man (and his companions) had a right to avenge assaults, injuries, and killings in which he would be the plaintiff up to the time of the next Allthing.[15] Sometimes this right was limited to the place of the incident; sometimes it was granted to the world at large for twenty-four hours after the event. The right to kill was also given a man to avenge sexual assaults or attempted sexual assaults on six women: wife, mother, daughter, sister, foster daughter, and foster mother.[16] The right to kill, however, like a legal judgment, limited the class of expiators to those who actually did the wrongful act.[17] The law was thus willing to waive its own obsession with procedure and admit that results were the important thing. For our purposes, the point is that law can go a long way toward countenancing revenge and still remain law. The wronged person could kill now within limits, but he would have to prove later that he had the right to kill. This, in fact, does not look all that different from our rules of justification; it's only that these people had much broader notions of what constituted justified killing. In this respect the law was very much in touch with the values of honor.

Then there were feuding norms. Honorable people did not undertake revenge lightly. Since revenge left not only you but your kin open to reprisal, those kin had a genuine interest in your vengeance-taking designs; you might have to rein in your vengeful desires to accommodate their interests. Feuding norms departed from legal rules in one key respect. In feud, as indicated above, you were not required to kill the person who had wronged you; his brother, cousin, uncle, son, father, or even close friends could serve just as well. This principle of group liability did much to constrain wild revenge. If you could get killed for your uncle's jokes or your cousin's womanizing, then you had a very keen interest in your uncle's sense of humor and your cousin's sex life. You policed those with whom the other side was likely to lump you. Revenge was never properly an individual matter; people consulted with their kin and friends before taking it, thus socializing the decision-making process. It was not just up to the individual who felt himself wronged. Kin and others would let you know if you were being supersensitive, and they would goad you to do your duty if you were not being sensitive enough. What they were concerned with was the appropriateness of your response, and they were there to help you get it right. You also needed your kin and friends for more than just advice. Most likely, you needed their help in carrying out revenge, and you would surely need their aid when it was your turn to be on the defensive. Above all, you needed the audience, the public, the uninvolved, to recognize that you were behaving appropriately and not being supersensitive. For the uninvolved were the possible class of supporters of your enemy, and support him they would if you were being asocial or merely self-assertive. If your cause was just, you would have an easier time getting third-party support; if it wasn't, it was easier for your enemy to get that support.

Feud, of course, was more than just doing the justice of avenging wrongs. It was also a way of engaging in politics. To the extent that feud looked back on past wrongs, it was judicial in its aspect; to the extent that it looked forward to acquiring power, it was political. But in either case it was subject to strong normative constraints. The feud and general notions of propriety were governed by notions of balance and reciprocity. Although the notion of balance is rich in ambiguity there were still limits. If people didn't stay within them they attracted communal hostility as well as legal liability.

Right action, acting with right, means more than just acting in accord with substantive legal rules; it also means acting *properly* when doing right. Propriety inevitably brings us to the world of emotion, gesture, and display. With regard to revenge, propriety is a matter not only of selecting a proper target but also of proper timing and proper demeanor. Three Norse proverbs give us rules of thumb: "Blood nights are the hottest"; "Only a slave avenges himself immediately, but a coward never does"; and "The longer vengeance is drawn out the more satisfying it will be."[18] One can begin plotting an emotional configuration of revenge from these proverbs. Anger and the shame that generates anger are the first things felt. The saga characters and the sagas themselves are rather reticent about talking about inner mental states, but peoples' bodies give them away. Characters turn red; they faint; they burst into tears or even hysterical laughter; they swell and sweat. Grief, anger, rage, fury, and shame surge, and the surge excuses, even justifies, hasty action. Blood nights, it seems, extended no more than three days. We see one saga character thinking it wise to absent himself from a locality for three days after a killing.[19] After that, it was unseemly to rush to vengeance. This suggests that the emotional states that motivated seemly revenge were in accord with cooler blood. Most revenge in the sagas is not the result of irrational slashing back, but it would be equally wrong to think of it as purely calculated instrumentality, although plenty of calculation underscored a good portion of successful vengeance takings. Vengeance taking required planning. One needed support, one needed information about one's target, one needed to consult about the advisability of whom to hit and when. These were political matters as well as matters of honor. The saga world, however, would not have recognized a distinction between honor and politics.

The psychology of revenge was a rather complex affair, and it would misrepresent that complexity to situate it within any particular vengeance taker. Revenge was only rarely an individual matter, and the different members of the group consulted or assembled to undertake it would be variously motivated. Some members of the grouping, usually young males, would stay furious much longer than the period contemplated by blood nights. Their role was to urge quick, aggressive, and often disproportionate action. These in turn were restrained by older men and others recruited who were less stricken by the death or insult that needed avenging but still felt the necessity and the propriety of vengeful action. For these people vengeance is inseparable from a sense of determination, a sense of duty, fueled at times by hatred, at times by a kind of malicious delight in being able to terrorize one's opponent. Nonhasty revenge was strategically wise practice. Not only did it give you the time to think things through and get them right, it also was a period of wariness for the possible class of victims who had to live with apprehension and anxiety.

Within the complex of shame, anxiety, anger, and purposiveness that motivates revenge,[20] anxiety is more than the lot of the possible vengeance target. No small amount belonged to the vengeance takers, who, despite the proverbial counsel about the deliciousness of slow revenge, knew that between the act of shame done them and the taking of revenge for it was the period of dominance by their enemy, the period of gossip about their shame and doubt about their capacity to avenge it. This was the period of other people's pleasure in one's own pain. Such knowledge about others' delights in one's own misfortune is not easy to bear any time, but in an honor-based society it is truly not to be borne, because the gossip of others and their delight constitutes the process by which one's social rank is readjusted downward. Nothing is more painful, nor more important.

If vengeance was mingled with politics, that is, with peoples' claim for relative rank and domination, it was also mingled with grief and how grief was properly displayed. Grief is an emotion that has points of significant overlap with frustration. Nothing you can do can bring back the object of grief. But it is precisely the frustration about the finality of grief that propels a desire to do something, either as a vent for frustration, or maybe, more magically, in hopes that action will bring some kind of reversibility to nature. Grief, frustration, anger, hatred, and revenge are elements in a kind of syndrome. This is not peculiar to Iceland. Grief, rage, and head-hunting go hand in hand among the Ilongot;[21] in *Macbeth* Malcolm can urge Macduff thus: "Let's make us med'cines of our great revenge / To cure this deadly grief.... Let grief / Convert to anger; blunt not the heart, enrage it" (4.3.214–15, 228–29).

Is it by a cultural or linguistic fiction that we pretend to demarcate certain emotions from one another? The oxymoron pays tribute to the fact that we can experience contrary emotions at the same time, and although no one would confuse joy with remorse, the notion of joyful remorse or remorseful joy is not inconceivable. Just how do we constitute a pure grief that is not variously bound up with frustration, anger, vengefulness, or despair? We might suppose that there are different griefs appropriate to different cultures, and within cultures to different ages, statuses, and genders. In the sagas, grief was manifested properly in old men by their taking to bed, at times with exaggerated ritual display.[22] For younger men, grief went with rage and hatred or a grim sense of purpose.[23] Women were allowed tears, but these were often tears of rage. Women, more than anyone, were supposed to be vengefully furious.[24] It is of some note that the Germanic word *harm* meant "grief" in Old Norse and both "grief" and "an offense or injury" in Old English, and although *harm* lost the sense of grief in Modern English, the semantic history of the word reveals rather nicely the intimate association between grief and the occasion for revenge.

Whatever revenge was in saga Iceland it was not what the antihonor, antirevenge discourses of political theory, moral philosophy, and utilitarianism wish to make it. It is constrained by norm, by law, and by a firm sense of the emotional accompaniment that must attend it for it to be properly motivated. Without "harm" or "shame," that is, without wrongs and the proper attendant emotions, it was unwarranted. That is, revenge had to be just and proper or it was simply another wrong that needed to be avenged. Here is where the antirevenge tradition makes a telling and practical point. How, they ask, do just revenges not engender a counterrevenge? The innocent kin of the person who rightly dies at the avenger's hand also will be rightly aggrieved. Won't they now have a claim for blood? In fact the critique is not wrong, and the feud often works precisely in that way. Moreover, wrongs don't simply arrive preinterpreted. What was laughed off at the time as a pleasantry among friends could be later recalled and interpreted as an avengeable offense when relations had soured. If the temporal frame of reference was extended too far back in the past, virtually any presently aggressive behavior could arguably be claimed as revenge for some long-forgotten wrong.

The trick is finding a principled way to understand when an action is a justified reaction rather than simply an aggressive move. Icelandic law attempted to solve the problem in such a way as to give avengers an incentive to take the route of getting an outlawry judgment and then killing the culprit rather than doing it without legal confirmation. The law made the killing of an outlaw privileged. Any revenge taken for the death of an outlaw could not itself be legal.[25] Killing someone in revenge before securing the judgment, no matter how rightful, subjected you to an outlawry action brought by the corpse's kin. There you could raise the issue of the justifiability of your action by way of defense. But these defenses were not as wide-ranging in their coverage as the claims upon which you could have had your enemy outlawed in the first place.[26] Without the intervention of the law, however, it was not unusual that a justifiable revenge could give rise to an equally justified reprisal. If the law tried to put an end to an infinite series of reprisals, it did so at the cost of frustration of grieving kin and friends of the outlaw. They might still take revenge, illegal now, but honor sometimes parted with the law, even in Iceland. In fact, litigants recognized that if peace were to stand a chance, the grief of people who had done no wrong would have to be assuaged and compensated. As a result, most disputes of any seriousness tended not to end in a legal judgment so much as in more informal settlements in which the reasonable claims of grieving people could be taken into account. It is thus quite common for someone who rightfully killed an attacker in legal self-defense to compensate the attacker's kin for their loss.

Suppose the law has the capacity to worry and be annoyed. The Icelandic law, then, was less worried by the disorders of revenge than by the peace purchased by the compromise of outlawry claims. Settling out of court annoyed the law. The law, as we have seen, was rather generous in giving a right to kill, but was very stingy when it came to authorizing settlement. In fact it purported to subject to lesser outlawry anyone who settled any case involving killing or wounds without obtaining permission from the Allthing first.[27] The sagas show no evidence that the rule was anything more than wishful thinking, but it reveals a ranking of concerns: it shows the law more jealous of its own prerogative than of bringing peace. What do we make of this? It may simply evidence the culture's view that of all the problems facing it, killing was not as important as subjecting all serious dispute to some official public scrutiny, even if the cost of that scrutiny was greater loss of life. Or we may simply see it as an earlier instance of the sad tendency of institutions to prefer their own power to the substantive matters that give them their missions and justify their existence.

On that bleak note we move to the present to see how revenge fares in our public fantasies and whether its style confirms the straw-man view of revenge as mere self-assertion without order, mayhem without measure. We will examine the style of revenge and the character of the avenger in that genre of film classically represented by *Death Wish* and *Dirty Harry* and myriad others adopting their form. The modern revenge film is characterized by a specific emotional economy that marks the genre, in fact determines it. Emotion-based theories of narrative are as old as Aristotle. Tragedy takes us through pity and fear to catharsis; the revenge narrative takes us from indignation and outrage at a wrong, via fear and loathing of the wrongdoer, to a sense of satisfaction of having the wrong righted on the body of the wrongdoer. The outrage and sense of satisfaction are crucial and definitive of the genre, but along the way from outrage to satisfaction we also expect to experience some mix of apprehension, hopefulness, anxiety, despair, terror, disgust, and suspense.

These films are about justice, doing justice, with equal emphasis on the doing and the justice. They are related to action and horror films, but there are crucial differences that distinguish the genres. In the revenge genre the hero hunts down the wrongdoer; in action films the hero tries to escape a wrongdoer intent on harming him or her. An action film hero is the fugitive unjustly accused, or she, more likely, is the "final girl" in various slasher films[28] or big-budget action-horror films such as the *Alien* and *Terminator* movies. These hunted heroes often become avengers mostly as a matter of self-defense, but their situation is quite different from that of classic avenging types like Dirty Harry or Charles Bronson. The hero-as-hunted genre has a different emotional economy from the vengeance film. The vengeance film, as we noted, depends on indignation leading to a sense of satisfaction; in the hero-as-hunted it is apprehension and horror leading to the experience of relief. One is the experience of escaping injustice, the other the experience of righting it.

Villains in the action-horror genre often pretend to a claim of right; they style themselves as avengers in their own revenge dramas. This is Max Cady in *Cape Fear* or the villains in *Patriot Games*. These are would-be avengers who aspire to the status of avenger but who are not granted it. We, the third-party observers, are the arbiters in this matter. And the chief reason we do not grant them legitimacy is that we judge them to be acting in accord with the straw-man model of revenge. They are not reacting to wrongs, but either to punishments that they deserved or to imagined insults. In the hero-as-hunted genre in which they find themselves their claims are recognizably without right, their methods of revenge pathologically disproportionate, and their motivation inappropriate. They have idiosyncratic notions of their own right, and as a result they do not engage us sympathetically. Look how thoroughly we reject the straw-man conception of revenge constructed by political and moral philosophers. We do not call Max Cady an avenger; we do not even call him an evil avenger. We simply call him a villain. We value the avenger status too much to accord it promiscuously to anyone with some crazed unconfirmed sense of his own wrong. The avenger status carries with it right and legitimacy, and thus we confer it on those whose claims are deserving. As in the saga world, revenge must be bound up with publicly sustainable claims of right.

In the saga world honor and justice are inextricably linked to a notion of reciprocity by a foundational metaphor based on debt, obligation, and the exchange of gifts. A wrong, like a gift, must be repaid;[29] not to repay is to live in shame or to be forever lower than the person you owe. The notion that the wronged person is a debtor means the wronged person is obliged, has a duty, not just a right, to pay back. We too subscribe to debt metaphors in our basic theories of corrective justice. As in the saga world, we understand wrongs as obliging us to act, to pay back what we owe, a most honorable commitment unfortunately vulgarized among us in the idiom "payback time." But we talk rather loosely about paying and paying back. We equally think of the wrongdoer as owing; he too is a debtor. We thus speak of the villain as *paying for* his wrongs, as owing a debt. Yet notice what happens when we make the wrongdoer a debtor: we blur something that is rather clear when it is the victim who is the debtor. When the victim is cast as debtor he knows to whom he owes repayment; the wrongdoer is never quite clear to whom he owes his debt. It's all rather fuzzy. He may be understood to owe the Furies, the gods, the state, or society (only rarely is he thought to owe his victim). The fuzziness, we see, is not just a matter of determining to whom among various claimants the wrongdoer owes his debt, but that the entity to whom he owes the debt is not flesh and blood, but itself a fuzzy abstraction.

The idea of the victim as debtor is completely consistent with an ethic of honor and revenge. We should make that stronger: it seems to be a necessary feature of honor and revenge. Nor is the idea of the wrong-doer as debtor inconsistent with honor and revenge. It is surely possible to understand the wrongdoer as paying for his wrong as he gets paid back by the victim. Feuding societies were not above this confusion either, since the wrongdoer often could negotiate an option of paying compensation to buy off the avenger's ax. But the idea of wrongdoer as debtor is also consistent with claims of a central authority interested in claiming jurisdiction and asserting an overriding claim to people's claims against each other in a way that the notion of the victim as debtor is not. Our revenge genre mixes its metaphors. We have two types of avenging hero: one who avenges outrages done to himself or to his loved ones; another who is a kind of professional avenger, usually a renegade soldier or police officer. The former is Paul Kersey (Charles Bronson) in *Death Wish*; the ideal model for the latter is Dirty Harry (Clint Eastwood). Roughly speaking, one pays back; the other makes others pay. Bronson ultimately becomes a generalized avenger doing justice where it needs to be done, and Harry inevitably gets wronged in his own right by the villains he hunts down. Still, without regard to the precise type of hero, the revenge genre is attracted more to the model of wrongdoer as owing than victim as owing. The sense of satisfaction it depends upon for its conclusion is achieved more by seeing the victim get it than by seeing the avenger reclaim lost honor. This only seems natural, given that the real victim is usually dead (or a woman)[30] and the avenger is operating as an agent or surrogate for the original victim. These movies have strangely little to do with the hero's honor reclamation, in spite of the genre's commitment to a macho style; they are more fantasies of effective state-delivered justice. Harry, after all, gets his right to do justice from being an employee of the state.[31]

Films in the revenge genre derive additional force from their implicit and at times explicit critique of the law. In their view, the law has lost sight of justice. More concerned with its own internal coherence, the law is depicted as preferring form to substance, and not just any form, but form that always seems to favor wrongdoers over law-abiding citizens. Thus Miranda warnings and the exclusionary rule are understood to make a joke of a constitution now enlisted to the cause of villains and criminals and forgetful of the claims of victims. Constitutional principle and the rhetoric that maintains it become the rank muck from which lawyers construct their tricks. This is a vision of law as either so foolish as not to know when it has been had or so knavish as not to care. Another critique, less virulent, takes this form: Even when the law gets it right, gets the criminal and brings him to justice, that justice is only second-best justice. The problem is that legal conclusions are never quite as satisfying as purely vengeful ones. The law promises closure and gives us parole and probation instead; it locks up the rapist only to release him to come back and kill the complaining witness.[32] Revenge accords more aesthetically with our sense of an ending; our fantasy is that revenge provides true closure. Unlike the grimmer and more realistic view of revenge in the saga world, the revenge genre gives us finality by detaching the villain from anyone interested enough to avenge him once he is killed.

The avenger, we see, must have right, and having right, he generally works to assist a stricken, inept, or wayward law in doing justice. The avenger does not view himself as providing a complete alternative system to formal bureaucratic law. He views his role as interstitial. He comes to remedy and complete the law, not to replace it. He has no problem with the idea of legal rules when they deliver justice, with justice conceived in terms of satisfying the rightful indignation of third parties against predatory wrongdoers and remedying the harms of victims. He gets the law to fulfill its central mission when legalism prevents it. Dirty Harry does equity. He is not a law unto himself. He works where the law fails to deliver justice. Like a chancellor, his right to intervene depends on the law's getting a chance to get the right result; his actions are in every sense derivative of the law, secondary, complementary, and equitable. In fact, the idea of Harry would make no sense in a world of no law, for what drives his style of heroism in particular is its implicit critique of the legal system. He needs Miranda warnings, search-and-seizure rules, the right against self-incrimination to have a purpose. Without such rules (and with stiffer punishments), the genre suggests, the law would do just fine and avengers would be out of work. And like the chancellor, he acts upon the body of the wrongdoer or the person unjustly benefiting from legal rules that are producing offensive, shocking, and unconscionable results.[33] The equity that motivates Harry does not deny the emotional economy that drives justice. Rightful indignation demands to be compensated with a sense of satisfaction. Harry would lose his moral force (and box-office allure) if he could not satisfy this most moral of emotions.

The revenge that plays the straw man for various traditions of legal and political theory is, as indicated above, by definition anarchical, uncontrolled, unprincipled, unbalanced. That is not a description of avengers in the sagas or in our revenge films. As we noted earlier, only villains are attracted to the straw-man model of revenge. They are the ones who operate solely by their own inner light and against general norms of propriety, right, and proportion. Consider, in contrast, just how constrained and ruled the avenger is. He must, after all, do justice, and that is no small constraint. And he is not the sole determiner of justice's demands; we are. It is we who determine whether he is hero or villain by how we apportion right between him and his adversary. His actions must accord with our sense of justice or he is not a hero or the film is not a revenge film. He must right wrongs and not just any wrongs, but ones we tend to feel are inadequately remedied at law. Should his notion of wrong become too expansive, he becomes a meddlesome bully or pathological in the manner of Travis Bickle in *Taxi Driver*, for whom the mere existence of others was an avengeable offense: "You talkin' to me?"

Notice the significant contrasts between the film avenger and his saga counterpart. Unlike the saga avenger, the film hero cannot kill the innocent father, son, or brother of the villain unless they too have committed avengeable offenses. Also unlike saga avengers, ours are inevitably loners. This makes for a rather paradoxical contrast with the saga hero, who is always deeply embedded within kin group and community. Paradoxical because the saga hero ends up being more individualized for such embedding than our avenger, who becomes almost indistinguishable from his office. He is his role and nothing more, a pure avenger. The saga hero, on the other hand, is only called to be an avenger two or three times in his life; he must also manage his farm, be a father, brother, husband, adviser, friend, and leader. For him, as a result, taking vengeance is a psychological drama in a way that it is not for the film hero: the saga avenger is more Hamlet than Harry. He thus ends up more individualized than the film avenger, in spite of the traditional wisdom that denies the capacity for deep inner lives to denizens of honor cultures. Our avenger's parody of romantic individualism rather weakly individuates him. He postures as the most romantic of individuals, refusing to follow along with the general level of incompetent docility that characterizes the bureaucratic style, while at the same time molding himself seamlessly to his ministerial function as a doer of justice. There is no office/person distinction here because there is no person distinct from the office, just a principle and a mission: a doer of justice.

I do not wish to overstate the case. The avenger has some strong areas of disagreement with the law. Here is a partial list:

1. Avengers will hear of no insanity defense for the nonpathetic insane, that is, for those whose insanity makes them objects of fear and loathing rather than of pity. In the same vein, notions of diminished capacity that concede too much to determinist models of human behavior are not acceptable. There is thus opposition to lessened culpability or defenses for riot syndrome, junk food, Prozac, black rage, posttraumatic stress (except for Vietnam vets)—even, I would bet, for homosexual panic.
2. The Fifth Amendment right against self-incrimination is serviceable mostly to rogues.
3. There is a general view that the law is too obsessed with wrongful acts rather than with evil characters. Why not let juries hear evi-

dence of prior convictions and arrests, prior complaints, and so on? That teeming assemblage of awful people who continually give offense without ever committing any one particular offense that will bring sufficiently appropriate legal sanction to bear upon them, such as the bully and the pimp, are thus justified targets for the avenger.

4. As a corollary to the preceding, there is no presumption of innocence for people who don't deserve it. The hostility to the presumption of innocence is succinctly captured in *Unforgiven* by the tough sheriff, Little Bill, when he is accused of having "just kicked the shit out of an innocent man." Responds Bill: "Innocent? Innocent of what?" Bill's mean wit changes the meaning of innocence to guilt and makes it the condition to be accounted for, if not quite to be proved. Moreover, Bill was right. The "innocent man" had violated the town's firearms ordinance and had done so because he intended to kill. Innocence in this genre is a true moral and social condition, not a legal conclusion.

5. The criminal law's notions of proportionality do not accord with the demands of justice. Not all first-degree and second-degree murders are worse than all rapes. The notion that rape could never be a capital offense unless the victim is also killed is not an acceptable ranking of wrongs, which ranking must depend not on the internal coherence of the law, but on the sense of indignation and outrage the act elicits in third parties.

These disagreements tend mostly in one direction: they all evidence a belief that our law stacks the deck against justice by stacking it too much in favor of wrongdoers. But they can be further broken down into sets of rules designed to protect law-abiding citizens from an intrusive and hostile state—such as search-and-seizure rules, the right against self-incrimination—and rules that are concerned to prevent the horror of punishing the innocent. The genre dismisses the first set as simply not reflective of the real source of danger in contemporary society. It is not the state but our fellow citizen who threatens our liberty. The second—protecting the innocent—is disposed of by the formal demands of the genre itself, which defines the problem away. The innocent are thus, by definition, the victims of villains, not the victims of avengers. In this genre the avenger never gets an innocent person. If he does he compromises the form so drastically as to undo it. Avengers who kill the innocent are vigilantes who, when banded together, are the villains in a different and easily identified genre of which we may cite *The Oxbow Incident* as an example. Notice I did not say that avengers do not get the wrong man. It is just that the wrong man is never innocent. The genre finesses this issue (in accordance with a popular sense of justice) by taking "innocent" to mean decent people minding their own business; innocence is emphatically not just having the fortune of being found legally not guilty because of some juror's notion of reasonable doubt.

I have tried in this essay to show that the concept of revenge as articulated in various antihonor discourses, whether they be moral, legal, or political-philosophical, is not borne out by revenge and honor-based cultures themselves. It is not unconstrained individual self-assertion in response to injuries as defined by that individual. Nor is that view of revenge borne out by popular culture. Avengers in the sagas and avengers in our films are both regulated by the audiences that observe them, precisely because both the saga hero and the modern avenger need the support of their audiences. For all the official handwringing over our delight in depictions of revenge, those depictions—critical as they are about the legal administration of justice, the leniency and uncertainty of punishment, the lack of concern with victims and their satisfaction—are as a matter of substance not all that opposed to the law. If popular culture's rules for establishing who and what are eligible for expiation are somewhat broader, they are still quite narrow. The avenger's target still has to have done wrong or harmed another. The avenger still has to convince the neutral observer that he has right. In other words, there are rules, very strict ones. The wild justice of revenge, for all its so-called wildness, is strictly constrained by the fact that it is justice. The filmic form in which this justice is portrayed depends on winning the support of viewers to the avenger's claims. We must be indignant, we must be outraged on behalf of victims, and then be satisfied by justified payback. The avenger cannot go it alone, inventing his own rules, his own theory of offense and injury. If he does, he goes over the edge into psychopathology, and then we are no longer seeing a classic revenge film.

If the avenger of American film and his saga counterpart share a richly constrained and social notion of revenge, they are otherwise quite different. The saga hero is driven by shame and by fear of shame, which are caught up and overlap variously with grief and anger. The avenger of film seems unmotivated by a sense of shame. He is, however, angry, but more often than not his anger is directed against his superiors or the authorities who must bear the ultimate blame for the mayhem of villains simply because they restrict him. In the saga world, justice and honor were inseparable; the notion of honor and justice as reciprocity, as paying back what you owe, largely unified them both in a field of exchange relations. The modern avenger has honor, but it is not that which motivates him; it is the desire to make wrongdoers pay and in the process to shame his superiors, who insist on making it so hard for him to make wrongdoers pay. But it is not the superiors who owe us; it is still the wrongdoers who do. They owe us for their acts of predation, for the harm they cause, for the anxiety they instill. This is hardly the saga model of restoring honor; it is rather the suburban model of reducing risk to an insurable minimum. Finally, the saga form is too complex in the emotional demands it makes on the reader to be reduced to a single genus; not so the revenge film. Dirty Harry knows you will be outraged by the wrongdoer, hate him for what he has done and who he is, and experience the satisfaction of justice done when Harry makes your day by blowing him away.

Notes

1. See Susan Jacoby, *Wild Justice: The Evolution of Revenge* (New York: Harper and Row, 1983).

2. See Þorgils saga ok Hafliða, in vol. 1 of *Sturlunga saga*, ed. Jón Jóhannesson, Magnús Finnbogason, and Kristján Eldjárn, 2 vols. (Reykjavík: Sturlunguútgáfan, 1946); hereafter cited as S.

3. See II *Canute* 40 sec. 2: "It is the duty most incumbent upon a Christian king that he should avenge to the uttermost offenses against God, in accordance with the nature of the deed"; *The Laws of the Kings of England from Edmund to Henry I*, ed. A. J. Robertson (Cambridge: Cambridge University Press, 1925), 196.

4. *Prestssaga Guðmundar góða*, S1, chaps. 8–9.

5. Some saga characters were able to be generally forgiving and to be honored for their mildness of manner; e.g., Áskell goði in *Reykdæla saga* (F10) and Síðu-Hallr in *Njáls saga* (F12). But they were powerful chieftains. Clearly it was only honorable to be forgiving when one in fact was giving up something that one could take. Imagine just how ridiculous (or downright contumacious) it would be for, say, a serf to forgive his lord. Family sagas are cited by volume in the series *Íslenzk Fornit* (F) (Reykjavík: Hið Íslenzka Fornritafélag, 1933–). For translation of all family saga texts, see *The Complete Sagas of the Icelanders*, 5 vols. ed. Viðar Hreinsson (Reykjavík: Leifur Eiríksson, 1997).

6. On peacemakers and men of goodwill, see the discussion in William Ian Miller, *Bloodtaking and Peacemaking* (Chicago: University of Chicago Press, 1990), 264–66.

7. I make here the obligatory move of noting that the judgment of vulgarity is an imposition of one class on another. That is obvious, yet I wonder if there isn't truly a Platonic form of vulgarity that rightly essentializes the category. If we define aggressive self-assertion as that which must recognize its own success solely by the fact that it disgusts the other, then we have liberated the notion of vulgarity from such easy relativistic dismissal.

8. Ernest van den Haag, *Punishing Criminals* (New York: Basic Books, 1975), 10, quoted in John Kaplan and Robert Weisberg, *Criminal Law*, 2nd ed. (Boston: Little Brown, 1991), 29.

9. Robert Nozick, *Philosophical Explanations* (Cambridge, Mass.: Harvard University Press, 1982), 366–68. I have abridged Nozick's account and subjected it to some minor paraphrasing.

10. See generally Miller, *Bloodtaking and Peacemaking*, where I deal much more fully with the intricacies of vengeance.

11. The *Leges Henrici Primi* do not make this a matter of implicit norm, but formally articulate it (64, 2b): "For the oath of a thegn equals the oaths of six villeins; if he is killed he is fully avenged by the slaying of six villeins"; *Leges Henrici Primi*, ed. L. J. Downer (Oxford: Clarendon Press, 1972), 204.

12. For a rare exception in which all those complicit are either killed or outlawed, see *Laxdæla saga* (F5), chaps. 49–51 (family sagas are cited by chapter, since most editions and translations agree on chapter division). Most often little players bore the brunt. They would get outlawed while the bigger fry were able to settle for an arbitrated settlement that usually substituted a transfer of wealth or exile of limited duration for full outlawry.

13. See *Finnboga saga* (F14), chap. 41; *Íslendinga saga* (S1), chaps. 3, 25, 129; *Sturlu saga* (S1), chaps. 5, 23.

14. With *Víga-Glúms saga* (F9), chap. 19, compare *Þorsteins þáttr stangarhöggs* (F11).

15. *Grágás* Ia 147, 149; II 302, 303–4; cited by volume and page to the editions of Vilhjálmur Finsen: vol. 1: *Grágás: Islændernes Lovbog i Fristatens Tid, udgivet efter det Kongelige Bibliotheks Haandskrift* (Copenhagen: Berlings Bogtrykkeri, 1852; reprint, Odense: Odense University Press, 1974); vol 2: *Grágás efter det Arnamagnæanske Haandskrift Nr. 334 fol., Staðarhólsbók* (Copenhagen: Gyldendal, 1879; reprint, Odense: Odense University Press, 1974).

16. *Grágás* Ia 164, II 331.

17. The sagas give scant sense that prejudgment vengeance was governed by these rules. See Andreas Heusler, *Das Strafrecht der Isländersagas* (Leipzig: Duncker & Humblot, 1911), 54.

18. *Grettis saga* (F7), chap. 15; *Víga-Glúms saga* (F9), chap. 8; *Ljósvetninga saga* (F10), C-version, chap. 13.

19. *Víga-Glúms saga,* (F9), chap. 8.

20. William Ian Miller, *Humiliation* (Ithaca, N.Y.: Cornell University Press, 1993), chap. 3.

21. See Michelle Z. Rosaldo, *Knowledge and Passion: Ilongot Notions of Self and Social Life* (Cambridge: Cambridge University Press, 1980), and "The Shame of Headhunters and the Autonomy of Self," *Ethos* 11 (1983): 135–51; and Renato Rosaldo, *Culture and Truth: The Remaking of Social Analysis* (Boston: Beacon Press, 1989), 1–21.

22. See *Egils saga* (F2), chap. 24; *Hávarðar saga Ísfirðings* (F6), chap. 5; also in some respects *Njáls saga* (F12), chap. 129.

23. Þórhallr Ásgrímsson (*Njáls saga* (F12), chap. 132); Skallagrímr (*Egils saga* (F2), chap. 24).

24. I am referring to the well-known role of women as goaders of their reluctant men to aggressive action; see Miller, *Bloodtaking and Peacemaking,* 212–14, and *Humiliation,* 104–5.

25. But that does not mean it did not happen; see, e.g., *Njáls saga* (F12), chap. 78.

26. There was a legal way around this. You could summon the person you killed posthumously for the act that he had committed that incurred your revenge. In this way you could have your revenge redefined as, in effect, the killing of an outlaw. See Miller, *Bloodtaking and Peacemaking,* 252, 363 n. 50.

27. *Grágás* Ia 174.

28. The term comes from Carol Clover's definitive study of the slasher genre in *Men, Women, and Chain Saws: Gender in the Modern Horror Film* (Princeton, N.J.: Princeton University Press, 1992), chap. 1.

29. *Njáls saga,* chap. 44. See Miller, *Bloodtaking and Peacemaking,* chap. 6. Note that seeing the wronged person as the debtor makes it difficult as a conceptual matter for the wronged person to forgive the wrongdoer. It is not debtors who are in the position to forgive what they owe.

30. As Clover points out, in *Men, Women, and Chain Saws,* in low-budget B films women can avenge themselves; in mainstream big-budget films men or the law take over on behalf of the female victim.

31. The villains in these films are often so execrable that they are not meaningfully engaged in a competition for honor with the hero. That the hero suffers beatings at their hands does not lessen the avenger's honor so much as make the villain even more execrable. Where the hero's honor is engaged is usually against his commanding officer, and the triumph of the hero is often depicted as more a shame to the commanding authorities who doubted or obstructed the hero than to the villain who lies dead. This fact shows just how central the critique of legal institutions is to the form.

32. Clover (*Men, Women, and Chain Saws,* 148–49) asks us to compare the knowing smile of satisfaction on the face of the avenging rape victim that closes out *I Spit on Your Grave,* a low-budget pure rape-revenge film, with the picture of a courthouse, the closing

shot of *The Accused*, a big-budget softening of the rape-revenge genre. The rape victim in the former has nothing more to fear from her tormentors. I would add that legal endings usually make for a distinctly weaker sense of satisfaction. The death of the wrongdoer brings serious closure to the business at hand; a guilty verdict is only a stay, a promise of closure, unless it ends in capital punishment.

33. Popular culture has not yet gotten around to blaming juries for failings in the system. The failings are still attributed to corrupt and inept officialdom, not to lay people who are just trying to do their best but getting it wrong. Surely one could make films blaming the five or six Menendez jurors who were willing to give credence to any claim, no matter how unsubstantiated, of child abuse, or those willing to slap the wrist of the man who put a brick through Reginald Denny's head, but that has not happened. Rather, I suspect, the critique will continue to follow the *Dirty Harry* and *Death Wish* line: what is wrong is that the law keeps evidence of the defendant's prior wrongs from the jury, but lets them hear any outlandishly manufactured claim of the wrongdoer's victimhood.

CHAPTER 4

❖

"The Doom of Resoun"
Accommodating Lay Interpretation in Late Medieval England
James H. Landman

Interpretation always takes place in the shadow of coercion.
— Robert Cover

*Lete al the clergie of divinite bese hem silf wiseli in this mater...for to
bi cleer witt drawe men into consente of trewe feith otherwise than bi
fier and swerd or hangement.*
— Bishop Reginald Pecock

Bishop Reginald Pecock and Sir John Fortescue share, among many
things, an interest in lay interpretation and the desirability of maintaining — or tolerating — a lay interpretive role in ecclesiastic doctrinal debate and common law adjudication.[1] Pecock and Fortescue also share
a concern with defending their respective institutions of the church and
the English common law from what they perceive as a detrimental reliance on extreme forms of physical coercion in place or in suppression
of lay interpretive voices. Neither writer denies coercion a role in the
maintenance of institutional authority; instead, the issue for both is the
effect of too great an application of coercive force in the church's quest
for doctrinal conformity and the law's search for proof of guilt. Equally
troubled by the implications of interpretive multiplicity, on the one hand,
and of coercively constraining or silencing variant lay voices, on the other,
Pecock and Fortescue each attempt to fashion an accommodation between
lay interpretation and institutional coercive force.

Qualifying his preference for consent to church doctrine produced by
"cleer witt" over that produced by "fier and swerd or hangement," Bishop
Pecock acknowledges "that the bothe now seid meenys ben good," urging only "that the former meene be parfitli excercisid, eer it schal be
come into the ii^e."[2] Coercion, in other words, is a force to be held in reserve — or kept in the shadows — to be called upon when a failure of "cleer
witt" compels reliance on a more severe form of persuasion. Nonetheless,
Pecock's preference for the consent of "cleer witt" over coerced consent
marks an important concession, one that is thoroughly explicated in a

series of texts written by Pecock in the English vernacular and addressed to persons of the "lay parti."[3]

The idea that the clergy can draw people to the "trewe feith" with "cleer witt" presumes both that church doctrine should be explained to the laity and that the laity can understand such explanations. It is an idea central to Pecock's arguments and is concisely represented by Pecock's emphasis on the "doom of resoun": the human capacity to make rational judgments.[4] Recognizing that the laity's own participation in the "doom of resoun" renders unsupported doctrinal statements by the church vulnerable, and acutely conscious of lay interpretive challenges to the authority of church doctrine, Pecock seeks to restore the church's authority by defining and accommodating a limited lay interpretive role in the ongoing production of church doctrine.

Slightly more than a decade after Pecock's proposals were decisively rejected by the English church hierarchy,[5] Sir John Fortescue (Henry VI's former chief justice of the King's Bench and subsequent chancellor in exile) takes up the subject of interpretation and coercion in a different context. Fortescue's *De laudibus legum Anglie* is presented as a dialogue between the chancellor and Henry VI's son, Prince Edward, and is intended to resolve the prince's uncertainty as to whether he should study English law or the "civil laws" of continental Europe. Comparing the common law of England with the laws and procedures of continental legal systems (especially France), the *De laudibus legum Anglie* devotes much attention to the determination of truth in the two systems. Whereas England entrusts the determination of truth to the deliberations of a panel of "twelve good and loyal men," continental procedure, at its most extreme, employs torture to extract the confession of the accused. In a famous passage from the *De laudibus*, Fortescue condemns the practice of torture and its supposed efficacy in producing a true confession: "Such confessions, alas! many...wretches make, not because of truth, but only because compelled by irresistible torments" (*De laudibus*, 51).

Fortescue's condemnation of torture—a condemnation of seemingly unquestionable conviction—nonetheless proves remarkably contingent as the arguments of the *De laudibus* develop. Determination of truth can be entrusted to a panel of English laymen only because England, uniquely blessed with natural and material riches, is also uniquely (and consequently) blessed with an adequate concentration of men whose reason and moral character are trustworthy. As the *De laudibus*'s student, Prince Edward, concludes with respect to continental procedure,

the civil law in the comparison made by you is delivered from all blame, because, though you have preferred the law of England to it, yet it does not deserve odium, since you...have shown only that the land where it rules is the cause of its not eliciting the truth in disputes by so good a procedure as the law of England does. (*De laudibus*, 71–73)

Coercion, explicitly condemned in the *De laudibus*'s vivid description of torture's force, reappears in the shadows of the prince's conclusion, filling in the spaces where men are less "dispositi ad discernendum" (disposed to understanding) than the materially blessed men of England.[6]

This chapter focuses on the tension between accommodating lay interpretation and preserving institutional authority in the writings of Pecock and Fortescue. Pecock's "doom of resoun" and Fortescue's disposition *ad discernendum* are concepts both necessary and potentially threatening to the balance each author seeks to achieve between the authority of his respective institution and a lay interpretive role within that institution. By acknowledging with these concepts the rational capacity of the "lay parti" of the faithful and the laymen of the jury, Pecock and Fortescue are able to justify lay participation in the production or application of church doctrine and the common law. But while this acknowledgment is necessary to accommodate lay interpretation, it also undermines the exclusivity of clerical and professional authority within these two institutions. That is to say, if, as both Pecock and Fortescue insist, the doctrine of the church and the rules and procedures of the common law are (for the most part) rational, and if the laity is deemed capable of making rational judgments, claims by church officials or common law professionals to the exclusive power of determining the meaning and proper application of religious doctrine or legal rules are, at the very least, contestable.

The implications of the "doom of resoun" or disposition *ad discernendum*—the notion that the capacity to make rational judgments is possessed at some level by everyone—thus directly pertain to central issues of social control: by whom such control is exercised and by what authority. Accommodating lay interpretation within an institution whose power is derived from the authority of its members' interpretations of a text or texts grounding the regulation of social relations inevitably entails the partial relinquishment of control to persons outside of, but subject to, that institution. As we shall see, this conclusion was lost to neither Pecock nor Fortescue, and their efforts to qualify their respective conceptual accommodations of lay interpretation help us to trace the shifting and highly contested bases of social control in fifteenth-century England.

Mirrors and Shadows: Interpretive Normativity and Coercion

The complex relationship between interpretation and social control in the specific context of legal institutions is a dominant and troubling concern of the theorist Robert Cover. Legal interpretation in Cover's theory refers to interpretive acts within an institution sanctioned to enforce its interpretive commitments with political coercion or violence. "It is," Cover writes, "precisely this embedding of an understanding of political text in institutional modes of action that distinguishes *legal* interpretation from the interpretation of literature, from political philosophy, and from constitutional criticism. Legal interpretation is either played out on the field of pain and death or it is something less (or more) than law."[7] Cover's emphasis on the institutional context of interpretive acts is not misplaced. The real distinction between legal and other forms of interpretation in Cover's theory derives not from the inherent qualities of a text, but from considerations extrinsic to the text. The first of these considerations is the designation of a text as "political," a designation loosely defined in Cover's theory, but seemingly meant to denote a text the interpretation of which is used to ground and articulate the social relations of a given culture. Second is the "embedding" of interpretations of such a text within an institution authorized to support its interpretive commitments to the text, and to regulate those of others, with coercive, often physically violent, practices.

In his essay "Nomos and Narrative," Cover describes the countervailing "jurisgenerative" and "jurispathic" impulses in legal interpretation. The jurisgenerative impulse refers to "the creation of legal meaning," while the jurispathic impulse describes "the process that destroys legal meaning in the interest of social control."[8] Jurisgenesis is associated with a "world-creating" or "paideic" pattern, that is, the building of a normative universe around "a common body of precept and narrative" (presumably an alternate description of the "political" text) through personal and communal pedagogical and experiential processes.[9] Yet the unity of Cover's paideic entity is threatened from the moment of its inception by "the problem of multiplicity of meaning—the fact that never only one but always many worlds are created by the too fertile forces of jurisgenesis." This, in turn, "leads at once to the imperial virtues and the imperial mode of world maintenance," associated with the jurispathic impulse and directed toward containment of "the potent flowers of normative meaning" produced through jurisgenesis.[10] It is important to note Cover's emphasis on the necessity of this world-maintaining mode and the perceived threat of unchecked jurisgenesis:

> Let loose, unfettered, the worlds created [through the forces of jurisgenesis] would be unstable and sectarian in their social organization, dissociative and incoherent in their discourse, wary and violent in their interactions. The sober imperial mode of world maintenance holds the mirror of critical objectivity to meaning, imposes the discipline of institutional justice upon norms, and places the constraint of peace on the void at which strong bonds cease.[11]

So, at least, in theory. In practice, "the mirror of critical objectivity," "the discipline of institutional justice," and "the constraint of peace" all can be easily distorted, and threaten to expel or destroy, instead of to regulate, "the potent flowers of normative meaning." Institutions given the power to regulate the meaning of a society's "common body of precepts and narrative" exercise a jurispathic function to the extent that they impose their hermeneutics on communities producing variant meanings. And when this function is fortified by the sanctioned use of coercive force, the regulating institution threatens not only to contain but to stifle the jurisgenerative production of meaning. "The question, then," for Cover, "is the extent to which coercion is necessary to the maintenance of minimum conditions for the creation of legal meaning in autonomous interpretive communities."[12]

Cover's definitions of the jurisgenerative and jurispathic impulses, and his own preference for the former impulse in his vision of pluralistic normativity, provide a vantage point from which the comparatively jurispathic tendencies of Pecock and Fortescue could be easily critiqued. But even more valuable for an analysis of Pecock's and Fortescue's theories, and for theories of social control in general, are the implications of Cover's move from the ideal "mirror of critical objectivity" to the "shadow of coercion," and his own ultimate reliance on coercion to maintain his vision of pluralistic normativity. For in making this move, a move Cover regrets but considers necessary in a violent world of fragmented paideic entities, Cover acknowledges that coercion in the name of social control cannot be justified in the name of the superior hermeneutical principle implied in the ideal mirror of critical objectivity. Instead, coercion must be defended in terms of "the need to maintain a sense of legal meaning despite the destruction of any pretense of superiority of one *nomos* over another,"[13] as a necessary alternative to the imagined "unfettered,... unstable and sectarian,... dissociative and incoherent,... wary and violent" normative worlds produced through an unchecked jurisgenerative impulse. Coercion, in short, is justified by the need to maintain social order.

The irreconciled tension in Cover's work between a valued proliferation of meaning and the feared violent disruption of order if meaning proliferates uncontrollably also pervades the writings of Pecock and Fortescue. The more constrained visions of interpretive normativity in these texts do not preclude consideration of the jurispathic impulse or criticism of the stifling effect of its unrestrained exercise. Both theorists depend explicitly on legal models to critique the unrestrained exercise of coercive force and to describe or imagine alternative methods for the interpretive production of meaning. Both recognize, as does Cover, the countervailing jurispathic and jurisgenerative impulses of legal interpretation, and both attempt to fashion a place for the latter impulse by seeking to circumscribe the exercise of the former.

Pecock's and Fortescue's institutional commitments are, however, clearer than those of Cover, and jurisgenesis's perceived challenge to social order produces more ready endorsements of the jurispathic impulse in both theorists' texts. The erosion of a superior hermeneutical principle grounding the authority of the church and the common law — both threatened by the admission of lay interpretation — provokes a reaction in, and to, Pecock's and Fortescue's texts that attempts to shore up such authority. It is a reaction characterized, in both cases, by attempts to define lay interpretive communities restrictively and to assert the priority of an institutionally sanctioned hermeneutic, a reaction often accompanied by the reencroachment of the shadow of coercion.

Fortescue and the "Lay Gentz" of the Jury

Sir John Fortescue has been described as "an English lawyer and the kind of amateur of philosophy who helps us understand the ideas of an age by coarsening them slightly."[14] This coarsening virtue is evident in Fortescue's discussions of the common law jury and the role of reason in legal interpretation, and the clear lines of his analysis are better considered before the more tentative, and vulnerable, discussions of lay interpretation in Pecock's texts, which slightly predate Fortescue's writings.

The text at the center of the following discussion, Fortescue's *De laudibus legum Anglie,* is not so much a theoretical accommodation of a lay interpretive role in common law adjudication as an advocate's defense of an institution whose insularity from the mainstream of European jurisprudence has become pronounced. A sense of this insularity is conveyed when Prince Edward, the *De laudibus*'s student, asks his father's chancellor whether he should devote himself to study of the laws of England or of the "civil laws" that are "renowned throughout the world" (*per orbem percelebres*).[15] In response, the chancellor initiates a comparative analysis of the two laws, seeking to establish the superiority of the English common law at its points of contrast with the civil laws.[16] The *De laudibus* is thus as much a defense as an acclamation of the English common law, and it is a defense not intended to change the course of civilian jurisprudence, but to persuade the English prince to guide himself and his royal courts according to the conventions of the common law when he assumes the throne.

The first point of contrast selected by the chancellor is determination of truth under the two systems: the English trial by jury is compared, first, to civilian deposition of witnesses, and, second, at the extreme of civilian procedure, to the procurement of a suspect's confession under torture. The priority given and attention paid to this topic is itself noteworthy and hints at the vulnerability of the common law jury the chancellor defends. This vulnerability is, of course, not conceded by the chancellor. The *De laudibus*'s vigorous advocacy — enthusiastic praise of the

English jury and critical descriptions of the civilian methods of deposition and torture—excludes consideration both of contemporary complaints regarding abuse of the trial jury and of close, if not exact, correspondences between the two systems. Yet even the vigor of Fortescue's advocacy cannot completely dispel doubts about the powerful interpretive role given to the laymen of the jury.[17]

The Limits of Legal Coercion

The *De laudibus*'s harshest criticisms come with the chancellor's denunciation of torture, a practice that, as described by the chancellor, takes the jurispathic impulse to the point of legal self-destruction, destroying not only the meaning of the victim's confession, but also the authority of the supervising judge and the law he administers. The chancellor's opinion of the meaninglessness of the confession produced under torture was noted earlier, but bears repeating: the victim of torture confesses "not because of truth, but only because compelled by irresistible torments."[18] Moreover, with a rhetorical question that attacks the central justification for torture's use, the chancellor asks, "What certainty results from the confessions of people under such pressure?"[19] The implied answer, of course, is the certainty of the confession itself, but a certainty dissociated from the truth of guilt or innocence by the "irresistible" compulsion of torture.

By destroying in its pursuit of certainty the confession's reference to the victim's understood guilt or innocence, torture thus destroys meaning for the sake of conformity in an extreme expression of the jurispathic impulse. It produces confessions that conform to and complete the minimum legal suspicion of guilt necessary for torture's application, converting suspicion of guilt to conviction. Yet the very meaninglessness of the confession enabling conviction attaches to the law according to which the confession is produced, destroying the law's superior hermeneutical position as a privileged producer of truth. And if the accused endures the torture, "and will not lie to the peril of his soul, so that the judge pronounces him innocent," the desire to condemn expressed in torture's force turns back against the judges themselves, rendering them as "thoroughly base" (*perignobiles*) as the executioners who physically carry out judgments against the convicted and, "by that very deed," are made "infamous" (*infames*) and "unfit for judicial status."[20] An "unsuccessful" use of torture thus effects a legal inversion: the innocent victim's endurance condemns the judge, marking his conscience with a wound that never heals "as he remembers the agonies of pain of a poor wretch so afflicted" (*De laudibus*, 53).

Perhaps the most significant (and strategically useful) element of the chancellor's critique of torture is its rejection of a principle of absolute certainty in legal adjudication as an unattainable ideal, or an ideal attainable in the name of certainty alone. The "full proof" of the confession procured by torture rests atop a pyramid of lesser, unreliable proofs, proofs whose unreliability is compounded by the lack of the particular knowledge necessary to evaluate those proofs. The chancellor questions civilian reliance on the deposition of two witnesses: "feeble indeed in power, and of less diligence, may he be deemed, who cannot find, out of all the men he knows, two who are so lacking in conscience and truth that, for fear, love, or advantage, they will contradict every truth" (*De laudibus,* 45). Moreover, the testifying witnesses and their reputation may well be unknown to the opposing party, let alone the judge, and consequently "the perversion of judgements by false witness" can occur "even under the best judges" (*De laudibus,* 47). Torture is intended to compensate for this unreliability in capital cases (*ubi mors imminet*) "lest innocent blood be condemned by the testimony of liars" (*De laudibus,* 46–47). But the result, as the chancellor demonstrates, is that innocent and guilty alike are condemned by the equally unreliable testimony of pain. There is, however, an alternative at hand, and the chancellor's attentions turn to a commendation of England's trial by jury.

The distinctions between confession under torture and trial by jury are many, but the contrast between the underlying assumptions of the two procedures is not as pronounced as the rhetoric of the *De laudibus* suggests. As regards the suspect, the contrast is between the violent eliciting of the suspect's speech and the subordination of the suspect's speech to the verdict of the jury, as the search for factual truth is deflected from the suspect's body to the panel of jurors assembled to determine this truth. This does not mean that the rights of the suspect improve as we cross the Channel from the continent to England; indeed, the suspect's very presence at trial might be the result of a process as brutally coercive as torture. Because trial by jury remained, in theory, a procedure chosen by the suspect, the inducement of *peine forte et dure* (pressing and starvation) was developed to encourage the suspect reluctant to "choose" trial by jury.[21] This particular violence was, however, preparatory to the determination of factual truth, which was entrusted to the jury.

Common law coercion thus facilitates, but does not claim an active role in, the determination of truth: the necessity for legal coercion of the suspect does not extend to a confession because of the common law's designation of the jury as the locus of factual truth. That is, because the understanding of fact represented by the jury's verdict determined conviction or acquittal, and because the verdict was not subject to a minimum standard of proof (the jury was not required to specify the factual basis of its verdict), the suspect's "certain" confession — the necessity of which was dictated by the civilian requirement of "full" proof in a capital case — did not become a requirement for conviction in England.[22] In a comment underscoring the chancellor's strategically apt critique of torture and the "certain" confession, John Langbein has noted that "the trial jury required for condemnation not certainty, but only persuasion."[23]

To ground the search for truth on "only persuasion" is, of course, to justify the jury, whose particular understanding of local circumstances provides the basis for the evaluation of trial testimony, local rumor, circumstantial evidence, and all the other persuasive information the medieval jury could draw upon in fashioning its verdict. And it is precisely this particular understanding that the chancellor cites in his defense of the common law jury. The "witnesses" of the jury, subject to challenge by the litigants or criminal defendant, are "neighbors" (*vicini*), not "unreliable hirelings, paupers, vagrants, nor any whose condition and cunning is unknown."[24] They, in turn, are able to evaluate the testimony of deposed witnesses: "These know all that the witnesses admit in their depositions, and they know the reliability, unreliability, and repute of the witnesses brought forward" (*De laudibus*, 63). Moreover, in criminal cases, the local jury safeguards the defendant ("who...in England can die unjustly for a crime, when...none save his neighbours, good and faithful men, against whom he has no manner of exception, can condemn him?") and ensures the application of justice ("it cannot be supposed that a suspect accused in this form can escape punishment, when his life and habits would thereafter be a terror to them who acquitted him of his crime") (*De laudibus*, 65).

The chancellor's explication of the jury's local, particular virtues raises, however, a new set of issues. The juror should be a neighbor, but at the same time be identified as "impartial" (*indifferens*) (*De laudibus*, 56–57); his empanelment must be overseen by the sheriff, himself of the locality, but by virtue of his oath, theoretically committed only to the interests of the king;[25] the jurors must, during their deliberations, be kept "in the custody of the officers of the court...lest in the meantime anyone should suborn them" (*De laudibus*, 61). And, Fortescue reassures his audience, if these safeguards do not work, the punishment of attaint is available against the suborned jury.[26] Called upon to bring their local knowledge to bear on the case and yet to remain above the influence of local, partial interests, the jurors occupy an ambiguous space, of the locality yet sworn to apply their understanding of the facts to the fulfillment of the king's law; supposedly impartial yet feared subject to subornation.

Bubbling beneath the surface of Fortescue's discussion, and seeping through in his careful reassurances that jury deliberations are adequately safeguarded against unwelcome influences, is the fear that these safeguards are, in fact, inadequate, a fear often voiced in contemporary complaints of jury corruption or partiality. Fifteenth-century petitions to Chancery alleging jury corruption question both the virtues of the local jury[27] and the deterrent effect of the attaint.[28] Early in the fifteenth century, Parliament itself proves willing to intervene in common law procedure and forgo the advantages of locality in a case where the pull (or push) of local influence could be irresistible.[29] And significantly, as Parliament deemphasizes the virtues of local knowledge in this case, it emphasizes material wealth as a criterion for jury service in response to a petitioner's complaint that "poor men" (*povere hommes*) on the jury "would not dare speak the truth" against the alleged wrongdoer.

We will return shortly to this emphasis on potential jurors' material wealth, an emphasis very much to Fortescue's liking. First, however, we should consider in greater detail this fear of the inadequately safeguarded, corruptible jury, a fear that speaks in part to the fear of jurisgenerative difference. The tendency of medieval juries to deviate from the strict letter of the law may indeed, in any individual case, have been the product of corruption or intimidation, which undoubtedly occurred. This tendency can also be attributed to the phenomenon typically referred to as "jury nullification."[30] As most thoroughly described by Thomas Green, medieval jury nullification, at least in the area of criminal law, operated primarily as a benign force, resulting in a high number of acquittals in cases where conviction meant capital punishment for the defendant.[31] It is this phenomenon that Fortescue seems to acknowledge when, in the *De laudibus*, the chancellor comments that he would "prefer twenty guilty men to escape death through mercy, than one innocent to be condemned unjustly."[32] At the same time, the chancellor's reference to "guilty men" (*facinoros*) escaping death "through mercy" (*pietate*) makes clear the chancellor's commitment to the law, which, despite the jury's tempering of its provisions, still holds guilty those fortunate enough to escape death.

The chancellor's use of *pietas* to describe the jury's tempering of the law's capital sanction associates the jury's behavior with the closely related concepts of *misericordia* (mercy) and *aequitas* (equity). Equity refers to the legal doctrine by which the rigors of the law are relaxed to prevent an unjust application of the law's general provisions based on specific circumstances not considered or foreseen when the law was enacted. As Christopher St. German, writing early in the sixteenth century, states: "Equytye is a [ryghtwysenes] that consideryth all the pertyculer cyrcumstaunces of the dede the whiche also is temperyd with the swetnes of mercye" ("mercye" here being a translation of the Latin *misericordia*).[33] Fortescue himself defines equity as an absolute power of the prince, to be applied at his wisdom, "lest the strictness of the words of the law, confounding its intent, should hurt the common good."[34] In neither case, however, is equity associated with *pietas*.

The connotative history of *pietas* in the Middle Ages is an ambiguous one.[35] *Pietas* and *justitia* are identified by Isidore of Seville as the two principal royal virtues in an early and influential formulation. As this formulation is developed by Alcuin in letters to Charlemagne, *justitia* is associated with paternal authority, and *pietas* with maternal mercy. This gendering of *pietas* is significant, for as its usage develops, so does "the connotation of political weakness."[36] Peter Damian comes to associate "excessive piety" (*inordinata pietas*) with the "disorder of the people" (*confusio plebis*), and when John of Salisbury "turns his attention specifically to the received formula of Isidore, he...updates the comple-mentary terms, retaining *iustitia* but finding alternatives to *pietas: mis-ericordia, moderatio, patientia,* and especially *clementia.*"[37] *Pietas* thus has at least two connotations that seem potentially troubling when asso-ciated with the jury: first, its equitable connotation, suggesting the jury's improper appropriation of a princely power, and second, its connotation of weakness and, if relied upon excessively, social disorder.

The *De laudibus*'s acknowledgment of the jury's willingness to judge a case through the prism of *pietas* instead of the law seems intended to cast a positive light on the underlying concern that the institution of the jury might indeed be out of control, unrestrained by the interpretive tethers of a law supposed to shape its statement of the facts. But given the ambiguous connotations of *pietas,* this acknowledgment does little to address the concern that the law is being subverted by such interpre-tive variances. Fortescue himself seems unconvinced: concerns over the reliability of the lay jury and, more generally, the threatened subversion of the law by the jury's hold on the facts appear elsewhere in Fortescue's writings. If the *De laudibus* admirably identifies the limits of legal coer-cion's trustworthiness, Fortescue's endorsement of economic limita-tions on England's common law alternative to the tortured truth give ample range to the shadow of coercion. And in his strong assertion of law's "natural" hermeneutical priority over fact, he leaves little doubt as to his conception of the jury's proper role.

Freed from the Soil: Rusticity and the Sufficient Juror

Lingering concerns over the reliability of the English jury's determina-tion of truth as described in the *De laudibus* are voiced by Prince Ed-ward when he asks the chancellor the obvious, albeit bothersome, ques-tion: "But still I wonder very much why this law of England, so worthy and so excellent, is not common to all the world" (*De laudibus,* 67). In response, the chancellor further refines the definition of the jury and the jury's role, building on work begun in Fortescue's *De natura legis natu-rae* and continued in his *Governance of England.* What emerges from these texts is a definition of the jury strictly limited by considerations of sex and economic class. Within these limitations, the standard for jury service is remarkably undifferentiated (and materialist in every sense of the word). But the promise of the jury as an alternative to the tortured truth is compromised for those outside of these limitations. And for those persons outside of England, subject to the institutional system of torture so strongly critiqued earlier in the *De laudibus,* the chancellor's response to the prince does little to dispel the shadow of coercion.

The chancellor responds to the prince's question by resting his defense of the English jury's superior ability to determine the truth upon the material blessings of England: "England is...so fertile that, compared area to area, it surpasses almost all other lands in the abundance of its produce; it is productive of its own accord, scarcely aided by man's labour." Consequently,

> the men of [England] are not very much burdened with the sweat of labour, so that they live with more spirit, as the ancient fathers did, who preferred to tend flocks rather than to distract their peace of mind with the cares of agriculture. For this reason the men of that land are made more apt and disposed to investigate causes which require searching examination than men who, immersed in agricultural work, have contracted a rusticity of mind from familiarity with the soil. (*De laudibus*, 67–69)

Material prosperity is not to be praised only for its salutary liberating effect on the disposition *ad discernendum*, however, for material wealth also imposes important constraints on the individual juror. Having something to lose, the juror will not venture to lose it: "It is unthinkable that such men could be suborned or be willing to perjure themselves, not only because of their fear of God, but also because of their honour, and the scandal which would ensue, and because of the harm they would do their heirs through their infamy" (*De laudibus*, 69). Threat of harm done to heirs—the stripping of material possessions from the juror convicted in an action of attaint—will keep jurors honest.

The balance of freedom and constraint to which materially qualified jurors (or "sufficeantz gentz")[38] are subject is reversed for persons below the minimum income qualifications. Blinded by "rustic ignorance" (*ruditas rusticitatis*), such persons "cannot clearly perceive the truth" from beneath the weight of the soil in which they are mired. At the same time, unencumbered by material wealth, these poor men (*pauperes*) "have neither shame of being infamous nor fear of the loss of their goods, since they have none."[39] Because of an inadequate concentration of personal wealth in most realms, use of the jury is simply not feasible. Jurors would either be drawn from so large an area that they would have little familiarity with the parties and witnesses or they would be drawn from a local pool of blinded, untrustworthy *pauperes*. Given these arguments, the prince concludes that "the civil law ... is delivered from all blame" (*De laudibus*, 71), a delivery that presumably includes civilian use of torture. And the chancellor's earlier censure of torture looks increasingly like a hyperbolic magnification of civilian procedure's evils that the virtues of the English jury can be contrasted against.

As we have already seen, Fortescue is not alone in linking material wealth to the jury's trustworthiness and discernment. In the preceding section, a petition to Parliament was discussed that, in response to its complaints of intimidation of the local "povere hommes" deliberately placed on the jury, secured a proclamation ordering that requirements of

juror locality be disregarded and that minimum juror income requirements be enhanced. Another fifteenth-century petition reiterates the chancellor's argument: "It is to suppose by reson, that the more sufficient
that men be of liflode, of Londes and Tenementes, ye more unlikly they are
by corruption, brocage, or drede, to be treted or moeved to perjurie."[40]

Similarly, the *De laudibus* is not alone among Fortescue's writings in
linking material prosperity to the maintenance of order, legal and otherwise, within the realm. In the *Governance of England*, Fortescue argues
against taxing the commons into poverty to support the king, noting that
"whan any rysinge hath be made in this londe be ffor theis dayis by commons, the pouerest men þeroff haue be þe grettest causers and doers ther
in." "Thryfty men," in contrast, "haue ben loth therto, ffor drede off
lesynge off thair gode."[41] Anyone doubting these conclusions need only
look to the realm of Bohemia, "wher the commons ffor pouerte rose apon
the nobles, and made all thair godis to be comune" (*Governance*, 139).
To be freed from the soil, from a state of rustic poverty, is thus to be
constrained by wealth. And the disposition *ad discernendum* seems to
be as much a function of fear of loss as a product of unsullied vision.

The *Governance*'s arguments augment our understanding of Fortescue's emphasis on wealth in another way. Poverty, in the *Governance*,
does not so much produce burdened rationality as differing interpretations of justice, interpretations that, as the case of Bohemia demonstrates,
put material "godis" at risk. "Nothyng," Fortescue argues, "mey make
[the king's] people to arise, but lakke off gode, or lakke off justice. But
yet sertanly when thay lakke gode thai woll aryse, sayng that thai lakke
justice" (*Governance*, 140). One's interpretation of justice, in other words,
depends on one's material wealth. Accordingly, the perceived justice of
laws implemented to regulate and protect the ownership of material goods
will be determined by one's participation in such ownership.[42]

To make the disposition *ad discernendum* a function of material wealth
is, of course, to make it an extremely plastic faculty, susceptible both to
expansion and to contraction, as well as to easy redefinition (just adjust
the qualifying amount). Material wealth also defines juror sufficiency
by a remarkably undifferentiated standard. This lack of differentiation
is not without problems. Fortescue himself asserts the importance of the
source of wealth in other contexts: lawyers, he maintains, are almost
exclusively the product of noble wealth, as the costs of legal education
generally exclude the sons of "poor and common people," who cannot
afford the expense, and of merchants, who "rarely desire to reduce their
stock by such annual burdens" (*De laudibus*, 119). And at least one fifteenth-century petition to Parliament questions the sufficiency of material wealth as an indicator of juror trustworthiness when the source of
that wealth is participation in illicit practices.[43] This petition, however,
does little to question the basic assumption that material wealth is the
best guarantor of a sufficient—or sufficiently constrained—juror.

It is this notion of wealth as a constraint—a constraint that the *Governance* defines as a constraint against variant interpretations of justice—that particularly expresses the jurispathic impulse underlying Fortescue's endorsement of the materially sufficient juror. Such a juror reflects the interests that the laws are designed to protect, and he consequently can be entrusted to protect the laws. The interests of the law and the interests of the sufficient juror, in other words, reflect each other with little distortion. But those outside of this material world, those who "lakke gode" and see a "lakke off justice" in the laws protecting the goods of others, see neither themselves nor their sense of justice reflected in the interests of the law. The laws and the jurors deemed sufficient to answer to their questions maintain a world from which "povere hommes" are excluded. Sensing the threat of the violent assertion of an alternative hermeneutic, Fortescue hopes to keep those who might assert such a hermeneutic in the shadows.

Changing the Sex of Justice

The exclusionary intent underlying Fortescue's discussion of the materially sufficient juror also informs his *De natura legis naturae*, a polemic set within a theory of natural law that, among other things, attempts to justify the exclusion of women from legal service. Exploiting the distinction between sex and gender, Fortescue in the *De natura* reads the female body as an inferior vessel incapable of containing the higher faculties of reason necessary for the discernment of legal, as opposed to factual, truth. At the same time, by gendering the discernment of factual truth as a feminine characteristic, Fortescue subordinates fact to the ordering masculine virtue of legal interpretation and, by implication, subordinates the role of the fact-finding jury to that of the legal professional.

As an attack on the Yorkist claim to the throne, the second part of the *De natura* is among the polemical texts written by Fortescue during his stay in exile with the court of Henry VI.[44] The first part is an abstract discussion of the natural law's characteristics; the second part applies natural law to a fictional dispute over title to the deceased king of Assyria's throne. The three disputants are the dead king's brother, daughter, and grandson (the daughter's son). Presided over by *Justitia*, at least initially, the dispute ends in the ruling that because a kingdom cannot descend to or through a woman, the deceased king's brother should ascend to the throne. Many of the arguments concern the two primary duties of the king—to fight and to judge—and it is in connection with the latter duty of judging that the inferior rational capacity of women is posited.

The king's daughter becomes the lightning rod in the *De natura*'s fictional dispute for arguments designed to prove, in preparation for the judgment in favor of the king's brother, woman's essential inferiority to man. As part of her son's and her uncle's individual efforts to discredit

103

her claims, the daughter is represented as emblematic of the deficiencies that, among other things, prove women unfit for judicial office. For example, the daughter's complaint that she alone among women, in the absence of male heirs, would be excluded from inheriting from her father is critiqued by her son as indicative of what becomes defined as a feminine inability to comprehend matters of law:

> My most dread mistress and mother stated throughout her speech the truth concerning the matter of fact which is the exciting cause of this disagreement. Would that she knew the ruling of the law as well as she knows the truth of the facts!...It is ignorance of the law and not of fact which urges her on to this suit, for, without an adviser, the pious simplicity of a woman cannot distinguish the difference that exists between the rights of succession to a kingdom and the rights of succession to a private estate.[45]

The son's criticism of his mother's "ignorance of law" (*ignorantia juris*) is echoed by the king's brother, who asserts that "although the mother hath of her own accord related the truth as to the matter of fact (*facti...veritatem*) about which we are contending, the truth touching the right (*veritatem juris*) which we are in search of she has hidden under thick clouds of error" (*De natura*, 121, 256). This opinion is bolstered by the *auctoritas* of Aristotle, who states "that the woman is a mulcted male (*mas occasionatus*), that hence, as she is deficient in her physical framework, so she is in her reason" (*De natura*, 121, 257). Consequently, women are unfit for the two primary kingly duties: to fight and to judge. Nature has endowed man with superior physical strength "for the performance of the greatest actions of the body...; and for the greatest achievements of the spirit nature has given to man a perfect reason, in respect of which she has made the woman the weaker vessel" (*De natura*, 122, 258).

These essentialist readings of the female body nonetheless belie Fortescue's own struggles to suppress contradictions of these opinions within his text. The daughter, for example, continuing her insistence upon raising inconvenient points of fact, argues that women rule men as duchesses and marquesses; her son, in a telling display of masculine legal rationality, counters that this is only because such women are subject to a supreme male ruler, "and thus obeying men they are able to govern men, because then their government is not deemed to be that of women, but rather that of men" (*De natura*, 139, 278). But even more troubling than the confusing gender performance of a female duchess ruling by the "government of men" is the feminine gender of *Justitia*, who presides over the dispute as judge throughout most, but not all, of the text.

It is not, the *De natura*'s author assures us, "any obstacle to [*Justitia*'s] power that women are by law excluded from the judicial office; for although the word justice (*justitia*) be of the feminine gender, she herself is not a woman, nor of the female sex; for sex hath no place in virtues any more than in spirits" (De natura, 115, 249). Yet the unsexed Justitia's gender continues to trouble the De natura, especially when she (it?) is called upon to pronounce the final judgment. Up to this point in the text, Justitia is described by terms such as "judicum doctissima," "judicum optima," and "judicum prudentissima": the superlative's declension is determined by the feminine gender of Justitia, the implied nominative, while the masculine judex that signifies Justitia's role is relegated to the genitive. When the moment of judgment arrives, however, the feminine superlatives disappear, judex asserts itself in the nominative position, and the troubling feminine gender of Justitia, along with Justitia herself, is relegated right off the page.[46]

What happens to Justitia on the manuscript page recalls the son's argument regarding a woman's governance, with a slight variation. A duchess's governance of men, the female performance of a masculine duty, can be stabilized through the subordination of the duchess to the masculine power, and male body, of a supreme ruler. No such stabilizing body is available, however, in the text of De natura: Justitia is a virtue without physical sex, but that leaves her defined solely by her feminine gender. When she is to perform the masculine duty of legal judgment, this lack of a stabilizing body proves too much for Fortescue's reassuring distinctions between sexus and genus to bear. Masculine judex must ultimately be summoned from the genitive to stabilize the judicial performance that threatens to destabilize one of the De natura's central arguments against women. Needless to say, Justitia's ouster from the page does not contradict the position (or lack thereof) of women — "by law excluded from the judicial office" — on the jury or elsewhere in the administration of justice.

Female bodies actually serve a stabilizing function in the De natura, by representing the roles that Fortescue wants to establish as feminine, and subordinate. Specifically, female bodies gender the role of discerning the truth of facts as feminine, while male bodies gender the "higher" faculties of reason as masculine. Drawing on the combined auctoritas of Saint Augustine, Saint Gregory, Saint Paul, and the "Master of the Sentences" (Peter Lombard), the judex in his final judgment asserts:

The Master himself, ... when treating of this subject, seems to compare the higher part of the reason to man, and the lower part to woman. So that the higher part, cleaving to God, and stretching itself out toward that which is eternal, in the contemplation of unchangeable truth, is held to be made after God's image; but it was not good for it to be alone, and therefore there was made as a help for it something like unto itself, the lower part, namely, of the reason, that takes thought of things temporal, which cannot, any more than woman, be called the image of God; but as the woman is the

glory of the man, it too deserves to be called the glory of the superior part of the mind, seeing it is subject and obedient to it. (*De
natura*, 178, 326)

Woman is subordinate to man, things temporal are subordinate to things
eternal, the truth of fact is subordinate to the truth of law. Or, to paraphrase the daughter's son's earlier argument, the pious simplicity (*simplicitas pia*) that can discern truth of fact, but is ignorant of law, cannot
be trusted to reach the truth without guidance, even though it can serve
the higher process of legal judgment. To violate this order, an order ordained by God, "would...be sin [*peccatum*], which is defined to be a
desertion of order" (*De natura*, 175, 323).

There are, of course, clear echoes of the *De natura*'s reference to a
feminine, factually circumscribed *simplicitas pia* in the *De laudibus*'s
reference to jury *pietas*. Indeed, as the *De natura*'s *judex* states, a man
"who holds an office is set over...a free man, directing him to his (the
free man's) interest, or to the common good" (*De natura*, 176, 323), as
man was set over woman, and other men, before the fall into sin. In the
abstract world of the *De natura* at least, an official man of law can direct
the behavior of those below and, with some effort, can keep the varying
details of fact contained in, and subordinate to, the all-embracing "natural" order of the law of God and man.

Pecock and the "Lay Parti"

The nightmare of jurisgenerative difference turned violent also troubles
the writings of Bishop Reginald Pecock. If the "lay parti" relied on its
own wits and studied the text of the Bible exclusively, without reference
to other disciplines in which the Bible's text is "groundid,"

> so many dyuerse opinions schulden rise in lay mennys wittis bi occa-
> sioun of textis in Holy Scripture...that al the world schulde be
> cumbrid therwith, and men schulden accorde to gidere in keping
> her seruice to God, as doggis doon in a market, whanne eche of
> hem terith otheris coot.[47]

And as in Fortescue's *Governance,* this nightmare seems convincingly
realized in the example of Bohemia:

> Certis in this wise...bifille the rewful and wepeable destruccioun
> of the worthi citee and vniuersite of Prage, and of the hool rewme
> of Beeme, as y haue had ther of enformacioun ynouȝ. And now, aftir
> the destruccioun of the rewme, the peple ben glad for to resorte
> and turne aȝen into the catholik and general feith and loore of the
> chirche. (*Repressor*, 86)

Elsewhere in Pecock's writings, however, this jurisgenerative night-mare is countered with an equally disturbing vision of the jurispathic repression of disputation. Paralleling Fortescue's later reliance on civil-ian procedure to critique the violent coercion of truth, Pecock turns to "the lawe of Macomet and of Sarazenis":

> The law of Macomet biddith, vndir greet peyne of horrible deeth suffring, that no man aftir he hath receyued the feith of thilk lawe dispute or argue with eny other man upon eny point, article, or con-clusion of thilk lawe: and bi this wrecchid and cursid maundement the peple of thilk secte ben so miche lockid up vndir boond, that manie mo of hem my3ten be conuertid into trewe feith than 3it ben, if thilk so vnresonable maundement of the same lawe ne were. (*Repressor*, 99–100)

In the *Repressor of Over Much Blaming of the Clergy*, Pecock some-what incongruously applies this law to laypersons who refuse to hear arguments against their interpretation of Scripture.[48] More fittingly, in the *Book of Faith* this law is used implicitly to chastise those who actu-ally have at their disposal "fier and swerd or hangement" and might pre-fer these means over "cleer witt" to bring a straying laity "into consente of trewe feith."[49]

These passages express a central tension in Pecock's work. Pecock rec-ognizes and accepts lay access to the texts of Scripture translated into the vernacular as an irreversible development. Yet he is acutely aware of the interpretive indeterminacy of texts, and specifically of the Bible's susceptibility to multiple, variant interpretations. Moreover, he recog-nizes the threat of this interpretive multiplicity to the institutional au-thority of the church, an authority dependent on the ability to assert the primacy of church interpretations of the Bible; an authority, that is, sup-ported by embedded interpretations of a distinctly "political" text. To open such institutionally embedded interpretations of the Bible to dispute threatens, at the very least, the reconfiguration of church authority and the social relations it governs. But to prohibit disputation of such inter-pretations is equally, if not more, threatening to church authority. Co-erced adherence to interpretations closed to dispute becomes "a ful sus-pecte thing to alle hem that schulde be convertid therto," and throws into question claims that such interpretations constitute a "trewe feith" (*BF*, 132).

In response to this dilemma, Pecock proposes a two-pronged accom-modation of lay scriptural interpretation. First, rather than limiting lay access to texts written or translated into the vernacular, Pecock insists that more materials should be made available in the vernacular, under clerical supervision, in order properly to ground lay interpretations of the Bible. Second, Pecock calls for the open expression of lay scriptural interpretations so that such interpretations can be monitored and, if necessary, corrected by the clergy.

Underlying Pecock's acceptance of lay interpretation is his concept of the "doom of resoun": the idea that the capacity for rational judgment is common to all persons, if not equally developed in all. This qualification is important to Pecock's theory, for the posited need to develop the "doom of resoun" enables Pecock to justify the role of a learned clergy and to preserve in them the authority to judge the validity of lay interpretations. It also proves to be an insufficient qualification. Notwithstanding Pecock's assertion that the laity must ultimately submit to the authority of the church in matters of scriptural interpretation, the recognition he gives to the potential of lay interpretation and the emphasis he places on the "doom of resoun" provoke a distinctly unaccommodating response from his clerical peers.

The "Doom of Resoun"

A crucial, if not the crucial, element of Pecock's writings is his emphasis on the "doom of resoun" as a fundamental aspect of scriptural interpretation.[50] The doom of reason — the capacity to understand and to make rational judgments — is closely associated with, and often used synonymously for, the concepts of the "lawe of kind" and "moral philsophie." The association is particularly close between the doom of reason and the law of kind; moral philosophy tends to represent the discipline that retrieves and compiles the truths offered up by the "doom of natural resoun, which is moral lawe of kinde and moral lawe of God, writun in the book of lawe of kinde in mennis soulis, prentid into the ymage of God."[51]

The doom of reason, as defined by Pecock, serves to justify both lay access to Scripture and clerical oversight of lay interpretive activity. As inherently human resources, "writun . . . in mennis soulis," the truths of the doom of reason and law of kind are available to all persons, especially when those truths have been established by the irrefutable, or highly probable, logic of the syllogism.[52] It should not, therefore, "be vnleeful laymen forto reede in the Bible and forto studie and leerne ther yn" under proper supervision; what Pecock seeks to remedy is

> the presumpcioun of tho lay persoones, whiche weenen bi her in-reding in the Bible forto come into more kunnyng than thei or alle the men in erthe — clerkis and othere — mowe come to, bi the Bible oonli withoute moral philsophie and lawe of kinde in doom of *weel disposid resoun*. (*Repressor*, 37; my emphasis)

Pecock's accusation of the presumption of "tho lay persoones" who study the Bible without a "weel disposid resoun" identifies another important aspect of the doom of reason and its related concepts. Although written within the potential understanding of every human, the truths of the doom of reason do not easily make themselves known, nor is reason a stable faculty, impervious to other influences. Moreover, the doom of reason's truths cannot be discovered in the text of Scripture alone: Scripture, with the exception of certain articles of God's "positijf lawe of feith," is not the grounding of God's laws generally, which "in huge quantite . . . ben fyndeable and knoweable bi mannis resoun withoute help of Holi Scripture" (*Repressor*, 41). But if these laws can be found "withoute help of Holi Scripture," they cannot be found without the help of the knowledge harvested from the law of kind and stored in the disciplines that help to ground the interpretation of Scripture.

By situating the Bible's text within a much larger disciplinary field of knowledge, a field ultimately grounded by the "inner text" of the law of kind, Pecock is thus able to assert the inadequacy of lay interpretations based on the text of Scripture alone, and to elevate the position of learned disciplines and clerics deemed necessary for an adequate understanding of Scripture. These arguments are vividly brought together in the *Repressor*'s extended metaphor of Midsummer Eve in London. If Christ and his apostles were now living in London and brought into the city boughs from the forest and flowers from the field to decorate Londoners' homes, "ȝit tho men of Londoun receyuing so tho braunchis and flouris ouȝten not seie and feele that tho braunchis and flouris grewen out of Cristis hondis, and out of the Apostlis hondis" (*Repressor*, 28). So it is with the text of Scripture: rather than the "fundament" of most of the truths expressed in its text, Scripture is a collection of truths harvested from the "trouthis of lawe of kinde" growing in the "the feeld of mannys soule":

> And out of this forest of treuthis mowe be take treuthis and conclusiouns, and be sett into open knowing of the fynder and of othere men, thouȝ not withoute labour and studie thoruȝ manie ȝeeris. And herto seruen clerkis of moral philsophie whiche now ben clepid Dyuynes riȝt as forresters and othere men seruen for to hewe doun braunchis for hem silf, and for to delyuere hem to citeseins in Londoun that her housis be maad the more honest ther with and therbi. (*Repressor*, 29–30)

Scripture, in other words, represents only part of the truths grounded in the law of kind in the human soul, and other truths harvested from the law of kind's forest inform the proper interpretation of Scripture. The forest, however, is a bit overgrown, and the harvesting of its truths is most ably accomplished by the experienced prunings of those learned in "moral philsophie." Hence,

> ful weel ouȝten alle persoones of the lay parti not miche leerned in moral phisophi and lawe of kinde forto make miche of clerkis weel

leerned in moral philsophi, that tho clerkis schulden helpe tho lay persoones forto ariʒt vndirstonde Holi Scripture in alle tho placis in which Holi Scripture rehercith the...conclusiouns and treuthis of moral philsophi, that is to seie of lawe of kinde. (*Repressor*, 46)

The net effect of these arguments is to subordinate much of the text of Scripture to the doom of reason. And indeed, Pecock makes precisely this point, arguing that wherever in Holy Scripture "be writen eny point or eny gouernaunce of the seide lawe of kinde it is more verrili writen in the book of mannis soule than in the outward book of parchemyn or of velym." Moreover, if there is "eny semyng discorde...bitwixe the wordis writen in the outward book of Holi Scripture and the doom of re-soun,...the wordis so writen withoutforth ouʒten be expowned and be interpretid and brouʒt forto accorde with the doom of resoun" (*Repressor*, 25).

The primacy of reason in Pecock's writings proves to be, as we shall see, one of his most vulnerable points. But at first glance, this elevation of reason hardly seems to constitute a radical endorsement of lay inter-pretation. The many qualifications deemed necessary to make the rea-son "weel disposid" serve to highlight the inadequacy of any lay in-terpretive activity that draws its authority from the text of Scripture without recourse to learned disciplines. Pecock also casts scriptural in-terpretation tied to the letter of the Bible in the familiar terms of a stunted feminine rationality[53] and of infantile irrationality. The text of Scripture, "miche delectable and sweete," has deluded the laity, who be-lieve too readily that something so sweet must contain everything nec-essary for spiritual nourishment. And thus,

thei puttiden al her motyue in her affeccioun or wil forto so trowe; and not in her intelleccioun or resoun; and in lijk maner doon wommen, for thei reulen hem silf as it were in alle her gouernaun-cis aftir her affeccioun and not aftir resoun, or more aftir affeccioun than after doom of resoun; bi cause that affeccioun in hem is ful strong and resoun in hem is litle, as for the more parti of wommen. (*Repressor*, 67)

In like manner, the laity's addiction to the sweetness of Scripture ren-ders them like children, who "louen sweete meetis and drinkis ful miche," and "whanne thei comen to feestis...feeden hem with sweete stonding potagis and with sweete bake metis, and leuen othere substancial and necessarie metis" (*Repressor*, 67). In contrast to such feminine, infantile lay understandings of Scripture are the well-reasoned interpretations of learned clerics, nourished by a less toothsome but more edifying diet of moral philosophy.

Yet even though there is little threatening to the authority of clerical interpretation of Scripture in these passages, there is also the suggestion of a characteristic of Pecock's writings that makes them susceptible to criticism by the "hasty unconsiderers" of his texts addressed in the *Book of Faith.*[54] This characteristic is Pecock's tendency to qualify statements that tend toward generalizations. It can be seen operating in Pecock's misogynist representations of feminine rationality: women rule themselves "in all her gouernauncis aftir her affeccioun and not aftir resoun, *or more aftir affeccioun than after doom of resoun"*; "affeccioun in hem is ful strong and resoun in hem is litle, *as for the more parti of wommen."* The antifeminist clerical hermeneutic is affirmed by Pecock; at the same time, he cannot resist acknowledging possible degrees of difference and exceptions to the rule.

Sharp lines between unschooled lay rationality and learned clerical reason blur further when Pecock considers members of his lay audience whose secular skills and training invite comparison with the "sotilte and heiȝte of witt" of the clergy. "Weel y wote," writes Pecock,

> þat so myche sotilte and heiȝte of witt muste ech weel leerned man in þe kyngis lawe of ynglond, and ech wijs greet mercer, in hise rekenyngis and bargeyns making, haue, howe grete, hiȝe and sutel witt he muste bisette vpon the hiȝest maters whiche y write, after þat þe signifiyng of þe wordis ben to hem knowun.[55]

Pecock's identification of legal and mercantile learning as an indicator of lay perspicacity has a certain resonance with Fortescue's defense of material wealth as the determiner of juror sufficiency, but the implied equation of this learning with clerical learning was not without controversy among Pecock's fellow clerics.[56] And, unlike Fortescue, Pecock does not use legal and mercantile "heiȝte of witt" as a means of limiting lay rationality. Experience with legal and mercantile affairs only indicates, but does not determine, the ability to comprehend complex matters, for "certis þe sooþ to seie, it is hard to mesure of al hem in þe layfe whiche schulen reede my writingis, þe capacite." Addressing "the comoun" in "comoun peplis langage" is not blameworthy, even if the subject matter is complex, "but it schal be þouȝt þus: who may take, take he."[57]

The blurring of lines between learned and lay "capacite" intensifies when Pecock attempts further to articulate proper clerical and lay roles in scriptural interpretation, a subject taken up in the following section. But there is a final element of the doom of reason that complicates Pecock's efforts to convince the laity to acquiesce to the ultimate authority of clerical interpretation and makes his texts vulnerable to hostile criticism. This is his insistence that, because human reason is fallible, even clerical interpretations of Scripture may be in error, and consequently, it is futile for the clergy to insist on the certainty of their positions.

Acknowledging (albeit with disapproval) that some laypersons say "hem knowe wel that the clergie may faile and erre as weel as thei, teching the feith," Pecock asserts that those clerics who labor to justify "that the clergie, namelich gaderid togidere in a general counseil, may not erre and faile aȝens eny article of feith, neither may determyne amys aȝens trewe feith, tho clerkis...laboren in veyn" (*BF*, 110–11). This fallibility is not limited to Pecock's contemporaries: "holi men, and ful kunnyng men, at sumtyme fillen upon the treuthe and founden it, and at sumtyme thei faileden from it, whanne thei weneden that thei hadden founde it" (*BF*, 146). The further one moves from those truths revealed "bi the auctorite of a teller or of a denouncer...whiche is so trewe that he may not lie,"[58] the more a claimed truth must be supported by "evydencis" sufficient to constrain the reason to believe the truth.

The fallibility of human reason would not, of course, be a revelation to Pecock's fellow clerics, nor does Pecock accept the argument that clerical fallibility puts clerical interpretation on the same level as lay understandings of Scripture. He is insisting only that the possibility of error be conceded in order that the clergy might turn its attention to strengthening the authority of its interpretive positions by producing "evydencis" sufficient to counter divergent lay readings, to convince by the constraining power of "cleer witt" instead of the less subtle power of "fier and swerd or hangement." But he is insisting on the recognition of clerical error in a text written in the vernacular, addressed as much to the "lay parti" as to the clergy. And the pressure of his concessions on his efforts to maintain distinct clerical and lay interpretive roles forces a telling acknowledgment of the comparative values of the reasoned truth and the maintenance of social order.

The Limits of Reason: "Correpcioun" and "Correccioun"

The problems of consent encouraged by the threat of "fier and swerd or hangement" are as apparent to the scholar of English religious dissent as they were to Pecock. Abjurations of heresy that followed upon a conviction provide much information about official church perspectives on the Wycliffite and Lollard movements of the late fourteenth and fifteenth centuries, and might even suggest, in a general fashion, the particular beliefs held by the convicted heretic. Yet the specific formation, and even the existence, of an individually held belief may well be permanently off the record. Abjurations were made under the threat of death, and their texts followed the form of questions put to suspects by prosecuting church officials.[59] They were not voluntary confessions of belief, and the most that can be claimed for them is that "the views confessed or abjured were held *in some form* by the suspect."[60] The distance between the official finding of a heretical belief as confessed in the abjuration and the particular formation of the individual's belief is often underscored in the text of the abjuration, when the convicted heretic appoints a cleric as the "organum vocis sue" (instrument of his or her voice) because he or she is unable to read the text of abjuration.[61]

While Pecock himself expresses little sympathy in his writings for convicted heretics, a text such as an official abjuration of heresy, acknowledged by the convict "vndir greet peyne of horrible deeth suffring," is nonetheless illustrative of the "ful suspecte thing" resulting from a legal ban on disputation of matters of faith. Although Pecock does not disapprove of such abjurations, he clearly views them as an inferior expression of the "consente of trewe feith," subordinate to an understanding of church doctrine forged between cleric and layperson on the basis of "cleer witt." Negotiating the terms of this understanding, however, while maintaining clerical authority proves a difficult, and dangerous, task.

Pecock asserts a primary distinction between clerical and lay roles in the interpretation of church doctrine in the difference between "correccioun" and "correpcioun." As defined in the prologue to the *Repressor,* "correpcioun" is a rebuke "which not oonli longith to an ouerer [superior] anentis his netherer [inferior], but also to a netherer anentis his ouerer," and is made "in neiȝbourli or brotherli maner" (*Repressor,* 1–2). One who wishes to "corrept" another does so "with such doctrine, knowing, or kunnyng, wherbi he canne shewe and proue it to be a defaute for which he undirnymeth and blameth, and the persoone so vndirnome and blamed to be gilti in the same defaut and synne."[62]

"Correccioun," in turn, carries a coercive or punitive valence ("correcting bi threatenyng and punyschinge"), and "longith oonli to the ouerer anentis his netherer, and not to the netherer anentis his ouerer" (*Repressor,* 1). The *Repressor* is intended to correct lay "correpciouns" of the clergy that lack a proper basis in "doctrine, knowing, or kunnyng," but it acknowledges the propriety of other lay "correpciouns": "alle othere gouernauncis of the clergie, for which the clergy is worthi to be blamed in brotherly and neiȝbourly correpcioun, y schal not be aboute to excuse neither defende" (*Repressor,* 4).

The concept of lay "correpcioun"—the "neiȝbourli" identification of defaults and sins deserving of "correccioun" by a superior authority (or "ouerer")—thus identifies a role for the laity that permits the voicing of critical opinions or accusations, but makes that role subordinate to the superior power of "correccioun."[63] The *Repressor,* addressed to a lay audience, deemphasizes the punitive connotations of "correccioun," emphasizing instead the authority of clerical "ouerers" in the definition and "correccioun" of lay doctrinal error. The hierarchical relationship between "correccioun" and "correpcioun" models the pedagogical program of the *Repressor* and the relationship between cleric and layperson in that program. Lay study of texts in disciplines supporting the reasoned interpretation of Scripture must not go unattended: the dangerous multiplicity of interpretation to which the Bible is subject also applies to other texts. Thus the layperson must seek out "substanciali leerned clerkis in logik and in moral philsophie and in dyvynyte" (*Repressor*, 85), who can correct variant interpretations and avert the dogfights and Bohemian breakdowns of uncontrolled jurisgenesis.

Yet in another of Pecock's characteristic qualifications, the hierarchy that authorizes clerical "correccioun" of lay "correpciouns" and stabilizes scriptural interpretation proves difficult to maintain. The layperson seeking learned counsel is advised that "ȝe must be waar her of, that euen as oon sterre is different from an other sterre in cleernes, so oon clerk is different from an other in kunnyng" (*Repressor*, 87–88). Many persons who bear the trappings of clergy, especially those who preach popular sermons, do not actually possess sufficient grounding in the many learned disciplines necessary for the "leding and reuling and the firme stabiling of al the chirche, both in the clergie and in the layfe" (*Repressor*, 91).

Indeed, Pecock suggests a causal link between the unevenness of clerical "kunnyng" and "the wickidli enfectid scole of heresie among the lay peple in Ynglond" (*Repressor*, 89), because many of those ostensibly qualified to correct lay error are themselves in need of "correccioun." The laity is left with the unsatisfactory advice to do the best they can to choose "a wijs and a sufficient clerk into her counseiler," being "excusid anentis God" if "his counseiling be vntrewe, vnto tyme thei mowe aspie the defaut of the same counseil" (*Repressor*, 92). But this advice implies a reversal of the hierarchical relationship between cleric and layperson: the layperson, expected to submit to the counselling of the cleric, might also reject the truth of such counsel if it is in error.

In the *Book of Faith*, the *Repressor*'s hierarchical model of "correccioun" and "correpcioun" is further flattened as Pecock tries to articulate how the laity might dispute opposing interpretations with the clergy. Using lay familiarity with common law litigation as his model, Pecock tries to convince the laity that opening their opinions to the arguments of "adversarie counseil" is necessary:

> If it seme to thee that thou hast sufficient proof aȝens the chirche, truste thou not to thin owne seemyng oonli, neither to thin owne, and to the semyng of hem whiche ben like wise affectid with thee, and holden at first with thee; but uttre thi mociouns to thin adversaries, and lete thin evydencis or mociouns be disputed, and pledid bitwixe men of thi counseil, and men of the adversarie counseil at ful, eer thou trust thee to have sufficient proof aȝens thi adversaries. (*BF*, 231–32)

Casting the clergy as "adversarie counseil" addresses a problem identified earlier in the *Book of Faith*; namely, that "it semeth to the lay persoonys that tho clerkis ben over favorable in mater longing to her favour and worschip, and ben not iugis indifferent, and stonding for the parti which hath the treuthe, whiche ever thilk party be" (*BF*, 112). But it also casts the disputing parties as coequals and opens the new problem of who is to judge the dispute. Having acknowledged that the laity views the clergy as partial judges and having implicitly recognized the church's limited tolerance for the lay expression of heterodox opinion,[64] Pecock can offer nothing more than a duty to submit to the church until its position has been sufficiently proved to be, and acknowledged to be, wrong.

But this duty to submit is precisely what Pecock has offered the laity in an earlier passage that drastically undercuts his assurances of clerical willingness to be party to, and impartial judges of, disputes with the laity. The *Book of Faith* is the last of Pecock's surviving texts, and it also seems the most conscious of growing clerical hostility toward Pecock's arguments. The anxious appeals to "hasty unconsiderers" of its dialogue between father and son have already been mentioned; it is significant that this dialogic structure is abandoned when the father stops addressing his son and, in the passage in question, speaks to a disobedient layman "whiche holdist the now late brenned men in Ynglond to be martiris."[65] Unlike the son, the layman is given no opportunity to respond.

The layman's sympathies for the "late brenned men" are misplaced: all those burned "in unobedience aȝens her prelatis" died "in dampnable synne, as bi the comoun lawe of God, notwithstonding al her holi lyvyng in other sides, and notwithstonding al her devocioun had to her opiniouns . . . ; ȝhe, more forto seie, *thouȝ it hadde be so that her seid opiniouns hadden be trewe*" (*BF*, 192; my emphasis). And what is the "comoun lawe of God" that has been violated by such obstinate, even if truthful, holdings of opinion? It is the law of hierarchy, heavenly and earthly, the "many foold ordre of overte and netherte, and obedience of the netherers to the overers" (*BF*, 193). It is the law violated by Lucifer and by Adam, and if they "were in dampnable synne for her pride, and presumpsioun, and unobedience," so too are these "aȝenstonders to prelatis . . . and ellis the seid comoun lawe of God were not trewe" (*BF*, 194).

To return to a restatement of the question posed by Robert Cover—to what extent is coercion necessary to the maintenance of a social order?—it would seem that the answer depends on one's investment in the order to be maintained. Pecock's own declaration of his investment in the hierarchical order of God's common law proved to be too little, too late. Shortly after the *Book of Faith* was completed, Pecock's opinions were declared heretical, and he was given the "choice" of abjuring his opinions and watching his books be burned or being burned himself. Choosing the former option, he was eventually locked away in a room at Thorney Abbey, Cambridgeshire, deprived of writing materials, and given only a Bible and a few devotional texts to read.[66]

Thomas Gascoigne's hostile account of Pecock's life contains a few lines supposedly spoken by Pecock following his abjuration. Emblematic of the jurispathic repression of Pecock's attempts to accommodate a lay genesis of scriptural meaning, they read:

> Wyt hath wundur that reson kan not tel;
> How a moder is mayd and God is man,
> Leve reson, beleve ye wonder;
> Beleve hath mastry and reson is under.[67]

And, of course, these lines represent a quite literal "doom" of reason. Like Pecock, whose attempts to speak rationally to disaffected members of the "lay parti" lead to the condemnation and suppression of his writings and his person, so too is reason judged and found wanting, subordinated to belief's "mastry" and condemned (or so its condemners hope) to silence.

Notes

My research and writing of the essay were supported by a United Kingdom Fulbright student research fellowship, a William B. Schallek Memorial Graduate Fellowship, and the University of Minnesota's Norman Johnston DeWitt Fellowship.

1. For an extensive discussion of Fortescue's and Pecock's common interest in questions of legal theory, see Norman Doe, *Fundamental Authority in Late Medieval English Law* (Cambridge: Cambridge University Press, 1990).

2. Bishop Reginald Pecock, *The Book of Faith*, ed. J. L. Morison (Glasgow: James Maclehose, 1909), 139 [hereafter cited as *BF*, with page number in the text]. The availability of "fier and swerd or hangement" as an inducement to consent to church doctrine was a reality in England throughout the fifteenth century and beyond, pursuant to the terms of the statute *De heretico comburendo* (1401). The statute permitted the surrender to the secular arm of convicted heretics who refused to abjure, or who had relapsed into heresy, for capital punishment by burning. It was enacted in response to the Wycliffite, or Lollard, movement, which "devoted much attention to attacking [the boundary of belief between Latin and English]" by translating the Bible into the English vernacular, and thus making the text of Scripture available to the laity; Margaret Aston, "Lollardy and Literacy," in *Lollards and Reformers: Images and Literacy in Late Medieval Religion* (London: Hambledon Press, 1984), 197.

3. As a starting point, the term *laity* can be defined as describing those persons who are not specially educated for, and do not hold, positions in the institutions of the church and the common law. The term has similar, but distinct, meanings in reference to the writings of Pecock and Fortescue. Pecock uses the term "lay parti" simply to describe persons who are not clerics, although occasionally the term is narrowed to refer to the "Bible men" or Lollards against whom his arguments are at times specifically directed. The term *laity*, with respect to Fortescue's writings, serves a similar descriptive function, although Fortescue himself does not use the term in the texts to be discussed. The concept of a laity defined in opposition to members of the English legal profession was nonetheless established by the later Middle Ages. By the fourteenth century, English lawyers are, for example, occasionally referring to the "lay gentz" of the jury. An example of such usage is the Year Book entry for Hil. 2 Richard II, pl. 3, in which Justice Skipwith argues that it is not proper for the court to "encoumbre" (burden) the "laiez gentz" of the jury with a question of bastardy unless the pleading lawyer specially pleads facts that would isolate bastardy as a specific legal issue to which the jury could respond with a limited verdict; see *The Year Books of Richard II: 2 Richard II, 1378–1379*, ed. and trans. Morris S. Arnold

(Cambridge, Mass.: Ames Foundation, 1975), 96–97. See also the *Manual of Law French*, 2nd ed., s.v. "lay."

4. "Doom" was a standard Middle English term for judgment and the act of judging. See the *Middle English Dictionary*, s.v. "dom."

5. Pecock's writings were declared heretical, and he abjured his opinions, late in the year 1457. The two Pecock texts that will be the focus of this discussion, the *Repressor of Over Much Blaming of the Clergy* and the *Book of Faith*, are the last written of Pecock's surviving works, completed in 1455 and 1456, respectively. See the biographical outline of Pecock's life in Charles Brockwell, *Bishop Reginald Pecock and the Lancastrian Church: Securing the Foundations of Cultural Authority*, Texts and Studies in Religion (Lewiston, N.Y.: Edwin Mellen Press, 1985), 25:239–42. Fortescue's literary efforts date from the period of his exile with the court of Henry VI. The *De laudibus legum Anglie* was probably written c. 1468–71, and the *De natura legis naturae*, c. 1461–63. The *Governance of England* was written after Fortescue's return to England and reconciliation with Edward IV, in 1471 or later. See the chronology of Fortescue's life in Sir John Fortescue, *De laudibus legum Anglie*, ed. and trans. S. B. Chrimes (Cambridge: Cambridge University Press, 1942), lix–lxvii; citations to the *De laudibus* will be from this edition and, unless otherwise noted, Chrimes's translation.

6. The sentence from which this quotation is taken reads in full: "Ex quibus homines regionis istius apti maius redduntur et dispositi ad discernendum in causis que magni sunt examinis, quam sunt viri qui telluris operibus inherentes ex ruris familiaritate mentis contrahunt ruditatem" (For this reason the men of that land are made more apt and disposed to investigate causes which require searching examination than men who, immersed in agricultural work, have contracted a rusticity of mind from familiarity with the soil); Fortescue, *De laudibus*, 68–69. I have translated *discernendum* as "understanding" to emphasize the cognitive and judgmental connotations of *discernere*, not fully suggested by Chrimes's translation of the verb as "to investigate." See the *Revised Medieval Latin Word-List from British and Irish Sources*, s.v. "discret/io."

7. Robert Cover, "Violence and the Word," in *Narrative, Violence, and the Law: The Essays of Robert Cover*, ed. Martha Minow, Michael Ryan, and Austin Sarat (Ann Arbor: University of Michigan Press, 1992), 210; emphasis in original. In a footnote to the quoted material, Cover acknowledges that "every interpretive practice takes place in some context" and specifically acknowledges the work of Stanley Fish and Fredric Jameson in foregrounding, respectively, "the dominance of institutional contexts *even in understanding literary texts*" (my emphasis), and (quoting Jameson), "the priority of the political interpretation of literary texts"; see Jameson, *The Political Unconscious: Narrative as Socially Symbolic Act* (Ithaca, N.Y.: Cornell University Press, 1981), 17. "But," Cover argues, "while asserting the special place of a political understanding of our social reality, such views do not in any way claim for literary interpretations what I am claiming about legal interpretation — that it is part of the *practice* of political violence" (emphasis in original). Cover's insistent separation of legal and literary interpretation reflects the same tendency to essentialize the historically constructed disciplines of legal and literary hermeneutics that Stanley Fish has criticized in his essay, "Don't Know Much about the Middle Ages: Posner on Law and Literature," in *Doing What Comes Naturally: Change, Rhetoric, and the Practice of Theory in Literary and Legal Studies* (Durham, N.C.: Duke University Press, 1989), 294–311. However, Cover's model of legal interpretation is more expansive than the model of legal interpretation proposed by Judge Richard Posner and criticized by Fish.

8. Cover, "Nomos and Narrative," in *Narrative, Violence, and the Law*, ed. Minow, Ryan, and Sarat, 103.

9. Ibid., 105.

10. Ibid., 109.

11. Ibid. As we shall see, Pecock and Fortescue share equally pessimistic visions of unchecked jurisgenesis.

12. Ibid., 144.

13. Ibid. For an analysis of Cover's ultimate reconciliation with legal violence, see Austin Sarat, "Robert Cover on Law and Violence," in *Narrative, Violence, and the Law*, ed. Minow, Ryan, and Sarat, 255–65, and Austin Sarat and Thomas Kearns, "Making Peace with Violence: Robert Cover on Law and Legal Theory," in *Law's Violence*, ed. Austin Sarat and Thomas R. Kearns (Ann Arbor: University of Michigan Press, 1992), 211–50.

14. J. G. A. Pocock, *The Machiavellian Moment: Florentine Political Thought and the Atlantic Republican Tradition* (Princeton, N.J.: Princeton University Press, 1975), 9.

15. Fortescue, *De laudibus*, 20–21. Fortescue uses the term "civil laws" (*leges civiles*) to denote systems of law based on Romano-canonical procedure, and relies on France for his model of such laws. The integration of these laws within European legal systems, as well as a sense of England's insularity from this integration, is illustrated by Raoul C. van Caenegem's map of the introduction and diffusion of judicial torture (map 3) at the end of his essay "La preuve dans l'ancien droit belge des origines à la fin du XVIIIᵉ siècle," in *La Preuve: Recueils de la société Jean Bodin pour l'histoire comparative des institutions* (Brussels: Librairie Encyclopédique, 1965), 18:375–430. Fortescue's contrast between civilian use of judicial torture and the English common law's trial by jury is one of his fundamental points of contrast between the two systems.

16. "When both laws agree," the chancellor states, "they are equally praiseworthy, but in the cases wherein they differ, the superiorities of the more excellent law will appear after due reflection"; Fortescue, *De laudibus*, 43.

17. Tracking the specific development of the jury's interpretive role and the developing distinction between its fact-finding and professional law-finding functions is notoriously difficult, given the laconism of English legal records on trial procedure. Originally defined as a panel of community witnesses, a definition that stays with the jury for a very long time, the jury held control over the facts that would determine the legal outcome of the case. The rendering of twelve individual factual accounts into a communal verdict would itself, of course, require some interpretation. However, it seems clear that by the fourteenth century, if not earlier, evidentiary procedures were developing that indicate that the jury was no longer a completely self-informing body, that it was also being asked to bring its understanding of local affairs to the interpretation of introduced evidence. In addition, the emergence of an "elite lawyer class" over the fourteenth and into the fifteenth century—a class "jealous of its prerogatives and insistent on preserving to itself the function of lawmaking and lawfinding"—sharpened the distinction between professional lawfinding and lay fact-finding functions; Morris Arnold, "Law and Fact in the Medieval Jury Trial: Out of Sight, Out of Mind," *American Journal of Legal History* 18 (1974): 279.

18. Fortescue's acknowledgment that a confession produced under torture has no reference to the victim's understanding—that it is, in other words, a statement whose content refers only to the torments that produce it—bears close resemblance to Elaine Scarry's theory of torture's "world-destroying" effect on its victims; see Elaine Scarry, *The Body in Pain: The Making and Unmaking of the World* (New York: Oxford University Press, 1985), 29 and, on the topic of torture generally, 27–59.

19. "Quid tunc certitudinis resultat ex confessionibus taliter compressorum?" Fortescue, *De laudibus*, 50–51. Torture itself was recognized as a *res fragilis et periculosa* (a fragile and risky thing), but proved an extremely effective means to secure the confession, the "queen of proofs" that was at the top of the hierarchy of proofs developed by Romano-canonical jurisprudence; see Edward Peters, *Torture* (New York: Blackwell, 1985), 40–73. The "certain" confession was separated from the "fragile and risky" process of torture by the requirement that the confession be repeated away from the place of torture (subject, however, to the reapplication of torture in the event that the victim recanted his or her confession). Fortescue's linking of certainty, the confession, and torture in the quoted passage appropriately elides the artificial separations of Romano-canonical procedure.

20. Fortescue, *De laudibus*, 50–51. Fortescue's use of "infames" has special resonance within the jurisprudence of torture. As Edward Peters notes, the Roman doctrine of *infamia* expanded substantially during the fifth and sixth centuries, an expansion that "paralleled

the extensions of the occasions when slaves could be tortured, when freemen might be interrogated and punished by formerly servile methods, and when 'low' condition exposed more and more freemen to torture itself"; Peters, *Torture*, 31. Revived in the Middle Ages and aligned with other theories of *mala fama, infamia* and these related theories "created substantial inroads into the idea of the inviolability of the defendant"; ibid., 45. In R. I. Moore's summary of the doctrine, "infamy diminished or destroyed the credibility of a man's testimony, depriving him of the protection of the courts, and exposing him to the torture which was otherwise held inconsistent with the dignity of a free man"; Moore, *The Formation of a Persecuting Society: Power and Deviance in Western Europe, 950–1250* (Oxford: Blackwell, 1987), 132.

21. The theoretical choice of trial by jury was a remnant of jury procedure as it developed in the years before 1215, when the jury's verdict was constructed as an alternative, available at the defendant's option, to physical modes of proof supported by theories of divine intervention. Even after these alternatives to jury trial were effectively abolished by the Fourth Lateran Council in 1215, the criminal suspect had affirmatively to choose trial by jury. To compensate for the absence of alternatives, the suspect who refused to so choose was subjected to the combined force of pressing beneath weights and slow starvation on a diet of stale bread and dirty water—the *peine forte et dure*. The only advantage to the suspect was death without conviction, and thus without forfeiture of property. In 1772, refusal to plead became grounds for a conviction; in 1827, it became a plea of not guilty, and jury trial was imposed without the defendant's choice; see S. F. C. Milsom, *Historical Foundations of the Common Law*, 2nd ed. (Toronto: Butterworths, 1981), 411.

22. As John Langbein notes, the English "were the beneficiaries of legal institutions so crude that torture was unnecessary." And the effects of this crudity could cut both ways for the criminal suspect. While "the jury standard of proof gave England no cause to torture," the suspect had few grounds upon which to appeal the jury's verdict: "To this day an English jury can convict a defendant on less evidence than was required as a mere precondition for interrogation under torture on the Continent"; Langbein, *Torture and the Law of Proof: Europe and England in the Ancien Régime* (Chicago: University of Chicago Press, 1977), 77–78.

23. Ibid., 80.

24. Fortescue, *De laudibus*, 62–63. The description of jurors as witnesses who judge the testimony of other witnesses indicates the dual function of the medieval juror. The juror, himself a "witness" in that his personal knowledge of the matter at issue could be considered in reaching the verdict, was also required to try the validity of other witnesses in reaching that verdict.

25. The sheriff, nominated by the king's counselors and selected by the king himself, "shall swear upon the holy evangels of God that, among other things, he will exercise and perform his office during the whole year properly, faithfully, and impartially, and that he will accept nothing by colour or reason of his office from anyone but the king"; ibid., 55.

26. The attaint was an action brought against a jury for a false verdict, tried before a new jury of twenty-four men who judged the verdict of the original twelve. The prescribed punishment for attaint was severe, including imprisonment and the loss of chattels. Its efficacy in practice is another matter. F. W. Maitland observes that "we may sometimes see attainted jurors escaping with moderate fines"; Sir Frederic Pollock and F. W. Maitland, *The History of English Law before the Time of Edward I*, 2nd ed. (Cambridge: Cambridge University Press, 1968), 2:542. J. H. Baker notes that "the procedure was rarely used even in medieval times...because the punishment of perjured trial jurors was so severe that attaint juries would seldom find against them"; Baker, *An Introduction to English Legal History*, 3rd ed. (London: Butterworths, 1990), 156. And because, in criminal cases, the jury was the defendant's theoretical "choice" of proof, "attaint was in principle not available in criminal cases"; Milsom, *Historical Foundations of the Common Law*, 411.

27. The questioning of local virtue is particularly, and not surprisingly, common when the petitioner is not from the same locality as the jury. John Wilson, for example, complains

that his dispute with John Harvy is to be determined by "a quest" made up of "dwellers in the parisshe where that the seid John [Harvy] dwelleth the whiche quest beyng so parciall that fereth nother god ne periure"; PRO C1/32/413.

28. William Kynge, "parson of the parische chirche of Saint Pancras in London," complains that one William Fresur "laburith dayly by vntrewe meanes to cause your seyde besecher to be endyted of rape." Not only is Fresur "a comyn Jurror" who allegedly has made a deal to trade favorable verdicts with "certeyn Jurrours of hys speciall and dayly acquayntance"; in addition, "ther lyeth none attaynte" upon a "false verdyt gevyn in London"; PRO C1/32/273.

29. Two separate petitions to the 1402 Parliament (3 Henry IV) seek relief against Sir Philip de Courtenay in property cases situated in the county of Devonshire. Both petitions allege Philip's seizure of the petitioners' property with, in the first case, the assistance of a "grand nombre des gentz armez," and in the second, a "fort mayn." The second petition more specifically describes Philip's legal tactics in the ensuing trials. Securing an array of potential assize jurors made up of "des pluis sufficeantz Chivalers & Esquiers du dit Counte, & auxi des meyns sufficeantz & poveres hommes entremellez," Philip allegedly trusted that "les pluis sufficeantz duissent faire defaute" ("the more sufficient would endeavor to make a default"), while the "poveres hommes n'oisent envers le dit Sire Philipp la verite dire" ("the poor men would not dare speak the truth against the said Sir Philip"). Parliament's solution is to set a £40 annual income minimum for persons sworn to judge the assize, and to empanel men from throughout the county of Devonshire, the challenge of the hundred (a challenge based on the number of jurors from the immediate locality) or any other challenge notwithstanding; *Rot. parl.*, 3:488–90.

30. As Marianne Constable has recently noted, the term *jury nullification* is based on the assumption "that 'law' is what the officials say it is"; Constable, *The Law of the Other: The Mixed Jury and Changing Conceptions of Citizenship, Law, and Knowledge* (Chicago: University of Chicago Press, 1994), 166, n. 16. Constable's point "is not that such accounts [of jury nullification] are incorrect, but that in the construction of their questions, they make particular assumptions which, correct or incorrect, are worthy of thought."

31. See Thomas A. Green, *Verdict According to Conscience: Perspectives on the English Criminal Trial Jury, 1200–1800* (Chicago: University of Chicago Press, 1985), 28–64.

32. Fortescue, *De laudibus*, 65. Elsewhere, however, Fortescue cites the high number of hangings for robbery and manslaughter in England as evidence of the Englishman's superior "corage" in comparison with the French and the Scots, who hang very few men for these crimes; Sir John Fortescue, *The Governance of England: Otherwise Called the Difference between an Absolute and a Limited Monarchy*, ed. Charles Plummer (Oxford: Clarendon Press, 1885), 141–42.

33. Christopher St. German, *Doctor and Student*, ed. T. F. T. Plucknett and J. L. Barton, Publications of the Selden Society, vol. 91 (London: Selden Society, 1974), 95. The corresponding text of the Latin version is printed on page 94.

34. Sir John Fortescue, *De natura legis naturae*, ed. and trans. Chichester Fortescue, in *The Works of Sir John Fortescue, Knight*, ed. Thomas (Fortescue), Lord Clermont (London: privately printed, 1869; translation reprinted, New York: Garland, 1980), 85, 214 (citations of the *De natura* will be from the 1869 edition, giving the page number of the Latin original first, and of the translation second). It is important to note that Fortescue, first, reserves this power to the prince absolutely, and second, urges him to use it cautiously, lest "he enact new laws without consulting the chief men of his kingdom, or bring in foreign laws, so that, refusing for the future to live politickly, he oppress his people with his *jus regale*"; ibid., 86, 215.

35. The discussion of *pietas* in this paragraph is taken from James D. Garrison, *Pietas from Vergil to Dryden* (University Park: Pennsylvania State University Press, 1992), 94–101.

36. Ibid., 96. Given its definition as a feminine principle, Garrison argues, "the *pietas* of the early medieval period moves away from the patriarchal and heroic context of the

Aeneid. The development of the connotation of political weakness is enhanced by the term's association with Louis the Pious" (ibid.).

37. Ibid., 101.

38. The term *sufficeant* is often used to describe an economically qualified juror. An example of such usage is in the petition to the 1402 Parliament discussed earlier.

39. Fortescue, *De laudibus,* 71. Fortescue's use of *rusticas* exploits a range of connotations, most of them pejorative. *Rusticas mentis* (rusticity of mind) results *ex ruris familiaritate* (from familiarity with the soil), and is contrasted with the idyllic pastoralism and disposition *ad discernendum* of the ancient fathers and their English successors whose wealth comes from the earth, but need not be worked out of it. Moreover, as rustic ignorance (*ruditas rusticitatis*) becomes a generalized trait of the poor (*pauperes*) near the end of the chancellor's speech, the concept of rusticity broadens to connote a wider, less specifically agricultural, trait. On the expansion of the connotations of *rusticus* in the Middle Ages to describe class distinctions, see Alexander Murray, *Reason and Society in the Middle Ages* (Oxford: Clarendon Press, 1978), 237–44.

40. From a petition of the Commons to Parliament, 15 Henry VI (1436); *Rot. parl.,* 4:501.

41. Fortescue, *Governance,* 138. The "thryfty men," Fortescue argues, take part in such risings only at the instigation of the poor, who threaten the better off with loss of their goods if they do not take part in the rising.

42. The law's association with protection of material wealth is concisely summarized in a 1421 (9 Henry V) petition to Parliament by a group of physicians eager to prohibit "unconnyng" and "lewed" men from "practyse in Fisyk." The physicians state, "[a] man hath thre things to governe, that is to say, Soule, Body, and wordly [sic] Goudes, the whiche ought and shulde ben principaly rewled by thre Sciences, that ben Divinite, Fisyk, and Lawe, the Soule by Divinite, the Body by Fisyk, wordly Goudes by Lawe"; *Rot. parl.,* 4:158.

43. A 1433 (11 Henry VI) petition to Parliament requests that "untrewe lyvers" in Southwark who made their fortune "by recettyng of comon women, thefes, mansleers and avoutoures, as by murdererys, and prive robberyes," and are now "sufficeaunt of frehold" to be returned to serve on juries of inquest, be subject to challenge and exclusion from jury service; *Rot. parl.,* 4:447.

44. The *De laudibus* also dates from this period, but lacks the *De natura*'s polemical tone. The polemical nature of the *De natura* certainly must be considered in any interpretation of its arguments: Fortescue himself later confesses that the opinions expressed in the *De natura* were "but arguments," and he "but a parcyall man"; Fortescue, "The Declaracion made by John Fortescu, Knyght, upon Certain Wrytinges Sent Oute of Scotland, Ayenst the Kinges Title to the Roialme of Englond," *Works of Fortescue,* 532. Yet the "Declaracion"—a recantation of certain positions written at the behest of Edward IV as a condition of the restoration of Fortescue's estates after the deaths of Henry VI and Prince Edward—keeps the basic "arguments" of the *De natura* intact and turns them in Edward IV's favor by means of a minor factual adjustment. The realm of England, unlike the realm of Assyria at issue in the *De natura,* is a Christian realm. Thus, English rulers are subject to the pope (a man), and title to the English throne can pass through a woman because she is subject to the governance of a man.

45. Fortescue, *De natura,* 116, 251. The daughter's argument is based on Numbers 27: "When a man shall have died without leaving a son, the inheritance shall go to his daughter."

46. The shift of subject from *Justitia* to *judex,* and from feminine to masculine grammatical gender, is especially apparent in the manuscript of the *De natura* where, from fol. 93v on, the now controlling masculine gender of *judex* is signified by the use of the standard abbreviation (resembling the arabic numeral "9") for the "us" masculine nominative termination of participles and adjectives modifying *judex* (e.g., "*Iudex . . . exors9 est*"); London, Lambeth Palace Library, MS 262.

47. Bishop Reginald Pecock, *The Repressor of Over Much Blaming of the Clergy,* ed. Churchill Babington, Rolls Series, vol. 19 (London: Longman, Green, 1860), 85–86.

48. The incongruity of this application arises from the position of the laypersons criticized by Pecock. The *Repressor* is directed primarily toward the "Bible men" or Lollards, individuals who hardly had the power to impose the "greet peyne of horrible deeth suffring" to enforce their interpretations of Scripture and who, instead, were themselves threatened by such pain under the provisions of the statute *De heretico comburendo*.

49. Pecock, 139. The law of "thilk wickid man Mahumet" and its suppression of argument is discussed in ibid., 132.

50. V. H. H. Green argues that "the 'doom of reason' is the central feature in [Pecock's thought]"; Green, *Bishop Reginald Pecock: A Study in Ecclesiastical History and Thought* (Cambridge: Cambridge University Press, 1945), 130. Charles Brockwell, although reluctant to accept Green's description of the doom of reason as the "essential factor in Pecock's viewpoint," nonetheless states that "there can be no quarrel with the claim that reason is the first principle of Pecock's theological method"; Brockwell, *Pecock and the Lancastrian Church*, 94–95.

51. Pecock, *Repressor*, 18. This quotation is illustrative of the way in which Pecock moves between the seemingly interchangeable concepts of the doom of reason and law of kind.

52. The syllogism, "mad of twey proposiciouns dryuyng out of hem and bi strengthe of hem the thridde proposicioun," is Pecock's favored tool for constructing his arguments. If the first two propositions, or premises, are certain, the third, or conclusion, is irrefutable. If the premises are merely probable, so too is the conclusion. "Miche good," Pecock argues, "wolde come forth if a schort compendiose logik were deuysid for al the comoun peple in her modiris langage"; *Repressor*, 8–9.

53. The clerical association between the feminine and the literal—and clerical denigration of this feminized literalism—has been well established. For an overview of the philosophical tradition informing this clerical hermeneutic, see Carolyn Dinshaw, *Chaucer's Sexual Poetics* (Madison: University of Wisconsin Press, 1989), 3–27. For an analysis of the very real ramifications of this hermeneutic in the context of the Lollard heresy trials, see Rita Copeland, "Why Women Can't Read: Medieval Hermeneutics, Statutory Law, and the Lollard Heresy Trials," in *Representing Women: Law, Literature, and Feminism*, ed. Susan Sage Heinzelman and Zipporah Batshaw Wiseman (Durham, N.C.: Duke University Press, 1994), 253–86. We have already seen a similar hermeneutic operating in Fortescue's *De natura*.

54. The *Book of Faith*, like many of Pecock's texts, is structured as a dialogue between father and son. The nature of "dialogazacioun"—the expression of opposing opinions eventually reconciled—provokes an immediate justification of the form in the *Book of Faith*, aimed at "hasty unconsiderers" who might quickly judge expressed opinions without considering their place in the dialogue; Pecock, *BF*, 121–22.

55. Bishop Reginald Pecock, *The Reule of Crysten Religioun*, ed. William C. Greet, EETS, o. s., no. 171 (London: Oxford University Press, 1927), 21. Pecock's approbation of legal and mercantile wit probably reflects his acquaintance with lawyers and merchants in London, where he lived as an absentee bishop. Wendy Scase's study of "common-profit" book circulation schemes in London, for example, describes Pecock's associations with the Mercers' Company and with John Carpenter, "Common Clerk of London 1417–38, compiler of the *Liber Albus*, . . . lawyer, associate of the London Charterhouse, and chief executor to the merchant and Mayor of London Richard Whittington"; Wendy Scase, "Reginald Pecock, John Carpenter and John Colop's 'Common-Profit' Books: Aspects of Book Ownership and Circulation in Fifteenth-Century London," *Medium Aevum* 61 (1992): 267.

56. Thomas Gascoigne, one of Pecock's fiercest critics, condemned another of Pecock's fellow bishops, William Booth, "for his lack of learning and his legalistic bent—'nor is he a good scholar nor a man of learning, nor considered to be virtuous, nor a graduate, but a common lawyer who confers benefices culpably on boys and comparative youngsters'"; E. F. Jacob, "Reynold Pecock, Bishop of Chichester," *Proceedings of the British Academy* 37

(1951): 132, quoting Thomas Gascoigne, *Loci e libro veritatum* (Oxford: Clarendon Press, 1881), 52.

57. Pecock, *Reule*, 20–21.

58. Pecock, *BF*, 124. Examples of such trustworthy tellers or denouncers are God and angels or apostles of God.

59. Anne Hudson, discussing the list of questions deduced from Bishop William Alnwick of Norwich's courtbook from the Norwich heresy trials (1428–31) and the abjurations of convicted heretics, notes that "very few of the abjurations cover views other than those mentioned [in the deduced list]. This fact . . . reveals how much the form of the questions asked determined the amount and content of the information given"; Hudson, "The Examination of Lollards," in *Lollards and Their Books* (London: Hambledon Press, 1985), 131.

60. Ibid., my emphasis. Hudson, on the same page, also warns against the use of negative evidence when interpreting abjurations of heresy: "It should not be assumed that a Lollard view omitted from a particular confession or abjuration was not held by the suspect. The omission may be simply the result of a failure to ask the necessary eliciting question."

61. For example, Hawisia Mone, convicted of heresy in Norwich, "constituit . . . magistrum Johannem Wylly organum vocis sue" (appointed master John Wylly as the instrument of her voice) after "asserens se nescire legere tenorem dicte abiuracionis sue" (declaring that she did not know how to read the contents of her said abjuration); *Heresy Trials in the Diocese of Norwich, 1428–31*, ed. Norman P. Tanner, Camden Fourth Series, vol. 20 (London: Royal Historical Society, 1977), 139.

62. Pecock, *Repressor*, 2. In the glossary to the *Repressor*, Babington defines "undirnyme" as "to reprove; find fault with"; ibid., 675.

63. There is, of course, a distinct, if not exact, resonance between this dynamic of lay "correpcioun" and authoritative "correccioun" and the dynamic between the common law jury and the legal and judicial officers of the king's court, a resonance intensified by the "nei3bourli" modification of Pecock's definition of lay "correpcioun." The jury, like the layperson seeking "correpcioun," is assigned the role of ascribing or withholding blame based on its collective, "nei3bourli" understanding of the circumstances; definition of the terms of blame and the execution of punishment against those found guilty are roles reserved for those in positions of legal and judicial authority.

64. When urging the laity to air their interpretations of Scripture, Pecock instructs them "to bringe thou forth thilke evydencis bi mouthe speking, *if thou dare appere*, or ellis bi writing *if thou dare not appere in speking*"; Pecock, *BF*, 198; my emphasis.

65. J. L. Morison, editor of the *Book of Faith*, marks this shift at the beginning of part 1, chapter 8, noting that "in this chapter the form of the book completely changes, and a Lollard takes the place of the son, without his privilege of questioning." It is in this chapter that the father proposes the adversarial disputation between layman and cleric. However, the dialogue structure is actually dropped in the middle of the preceding chapter, where Morison notes that "as Pecock kindles to his argument, he inclines to forget the dialogue with its didactic tone, and substitutes an argumentative monologue." This monologue is directed at the man who holds burned Lollards to be martyrs; Pecock, *BF*, 195, 192.

66. For the text of the archbishop of Canterbury's instructions consigning Pecock to Thorney Abbey, see *English Historical Documents, IV (1327–1485)*, ed. A. R. Myers (London: Eyre and Spottiswoode, 1969), 877.

67. Gascoigne, *Loci*, 217.

CHAPTER 5

⚜

Chaucer's Hard Cases

Elizabeth Fowler

D ominion (Latin *dominium*) is a fundamental concept of medieval and early modern political philosophy, and for all its importance, it is exquisitely volatile. The topic of dominion lies at the center of the most important debates in European jurisprudence: it is an issue that retains its urgency across the span that stretches from the investiture controversies of the High Middle Ages to the fourteenth-century conflicts over religious poverty, and from the cultural, medical, and commercial crises of European colonial expansion to the Reformation. Theories of dominion consider the sources, limits, institutions, and justification — in a word, the constitution — of power.[1]

Dominion is best understood as a relationship rather than an idea or a quality attributed to the person.[2] All social relations or bonds, including those between people and things, necessarily reflect a form of dominion insofar as they model and contain rights and powers: *dominium* is not the same word as our *domination,* but a category that includes it. In its narrowest legal definition, *dominium* refers to ownership in its perfect or complete sense. In use both in and out of the law, however, its semantic field is much wider. Dominion means the legal right to possession of a thing or of knowledge, as in the modern words *title, possession, ownership, proprietorship, mastery*; it means the exercise of a controlling power or the condition of that control, as in the words *imperium, lordship, rule, command, dominance, sway*; it means the right or power to command, decide, rule, or judge, as in the words *sovereignty, authority, jurisdiction, domination, might, prerogative.*

Medieval and early modern English writing offers a tradition of thought heavily marked by what I will call *jurisprudential topoi*: scenes, motifs, concepts, or formulas that raise philosophical questions about legal principles.[3] These topoi were alive in the romance and other popular literary forms, in sermon literature, in the chronicles, in theology, and in jurisprudence. To take three examples: first, the origins of both sexual and political dominion are explored through the topos of Eden (and its offshoot, the *hortus conclusus*) by canon lawyers and theologians in commentaries on Genesis, by the rebels of the 1381 rising, by Hooker in *The Lawes of Ecclesiastical Politie,* by colonial writers about Ireland, and by countless medieval and early modern poets, including Milton in *Paradise Lost,* a poem directly responsive to the powerful natural jurisprudence of Hugo

Grotius. Second, the claims of the kind of dominion that is established by conquest are considered through the triumph, in its literary, ceremonial, architectural, painted, and chronicled forms. Third, the role of consent in sovereignty is probed through plot parallels between political and sexual vows that appear in the early English romances; in the political writings of Langland, Gower, Hoccleve, Lydgate, and Elyot; in the radical university philosophy of Wyclif; in the Arthurian cycles; in the epic romances of Sidney and Spenser; and in plays by Marlowe, Shakespeare, and their competitors. Once we recognize a few of the lost topoi and terms of the debates about dominion that so occupied these centuries, a new alignment of legal and literary works becomes visible. It is a tradition of political thought that is obscured by twentieth-century political historiography, which establishes its touchstone in the seventeenth-century contractarians.[4]

Edenic Dominion

Let me explore my first example more closely. For medieval and early modern commentators of all classes, the Genesis story of the fall provided an opportunity to theorize dominion explicitly. It became the story of the origin of God's dominion over creation, of men's dominion over women, of human dominion over animals and land, of human dominion over knowledge, and of the dominion conveyed by labor. The absence of political dominion from this list is so significant that it helped to justify riots. One motto of the rising of 1381 was the famous "Whan Adam dalf and Eve span, / Who was þanne a gentil man?" John Ball took this proverb as the text of his sermon at Blackheath.[5] The couplet draws our attention to the absence of class-based sovereignty in Genesis,[6] and goes further, to the point of calling upon the primacy of the dominion created by labor that the biblical text also establishes. However, the couplet's gendering of labor—"Whan Adam dalf, and Eve span"—seems to qualify the call to revolt, specifically, if implicitly, admonishing women that their labor is not a license to dominion over men, since Adam's sovereignty over Eve is more primary than that dominion workers enjoy over the wealth their labor creates.

In the brilliant compression of this powerful maxim, three kinds of dominion are compared: (1) sexual relations (uninflected by class because all human beings descend from these same parents), (2) ownership (construed as a relation between labor and wealth rather than as a common law question of inherited, taxed, escheated, or contractually transferred title), and (3) lordship or estate. According to the couplet, Genesis elevates the first two kinds of dominion by underwriting the authority of men over women and of laborers over property. Conversely, it discredits the third by means of the embedded corollaries of the first two kinds of dominion, as well as the simple absence from Eden of feudal class structure.

If property law is a prop for a specific order of dominion, say feudalism, then the rhetorical question of John Ball's sermon presents a particular kind of hard case, pitting feudalism against Genesis. Hard cases make bad law, as the legal maxim goes, because they invite judges to act willfully on the basis of the unusual. But hard cases make excellent narrative art and deliberative occasions: they are an invitation to us all to practice good jurisprudence, because they take us beyond indifferent descriptions of legal and political practice. We are challenged to think, to evaluate, to measure the practices that make up our social institutions and ideals. In *The Canterbury Tales*, dominion is very much a live issue: like philosophers, rebels, kings, lawyers, and other poets, Chaucer frequently enters into the vigorous medieval tradition that considers the limits, sources, and kinds of dominion. Rather like John Ball's proverb, *The Canterbury Tales* comprise a tangle of arguments about social relations. The first clause of the proverb sets the parameters of its thought experiment: let's take Eden, it says, what do you think of dominion in that case? In Chaucer's narratives, questions of bonds, voluntarism, and social roles are turned over and over in the same kind of hypothetical environment. The tales take up the issue of dominion directly, worrying certain words that are familiar to Chaucerians as epitomes of critical issues: *possessioun, dominacioun, soveraynetee, libertee, deite, maistrie, daunger, commaundement, lordshipe, regne, fredom*. These are all terms with jurisprudential force; most can be found in a current legal dictionary. Whether it be a question of dominion as it is experienced in marriage or in the polity, Chaucer's hard cases always invite us to think jurisprudentially and politically.

Chaucer frequently raises the issue of dominion through lexis, topos, and genre, but there is another strategy I would like to identify, one I will call deliberative. The deliberative strategy takes place at a level that Mary Carruthers terms the "macro-rhetorical."[7] V. A. Kolve has equipped us to roam freely between vastly different kinds of artifacts by stressing the iconographical significance of images as they appear both verbally and visually. Carruthers's work on memory urges us to reconsider the larger roles of rhetorical colors. According to her account, in the encounter with an ornament of style the reader is asked to collate, or recollect, a series of texts drawn from research and experience, and then to make judgments (ethical in their core) about the matter this chain of texts evokes. Together the interpretive techniques of Carruthers and Kolve offer a purchase upon what I am calling the deliberative process in Chaucer's poetry and upon how it incorporates the jurisprudential topoi. Setting up the hard case in the narrative is part of that deliberative strategy. This mode has made Chaucer seem indifferent or apolitical to many readers who expect political statements to support or condemn particular fourteenth-century events, persons, and policies.

The impression readers have had of indifference (or worse) is increased by the fact that when scholars have recognized and researched Chaucer's use of legal and political diction, allusion, topic, or figure, they often seek to establish a key to medieval beliefs. This useful scholarship has too often, no doubt inadvertently, been like a finger in a dike, stopping up the issue at the very moment it is broached by drying up the controversial and interrogative aspects of Chaucer's citations. Difficulties arise when we acknowledge the political nature of such language; sometimes those difficulties seem overwhelming.[8] It is easy to feel that one navigates between a Scylla and Charybdis of conspiracies: "power" is either doing all kinds of darkly agentless consolidating and dispersing, or certain agents (such as the Crown) attain an artificial surplus of agency and others an unaccountable deficit. It is good to recall us, as Larry Scanlon has done, to observing politics in the context of the ideological purposes of "power," but in order to do so with any reach we need to be able to define power more precisely than we have done.[9] Fortunately, power is not just a motive, it has forms, and those forms should be part of its description. Late medieval England was full of people using, suffering, and making arguments about power, or, to be both more ideationally and materially precise, about dominion. Conceptual deliberations upon its forms are not the sum of what we can know about dominion, by any means, but written records give us special access to ideas, and I think that, alongside a more materialist history, they are interesting and important. This essay tries to illuminate the relation of *The Canterbury Tales* to ideology.

By suggesting that *The Canterbury Tales* lack a forensic or an epideictic political mode, I also intend to praise, and to assume, the deliberative. This is the mode that I believe best characterizes Chaucerian narrative, and I see it as no less political (and no more ideologically obfuscating) than the other two kinds of argumentation. Its main political asset is that it invites dialogue, an intensely characteristic Chaucerian effect. That Chaucer poses his hard cases interrogatively does not mean that the writing refrains from critical judgment. I propose to look briefly at one of Chaucer's thought experiments, *The Knight's Tale,* with an eye to the way that he uses jurisprudential topoi to draw us into the deliberations. As we shall see, the triumph represents the claim of conquest and the exchange of marital vows counters that claim with a model of consent.

The Lancastrian Repudiation of Conquest

Perhaps the invasion of sexual ethics into the sphere of constitutional thought was a result of the way tyranny was defined throughout this period. A tyrant is conceived as a ruler who acts for his personal pleasure rather than for the common good. This is an important response to and defense against the enduring, ambiguous legal maxim *Quod principi placuit, legis habet vigorem,* what pleases the prince has the power of law.[10] In order to combat abuses of this maxim and to set limits to the prince's justification of his "pleasures" through law, private pleasures had to be distinguished from public goods. The opportunity for sexual connotation is obvious, and the ability of narrative to characterize a ruler as a tyrant by a single stroke of sexual aggression is recognized by all readers of romance. It is a truth romances universally acknowledge that the power of virtuous Christian beauty produces the urge toward *raptus* in evil sultans, stewards, and judges everywhere. As Aristotle says, it is wrong to think that "pleasant and fine things force us."[11] Beauty does not make actions upon it involuntary. The symbolic relation between virtue and attributes such as *puissance* and beauty is central to the romance mode, and conveys title to worldly, or otherworldly, sovereignty with such frequency that I hardly need cite examples.

Yet if beauty is an icon for Christian virtue (coalescing, perhaps, in the pictorial halo) it is even more specifically true that *raptus* is an icon for dominion established by conquest, one that survives for centuries in the graphic arts. While dominion claimed by conquest is not necessarily a crime, *raptus* certainly is, and the analogy between rape and conquest that is part and parcel of the genre of romance eventually served not only to eroticize conquest, but also to criminalize it. Thus, rape is a sign of an unjust war; the sexual depredations of the Bosnian Serbs in the early 1990s, for example, were effectively cited to convey the illegitimacy of their political aggressions. The most important operation of romance in this regard is the analogy it makes between sexual dominion and political dominion. While particular romances can come down hard against consent and for the legitimacy of absolute rule by conquest, over the long run the effect of these analogies has been a forceful affirmation of consent in the conception of social bonds of all kinds.

One of the tools for constraining English kings from abusing their power was the coronation oath, in which the king swore to maintain the powers of the church and the law. Bracton explains it this way:

> For at his coronation the king must swear, having taken an oath in the name of Jesus Christ, these three promises to the people subject to him.
>
> *Of the oath [sacramento] the king must swear at his coronation.* In the first place, that to the utmost of his power he will employ his might to secure and will enjoin that true peace shall be maintained for the church of God and all Christian people throughout his reign. Secondly, that he will forbid rapacity to his subjects of all degrees [*ut rapacitates et omnes iniquitates omnibus gradibus interdicat*]. Thirdly, that he will cause all judgments to be given with equity and mercy, so that he may himself be shown the mercy

of a clement and merciful God, in order that by his justice all men may enjoy unbroken peace.[12]

These three aspects of the vow are evident in the older Anglo-Saxon coronation oaths and in the later oath of Edward II, which is cited in the records of the depositions of both Edward and Richard II.[13] Edward was held to have perjured his oath; Richard to have done that and much more. In Bracton, the word *rapacitates* stands generally for injustice that must be restrained; it is closely related to *raptus* and appears under the same heading (*rapacitas*) in R. E. Latham's *Medieval Latin Word-List*.[14]

The erosion of the legitimacy of conquest was well under way by Chaucer's time, and we have both lawyers and poets to thank for that. One of the curious results of this ideological struggle lies in the records of the constitutional struggle of 1399. The parliamentary rolls for that year describe Richard II's deposition in Latin, but are interrupted by a curious section in English. Here Henry, duke of Lancaster, presents a brief "chalenge" in English to claim the realm and crown. A Latin sermon by the archbishop of Canterbury follows, explaining that Henry will rule not according to his own will but according to God's (presumably the archbishop expected to communicate a significant portion of that will). According to the articles of deposition and other records, Richard was fond of saying that his will was law.[15] Then the rolls momentarily break back into English again, as Henry makes a pointed disclaimer:

> Sires, I thank God and yowe, spiritual and temporal and all the astates of the lond, and do yowe to wyte it is noght my will that no man thynk that be waye of conquest I wold disherit any man of his heritage, franches, or other ryghtes that hym aght to have, no put hym out of that that he has and has had by the gude laws and customs of the rewme—except thos persons that has ben agan the gude purpose and the commune profyt of the rewme.[16]

Why, just in the moment of making his strongest claims to dominion, does Henry explicitly disavow conquest? His disavowal is reinforced by the fact that the rolls take pains to characterize Richard as acting more like a conqueror of England than Henry had. For example, the indictments against Richard include his encouragement of his personal mob, the Cheshire Archers, for pillage, murder, and rape of English subjects.[17] Such actions fly in the face of Bracton's representation of the English coronation oath and its injunctions against rapacity. Certainly, from a legal point of view, Henry needed to reassure the legal advisers of the barons, whose own claims to lordship and property would have been interrupted by an absolute claim of conquest. The disavowal, however, is not in Law French or Latin and thus apparently not aimed at the specialized audience who would have understood the legal difficulties involved in the extension of Richard's institutional arrangements to Henry. The sudden turn to English is accompanied by an elaborate formal address that repeats throughout the passage. Henry speaks to those present in their formal, representative capacities: "yowe, spiritual and temporal and all the astates of the lond." He follows this address with an imperative that includes all men not present individually: let "no man thynk" that Henry takes by conquest. The second person yields further to a widely inclusive "any man" as Henry characterizes his protection of current political and property rights, leaving his audience with an assurance and a threat against those who have defied the jurisprudential and Chaucerian virtue of "commune profyt." This insistently masculine appeal to his audience bows to the upholding of common profit and the abnegation of conquest in a way that I think goes far beyond what Henry needed to do to reassure the barons. A full understanding of the political language this extraordinary English outburst employs must, I think, consider jurisprudence as it is developed in the history of the romance.

The Interrupted Triumph

The very first of *The Canterbury Tales*, *The Knight's Tale*, introduces the topic of dominion by considering the question of conquest, that strong claim which would be both courted and disavowed by Henry in 1399. I propose to describe *The Knight's Tale* as a thought experiment that considers the strengths and the limits of such an establishment of rule. Seeing the tale in the context of jurisprudence allows us to reframe traditional questions about Theseus, so that we can better understand how the tale's politics work. The topic of conquest is raised by attributing the narrative to a crusading knight and by the figure of Theseus itself. As so often, Chaucer finds political ideology in genres and in the traditions attached to certain stories, authors, and characters.

In choosing to rewrite part of Theseus's story, Chaucer takes on a figure out of political philosophy. His Theseus exemplifies a category in Aristotle's *The Politics* as it is explicated by Marsiglio of Padua:

> There is and was a fifth method of kingly monarchy, whereby the ruler is made lord (*dominus*) over everything in the community, disposing of things and persons according to his own will, just as the head of a family disposes at will of everything in his own household.[18]

This kind of absolute monarchy is inimical to the English political settlement, which John Fortescue will soon praise as a mixed or limited monarchy, *dominium politicum et regale*. His fifteenth-century formulation of the English version of the mixed constitution plays upon an ideal that is well accepted by Chaucer's time, one given strong impetus by the interpretations of Aristotelian constitutional theory established by Thomas Aquinas. The ideal of the mixed constitution is expressed in late medieval English government by the elevation of Parliament's role in circumscribing the autonomy of the monarch. In a passage that strictly curtails interpretation of the Roman maxim *quod principi placuit*, Bracton places much stronger constraints upon the English king than those Richard II wished to recognize:

> For the king, since he is the minister and vicar of God on earth, can do nothing save what he can do *de jure*, despite the statement that the will of the prince has the force of law [*quod principi placet legis habet vigorem*], because there follows at the end of the *lex* the words "since by the *lex regia*, which was made with respect to his sovereignty"; nor is that anything rashly put forward of his own will, but what has been rightly decided with the counsel of his magnates, deliberation and consultation having been had thereon, the king giving it *auctoritas*. His power is that of *jus*, not *injuria* and since it is he from whom *jus* proceeds, from the source whence *jus* takes its origin no instance of *injuria* ought to arise, and also, what one is bound by virtue of his office to forbid to others, he ought not to do himself.... For he is called *rex* not from reigning but from ruling well, since he is a king as long as he rules well but a tyrant when he oppresses by violent domination the people entrusted to his care. Let him, therefore, temper his power by law, which is the bridle of power, that he may live according to the laws, for the law of mankind [*lex humana*] has decreed that his own laws bind the lawgiver, and elsewhere in the same source, it is a saying worthy of the majesty of the ruler that the prince acknowledge himself bound by the laws.[19]

Richard II tested the limits of this institutional settlement severely throughout the height of Chaucer's career. In his Theseus we have not an evil holder of a limited monarchy, as Richard is often described, but something like its mirror opposite: a benevolent holder of an absolute dominion.[20] This is the kind of idealized representation that Richard's ideological campaigns attempted to create, but the figure is let loose in a story that offers a very bleak view of life under absolute dominion.

In the first lines of *The Knight's Tale*, Duke Theseus appears as an archetype of the quintessential *dominus* by conquest, the man on the top of every relation of dominion: the Knight tells us that, according to old stories, Theseus is "lord and governour, / And in his tyme swich a conqueror / That gretter was ther noon under the sonne" (861–63).[21] He has "conquered al the regne of Femenye," "weddede the queene Ypolita," and within fifteen lines, as we move into the present tense of the narration, he is leading his wife-prize and her sister home in a triumphal procession. This is a scene that, were it one of Petrarch's *Trionfi* (1351–74), would have to be called "the triumph of triumph." The form we call "the triumph" crosses over the boundaries between media and has important manifestations in music, architecture, drama, lyric poetry, and civic and religious ceremony. All these triumphal forms are associated with dominion established by conquest. Yet look what happens to the triumph that opens *The Knight's Tale*: it is suspended nearly as soon as it is established. Theseus is not allowed to complete his triumph or to bring his wife to bed. First the poetry freezes the frame with the ambiguous word "lete" ("And thus with victorie and with melodye / Lete I this noble duc to Atthenes ryde, / And al his hoost in armes hym bisyde"). "Lete" here suggests both "allow" him to ride to Athens and "prevent" him from riding to Athens. It turns out, of course, that Theseus is interrupted both by the narrator's rhetoric and by the plot.

Here, as we pause with Theseus, I remind you that much criticism of *The Knight's Tale* has focused on Theseus and whether he is understood to be idealized or satirized, whether he is a philosopher, a mercenary, or a tyrant.[22] There are, of course, reams of criticism justifying Theseus's role in terms of his aspirations to civilize the brutal disorder of life, but these critics take a view that must ignore Theseus's role as the source of much of the brutal disorder of life.[23] This view cannot account for the Theseus of *The House of Fame* (405–26), *The Legend of Good Women* (VI, VIII), or *Anelida and Arcite*. The few important essays that are disturbed by tyrannical aspects of Theseus's behavior encounter the problem of explaining why Chaucer makes him so sympathetic. Jill Mann explains the importance of Chaucer's attribution of pity to Theseus within the sphere of sexual relations and the emotions, an interpretation that must be extended, I think, into the realm of politics if it is to acknowledge the political scope of the tale.[24] The project of my reading of *The Knight's Tale* is to shift attention away from the traditional problem of the characterization of Theseus and to focus upon his role as the plot's embodiment of a *dominus* who holds by conquest; he is, as the Knight says, the "conqueror."[25] The task that Chaucer sets the reader is, I think, not to decide whether Theseus's character is good or bad, a dilemma perceived as central by most of the criticism of *The Knight's Tale* to date, but rather it is to decide whether conquest can be compatible with good governance, whether it can be detached from absolutism, and whether, as a justification for rule, it can make a good showing against the competing argument, that the proper establishment of dominion lies not through conquest, but through consent.

In sum, I propose to read *The Knight's Tale* not as an exemplification of jurisprudence, but as a test of it, a hard case that pits the institutional arrangements of dominion by conquest against the ameliorating influence of a benevolent ruler. It offers, in this sense, the best case that can be made for conquest; however, it is a case that never amounts to a defense. What Chaucer demonstrates in *The Knight's Tale* is that even under the most benevolent, virtuous, "pitous" *dominus*, dominion by conquest is incapable of civilizing. It can command, it can revenge, it can take, it can bring the half-dead to life and the half-living to death, but it is incapable of compelling consent and conjuring community in any meaningful interpretation of the terms. Conquest is, by definition, supremely uninterested in consent; thus, in the brilliant argument of *The Knight's Tale,* conquest is incapable of coming to political satisfaction. Revenge, victory, and pillage are its sole rewards; it cannot form secure, reciprocal social bonds. Conquest can build triumphs, monuments, prisons, enclosed gardens, and tournament stadiums, but it cannot build cities; it cannot build secure, functioning polities. Perhaps most decisively, although Theseus can arrange a marriage, we are aware that it is a marriage that falls far short of the kind of sexual bond that Chaucer idealizes on political grounds—that blissful union "by evene acord" achieved by the Commons at the end of *The Parlement of Foules.* You will remember how that accord is achieved through the validation of voluntary consent, above all else.

Meanwhile, back to the freeze frame that interrupts Theseus's progress. Very near the opening of the tale, just as Theseus's triumphal procession is approaching Athens, the narrator indulges in a long *occupatio* (or *occultatio,* as H. A. Kelly and R. A. Lanham prefer) that makes a great show of its own interruption.[26] To double this narrative interruption, a group of widows stops Theseus's progress in the plot, just "Whan he was come almoost unto the toun" (894). The minute he is about to reach his seat of power, they send him back out to war, and he is not allowed to *enjoy*—as lawyers say of real estate and priests say of wives—his triumph. *The Knight's Tale* begins, then, with a fine example of what we might call *contractus interruptus,* one that later fascinated both Spenser and Shakespeare: Theseus suffers an interrupted resumption of his throne, an interrupted assumption of a newly expanded sovereignty, and an interrupted contract of marriage with Ypolita.[27]

Sexual Vows and Political Dominion

It has often been noted that *occupatio,* which provides the first interruption, is one of the narrator's characteristic rhetorical moves. "If it nere to long to heere," he says, he would tell how all this happened, how the government of women was brought down, about the great battle between Athenians and Amazons, about the siege against the Queen Ypolita, about their wedding and the tempest at their homecoming—"but," he says, "al that thyng I moot as now forbere" (885). Without contradicting his lavish praise of Theseus, the narrator does say that there is another story he is repressing, one that he will not tell. That is Ypolita's story, the story of her reign and of the reign of women. Why does Chaucer deliberately lower this epistemological veil? Usually he glories in pursuing the stories of women and what they most desire, the conditions of their consent, their "queynte" fantasies, their heroism, their ambition, their tragedies, and their victories. The story of Ypolita's losses during the war is in fact a more typically Chaucerian story than the story of Theseus, and his main source, Boccaccio's *Teseida*, gives it full play. Why does Chaucer set it apart in ostentatious brackets right at the very beginning of *The Knight's Tale?* He does so in order fully to test the claims of conquest. The reader must focus upon the plot of conquest as it carries the narrative, but, lurking in spaces like the *occupatio*, there remains a continuous, implicit recourse to the canon law standard of mutual consent in sexual love.

Chaucer epitomizes his jurisprudential thought experiment by combining the political with the sexual in Theseus's opening victory over the Regne of Femenye. The victory and the wedding necessarily pit the two extremes of dominion theory against each other: war proceeds upon an implicit justification of dominion by conquest; legitimate marriage, however, as all good readers of romance know, proceeds upon the justification of dominion by consent. These two principal motives of the tale's trial of dominion, the political and the sexual, are first happily combined in the glorious description of Theseus in the first lines, then they are subtly unraveled and distinguished by the *occupatio*; next, they are drawn into conflict with each other, and with other forms of social bonds, by the philosophical plot.

Chaucer builds the jurisprudential principles he is testing into the tale through competing generic structures and sets of values. For example, look at the Knight's despairing apostrophe as it breaks through the narrative crux at the center of the episode in which Palamoun and Arcite nearly destroy each other in the grove. Here the several sets of values that are the motor of the story are brought, like the plot itself, to a pitch of conflict:

> O Cupide, out of alle charitee!
> O regne, that wolt no felawe have with thee!
> Ful sooth is seyd that love ne lordshipe
> Wol noght, his thankes, have no felaweshipe.
> Well fynden that Arcite and Palamoun.
>
> (1623–27)

Here, in a crux of tangled apostrophes at the center of the tale, both the romance and the epic plots are declared to be incompatible with "felawschipe," with relationships "by evene acord." "Felawschipe" signifies the voluntarily created mutual bonds that are dissolved here in the grove with the loss of blood between the artificially resurrected Arcite and Palamoun. It is not Theseus who is decried in this scene; he is a benevolent ruler in terms of his ethical character, exemplary in his pity. Rather, what is destructive of fellowship is the kind of lordship that will have no fellowship, the form of rule that Theseus has chosen. Together with the idealized, anti-Petrarchan concept of marriage as mutual, fellowship haunts the tale in the plot of dissolution and in the literary form of the complaint.

Arcite becomes a *dominus* by conquest when he wins Emelye "with strengthe," as he prayed he would ("I moot with strengthe wynne hire in the place" [2399]). In his victory we are invited to recall the self-destructive figure of Conquest as it appears in the Temple of Mars. We know from the description of Theseus's banner before the sack of Thebes that a red statue of Mars is the duke's emblem:

> The rede statue of Mars, with spere and targe,
> So shyneth in his white baner large
> That alle the feeldes glyteren up and doun.
> (975–77)

Describing the Temple of Mars, the Knight reports a vision:

> And al above, depeynted in a tour,
> Saugh I Conquest, sittynge in greet honour.
> (2027–28)

As many readers have noticed, this sight casts back to the opening description of the duke ("swich a conquerour / That gretter was ther noon under the sonne" [862–63]) and forward to his appearance, "Arrayed right as he were a god in trone," appearing in his palace window (2529). In the temple, Chaucer adds a salient iconographical detail to the picture of Conquest that must color our perception of Theseus. Conquest sits

> With the sharpe swerd over his heed
> Hangynge by a soutil twynes threed.
> (2029–30)

As the parallel courtship plot of *The Parlement of Foules* acknowledges, only the robust twine that is fellowship "by evene acord" can properly knit together a polity, and the quandary of *The Knight's Tale* is that—no matter how honorable the conqueror—conquest unravels such bonds, leaving itself vulnerable to falling under its own instrument, the sword.

Together with the Aristotelian notion of friendship ("felawschipe"), the figure of marriage is crucial to understanding the representation of social bonds in Chaucer. *The Knight's Tale* begins with a marriage, yet it does not describe the performance of this marriage: our suspicion is drawn to the significant omission of Ypolita's consent by her military resistance, chronicled and not chronicled by the *occupatio*. The answer to whether the queen has consented to the marriage lies irretrievably behind the epistemological veil of the *occupatio*. In fact, her consent is irrelevant to Theseus's story: the withholding of this information is another sign of Chaucer's insistence upon *The Knight's Tale* as a proper test of conquest. Conquest drowns consent absolutely. Theirs is a marriage established by conquest: thus it is indifferent to consent and, strictly speaking, it is a rape — a *raptus*, the privileged ancient and medieval iconographical sign for dominion by conquest. Ypolita loses the war, and thus she loses the capacity for consent. She becomes a "caityf" to Theseus's "lord" and a spoil of war to his pillaging. Chaucer carefully omits her consent, yet under such coercion, as under dread or fraud, a "yes" would hardly ring true. Consent under the pressure of such impediments would not suffice for his romance-fed, Christian audience, just as it would not hold up under canon law. As that other great romance epic *Gone with the Wind* asks in equally hybrid terms: can the female personification of a conquered territory, be it Scarlett or Ypolita, really make a go of a new Union with her rapist? *The Knight's Tale* goes further in giving the conqueror every ethical and political advantage that can accrue to what is, after all, a conqueror: he appears as a gentleman of honor. *The Knight's Tale* bundles up a number of parallel questions for its readers: How good can pagan culture be? How good can a *dominus* by conquest be? And how good can a marriage by *raptus* be? Last but not least, the really interesting question for the sixteenth-century writers who extend Chaucer's analysis is, Can conquest be converted to consent?

This is a question that is taken up by centuries of romance writers up to the present day. When Catharine MacKinnon diagnoses modern sexuality as essentially the eroticization of dominance behavior, she is right there with Chaucer's Emelye in the Temple of Diana, taking a firmly jurisprudential position that is well mapped out in the landscape of epic and romance.[28] It is good, if a bit frightening, to see the critique revived in this form. I think it is important that the analogy between sexual bonds and constitutional political bonds, repeatedly worked through in all forms of romance, has over the long run been a most fertile source of a jurisprudence that protects the agency and voice of women and the less powerful. This is a jurisprudence that has been crucial in defining and creating an environment for consent that makes it as meaningful as possible.

The Knight deliberately does not describe Ypolita's conversion from military adversary to wife; we are merely informed that she is vanquished. The reader's sense of the missing story thus only becomes more urgent during the course of the tale — not only do we wonder whether Ypolita's resistance was ever truly transformed to meaningful consent, but the question of whether her sister Emelye will ever consent to marriage motivates the plot and is left openly hanging in the last lines like an unspoken *demande d'amour*. We do not hear Emelye's story—the narrator makes us very aware of that—and the glimpse of her wishes that we are allowed in the Temple of Diana merely underscores that absence by expressing her dread.

Finally, in the conclusion to the tale, we do witness the performance of a marriage. But what kind of marriage? The vows themselves are imperatives uttered by Theseus in a complicated and indirect speech act that leaves us questioning the conditions of such social bonds and the relations of dominion they make concrete. Famously, just as the *occupatio* leaves Ypolita loudly unheard in the first lines, Theseus's speech leaves Emelye loudly unheard:

> "Suster," quod he [Theseus], "this is my fulle assent,
> With al th'avys heere of my parlement,
> That gentil Palamon, youre owene knyght,
> That serveth yow with wille, herte, and myght,
> And ever hath doon syn ye first hym knewe,
> That ye shul of youre grace upon hym rewe,
> And taken hym for housbonde and for lord.
> Lene me youre hond, for this is oure accord."
>
> (3075–82)

As a speech act, this utterance performs a marriage. But in this marriage, it is Theseus who says "I do," as he says "this is my fulle assent." Instead of the voluntary and symbolic joining of the couple's hands, Theseus issues an imperative "Lene me youre hond" to Emelye. A clause controlling marriages forced by feudal lords is incorporated into the common law by Magna Carta. More stringently, canon law requires an exchange of mutual consent in the performance of Christian marriage, and has done since the twelfth-century decretals of popes Alexander III and Innocent III, whether or not that consent is ratified and underwritten by the community. In place of what fourteenth-century Christians would recognize as a lawful, mutual contract between Emelye and Palamoun, then, we are given Theseus's contract, which engulfs all else in its expansive, royal, first-person plural: "for this is oure accord."

Emelye does experience an emotional reversal at the end of the tale; she screams and swoons at Arcite's deathbed. At the funeral she appears after Palamoun:

> passynge othere of wepynge, Emelye,
> The rewefulleste of al the compaignye.
>
> (2885–86)

We are carefully reminded of her vows in Diana's temple when the scene is echoed by the complex *occupatio* that describes the funeral. The narrator will not tell us

> how Arcite lay among al this,
> Ne what richesse aboute his body is;
> Ne how that Emelye, as was the gyse,
> Putte in the fyr of funeral servyse;
> Ne how she swowned whan men made the fyr,
> Ne what she spak, ne what was hir desir.
>
> (2939–44)

Although we never hear her consent to Theseus's enforced vow, we are told that she and Palamoun are wed, and that "Emelye hym loveth so tendrely" that "nevere was ther no word hem bitwene / Of jalousie or any oother teene" (3103–06). But Emelye's emotional reversal has already occurred by the time that Theseus asks for her "wommanly pitee" (3083). Her emotions and her final obedience to heterosexual custom are commanded by the duke, but already evoked by the horrors of Arcite's death.

Theseus's usurpation of the roles and voices of Emelye and Palamoun should be considered together with another comment from Marsiglio:

> The fourth conclusion is that no one swearing an oath can by that vow bind another person to the observance of any vow, unless there has been an explicit mandate or precept to do this by a person who has reached the requisite age, as is apparent from the definition of a vow stated above. For a vow is and should be the voluntary and uncoerced swearing of a promise about the committing or omitting of some act which is known rather than unknown, on account of which no one can by the uttering of a vow bind another person involuntarily or unawares to the observance of some vow.[29]

This particular kind of tyranny, the substitution of the will of the sovereign for that of his people, is a close relative of the tyranny that Grisilde's Markis practices. While *The Knight's Tale* investigates the limits of conquest, other tales ask about neighboring aspects of dominion and its relationship to consent. Chaucer manages these political thought experiments not through discursive reason (which serves primarily as psychological description throughout *The Knight's Tale*), but by setting up the hard case and putting it before us, asking us to see these old stories through their jurisprudential topoi and to respond with our passions as well as our reason.

In *The Knight's Tale*, Chaucer employs a strategy opposite to the one that he takes after the identical opening gambit (the *contractus interruptus*) of *Anelida and Arcite*. There he gives full play to the anti-Theseus, anti-epic mode of complaint. His usual impulse is, I think, thus to further the Ovidian critique of Vergilian epic values, but in *The Knight's Tale* he gives fuller voice to the poetry of imperial conquest and still manages, I think, a better argument against absolutism than that which accrues to Theseus's other Chaucerian appearances in *The House of Fame* and *The Legend of Good Women*, where he is reviled openly and at length. Theseus cannot reach the sexual and political satisfactions of marriage and settled government because claims by conquest are corrosive of efforts to construct the good polity. If the bonds of friendship, as Aristotle says, are the basis of the polity, then rule by conquest, as it is shown to be inimical to friendship in *The Knight's Tale*, is also inimical to the polity.[30] In the grove, the Knight restates the Franklin's favorite aphorism in its fully political form: just as, according to the Franklin, love flees at the appearance of "maistrye," Aristotelian fellowship dissolves under the pressure of dominion wielded by conquest:

> O regne, that wolt no felawe have with thee!
> Ful sooth is seyd that love ne lordshipe
> Wol noght, his thankes, have no felaweshipe.
> (1624–26)

Chaucerian Grounds

Sometime after the coronation of Henry IV, Chaucer wrote a verse entitled "The Complaint of Chaucer to His Purse." It contains an "envoy" in which he directly addresses Henry with these words:

> O conquerour of Brutes Albyon,
> Which that by lyne and free eleccion
> Been verray kyng, this song to yow I sende,
> And ye, that mowen alle oure harmes amende,
> Have mynde upon my supplicacion.

Here Henry is apostrophized in imperial terms as the conqueror of the Albion of Brutus, as the translator, to put it technically, of the Roman imperial dominion to England. However, Chaucer does not include that credential among the two he then lists as qualifying Henry to be the true king: Henry is king *by lineage* and *by free election*.[31] The ambiguous treatment of the epithet "conqueror" must have been designed to please, because it is contained in a request for the payment of Chaucer's pension. But it must be noted that the triumph of conquest, trumpeted so loudly in the first line, is sharply limited by the clause that gives Henry's two common law claims to the crown. In the tradition of English advice to princes that Henry himself takes up, then, the "Complaint"—like *The Knight's Tale* before it—stresses the inadequacy of conquest. As the *General Prologue* moves to its end and introduces the first speaker, it takes up the question of causal determination that will underline all of the narration of *The Knight's Tale*:

Were it by aventure, or sort, or cas,
The sothe is this: the cut fil to the Knyght,
Of which ful blithe and glad was every wyght.
(844–46)

The observant jumble of these lines is perfectly matched by the opening lines of the "Complaint," where conquest, destiny, blood, and acclaim are thrown into a hyperbolic state of semicompatibility best described as overdetermination. Chaucer poses the Boethian philosophical issues of *The Knight's Tale*, not in the context of metaphysics but of political philosophy. Similarly, in light of Henry's English abjuration of conquest, Chaucer's apostrophe must be seen as only superficially and ambiguously epideictic. It teeters between praise and blame in a way that urges Henry, if he is to be truly more than a dominus by conquest, to pay Chaucer as a sign of that general obligation. I think Chaucer's songs, including *The Knight's Tale*, are best characterized as deliberative appeals to the hard case ("Were it by aventure, or sort, or cas"), requiring our ethical engagement under cover of a flourish of courtly, epideictic rhetoric. When Chaucer aligns his own wealth with the amendment of "alle oure harmes," it is markedly self-serving, but it also carefully limits the lawfulness of conquest and adds his voice, once again, to an important, political defense of consent that English poetry helped to keep alive in the common law.[32]

Notes

1. Introductions to these debates may be found in, e.g., John Gilchrist, *The Church and Economic Activity in the Middle Ages* (New York: St. Martin's Press, 1969); Brian Tierney, *The Crisis of Church and State, 1050–1300* (Toronto: University of Toronto Press, 1988); Brian Tierney, "Hierarchy, Consent, and the 'Western Tradition,'" *Political Theory* 15 (1987): 646–52; Norman Doe, *Fundamental Authority in Late Medieval English Law* (Cambridge: Cambridge University Press, 1990); Janet Coleman, "Property and Poverty," in *The Cambridge History of Medieval Political Thought: c. 350–c. 1450*, ed. J. H. Burns (Cambridge: Cambridge University Press, 1988), 607–48; J. H. Burns, *Lordship, Kingship and Empire: The Idea of Monarchy, 1400–1525* (Oxford: Clarendon Press, 1992); and Antony Black, *Political Thought in Europe, 1250–1450* (Cambridge: Cambridge University Press, 1992).

2. Cf. similar arguments by Thomas Aquinas, *Summa theologiae*, q. 57, and Aristotle, *The Politics*, 1252a25–35.

3. This chapter is part of a larger work in progress called "Conquest and Consent: The Grounds of Dominion in English Poetry and Political Thought, 1327–1649."

4. This historiography is now beginning to be altered by historians of ideas such as Brian Tierney and Richard Tuck and by the feminist critique of contractarianism, led by philosophers such as Carole Pateman. It may be that the most serious blow to the state of received ideas in the history of political thought will come from scholars who have begun to look at medieval and early modern Scottish, Irish, Welsh, and British histories in a comparatist way, rather than seeing constitutional history as either emanating only from Westminster, as the British legal historians have done, or seeing it as only a reaction against Westminster, as the nationalist historians of Ireland, Scotland, and indeed colonial America have done.

5. Thomas Walsingham, *Chronica maiora*, quoted from British Museum, Royal MS E ix, fol. 287a, in Albert B. Friedman, "'When Adam Delved...': Contexts of a Historic Proverb," in *The Learned and the Lewed: Studies in Chaucer and Medieval Literature*, ed. Larry D. Benson (Cambridge: Harvard University Press, 1974), 213. Friedman provides numerous citations of the proverb in English and other languages.

6. This is not a new argument in 1381 (for example, the equality of all men according to natural law is authoritative in Gregory the Great's sixth-century *Pastoral Rule*); however, the consequences of such a declaration vary widely. For example, it poses no essential threat to the legitimacy of slavery for Thomas Aquinas (*Summa theologiae*, q. 52). Although he admits there was no *dominium* (i.e., full or absolute dominion) in Eden, he restricts that claim to slavery and argues that other kinds of political dominion could have existed between men in the original state (*Summa theologiae*, q. 96).

7. Mary J. Carruthers, "Seeing Things: Locational Memory in Chaucer's *Knight's Tale*," in *Art and Context in Late Medieval English Narrative*, ed. Robert R. Edwards (Cambridge: D. S. Brewer, 1994), 106; and see Mary J. Carruthers, *The Book of Memory: A Study of Memory in Medieval Culture* (Cambridge: Cambridge University Press, 1990).

8. "Chaucerian politics," as Lee Patterson writes, are only "disingenuously and uncertainly apolitical"; introduction to *Literary Practice and Social Change in Britain, 1380–1530*, ed. Lee Patterson (Berkeley: University of California Press, 1990), 10.

9. About Ernst Kantorowicz and Michael Wilks, Larry Scanlon writes, "Because these scholars are interested in ideas rather than ideology, they have little to say about the way medieval ideas about kingship functioned culturally, how they maintained the power structure they conceptualized"; Scanlon, "The King's Two Voices: Narrative and Power in Hoccleve's *Regement of Princes*," in *Literary Practice and Social Change in Britain, 1380–1530*, ed. Patterson, 218. I might add that it is important to discover how ideas about kingship could also erode and interfere with the power structure they conceptualized.

10. E.g., Justinian, *Digest*, 1.4.1.

11. Aristotle, *Nichomachean Ethics*, trans. Terence Irwin (Indianapolis: Hackett, 1985), 1110b10.

12. Henry de Bracton, *On the Laws and Customs of England* (*De legibus et consuetudinibus angliae*), 4 vols., trans. Samuel E. Thorne (Cambridge: Harvard University Press, 1968–77), 2:304.

13. See the coronation oath of Edgar in the year 946, Carl Stephenson and Frederick George Marcham, trans. and ed., *Sources of English Constitutional History* (New York: Harper and Brothers, 1937), 18. The oath of Edward II is translated at 192.

14. R. E. Latham, *Revised Medieval Latin Word-List from British and Irish Sources* (London: Oxford University Press, 1965). On *raptus* and the law, see Christopher Cannon, "*Raptus* in the Chaumpaigne Release and a Newly Discovered Document Concerning the Life of Geoffrey Chaucer," *Speculum* 68 (1993): 74–94.

15. This habit is cited in the 33rd article of the parliamentary records of the deposition; *Rotuli parliamentorum*, 6 vols. (London, 1776–77), 3:415–34. Scanlon argues that the power of the article inheres in its narrative and rhetorical appeal to the ideological (rather than legal) fiction of the corporate nature of kingship and, further, that it is anachronistic to see the deposition primarily as "a matter of resisting tyranny" ("The King's Two Voices," 219–22).

16. Stephenson and Marcham, *Sources*, 254.

17. Compare the actions attributed to these characters to those of Theseus's men during the sack of Thebes.

18. Marsiglio of Padua, *Defensor pacis*, trans. Alan Gewirth (Toronto: University of Toronto Press, 1980), 31; cf. Aristotle, *The Politics*, 1287a1–1288b1.

19. Bracton, *Laws and Customs*, 2:305–6.

20. The role of Theseus in political philosophy continues into the early modern period. In *Il principe*, Machiavelli designates Theseus together with Moses, Cyrus, and Romulus as men who founded new states by means of "virtù" rather than "fortuna." Ac-

cording to Niccolò Machiavelli, Fortune gave Theseus the occasion and the dispersed (*dispersi*) Athenians, who then were, like Chaucer's Arcite and Palamoun, material to be shaped to the form of his dominion. See *The Prince: A Bilingual Edition*, trans. Mark Musa (New York: St. Martin's Press, 1964), 40–43.

21. All my references to Chaucer's poems are by line number to *The Riverside Chaucer*, ed. Larry D. Benson, 3rd ed. (Boston: Houghton Mifflin, 1987).

22. David Aers makes an excellent case for Chaucer's criticism of Theseus's militarism in *Chaucer, Langland, and the Creative Imagination* (London: Routledge and Kegan Paul, 1980), 174–95, and its "inquiry into problems of order in cultural and metaphysical dimensions, one which includes especial attention to the uses of metaphysical language by those in power, the transformations of metaphysics into an ideology of unreflexive secular domination" (195).

23. For example: "Order, which characterizes the structure of the poem, is also the heart of its meaning," according to Charles Muscatine, *Chaucer and the French Tradition* (Berkeley: University of California Press, 1969), 181. Not so Aers: "Although much of the misery the poet has displayed is based in specific human practices and choices encouraged by the culture over which Theseus presides, the duke never thinks of differentiating between 'that we may nat eschue' and what we *could* eschew with a change in outlook and practice"; *Chaucer, Langland, and the Creative Imagination*, 191.

24. Jill Mann, *Geoffrey Chaucer* (New York: Harvester Wheatsheaf, 1991), 165–85. On pity, see also Aristotle, *Nichomachean Ethics*, 1105b20–30. For an introduction to the bibliography of *The Knight's Tale*, see the explanatory notes of *The Riverside Chaucer* by Vincent J. DiMarco (826–28), and Lee Patterson, *Chaucer and the Subject of History* (Madison: University of Wisconsin Press, 1991), 165–68.

25. Lee Patterson's chapter "*The Knight's Tale* and the Crisis of Chivalric Identity," in *Chaucer and the Subject of History*, 165–230, provides an important social and historical analysis of characterization.

26. Richard A. Lanham, *A Handlist of Rhetorical Terms*, 2nd ed. (Berkeley: University of California Press, 1991), 104.

27. I am grateful to Katherine Rowe for coining the clever phrase *contractus interruptus* for me.

28. Catharine A. MacKinnon, e.g., *Feminism Unmodified: Discourses on Life and Law* (Cambridge: Harvard University Press, 1987), 46–62, and *Toward a Feminist Theory of the State* (Cambridge: Harvard University Press, 1989), 106–25. Romance has, I think, powerful resources for feminist jurisprudence.

29. Marsiglio of Padua, *Defensor minor*, 9.1, trans. Cary J. Nederman (New York: Cambridge University Press, 1993).

30. Aristotle, *Nichomachean Ethics*, 1155–72.

31. "Free eleccion" is an ambiguous term that carries a primary legal reference to the voluntary acclaim of the commons that had been staged at the coronation, but may also suggest Richard's purported designation of Henry as successor or Henry's choice to take the crown. I follow Paul Strohm's important example here by reading the complaint in the context of Lancastrian claims; Strohm, *Hochon's Arrow: The Social Imagination of Fourteenth-Century Texts* (Princeton, N.J.: Princeton University Press, 1992), 75–94.

32. I would like to thank Christopher Cannon, Larry Scanlon, David Wallace, and audiences at Stanford University, the University of Minnesota, and Harvard University for thinking this argument through with me.

❖

The "Unfaithful Wife" in Medieval Spanish Literature and Law

Louise Mirrer

No image of woman has been more frequently developed or cited in the history of Spanish literature than that of the unfaithful wife.[1] Collapsing the common notion of female lust as insatiable and uncontrollable[2] with the common definition of woman as "man's confusion," meaning that she is treacherous and deceitful,[3] the image appears and reappears across a broad spectrum of literary genres, from early lyric to contemporary drama.

In the Middle Ages, the image runs like a rich vein through popular as well as learned texts. For example, the medieval Castilian *Refranero* or proverb collection proffers women who deceive their husbands as protagonists in all but six of some eighty proverbs relating specifically to marital infidelity. These proverbs tend to generalize, denouncing married women without exception in such broad declarations as

Kada rratón tiene su nido, i kada muxer su abrigo i amigo[4]

[Every rat has its nest, and every woman her overcoat and her lover]

or

Muxer kasada, nunka asegurada.[5]

[A married woman is never a safe bet.]

The image also functions as the basis for the ballad of *La bella malmaridada* (The beautiful, unhappily married woman), a medieval text that has been glossed or cited with greater frequency than any other text in Spanish literary history.[6] This ballad reports a dialogue between a beautiful married woman and a man who begs her to take him as a lover. The man claims to have knowledge of her husband's faithlessness, and the woman, who apparently needs no further prompting, readily gives in, imploring the lover to take her away with him. At this point, the husband appears. One version of *La bella malmaridada*, probably dating from the fifteenth century but collected for the first time in Juan de Molina's *Cancionero* of 1527, reads as follows:

La bella mal maridada
de las lindas que yo vi
veote triste enojada
la verdad dila tu ami
si has de tomar amores
vida no dexes a mi
que a tu marido señora
con otra mujer lo vi
y besando y abraçando
mucho mal dize de ti
juraua y perjuraua
que te hauia de ferir
alli hablo la señora
alli hablo dixo assi
saquesme tu el cauallero
y sacasses me de aqui
por las tierras donde fueres
bien te sabre yo seruir
ellos en aquesto estando
su marido veyslo aqui.[7]

["Beautiful, unhappy wife
the most beautiful I've seen
I see you so sad and angry
tell me the truth.
If you are to take a lover
don't abandon me for another,
as your husband, my lady
with other women I've seen
kissing and gallivanting;
he speaks poorly of you,
he swore time and again
that he would do you harm."
At this, the lady spoke,
she spoke, and said this:
"Take me, oh, knight,
take me from here.
Wherever you may go
I'd know to serve you well."
While they were thus engaged,
Lo, the husband appeared.][8]

While not all versions and variants of *La bella malmaridada* have a denouement—some, like the above version, simply end with the appearance of the husband—many close by adding a second topic to the theme of the unfaithful wife. This is the criminal aspect of women's marital infidelity. Texts such as the *Bella malmaridada* variant collected in Lorenzo de Sepúlveda's 1551 *Romances nuevamente sacados de historias antiguas de las crónicas de España* provide graphic descriptions of the kinds of punishments unfaithful wives might receive. In Sepúlveda's text, it is the wife herself who articulates how her punishment might best be carried out:

> Con riendas de tu cauallo,
> señor açotes a mí.
> Con cordones de oro y sirgo
> biua ahorques a mí;
> enla huerta delos naranjos
> vida entierres tú amí.[9]
>
> [With your horsewhips,
> my lord, whip me.
> With golden towropes
> hang me alive;
> in the orange grove
> bury me alive.][10]

In other versions of *La bella malmaridada* and in such related ballads as *Albaniña* or *Blancaniña*, the husband, confronted with signs of his wife's infidelity, simply takes out his sword (or her lover's sword, which he has found in her bedroom) and kills her. In some texts, the husband returns his wife to her father, who takes out his sword and kills her.[11] Even when these ballads suggest that the woman's husband may truly be unfaithful and even cruel to her, punishment is often insisted upon. Women, as medieval male Spanish writers frequently declared, were supposed to learn to apply the restraints that God had given them.[12]

The insistence on punishment for female adultery—irrespective of surrounding circumstances—indeed comes into play in many medieval Spanish texts whose specific focus lies elsewhere. Many ballads relating to King Pedro I of Castile (known also as *el Cruel*), for example, although meant to highlight the king's despotic and bloodthirsty behavior, implicate his young wife—supposedly bludgeoned to death on her husband's orders—in her own horrific assassination, suggesting that her death was a punishment for an affair she had with the king's half brother. The alleged infidelity is seen as inexcusable, even though the texts thoroughly recognize the king's lack of sexual interest in his wife (he is said to have left her alone—and a virgin—on their wedding night, never to return), his long-standing relationship with a mistress, and the unproven nature of the accusation against the queen.[13] No matter how good a wife's reasons for taking a lover—and how uncertain her actual infidelity—female adultery remains a corporally punishable crime.

So obsessive could the concern with unfaithful wives and their punishment be that, in medieval Spanish literature, even a widow risked suffering the penalties of adultery. In the fourteenth-century *Libro de Buen Amor*, the widow Doña Endrina fears a "bad name"—and the punitive fines attaching to adultery—if she remarries before the close of a one-year waiting period:

> Si yo ante casase, sería enfamada,
> perdería la manda que a mí es mandada.
> (Sts. 759a-760b)[14]
>
> [If I should marry sooner, I would get a bad name;
> I would lose the inheritance that has been willed to me.][15]

Medieval Spanish law codes coincide with the literature's obsessive concern about unfaithful wives in their numerous prohibitions against, and punishments for, female adultery. The seventh-century *Fuero Juzgo*, for example, states that both the woman's husband and her father have the right to murder her with impunity (lib. 2, tít. 4, ley 9).[16] While the thirteenth-century *Siete Partidas*[17] discouraged men from taking the law into their own hands when it came to their wives' or daughters' adultery (part. 8, tít. 18, ley 13), it empowered the state to whip unfaithful wives publicly or to place them in a convent (part. 7, tít. 18, ley 15).[18] Recognizing that a woman could become pregnant as a result of an extramarital affair, the *Siete Partidas* also ruled that a widow must wait one year before remarrying so that paternity could be established for children born after a first husband's death (part. 4, tít. 6, ley 18, and tít. 7, ley 3; part. 4, tít. 12, ley 3).[19] When a woman broke these laws, she lost the rights granted her as a widow and faced punitive fines, including the forfeiture of the deceased husband's wedding gift to her (part. 4, tít. 12, ley 3). The municipal ordinances of the time also imposed punitive fines when the widow disregarded the one-year restriction on her remarriage.[20] In fact, the 1982 Spanish *Civil Code* maintains a similar restriction, stating that a widow may not remarry until three hundred days after the death of her husband or until after she gives birth, if pregnant.[21]

The coincidence of legal and literary discourses is so explicit and so direct in medieval Spain not only in the obsessive concern with female adultery, but also in the very punishments prescribed for adultresses—for example, death at the hands of a husband or father, public whipping, and financial penalties—that it is tempting to reread the literature as evidence for a particular theory of material culture. This theory would suggest that a society's official codes of behavior are reproduced in its literature, and that its literary works then serve the function of reinforcing and disseminating them to a wider audience. Inculcating in the populace society's official position, the literary texts simply channel the effects of power. Culture is accordingly identified as a series of mechanisms for controlling human behavior, with women, in this case, its subjects — that is, its subjects to control.[22] This would explain why women are so stereotyped in the literature; their depictions underline the uncontrollable sexuality and treachery of their gender and confirm the need for policing and controlling real women's behavior. The literature, in other words, both rehearses and rationalizes restrictive legal attitudes toward women, presenting a vision of them as requiring legal restraint.

It would seem, with respect to this theory, that the patterns of appropriate conduct laid out in the law codes and literary texts were actually followed by the population. One could reasonably assume that, while female adultery went on — otherwise, why all the concern about it? — when discovered, it was stamped out and dealt with viciously.[23] Medieval Spain, in this light, appears a monolithic culture, with direct correspondence at every level between the official codes and the types of behavior that they upheld and encouraged.

Indeed, medieval Spain is often seen this way. Lucy Sponsler, for example, identifies the status of married women during the period with the official legal positions of the various cultures that inhabited the peninsula. She concludes that "the Roman, Visigothic, Jewish, Arabic and Catholic influences during Spain's long history had combined to make the Spanish woman one of the most subordinated in all of Europe."[24] Anne Cruz also finds a direct relationship between official expectations of female behavior and women's everyday lives in her discussion of the ballad of *La bella malmaridada*. She indicates that the plight of the text's female protagonist responds specifically to the social expectations of Spanish women, and that the popularity of the text's theme "speaks eloquently to the situation of Hispanic married women."[25] Calling medieval Spanish proverbs exceptional in the context of other European traditions, Louis Combet draws a parallel between the relentless and strident hostility toward women manifested in the Castilian *Refranero* and the situation of real women in medieval Spain.[26] He writes, "Il est clair que c'est la femme, socialement moins bien armée, qui reçoit les plus rudes coups" (it is clear that it is the woman who, socially less well equipped, receives the harshest treatment).[27]

While, as Sponsler points out, "few people will be surprised to learn that the legal rights of women in Spain were...extremely restricted,"[28] many may be surprised to find evidence that medieval Spanish women not only ignored or broke the laws and precepts of literature regarding adultery, but they also appeared to get away with it. What's more, there seems to have been a standard legal way for letting them do so openly, and nonconformity with the laws and social codes prescribed for women in literature could actually be legalized.

Among the more than four hundred folia of a parchment-bound volume purchased by the Biblioteca Nacional in Madrid from the count of Miranda in 1757 are examples of fifteenth-century notarial formulae written expressly for the purposes of pardoning women for adultery.[29] The documents contained in this collection, marked on the back "Formulario antiguo de instrumentos públicos," do not appear to be aberrations — unusual or exceptional instances of charitable deeds. On the contrary, they are among numerous model agreements or templates specifically designed to accommodate the need for rapid redaction of the most frequent of juridical acts. Through such slight touches as the replacement of the words *fulano* and *fulana* ("John Doe" and "Jane Doe" would be the English equivalents) with the real names of the parties involved, or *de tal lugar* (of such a place) with the real name of a town or village, documents such as these allowed scribes and notaries to make the most common types of agreements legal without having to generate a new contract every time the names of plaintiffs, places, dates, witnesses, and so on changed. They are thus among the most important sources for the law as people actually lived it, and from them we may be able to intuit most fruitfully what really happened in medieval Spanish society.

One key document found in the collection is entitled "Nota de carta de perdón que da el marido a su esposa e a su muger de adulterio que le fiso" (Notary's letter of pardon that the husband gives to his wife and his woman for the adultery that she committed).[30] In the approximately two thousand words of this document, *fulano* (John Doe) exempts himself and his wife, *fulana* (Jane Doe), from all of the laws, statutes, rights, customs, decrees, and decretals regarding adultery in the ecclesiastic as well as secular realms — including the home, court, and chancellery of the king, and every city, town, and place in the kingdom. A sample taken from the very repetitious document reads as follows:

> Renuncio e parto e quito de mi e de mi favor e ayuda todaslas leys e fueros e derechos e costunbres e decretos e decretales usados e por usar asi eclesiasticos commo seglares, ansi en general commo en especial, e yo nin otro por mi, aya nin pudiese aver en contra lo que dicho es, nin contra parte dello sea, e que non acorra nin aprovechen en alguna manera nin de cartas que tenga ganadas o por ganar de aqui adelante del Rey o de Reyna o de Infante heredero o de otro sennor o sennora nin de omme poderoso nin de persona alguna.[31]

> [I renounce and depart from and deprive myself and my protection of the ecclesiastic as well as secular, general as well as special, laws and *fueros* and rights and customs and decrees and decretals used

and to be used, and neither I, nor another for me, shall be able to go against the aforesaid, nor against part of the aforesaid, nor be helped by nor take advantage of in some manner either the charters sustained or to be sustained from here on in by the King or Queen or Royal Prince Heir, or other lord or lady or powerful man or any person at all.]

In its wording, this particular document shows keen awareness of the very many official sanctions and judgments against adultery extant in medieval Spain. Indeed, before declaring the adulterous wife absolved, the document spells out a number of possible remedies available to—in fact, required of—an aggrieved husband, including criminal and civil proceedings resulting in corporal punishment and confiscation of the wife's property. But, in its explicit rejection of such remedies, the document makes it clear that Spanish society, at least in the fifteenth century, did not necessarily respond to unfaithful wives with the sword or the whip or stiff financial penalties, even if the written, official codes of behavior—enforced by the king, among others—insisted upon it.

There is, it is true, an appeal made to a "higher authority" in the document. *Fulano*'s renunciation of any and all earthly legal remedies is linked to the forgiveness of Christ, who, as the document points out, not only accepted a cruel death, but also pardoned those who meted it out to him:

Jesucristo que no solamente quiso la su muerte cruel sin merescimiento dada, el perdonó a los que gela dieron e fisieron dar, mas rogó a su padre muy santo nuestro sennor Dios que les perdonase.[32]

[Jesus Christ, who not only sought a cruel death which he did not deserve, but pardoned those who meted it out to him, and also begged his very holy father our lord God to pardon them.]

But the identification between *fulano* and Christ is not central to the document; on the other hand, *fulano*'s perceived independence from official codes of behavior is.

It is interesting that the document alludes to women's, as well as men's, capacity for independent action, repeatedly proclaiming women's liberty as well as their power to do as they wish. *Fulano* declares several times that his wife, released from the penalties prescribed for her crime, is free to do with herself, her body, her material goods, and her personal finances whatever any "honorable" woman would do: "que vos fagades e podades faser de vos e de vuestro cuerpo commo toda muger honrrada libre e quita e escrita e en su libre poderio" [that you may do with yourself and your body as would any honorable woman free of debt and judgments against her and acting in accordance with her own free will].[33] This expression of women's liberation, like the pardon itself, makes the law as it was actually lived in medieval Spain appear quite different from the law as reproduced in literary texts and from the law as set down in the *Fuero Juzgo, Siete Partidas, Ordenanzas Reales,* or even the municipal ordinances and local statutes that Heath Dillard, for example, has found so useful in nuancing traditional understandings of married women's status in medieval Spain.[34]

The theme of women's freedom to do as they wished with themselves, their bodies, their material goods, and their personal finances runs through a second fifteenth-century notarial letter of pardon found in the count of Miranda's collection, as well. This document similarly entails a *fulano* (John Doe) who renounces all laws regarding adultery in both secular and ecclesiastic realms. In this instance, however, the letter is meant to be signed by the wife as well as the husband. It is also even more exaggerated in its insistence on individuals' capacities for independent action, irrespective of written, official codes. *Fulano,* in fact, specifically renounces all the laws, statutes, and ecclesiastic rulings deliberately designed to prohibit a man from pardoning his wife's adultery:

Dixeron que renunciavan e renunciaron toda la ley e fuero e derecho eclesiastico seglar e general e especial que contra lo contenido en esta carta fuese e especialmente dixeron que renunciavan e renunciaron el derecho que dixe que non puede perdonar la injuria que le es por faser e aso mismo renunció el derecho que dixe que non puede el omme dar licencia a su muger para se casar o faser adulterio o pecado de carne con otro.[35]

[They said that they were renouncing and renounced all laws, *fueros,* and ecclesiatic, secular, general, and special rights that the contents of this letter contradict, and they especially said that they were renouncing and renounced the right that says that such harm cannot be pardoned and the right that says that a man cannot allow his wife to marry or to commit adultery or carnal sin with another.]

He, in addition, renounces the law that states that general renunciations (presumably such as the one made in this document) are illegal. In cosigning the document, *fulano*'s wife, *fulana,* pardons her husband for his adultery as he pardons her for hers. This is interesting because nowhere in the main body of laws or in literature is there much concern expressed about infidelity in the case of unfaithful husbands. We have already seen, in the ballad of *La bella malmaridada,* that a wife is punished for adultery even in cases where her husband is also unfaithful. No mention is made of any punishment for the husband in any of the many versions of this text. Moreover, in law codes such as the *Fuero Juzgo,* while a wife was allowed to punish her husband's consort if—and only if— she was an unmarried woman, no mention at all is made of her right to punish her own husband (lib. 3 tít. 4, ley 9).[36] The *Siete Partidas* does allow a couple to separate if either partner commits adultery (part. 5, tít. 2, ley 7); however, it does not allow a wife to accuse her husband of committing adultery with another man's wife, reserving this right for the other man alone (part. 7, tít. 18, ley 1). Indeed, this state of affairs did not change much until 1971, before which time the *Spanish Penal Code* stipulated exile for the husband who caught his wife in flagrante delicto and murdered her, but imprisonment until death for the woman who murdered her husband under the same circumstances.[37]

It is interesting to find that, in this second document, *fulana*, or Jane Doe, in a passage relating to her alone, specifically renounces the laws of the Roman emperors that spoke in favor of and in support of women ("la ley de los enperadores Justiniano e Valiano e Costantino que fablan en favor e ayuda de las mugeres").[38] Medieval Spanish society did not, it would appear, see women as so disadvantaged by the influence of Roman law as modern scholars seem to.

Written laws may be, as François Baume suggests, the smallest part of the legislative and juridical baggage of a people.[39] The brief and concise text of a general law cannot hope to elaborate the many and varied facts of everyday life. This is why such notarial documents as those cited above are so interesting and important to look at. But focusing on more than just the state's discourse radically alters the customary picture of medieval Spain as a rather monolithic culture, with direct correspondence at every level between official codes and the types of behavior these codes upheld and encouraged. It is interesting, in this context, to revisit the theme of the unfaithful wife in medieval Spanish literature, and to see if those moments when dissident subjects appear in the social text can similarly be traced.

Might, for example, a ballad such as *La bella malmaridada*, which appears transparently to reproduce the official legal position of unfaithful wives in medieval Spain, also project into the text female subjects who resisted that position?

As mentioned earlier, some versions of *La bella malmaridada* have no denouements and therefore fail to spell out a precise punishment for the unfaithful wife's crime. The traditional understanding of such truncation is that medieval Spanish audiences would already know the outcome of the story (in other words, they knew what was in store for the adulterous wife) and a denouement was therefore unnecessary and even undesirable within the artistic economy of the text. With or without a clear resolution, the ballad, according to this view, played a critical role in enforcing female social conformity, particularly as ballad audiences appear to have included women.

Yet, as we know from certain theories of reception,[40] "gaps" in literature allow listeners and readers actively to participate in the production of textual meaning. Thus it is not at all clear that, with or without a denouement, the texts subjected women to control. It is, indeed, possible to understand, in the truncated versions of this text and others like it, a deliberate rendering of the outcome as ambiguous and unstable and a therefore ambivalent attitude toward unhappily married women.[41]

While the options available to the unhappily married woman are of course not specified in the ballads without denouements, neither are any of the official legal solutions. Other popular medieval Spanish texts that describe husbands who are ridiculed as a result of their wives' infidelity hint at a similar ambiguity. Although almost always seen to operate strictly within the conventional discourses of law, religion, and, in particular, antifeminism, these texts may even criticize or undercut conventional values. Because they tend to focus more on husbands than on wives, women in them may even appear to get away with adultery. One popular proverb, for example, sets up a dialogue between an unfaithful wife and her cuckolded husband:

"Kornudo sois, marido" ["You've been cuckolded, husband"], the wife says.

"Muxer," ["Wife,"] the husband replies, ¿i kién te lo dixo? ["And who told you that?"].[42]

The *Disciplina clericalis* of Petrus Alphonsi (a Christian convert born Moisés Sefardi in 1062) is an early repository for examples of unpunished female adultery.[43] This text describes the various ruses used by unfaithful wives to conceal their lovers from their husbands (blinding them with a squirt of milk from their breasts, holding up a sheet or a pot that they claim needs mending, declaring that their lover is a refugee from criminals outside, and locking their husbands out of the house). In popular balladry, an entertaining variation on this theme incorporates a novel rendering of the "Puss in Boots" tale. In some texts, the treacherous wife, caught in flagrante delicto, insists to her husband that the figure sleeping beside her in bed is a cat, not a man. In the modern oral tradition, the perplexed husband replies:

Muchas tierras traigo andadas, Cataluña y Aragón,
y en mi vida he visto un gato de botas y pantalón.[44]

[Many lands have I traveled, including Catalonia and Aragon,
but never in my life have I seen a cat wearing boots and trousers.]

While texts such as these reproduce offical attitudes by reinforcing the stereotype of women as requiring external control, it is possible to see in them also women's alternatives. Indeed, these texts' female subjects appear to refuse subjection, so that even within the most conservative of conventions, women's liberation from male domination is explored.

The episode of the widow, Doña Endrina, in the *Libro de Buen Amor* may be another case in point. While the text leaves unclear whether or not Endrina's one-year waiting period is actually up and thus whether or not she is liable for penalties as an adulteress, it does underscore her resistence to the doctrinally inspired and legally approved model of chaste widowhood. Indeed, although the text reinforces and disseminates this model through a series of allegorical warnings against incontinence targeted specifically at a female audience, it also shows the contradictory effects of power, projecting, in its image of an independent widow, a woman liberated from male control—free to do, as the notarial documents say—as she wishes with herself, her body, and her finances.[45]

In an admittedly preliminary way, I hope to have questioned here—at least in the context of the popular theme of the unfaithful wife—the relationship among law, literature, and the subjects that the legal and literary discourses of medieval Spain were meant to control. While the culture's extraordinary focus on unfaithful wives and their punishment must still be seen as part of an official effort to demonstrate women's need for external control, medieval Spain must also be considered as a society whose subjects were inclined to see themselves, irrespective of officialdom, as autonomous and free. Thus, although there may have been in the society an extreme dependence on cultural production for reinforcing and disseminating official, legal positions, there may also have been more pockets of resistance and disruption within the social text than we often tend to think.

Notes

1. For discussion, see Louis Combet, *Recherches sur le "Refranero" Castillan* (Paris: Belles Lettres, 1971); Anne J. Cruz, "*La Bella Malmaridada*," in *Culture and Control in Counter-Reformation Spain*, ed. Anne J. Cruz and Mary Elizabeth Perry (Minneapolis: University of Minnesota Press, 1992), 145–70; Harriett Goldberg, "Two Parallel Medieval Commonplaces: Antifeminism and Antisemitism in the Hispanic Literary Tradition," in *Aspects of Jewish Culture in the Middle Ages*, ed. Paul E. Szarmach (Albany: SUNY Press, 1979), 85–119; Donald McGrady, "Análisis de *La bella malmaridada*, de Lope," in *Estudios sobre el Siglo de Oro en homenaje a Raymond R. MacCurdy*, ed. Angel González et al. (Madrid: Cátreda, 1983), 83–101; and Félix Lope de Vega, *La bella malmaridada*, ed. Donald McGrady and Suzanne Freeman (Charlottesville, Va.: Biblioteca Siglo de Oro, 1986), introduction, 22–30.
2. Some medieval Spanish writers likened women's uncontrollable lust to a runaway horse. See Fray Martín de Córdoba, *Jardín de nobles donzellas: A Critical Edition and Study*, ed. Harriet Goldberg, University of North Carolina Studies in the Romance Languages and Literatures 137 (Chapel Hill: University of North Carolina Press, 1974), 195; Luis de Lucena, *Repetición de amores*, ed. Jacob Ornstein (Chapel Hill: University of North Carolina Press, 1954). See also Goldberg, "Two Parallel Medieval Commonplaces," 93.
3. This definition of woman is found in the thirteenth-century *Historia de Segundo*; see Hermann Knust, *Mittheilungen aus dem Eskurial* (Tübingen, 1879), 503; Goldberg, "Two Parallel Medieval Commonplaces," 93.

4. Combet, *Recherches*, 430; unless otherwise noted, translations are my own.

5. Ibid., 428.

6. See Cruz, *"La Bella Malmaridada,"* 151.

7. Juan de Molina, *Cancionero* (1527), ed. Antonio Rodríguez-Moñino (Valenci: Castalia, 1952).

8. I have used here Cruz's excellent translation; *"La Bella Malmaridada,"* 151–52.

9. Lorenzo de Sepúlveda, *Romances nuevamente sacados de historias antiguas de las crónicas de España* (Antwerp, 1551).

10. Cruz's translation; *"La Bella Malmaridada,"* 153.

11. See, for discussion of this text in the modern tradition, Teresa Catarella, "Feminine Historicizing in the *romancero novelesco*," *Bulletin of Hispanic Studies* 67 (1990): 331–43.

12. De Cordoba, *Jardín de nobles donzellas*, 195. See also de Lucena, *Repetición*, 85; and Goldberg, "Two Parallel Medieval Commonplaces," 93.

13. I have discussed these texts at length in Mirrer, *The Language of Evaluation: A Sociolinguistic Approach to the Story of Pedro el Cruel in Ballad and Chronicle* (Amsterdam: Benjamins, 1986).

14. Juan Ruiz, *Libro de Buen Amor*, ed. Jacques Joset (Madrid: Espasa-Calpe, 1974).

15. I have used Willis's translation: Juan Ruiz, *Libro de Buen Amor*, ed. Raymond Willis, with an introduction and English paraphrase (Princeton, N.J.: Princeton University Press, 1972).

16. The *Fuero Juzgo*, promulgated in 654 A.D., blended Roman and Germanic law. See *Códigos españoles*, ed. Antonio de San Martín (Madrid, 1872), vol. 1.

17. The *Siete Partidas*, compiled in the thirteenth century by Alfonso X, was considered to have put into romance all ecclesiastical as well as secular laws; see *Códigos españoles*, vol. 3. The object of the work, as stated in its prologue, was to impose the *Siete Partidas* as the sole body of laws in Alfonso's kingdom. By the mid–fourteenth century, the *Partidas* was accepted as such, although the validity of urban *fueros* and noble privileges was still recognized. Alfonso X, in dating his work by the Hegira as well as by the Christian era, spoke as ruler of all Muslims as well as of all Christians.

18. The preoccupation with women's sexual behavior within marriage manifested in the legal codes probably stemmed from the belief that the married woman, as the bearer of children, was the chief guardian of the family. The *Partidas*, for example, give this as the reason for marriage being called *matrimony* and not patrimony; part. 4, tít. 2, ley 2. See also Lucy A. Sponsler, "The Status of Married Women under the Legal System of Spain," *Journal of Legal History* 3, no. 2 (1982): 125–52, esp. 127. The *Partidas* give the same reason in order to justify strict control over the married woman's sexual behavior. Indeed, the *Partidas* recognized that a woman could become pregnant as a result of an extramarital affair. Thus, when the married woman committed adultery, the entire family structure was at stake. She could produce offspring who might compete with a husband's own legitimate heirs. She might even, in the worst possible scenario, seek to do away with her husband in order to remarry a lover, and then mistreat or kill her first husband's children; part. 4, tít. 16, ley 5. Since female adultery raised the issues of paternity and inheritance in a way that male adultery did not, the law codes viewed the married woman, and not the married man, as a grave potential threat to the family structure.

19. The *Siete Partidas* dealt with this concern by outlining a complex series of steps to be taken in the case of a pregnant widow. They also put forth a number of laws designed to prevent a widow's mistreatment of her first husband's children — or indeed her consent to their deaths — in order to please a new husband; see Sponsler, "Legal Status," 148; part. 6, tít. 16, ley 5.

20. See, for discussion, Heath Dillard, *Daughters of the Reconquest* (Cambridge: Cambridge University Press, 1984), 98.

21. *Código Civil*, Boletín Oficial del Estado (Madrid: Ministero de Justicia, 1980), article 45. See also Sponsler, "Legal Status," 129.

22. See, for discussion of this concept in Spanish culture, Anthony J. Cascardi, "The Subject of Control," in *Culture and Control*, ed. Cruz and Perry, 231–54, esp. 235.

23. There is, in fact, strong disagreement among critics on the extent to which husbands did murder their adulterous wives. For two opposing points of view, see Melveena McKendrick, *Woman and Society in the Spanish Drama of the Golden Age: A Study of the "Mujer varonil"* (Cambridge: Cambridge University Press, 1974), and María Helena Sánchez Ortega, "La mujer en el Antiguo Régimen: Tipos históricos y arquetipos literarios," in *Nuevas perpectivas sobre la mujer*, Actas de las Primeras Jornadas de Investigación Interdisciplinaria (Madrid: Universidad Autónoma, 1980).

24. Sponsler, "Legal Status," 125.

25. Cruz, "*La Bella Malmaridada*," 149, 151.

26. "Même si les proverbes cité par Morawski et Le Roux de Lincy restent, dans leur majorité, dans la perspective misogyne médiévale, on n'y trouve pas — du moins de façon aussi systématique — l'âpreté hargneuse qui donne sa tonalité spécifique au *refranero* consacré à la femme"; Combet, *Recherches*, 277.

27. Ibid., 278.

28. Sponsler, "Legal Status," 125.

29. The folia are collected, but not edited, in Luisa Cuesta Gutiérrez, *Formulario notarial castellano del siglo XV* (Madrid: Ministerio de Justicia y Consejo Superior de Investigaciones Científicas, 1947). I give page references throughout to Cuesta Gutiérrez's text.

30. Cuesta Gutiérrez, *Formulario notarial*, 183–86.

31. Ibid., 186.

32. Ibid., 184.

33. Ibid., 185.

34. Dillard, *Daughters of the Reconquest*. See also Dillard, "Women in Reconquest Castile: The Fueros of Sepúlveda and Cuenca," in *Women in Medieval Society*, ed. Brenda M. Bolton et al. (Philadelphia: University of Pennsylvania Press, 1976), 71–94.

35. Cuesta Gutiérrez, *Formulario notarial*, 188.

36. In the *Fuero Juzgo*, adultery on the part of the wife was a grounds for separation (lib. 3, tít. 6, ley 2), but there is no mention of what happened in the case of adultery on the part of the husband.

37. *Leyes penales* (Madrid: Editorial Civitas, 1975), art. 405; Sponsler, "Legal Status," 144.

38. Cuesta Gutiérrez, *Formulario notarial*, 188.

39. François Baume, *Introduction a l'étude historique du droit coutumier français*, 141.

40. E.g., "reader reception" theory.

41. Catarella, "Feminine Historicizing," develops this point with respect to the modern oral tradition.

42. Combet, *Recherches*, 429.

43. Petrus Alphonsi, *Disciplina clericalis*, ed. Angel González Palencia (Madrid, 1948). See Goldberg, "Two Parallel Medieval Commonplaces," 93–94.

44. Catarella, "Feminine Historicizing," 337. In a number of versions, the husband proceeds to take out his sword and stab his wife three times.

45. While the episode, as I suggested earlier, rather faithfully reproduces the legal position of widows in medieval Spain — not to mention the stereotyped image of widows as less able to control their passions and therefore requiring the control of law and doctrine — it projects as its subject one of the medieval world's more powerful female types. In medieval Spanish law, widows were provided with a large number of capacities in which they could act on their own, including the right to assume administrative control over family property and the right to choose their own partner, should they decide to remarry; see Dillard, *Daughters*, 96–126.

CHAPTER 7

❖

The Rights of
Medieval English Women
Crime and the Issue of Representation

Christopher Cannon

*The Middle Ages were resolutely male. All the opinions that reach and
inform me were held by men, convinced of the superiority of their sex.
I hear only them.*

— George Duby

The written record of the Middle Ages resists our efforts to reconstruct what Carolyn Dinshaw describes in a clarifying phrase as
"lived lives," and it seems most to thwart us when the lives we
seek to reconstruct are the lives lived by women.[1] Inherent in the record
that we use for such reconstruction, says George Duby, is a kind of
"screen between our eyes and what our eyes want to see": we may "measure this distance" and "perceive the distortion," or we "must give up
the positivist dream of attaining past reality" and recognize that "this
screen can never be completely penetrated."[2] The law of medieval England, my main subject in this essay, proceeds by an even more general
logic of obfuscation, one that extends to the lives of medieval men as
well as women. This law leaves a legacy of the recorded word more vo-
luminous than historians have as yet been able to read in detail, but these
words are largely instrumental in their function, prompted by events often unmentioned or artfully concealed, designed to secure ends often unspecified or misrepresented. As William Maitland laments these general
distortions, the court may be "miraculously clear in our spotlight" but
"the world around it, . . . the world of fact," lies wholly "in the dark."[3]

But what if the screen itself signifies? In what follows I will argue
that distortions may themselves be "facts" miraculously clear in our spotlight, that — to abandon, finally, honest but misleadingly hypostasizing
images — the record's overt resistance *is* the resistance lived in the life
and, particularly, in the lives lived by women. I focus by design here on
the records of crime (in particular, on enrollments in the Court of King's
Bench) in order to seek such resistances where they appear to have been
most acute. The ground for a woman's recorded presence at law was generally a wrong directed at her possessions or her person: the nature and
ambit of the female lives court rolls describe begin in a woman's hurt.
The law often intensified this hurt in the instance of its legal recording

by severely limiting the forms in which a woman might rightly demand
or receive redress for her injury (irrespective of the general proof she
might offer of its occurrence). But in setting out these limitations in detail the criminal record also unfolds as an extraordinarily detailed narrative of lived limits, of the *experience* of legal restriction, and, as I will
also argue, of the recruitment of such restriction *by* women for their
own signifying purposes.

This last, more positive, ramification is given useful summary as
William Langland uses it to confect the allegorical legal proceedings involving Lady Mede in *Piers Plowman*.[4] Mede is made to "com to þe kynges court," and her presence "in þe myddes and [al þis meynee] after"
results in a predictable debate among male figures about her—but after
several hundred lines as the subject of legal proceedings, Mede pushes
her way forward and demands her own "space to speke" to "spede if she
myȝte."[5] Her demand and the court's recognition of it ("the kyng graunted
hire grace wiþ a good wille" [III.172]) have no large result since Mede is
finally silenced, but the episode nevertheless crucially records the limitations of the law on female action *as* the actions of a female figure press
against them. In the allegorical case, as in numerous enrolled cases, legal restraint is itself responsible for a document in which a woman (to
borrow a phrase Rita Copeland adapts from William Thorpe) "stretches
forth a life as a legible text."[6] As I will argue here, the general circumstances that allowed medieval English women to "com to the kynges
court" gave them the *right* (in the strictest legal sense) to stretch forth
their lives in this manner, that is, at and through legal boundaries. The
larger issue the criminal records finally disclose—both what is at stake
in and what results from women's presence in them—is the right that
even legal disability gave medieval women to such a "space to speke"
and, therefore, to the documentary representation of their lives. Langland's is not the only recognition of this right outside the criminal law,
either, and, in the most general terms, what the criminal records finally
show is how the theory that gave women this right in court could be addressed by medieval English women to all forms of textual authority in
order to gain access, finally, to documents of every representational kind.

Recovering Covered Lives

The English law ought to be the wrong place to search for evidence of
the lived lives of women, given the systematic exclusion of women from
most of the rights accorded by that law until relatively recently. The
roots of this long exclusion are clear enough in the monumental summary of the legal principle medieval England provided for itself, the *De
legibus et consuetudinibus Angliae,* a thirteenth-century treatise commonly attributed to Henry Bracton (and therefore commonly called *Bracton*).[7] *Bracton* begins with an outline of the relations the law regulated

between what are called "persons" (*personae*), who are considered first, of all issues in the law, because, *Bracton* says, all rights derive from them (*quarum causa statuta sunt omnia iura*). That rationale becomes the ground on which women are effectively excluded from all such rights by this treatise's initial mode of classification (the "*prima divisione personarum*"), in which women are not even mentioned (2:29). Only after lengthy definition of freemen and bondsmen, the nature of freedom, the nature of bondsmen, the source of bondage, the source of freedom, the proper designation of the free, and what *personae* are to be counted as children does this treatise finally arrive at a classification of persons that mentions women. They do not fare so well by this mention: "Mankind may also be classified in another way: male, female, or hermaphrodite. Women differ from men in many respects, for their position is inferior to that of men."[8]

Women exist in relation to the category of *personae* precisely as they are inferior, and later on in this section *Bracton* goes this categorical subjection one better by further excluding women even from regulated forms of servitude. *Personae*, *Bracton* suggests, may be either "free or bond," "*sui juris*" or within the *potestas* of another, within the wardship of lords, or the *cura* of relatives (2:35), and tacked onto this clear set of distinctions, neither clearly *sui juris* nor within the *potestates* or *curae* regulated by the law of persons, come women: "Some [persons] are under the rod [*sub virga*], as wives, etc."[9] Women are persons, *Bracton* implies, only as they *are* wives. Later, in a remark that predicts much of later legal theory about the status of English women, *Bracton* makes explicit what the phrase "*sub virga*" implies: "A husband and wife ... are, so to speak, a single person, because they are one flesh and blood."[10] This doctrine, often called "unity of person" in histories of English law, measures the extreme of a medieval woman's disability: her legal person was defined only when she was a wife, but, as a wife, she was excluded from the very rights that the theory of person existed to confer.

Small wonder then that legal history has remembered English women largely in terms of this doctrine, in the role of "wife," under the severe legal disadvantage marriage meant, as "unity of person" is sometimes also described, under the "coverture" of her husband. The *locus classicus* of this pervasive view is the section on "husbands and wives" in William Blackstone's *Commentaries on the Laws of England* (1765) devoted to the "rights of persons."[11] Blackstone's paternalistic condescension toward women there ("even the disabilities, which the wife lies under, are for the most part intended for her protection and benefit. So great a favourite is the female sex of the laws of England" [1:445]) is as legendary as his definitive summary of this doctrine. For Blackstone and, therefore, for much subsequent legal history, a woman is disabled from exercising most of the "rights of persons" precisely because the "husband or wife are one person in law": the "legal existence of the woman is suspended during the marriage . . . incorporated and consolidated into that of the husband: under whose wing, protection and cover, she performs every thing" (1:442). J. H. Baker's more recent *Introduction to English Legal History* updates Blackstone with a similarly stark summary of this legal theory:

> The origin of the doctrine, and its one-sidedness, may be found in the traditional inferiority of women, and the power which social custom vested in the husband over his wife. According to the scriptures, woman was created for man and bound to obey him. . . . her husband or *baron* was both her sovereign and her guardian. If she killed him it was not simple murder, but treason. He looked after her and her property during the "coverture," while she was incapable of owning separate property or of making her own contracts. She could not sue or be sued at common law without her *baron*, and this prevented her from suing him for any wrong done to her.[12]

It is a simple scheme that seems to put up an impenetrable screen not only between women and any legal rights they might exercise, but also between the historian and any evidence of the lives of individual women in earlier periods. Because "unity of person" has, as Maitland points out (and as Baker points out here), "the warrant of holy writ," it has been extremely easy to see it as a "ruling principle" of English law since the Middle Ages (2:406).

But there is a problem here, and Maitland notes it with a tenacity that has, I think, been too little recognized. He recommends that we be "on our guard" against regarding the doctrine as a "common belief" and works to disassemble the explanatory power of the doctrine in the medieval period in particular (2:405–6). Certain lines for that disassembly are clear enough in the summaries of the doctrine I have just given. Not all women were married, and even though the law tended to view them chiefly in such terms (as potentially "marriageable" even when unmarried), "unity of person" cannot, by definition, account for the legal status of unmarried women. Baker's summary demonstrates a second problem with the historical account of "unity of person" in two footnotes describing the weakening of the doctrine in the Married Women's Property Acts of 1870 and 1882 (398 nn. 22–23). These notes show that Baker's description of the doctrine is really a conspectus of the history of English law up until the twentieth century ("The *feme covert* was finally given the same contractual capacity as a *feme sole* in 1935" [399]). The strong medieval roots for the doctrine in *Bracton* notwithstanding, a broad historical view distorts the validity of "unity of person" to medieval law because that doctrine increased in power until the end of the last century; it was not yet in full operation during the Middle Ages. Maitland criticizes the "common assumption . . . that from the age of savagery until the present age every change in marital law has been favourable to the wife" (2:403). He suggests that "unity of person" describes the "final shape that [the] common law took" (2:403), that it was a "goal" of English law (2:405), but, he urges, "a consistently operative principle it cannot be" (2:406). There are chinks in the armature of "coverture" that even Blackstone must admit (husbands and wives, he points out in an aside, may act as "two distinct persons" in "civil law" [1:444]). Maitland attributes overreliance on the concept to its compelling rhetorical power (it serves "to round a paragraph") and its seductive simplicity (it "now and again leads us out of...a difficulty"), but, by his account, it was precisely *not* a doctrine in medieval law (2:406). In place of "unity of person" Maitland advocates a description of medieval law nuanced enough to account for women's legal abilities: "We cannot, even within the sphere of property law, explain the marital relationship as being simply the subjection of the wife to her husband's will. He constantly needs her concurrence, and the law takes care that she shall have an opportunity of freely refusing her assent to his acts" (2:407).

Balanced against the growing rigor of the doctrine of "unity of person," a door seems to open here to a history that finds advantage in the legal position of medieval women when compared with the strictures early modern and modern law would bring.[13] Such a view may have a claim where it focuses only on the law of property,[14] but *Bracton* alone sets a firm limit to any such contrast: women living *"sub virga"* were hardly living in a "golden age."[15] And Maitland is not really emphasizing medieval women's advantages so much as he is dismissing "unity of person" as a way of defining medieval women's *dis*advantages in the period; he suggests that the more complex specificities of medieval legal provisions—many of them explicit in the practice of law and discussed carefully nowhere in its theory—need to be defined in that doctrine's stead; he implies that the doctrine is *not* the screen in the law obscuring medieval women from legal history's view but, rather, the screen preventing legal history from seeing the activities of women that the record actually makes manifest.

A useful theory for describing those activities informs the method of a treatise of the early seventeenth century called, significantly, the *Lawes Resolutions of Womens Rights* (1632).[16] This treatise is ideally placed in the history of the law to take broad retrospect of medieval England without interference from the later changes that obscure the picture in Blackstone and Baker, and its provocative stance is to view women's general disadvantage under the law as precisely the opportunity to tease out what women *could* do as they lived within the confines of general strictures. Its point of departure for a discussion of "rights" is then, paradoxically, women's legal dependence: "[Women] have nothing to do in constituting Lawes, or consenting to them, in interpreting of Lawes, or in hearing them interpreted at lectures, leets or charges, and yet they stand strictly tyed to mens establishments, little or nothyng excused by ignorance" (2).

Its declared function is educative: it wants to make sure women "stand upon their owne guard" against laws that "are not more rigorously penned, than sometime put in execution against them" (399). But the larger point of its summary, as outlined in an introductory epistle "To the Reader" (a woman reader, it seems clear) is to understand the very rigor of the law's definition of a woman's disadvantage as a reflexively rigorous definition of her legal allowance. "Women's Rights," this epistle says, "comprehends all our Lawes concerning Women."[17] The treatise therefore contains a summary of all the "Lawes Provision for Woemen," be those provisions subjugating or empowering, as those provisions are laid out in precedent treatises, statutes, and the representative case-law.[18] As a result of this provocative stance, what are often represented as "rights" in this treatise are exactly the kind of provisions a modern reader would very much want to call "wrongs": "If a man beat an out-law, a traitor, a Pagan, his villein, or his wife it is dispunishable, because by the Law Common these persons can have no action" (128). And yet as a part of this stance, the treatise is also extraordinarily cagey in its interpretation of such disabling "rights." In the case of a husband's right to beat his wife, for example, the treatise wins through to this logical response:

> If it be in none other regard lawfaull to beat a man's wife, then because the poore wench can sue no other action for it, I pray why may not the Wife beat the Husband againe, what action can he have if she doe.... If he come to the Chancery or Justices in the Country of the peace against her, because her recognizance alone will hardly bee taken, he were best be bound for her, and then if he be beaten the second time, let him know the price of it on God's name. (128–29)

This is far from an ideal picture, as is the *Lawes Resolutions* definition of a right, but such argumentative tenacity on behalf of understanding women's position in the face of legal provisions that ostensibly constrain them makes a real claim. The treatise makes so bold as to read precedent law on the presumption that medieval English women *had* rights. For this reason it refuses to lament the law's restrictions on women's actions and turns them, instead, into a negative for which women's actions were the positive. It is a theory and a practice that might be further pursued.

Legal Allowance and Compunction as "Right"

Assume that medieval women had rights and the first thing that comes clear is that there is explicit warrant in medieval legal theory for attaching the Latin word commonly translated as "right" — that is, *ius* — to women. By and large — and this goes as much for men as for women — the word appears in medieval theory and case law to characterize rights in property: the "right" that medieval persons had to what *Bracton* calls the "dominion of things" (*dominia rerum*) (2:42). In a long discussion entitled "Of Acquiring the Dominion of Things" (*De adquirendo rerum dominio*) (2:42–281), *Bracton* makes clear that women acquired this dominion by "right" as a matter of course in two important ways. First and foremost they might inherit rights in land: "There is another *causa* for acquiring dominion called succession, which entitles every heir to everything of which his ancestors die seised as of fee, or of which they once were seised as of fee and hereditary right, which ought to descend to nearer heirs, male and female."[19] In this way a woman might become, by right, the "chief lord of a fee" (*capitalis dominus de feodo illo*), as the court of the king upheld in 1286 was the case for Milisent de Mouhaut for "one messuage, four acres of garden, one acre of parkland, and one pigeon-house."[20] Milisent is untrammeled in this record by the guardianship of either father or husband, but a married woman might even claim rights to land independent of her husband. This is clear in a case in King's Bench from 1291: "And on this there came Matilda, the wife of John of Waltham, saying that the aforesaid messuage was her right and perquisite and that her husband's default ought not to be prejudicial to her inasmuch as she was present in court before judgment was given and ready to defend her estate."[21]

Although such rights of dominion derived from property, they were not limited to property: rights over a thing, precisely because possession of land was a concentric right in the English Middle Ages (a tenant might possess land "from" and, therefore, at the same time as the lord who also possessed it), ramified directly in rights over persons. A woman's right in her property—her *ius in ipsa re*—brought her into precisely the kinds of personal relations from which the discussion of persons in *Bracton* carefully excludes her. These further rights are hinted at in the record concerning Milisent de Mouhaut and her property when Milisent is said to have sent "*her* bailiff" (*balliuus suus*) to answer a claim against her holding. The issue is more strongly put forward in an action of 1290, also concerning Milisent de Mouhaut's land, where pleas are said to have been entered against Milisent and what are called "*her* men" (*homines suos*).[22] The theory behind all this language is spelled out more clearly in *Bracton* when the second important way women acquired rights in property is described. "Unity of person" notwithstanding, this second set of rights accrued to women precisely because they *were* wives, since, as a result of marriage, women gained dominion over the property of their husbands through the "rightful" (*rationalis*) dower equal to a third of his property, to which they were entitled.[23] As a result of this right in property women also gained a clear set of rights over the persons attached to the land (as wards and tenants) over which they acquired dominion: "When a wife has thus been specifically endowed of some certain property, she begins at once, at the time the dower is constituted, to have a right in that property, and in all the appurtenances, in the advowsons and collations of churches, in wardships, reliefs and marriages, and in all other things, since nothing is specifically excepted."[24]

The clear subjection entailed in describing marriage as a "rod" begins to evanesce in *Bracton*, in other words, as soon as the terms by which that "rod" governed are themselves defined: marriage enters a wide range of rightful claims on a woman's behalf. A woman's claim to these rights was carefully defended by right as well. Should a husband alienate more than a third of his lands or fail to endow his wife with her rightful third at their marriage, a woman had recourse at law by an action of dower (*actio de dote*).[25] This action formed such a crucial part of English law, in fact, that a whole section in *Bracton* is devoted to its proper execution.[26] The realities of dominion's acquisition continually brought women into rightful possession of precisely those legal controls that the medieval theory of persons proposed to deny them.

Rights in property are useful in illustrating the problems with "unity of person" as a description of medieval English law, and they are significant in giving the phrase "rights of women" meaningful reference in the medieval period. These rights only relate to women who *had* property, of course, but they are also a point of entry into a wider set of rights that medieval theory and practice assigned to *all* English women. This second category of rights was a procedural ramification of property rights—the form in which those rights appeared in case law—and it extended the rights that possession of land conferred to other sorts of possessions and, finally, to women's very bodies. It is a right that might loosely be called a "right to plead." The definition of this right requires some recourse to the logic of the *Lawes Resolutions* because it is not assigned to women in theory and existed clearly only in practice, at the point where a woman was hurt. Pleading at law became possible as a result of injury (a wrong committed against a person gave that person the legal opportunity to seek redress): that is, the right to plead only came into existence for a woman when she had suffered *beyond* the normal disabilities to which she was consigned by the law. But the plea was itself advantageous to a woman since it aided her precisely at the point of her harm, compensating her legally because injury to rightful possession was rightfully redressed: "What is an action? It is nothing other than the right of pursuing in a judicial proceeding what is due to one."[27] This remark introduces the section of *Bracton* on civil actions and describes how infringement of a person's dominion might be defended. The action it refers to gave possessors recourse for a loss of possession whether that thing was an immovable (*res immobilis*), such as land, or a movable (*res mobilis*), such as a garment (2:292). Although women are nowhere designated in *Bracton* as benefiting from this right, women had property (as we have seen); property made things "due" to a person; so women could rightfully pursue this action.[28] Its employment is visible in the record in the case of possessed immovables when Milisent de Mouhaut and Matilda of Waltham enter pleas to defend their property in the cases I have already mentioned. It is visible in a case of possessed movables when, in 1280, Matilda le Lorimer enters a plea against Walter Comyn because he "robbed her of her goods and chattels... to the value of a hundred shillings."[29]

This right to plead extended beyond the redress of injuries to property to redress for those injuries medieval legal theory defined as criminal — generally speaking, violent hurt done to a person's body or property or to the bodies of persons related to them. This subcategory of pleading entered the record much like a "right of action," but, because it responded to an injury that medieval legal theory defined on entirely different grounds, it was never described as a "right." This theory could not see such an action in personal terms — as a "right of persons" — because it did not understand the person affected by crime to be the person to whom the injury was done; crime injured "every person, because of the king's peace and common welfare."[30] As a result of this thinking, appeals seeking redress for crime (appeals being the form that criminal pleas took) seek redress for injuries done to *all* persons (that is, technically, injuries done to the "king's peace"). Descriptions of such pleas focus, then, entirely on the obligations of officials to protect the peace on behalf of the king, slighting the stake of victims almost entirely. On the other hand, the way *Bracton* specifies these obligations makes clear that pleading in the form of an appeal *was* a right. Here, for example, is the specification of these obligations in cases where a "virgin" appeals a man for a rape: "This is their official duty in connexion with the rape of virgins: if a man has been appealed of rape by a woman and the deed is of recent occurrence, as may often be ascertained by certain signs, as where the hue has been raised and recently pursued, or her garments are torn, or if not torn, stained with blood, let the appellee be attached."[31] The official's specified duty — he *must* attach the appellee when a woman appeals such a rape — makes the woman's appeal an imperative triggering that duty; his legal compunction effectively endows a woman with the "right" to this appeal. By the logic of the *Lawes Resolutions*, moreover, the provisions in *Bracton* restricting women's appeals to "not more than two cases" (*non nisi in duobus*) are provisions endowing them with the right *to* appeal in the two cases specified: "We must see the cases in which a woman has an appeal. It is clear that there are no more than two by which one ought to be put to the duel or the grand assise, that is, only for a forcible harm done to her body, as for rape, as was said above, and for the death of her husband slain within her arms, and in no other way."[32] Since the perspective of such theory is the perspective of the court only — what it can and cannot allow procedurally — restriction must do duty for endowment. But, were the language more positive, the result would be the same: when a woman came into court, appealed someone for her rape or the murder of her husband, the court had an "official duty" (*officium*) to respond to the claim she was allowed to make. This is exactly what the language in a case of 1307 recognizes when it says that Cecily, widow of Alan le Day, "had good and lawful cause to make [an] appeal" (*bonam causam et iustam habuit appellum*).[33]

Women's rights in property and their implicit right to appeal were, in the largest sense, a right to written representation: the right to enter a court to redress a wrong by telling the story of that wrong and demanding that that story be both recorded and acted upon by officers of the court. The individual rights that add up to this larger one are worth recognizing for their own sake, as I have so far tried to do. With the unusual exception of the *Lawes Resolutions of Womens Rights,* legal history does not establish the category of "rights" as one on which medieval English women have any general claim. To be sure, women wound up in court for other reasons. If the rights I have outlined gave them voice to describe their dispossessions, their rapes, and the murder of their husbands, women were also accused as dispossessors, murderers, and even parties to the rape of other women. They came to court as the party sued or appealed almost as often as they came to right wrongs done to themselves — and they tell stories that require recording in such cases, too. It is worth emphasizing women's rights over their transgressions, and their right to plead over the rights from which that larger procedural right ramified, because of the way this right relates to the textual remains of the law. If the right to plead was, in practice, a right to representation, then medieval English law gave women a way to control the recording of their lived lives in the record: it gave women a right to speak about their lives, and it gave them a right to have that speaking made into a *text.* The verbs of record make this point eloquently enough. In 1281 Agnes le Mire is "asked" (*quesita*) and "says herself" (*dicit ipsa*) in response; in 1282 Rose le Savage comes to court and "appeals" (*appellat*); in 1292 Hawise ap Wenonwen "proffers" a charter "in these words" (*profert in hec verba*); in 1355 Blanche Wake comes to court and "while protesting... says" (*protestando... dicit*).[34] But the shockingly apposite textuality of one case from 1358 shows best how rightful pleading gave women a *useful* access to texts. In this case Nichola Godechepe enters a "plea of contempt and trespass" (*placit[um] contemptus et transgressionis*) against John of Offham and, "in her own person" (*in propria persona sua*), "complains" (*queritur*) of the following:

> The aforesaid Nichola was on her way to Westminster to prosecute as his guardian the right of Theobald, her son, against the aforesaid John and some others with respect to the advowson of Offham church.... The said John and others unknown... seized Nichola with force and arms,... tied her hands and feet and assaulted her and beat, wounded and ill-treated her so that her life was despaired of, and they made her eat a certain charter.[35]

The textual form of the injury done Nichola as a part of the physical violence directed more generally at her person endangers the right of her son to the advowson of Offham Church; that right is preserved in the textual warrant of the charter she is made to eat. Nichola's right to plead results in another text, however: the text of this record. Assume for a moment that Nichola Godechepe was illiterate (a reasonable, but not entirely necessary, assumption) and see in particularly stark relief how her right to plead struck back at John of Offham in precisely the textual form of his assault: that is, not only by seeking his punishment at law, but by restoring the charter to written form through the legal procedures of pleading. When Godechepe says that she was forced to eat the charter, she also "complains" in what appears to be exacting detail of the charter's contents:

> and they made her eat a certain charter (in which it was stated that John de Chydak, knight, enfeoffed Thomas Godechepe and Isabella of Offham and the heirs of the said Thomas, the lawful issue of his body, with two parts of the manor of Offham, together with the advowson of the aforesaid church, and that Thomas afterward married the aforesaid Nichola, and from them there was as issue the aforesaid Theobald as son and heir in accordance with the form of gift contained in the aforesaid charter).[36]

Nichola's right to plead gives her access to written record in which she can have the consumed charter rewritten. John of Offham clearly thought he could deny the right in property that Nichola protects by destroying the text that bestowed it, but Nichola's right to plead routs him by making the destroyed text exist, *as* a text, again. The legal implications of this reenrollment are probably not extensive—it is unlikely that Nichola could use this new record to any subsequent effect in enforcing her son's right—but it is nevertheless significant that the right of appeal, by its terms and in and of itself, compels the court to repair the textual damage John of Offham did through the forms in which it must hear *and* record Nichola's plea. In a strictly textual sense at least, she wins.

Of course we could doubt the veracity of everything that Nichola Godechepe or any woman or man like her says, even *in propria persona.* The reader of a text resulting from such a plea can make no mistake about the mediated status of the representation it provides: it is representation in the third person, a report of what a woman said, not her "complaint" but what "she complains."[37] The texts these women had a rightful access to through their legal speaking were, like the stories their speech tells, controlled by the men who wielded legal pen and parchment and who dictated the forms of speech allowable in court. In a plea of 1422 by Isabella Waye against Stephen Melya of Moreleigh (for wasting her grass to the value of forty shillings), Isabella "complains thereof by Thomas Foulhill, her attorney" (*per Thomam Foulhill' attornatum suum queritur*).[38] Where such attorneys are not said to speak for women in a record we can often suspect their presence at the elbow of pleading women, feeding them the language and even the content that will be appropriate to the procedures and forms of the court. The constraints legal procedures placed on the words allowed to any pleader are made clear in the appeal of Rose le Savage (mentioned earlier), which is at first rendered "null" (*nullum*), with the result that Rose is jailed for making a "false appeal," not because it was found that she was not raped, but because she "did not name a definite day or a definite year or a definite place" (*non nominauit certum diem nec certum annum nec certum locum*), as the form of appeal demanded.[39] An appeal by Elena Coventry in 1368 for the death of her husband bears the mark of the kind of legal advice Rose le Savage lacked: "Elena in her own person at once appeals Richard and William of this, that whereas John was in the peace of God and of the present king at Farnborough in the county of Kent by night, and on the Friday after the Feast of Saint Margaret the Virgin in the forty-second year of the present king's reign."[40] The warrant in the record for Elena's speech (that, "in her own person," she "appeals . . . *this*") is qualified by a precision in that speech that bears the marks of careful shaping by the kind of legal knowledge we would expect attorneys above all to have. The very Latin of the record enters a further qualification and interposes another figure between the life and its record: the scribe or scribes who translated and recorded pleaders' words.[41] We cannot know for sure, but we might imagine that Elena, like most appellants of the fourteenth century, entered her appeal in English, and that this English was then translated into the Latin of the record. Such translation would involve not only a translation of English forms but also their codification in the Latin formula that the records customarily used. With little effort we can imagine that Elena said, "John, who was in the peace of God, etc.," and this was then formalized and formulized to "*whereas* John was in the peace of God, etc."; with more daring we could imagine that she said nothing of the sort ("my husband John was doing nothing to provoke his attackers when, all of a sudden . . .") and the scribe simply organized what Elena said to sort with the forms he either expected to hear or knew he must write.

But, to the extent that this mediation determines the record and qualifies the stories women told as a result of their right to representation, that mediation and that qualification were also an important aspect of lives that pleas represent. There is a useful analogy here to the circumscription of women's right to plead by the violence—the wrongs and crimes—on which those pleas were predicated. As I have suggested, this right was in force only *by* force; it was always an injury that enabled women to plead in the generic instances I have outlined. Such precedent circumstances qualify the extent to which the rights medieval women exercised at law may be understood as legal abilities, but it is equally true that these qualifications were *lived* qualifications: the dispossession or the murder or the rape that essentially created a particular woman's right to plead was a crucial part of the lived experience that the record of her plea narrates. In a similar way, the constricting lines of force that work to obscure women's voices in court — the rules of law and its procedural forms, attorneys and their linguistic influence, scribes and their distorting Latin formulae — are crucial forces determining the part of life lived *at law*: in the court, in the process of pleading, on the way to asserting the rights to plead and appeal that women had. Part of what is interesting about these records of women's speech, then — and the reason I focus on them here — is not only the extent to which they purport to record what women said, but the extent to which they actually do *not* achieve this purported goal. These legal pleas are what can generally be called "acts of assertive representation," to adapt a useful phrase coined by Steven Justice for a different purpose.[42] A struggle for access to writing of the kind that the right to plead gave was an experience that medieval English women were living *as* they pled, and that struggle generally survives in the forms of the texts women's pleading managed to produce. The levels of countervailing resistance to which legal records testify are a skein that obfuscates the female voice and the life it speaks of, but that skein is itself the trace and sign of a mode of living hemmed in (itself obfuscated) by legal limits.

Acts of Representation

Records of pleading represent struggles in the lives of medieval English women because pleas were (and were experienced as) struggles for representation. Take, for example, a case of 1281 in which Agnes Colle appeals Henry le Ternur and Gilbert of Grafham for the death of her son. Henry and Gilbert's first gambit before denying that they killed Agnes's son (a denial they eventually make) is to claim that Agnes has no right to appeal. Here is their claim and its result: "It is contained in the Great Charter of the lord king that no woman ought to appeal anyone save for the death of her husband. Therefore it is awarded that the aforesaid Henry and Gilbert go thereof without day with respect to her appeal and the aforesaid Agnes be committed to gaol."[43] There is always the potential that any suit is purely instrumental (lodging an accusation in order to satisfy an entirely unmentioned motive), and that potential throws a presumption of doubt over any "fact" a pleader or a defendant adduces in a suit. Even a naive reader could agree that this record is hardly evidence that Henry le Ternur and Gilbert of Grafham killed anyone (the courts come to no conclusion about their guilt); a skeptical reader would have to point out that this record is not even evidence that Agnes Colle's son was murdered; a cynical reader would need to note that the record does not provide any assurance that her son is even *dead*. But the record's truth-value as testimony to procedure is rather different. We are more justified in learning from this record that the courts restricted a woman's right to appeal the death of any relative other than her husband: this record exists only to record that decision accurately and, should it fail of that, it fails of everything. In this sense the record is a transparent record of Agnes Colle's experience at law. She may well have lived the horrific experience of the murder of a son, but she surely experienced the silencing of her appeal as a result of having appealed the death of the "wrong" person. The same is true of the suits of Rose le Savage (whose appeal is at first nonsuited because she is not specific enough) and Elena Coventry (and her rigorous specificity in appealing the death of her husband), which I described earlier. These records may not give us sure information about the rape or the murder, but they do tell us with assurance about the *process* of representing the experience of those crimes, of the experience of the act of representation itself.

In this sense, the significance of such records extends well beyond the courts because the activity of representation itself can be seen to matter not only *at* law, but as the law generally circumscribes and determines all processes of living. As Catharine MacKinnon suggests in her extensive critique of modern American law, juridical limits are, in their nature, quotidian limits, insofar as daily life in a society governed by a rule of law must unfold within and by the strictures of that rule. In MacKinnon's phrasing, the "truth of women's reality"—and we might easily substitute "lived lives" for the "women's reality" here—is a "truth" that can *only* exist as a function of the law, that is *necessarily* determined by the "male perspective both systematic and hegemonic" that is that law.[44] Because this law generally "circumlocutes [a woman's] speech, and describes her life," the legal restrictions visible in court records are not simply the particularized restrictions of legal procedure but the *general* limits placed on (and determining) the full extent of women's reality.[45] What women live in that reality, according to MacKinnon, is a "struggle for consciousness," a "struggle for world," and, because that struggle is everywhere joined against legal restriction, it is a struggle that is everywhere recovered by "revealing, criticizing, and explaining" restrictions: a life that exists, as MacKinnon puts it, in "its impossibility" is *well* represented by defining that impossibility—by exposing and defining the law's general limits.[46] MacKinnon's method is the method of the *Lawes Resolutions of Womens Rights* pushed beyond the limits of the law's provisions to the living that only the law's provisions allow. Where the procedures of the *Lawes Resolutions* extract a *legal* position from the limitations of the law, MacKinnon argues that the *whole* lived life exists in (and may therefore be extracted from) those same limitations. It is a theory that makes the experiential testimony provided by the kinds of pleading I have been trying to call attention to relevant, in a sense, to everything: such pleading constitutes nothing less than representations of the limits that were (and, according to MacKinnon, are) the whole of women's lived lives.

MacKinnon's legal ontology neatly reverses traditional assumptions about the relationship between the law and the life: it understands that a woman who has "nothing to do in constituting Lawes" (to recall the language of the *Lawes Resolutions*) is a person whose life exists in the legal restriction or compunction constraining her action, in the "struggle for world" that legal limits necessitate. It is a bracing theory and one that, when applied to the English Middle Ages, discloses the plenitude with which the struggle for representation in women's pleadings testifies to something important. There are limits to this importance, of course. To understand representation as a central "impossibility" in the life of medieval women, to equate the "struggle for consciousness" *with* the life, threatens to slight the material struggles medieval women faced in the quotidian: struggles to protect their bodies, to guard their property, to survive in the most mundane (which, in the living, is the largest) sense. But it must also be remembered—and this parallels MacKinnon's point of departure in thinking about modern law—that the right to representation for medieval women emerged directly from the meager protections medieval law gave them in quotidian struggles. It was the simple right to own something that gave women the right to representation in the first instance (the one right only exists to protect the other). It was the right not to be raped that allowed women the right to appeal in the second instance (women spoke at law to defend their bodies). Not only did representation arise from daily struggle; its method was to signify that struggle in, and to, and for, the law; its goal was to recruit the law's protection in that daily struggle by *means* of representation. Representation was not all that was at stake for women in the Middle Ages, in other words—far from it—but representation of lives was the only ground medieval women had for asserting what was at stake for them so as to compel men to acknowledge those stakes by, at the very least, recording them.

There is, then, a telling indication of the general importance of a "struggle for consciousness" to the lived lives of women in the way that what MacKinnon calls the "male perspective both systematic and hegemonic" reacted to them. As I have already suggested, women's right to plead was a paradoxical result of the forms such hegemony took: the proprietary actions of women were a side effect of male control over other men (when women were unmarried), or a result of the male control exerted over women in marriage (as they were "*sub virga*"); the forms of appeal allowable to women could be understood to protect their marriageability or their status as property in marriage *for* men (in the case of appeals of rape) or to assure that widows pursued the murderers *of* men (in the case of appeals for the murder of a husband). But, by contrast, if women's pleas were important to women because such pleas allowed them to represent male restrictions of their lives at law, if women's representation of their lives in court could force men to yield to pleas precisely so as to coerce male control over lives to women's advantage, then it would make sense that the very hegemonies that had produced that right to plead only as a side effect would register this threat and view women's pleading as dangerous. This is, in fact, exactly what Langland registers with respect to Lady Mede in the final passages concerning her in *Piers Plowman*:

And modiliche* vpon Mede wiþ mytʒe þe kyng loked,	*angrily
And gan wexe wroþ with lawe for Mede almoost hadde shent* it,	*destroyed
And seide, "þoruʒ [youre] lawe, as I leue, I lese manye eschetes;	*properties
Mede ouermaistreþ lawe and muche truþe letteþ.*	*hinders
Ac Reson shal rekene wiþ yow if I regne any while,	
And deme* yow, bi þis day, as ye han deserued.	*judge
Mede shal noʒt maynprise* yow, by þe marie of heuene!	*act as surety for
I wole haue leaute* in lawe, and lete be al youre ianglyng."	*good faith
(IV.173–80)	

The problem of "mede" for Langland and the king exceeds Mede's gender of course — she represents the social and political dangers of "mede" and not simply of women — but the personification of mede as a "lady" everywhere informs both her actions and the reactions of others to her.[47] The king portrays a Mede with influence through pleading as a Mede who "overmasters law" and nearly destroys it ("almoost had shent it"). In suggesting that "janglyng" is dangerous to "leaute in lawe," the king places women's speech in general opposition to justice. And one of the dangers among the many I take Langland to show the king recognizing here is that a woman speaking in opposition to the law's provisions necessarily opens the law to the claims of the "truth of women's reality." To allow women in court, and to allow them to speak there, was to open the law to a mode of existence that its general conception was committed to restricting and, thereby, excluding. Mede's near success at the expense of the law ("Mede *almoost* hadde shent it") is central to the threat she poses: the king's outrage and his grounds for silencing Mede here are not least significant as they are figured as acts taken by male figures on behalf of "lawe."

The danger Lady Mede poses in *Piers Plowman* is a danger that provoked the English courts to police women's right to plead rigorously, to punish women for any attempt to jump outside the rails of the rights in which legal thinking tracked them. Cecily le Day's appeal of Gilbert of Hallington for the death of her husband in 1307 (a case I mentioned briefly earlier) shows this policing and this punishment at work. Gilbert gets clear of the king's suit for the murder by producing a charter in which the fact of the murder is granted but the king has pardoned Gilbert (*perdonavimus*) "for good service" (*pro bono seruicio*). Gilbert also gets clear of Cecily's appeal on the grounds that she "has a husband" (*habet virum*), the implication being that she cannot appeal the death of a husband because her remarriage has barred her claim by the very terms in which the appeal is granted. In this case, Cecily's lived circumstance, represented to the court, gets in the way of the court's ordinary procedures, and the court is forced to yield to the logic of her claim by acknowledging the realities of her life: "And because the said appeal was not quashed or proved false and it is quite evident that the same Cecily had good and lawful cause to make the aforesaid appeal and to prosecute it for the abovesaid reasons, although she could not prosecute it because she has a husband, and its cause is a certain foolishness rather than anything deceitful, it is conceded by grace of the court."[48] Despite this concession, the court does not really yield legally. It admits that the restriction on Cecily le Day's grounds of appeal is a "certain foolishness," but Cecily is still punished for the temerity of representing a life at odds with the provisions of the law. At the point where she comes to make this appeal, Cecily has been imprisoned for fifteen days for proffering the same suit against Gilbert of Hallington in the county court, and the king's court here only grants that she "may make fine" (that is, the wrong she committed by making a "false appeal" may be amerced). The restrictions imposed on Cecily le Day are similar to the restrictions imposed on the appeals of Rose le Savage and Agnes Colle. Rose's failure to follow correct procedure and Agnes's failure, like Cecily's, to describe a life that is allowably lived by the form of the appeal are both grounds for the court to silence and punish those women (recall that Rose le Savage and Agnes Colle were jailed, too). Where women represented lives to the court in forms that the law had not validated, the court might have to recognize that the lack of validation was "foolishness." This was the danger. And the response that registered that danger was a judgment that denied the eccentric claim and punished the woman who had pled—because she had lived—eccentrically with respect to the law's provisions.

The policing of women's speaking at law also registered the importance of that speaking on the larger scale of medieval legal theory and statute, which were changed in this period precisely to limit women's rights to plead. We have already seen the glimmers of the broad theoretical exclusion that was to emerge in the doctrine of "unity of person" as it formed part of medieval legal thinking in *Bracton.* As I have also mentioned, legal histories show how a full-blown expression of this doctrine was later destined to restrict a married woman's right to plead in almost every case. A separate but similar development in the marriage law of England also worked—with a minatory care—to restrict women's right to representation in the medieval period itself. As John Post has observed, provisions in the statutes called Westminster I in 1275 and Westminster II in 1285 worked to conflate the appeal of rape with what had been separate trespassory actions for "ravishment" (that is, abductions that might or might not involve sexual violence).[49] This change in procedure had the implicit result of converting rapes from crimes that harmed a woman victim into trespassory wrongs that damaged property. In this new form, of course, *women* were the property in question, wives or marriageable daughters "damaged" in their marriageability by sexual violence, daughters or wards withheld from the remunerative marriages arranged for them by fathers or guardians. According to Post, the Statute of Rapes of 1382 continued to erode the appeal of rape by a similar strategy: provisions in this statute essentially transferred the "right" of the appeal of rape itself from a woman to her family, and thus most probably to her father or male guardian.[50] Statutes in medieval English law do not translate directly into procedure: there were still appeals of rape by women in records subsequent to all of these statutes; to some extent the changes in these statutes simply resulted in a welter of legal confusion.[51] But the result that is potential in these changes shows that their target was first and foremost women's right to represent their lives under the law: simply put, the provisions of Westminster I and II and the Statute of Rapes converted the right to appeal rapes that had been held by women to a right of action that was held by *men*. The redefinition of wrong and the changed legal procedure for seeking recompense essentially absorbed one of two rights to appeal that women had into the more restrictive tenets of the marriage law. The fear that men addressed in these statutes, according to Sue Sheridan Walker, was that women might *let* themselves be "ravished" in order to exert some control over the marriage choice that was otherwise in the gift of fathers and male guardians. Because an appeal of rape could technically be settled if the victim of the rape agreed to marry the rapist, women could conceivably use their right to appeal a rape to choose their husband: to assert the circumstances of the lives they had chosen to live in a court of law, and to *force* the court, through their rightful pleading, to ratify the circumstances of those lives through its own procedures.[52] Westminster I and II and the Statute of Rapes take the measure of what a woman's right to appeal a rape could do, and they also show how that ability could be limited precisely by limiting women's rights. In taking square aim at one of the secure grounds on which a woman had a right to represent her life and by working to obliterate that right in the most sweeping terms possible, these statutes also demonstrate in the negative how useful that right could be to women's living. The forms of that living—conducted through and by a right to plead— could so qualify male control over female lives that men saw that they could increase that control precisely by limiting that right.

The importance of "the struggle for consciousness" in the lived lives of medieval women is most powerfully measured, however, not by the coercive reaction it engendered in statutes but in the way that struggle is visible outside the criminal law in other genres of record. These other textual kinds show that the referent for the legal conflict over the right to appeal was, more generally, a conflict born in the conditions under which medieval women lived, not within the legal limits of the courts, but within the broader limits of social life regulated by *language*. An episode in the records of the ecclesiastical courts offers a rare but explicit acknowledgment of this general linguistic referent. In the records for 1421 of the York consistory court, as Richard Helmholz notes, a woman named Agnes protested the court's judgment "publicly by means of oral evidence and in the vulgar language" (*viva voce et vulgari lingua publice protestabatur*).[53] That this is more than an isolated incident, as Helmholz also points out, is made clear in an early-fourteenth-century lyric that satirizes the consistory courts through a generic reproduction of Agnes's protest:

Ant heo* cometh by-modered* ase a mor-hen,	*she/covered with mud
Ant scrynketh* for shome,* ant shometh for men,	*shrinks/shame
Un-comely under calle.*	*headdress
Heo biginneth to shryke,* ant scremeth anon,	*shriek
Ant saith, "by my gabbyng ne shal hit so gon,	
Ant that beo on ou alle;	
That thou shalt me wedde ant wedde to wyf.*"[54]	*make me a wife

The abuse satirized here parallels the danger Lady Mede poses to the court of the king: "gabbyng" is what this woman uses to oppose the court's commands; the strictures the law means to impose on the way a woman lives her life (here in forcing this woman to marry) are threatened by a woman's very ability to protest them. But the satire of the poem calls attention to the *form* of this woman's speech, too (she "shrieks" and "screams"), and, in this, it subtly duplicates the point that the York consistory court record makes explicit: English men could learn Latin; English women, as a rule denied the linguistic education available to men, tended to know only English. Women's "space to speke," whenever granted, was an English space, and as the scribe of the York record notes (by noticing Agnes's vernacular speaking) and the author of this poem registers (in his disparagement), women's English speaking sorted ill with the court's Latinate decorum. These texts also suggest that English speaking was a threat to the courts because vernacularity posed a general threat to male control of the "space to speak": English proficiency was, in fact, the door through which all English-speaking persons—both men and women—were gaining a right to written narrative independent of their rights at law. It was a right that resulted directly from the way English gradually asserted a general right to textual preservation over against Latin (and French) in the thirteenth and fourteenth centuries. The positive form of the fact that these texts are only capable of registering in the negative is this: the works of Chaucer, the "father of English poetry," coincide with the first work by an English woman who names herself in her text. English women had increased access to representation in their lives through changes in linguistic culture that increasingly legitimized the only verbal and textual forms that were available to them. As Latin and French yielded linguistic ground to English they ceded territory on which women already securely stood. The right to representation mattered to women in this period, in short, because they were increasingly getting and using that right *out* of court.

At such a point of textual intersection—where the referent for women's legal struggle for world can be located as much in the social struggle for linguistic access as in the legal world of the courts—we can also see how the argument that women directed at the law to expose its limits and assert their narrative rights is only a particular form of the general argument that female disadvantage addressed to authority to claim legitimate access to *all* forms of the written word. In fact, that first English woman writer, Julian of Norwich, to whom I have just referred, claims her own right to represent lived experience in *A Revelation of Love* (1385–88 and 1393 or after) in terms almost exactly parallel to the legal theory for such rights that I have been tracing.[55] Julian's condition parallels women's conditions in court (she describes herself as "a symple creature unlettyrde" [2:285]), and, therefore, as in court records, her text is also mediated through a scribe. Julian also constructs her right to write—or, more exactly, to speak and to have written—out of the very disabilities that ought to prevent her from doing so: "For I am suer ther be meny that never hath shewyng ne sy3t but of the comyn techyng of holy chyrch that loue god better than I. For yf I looke syngulery to my selfe I am ry3t nought; but in generall I am, I hope, in onehede of cheryte with alle my evyn cristen" (2:321–22) Such humility is inherent to Christian devotion, of course, but what is crucial in Julian's case is the way its implications are subtly teased out—as they may be in the law—to license a devotional "space" for a woman's speech.[56] The material of dependence (to be "ry3t nought") is made to ramify in a warrant for the making of a text: "Thankyng is a true inward knowyng, with grett reuerence and louely drede turnyng oure selfe with alle oure myghtes in to the werkyng that oure lorde steryd vs to, enjoyeng and thankyng inwardly. And some tyme for plenteousnes it brekyth ou3t with voyce and seyth: Good lorde, grannt mercy; blessyd mott thou be" (2:466–67). The inspiration of the Passion in Julian's epistemology demands the spoken word that, finally, is the text. The outward "werkyng" is made equivalent to the inner "thankyng." The imperatives of devotion effectively necessitate the speech for which Julian figures herself as a medium only ("it brekyth out with voyce"): "And so the vertu of oure lordes worde turnyth in to the soule and quyckynnyth the hart and entryth by hys grace in to tru werkyng, and makyth it to pray fulle blessydfully, and truly to enioy in oure lorde" (2:467).

The moment of Julian's "impossibility" (the ways in which her belief drives her thinking inward to dwell on her disabilities) is the moment that produces her text. In all these ways, in other words, Julian's theology of speaking is a calque of the legal theory that gave women that right in a different "space"; it is the devotional equivalent of the right to plead. The critical difference is, of course, the linguistic difference: the words that Julian both hears and "cries" are English, and this means not only that Julian does not require the courts to make a text, but that she constructs a textual license that any English speaker might construct — which means, of course, that any *woman* might construct. Julian's *Revelation* provides a record, not only of "what happened" in "the yer of our lord a thousannde and three hundered and lxxiij, the xiij of Mai" (2:285), that is of the "revelations" themselves, but also of the process of representing those revelations in the written form of her treatise. The treatise claims powerfully but implicitly — saying nowhere but showing everywhere in its English forms — that Julian's right to representation exists in the increasing access that English proficiency is giving English speakers to textual production. Julian describes the process that representation entailed for women — her devotional argument for her own right to speak records her "struggle for world," the "struggle for consciousness" in her own life — and reports that "struggle" in the nonlegal sphere where it was increasingly being joined.

The Book of Margery Kempe (1436–38), the second major English text signed by a woman, makes this same point about vernacularity in different terms. The long struggle Kempe details at the beginning of her book to get her words written down intelligibly is the most explicit record we have of the "struggle for world" women of this period engaged in.[57] But the *Book* is even more searching than this in the forms it finds for expressing the struggle a woman might experience in the process of representing her life in English. Kempe's attempt to find, as she puts it, "understondyng" for her "language" because it *is* English results in numerous episodes where the intelligibility of English per se is precisely what is at issue. One episode may stand here for many:

> At þe last, þe seyd creatur, seyng & wel vndirstondyng þat hir confessour vndirstod not her langage & þat was tediows to hym, þan, in party to comfort hym . . . sche telde in hyr owyn langage in Englysch a story of Holy Writte whech sche had lernyd of clerkys. . . . Than þei askyd hir confessour ʒyf he vndirstod þat sche had seyd, & he a-non in Latyn telde hem þe same wordys þat sche seyd be-forn in Englisch, for he cowde neyþyr speke Englysch ne vndirstondyn Englisch saue only aftyr hir tunge. (97–98)[58]

This miracle (or fantasy) of hyperliteracy represents both the difficulty medieval English women had in having their English recognized by a culture that privileged the Latinity it denied them and Kempe's unbridled success in making that culture *hear* her. Margery finds "understondyng" in this episode as Kempe generally finds it in her book.[59] Kempe's notorious "cryings" are an important record of this struggle, too. They are portrayed as a constant annoyance to Margery's companions in the *Book,* and although they are often thought to be glossed by the "wepyng" and "sobbyng" that Kempe always mentions in connection with them, the "cryings" at times are given clear verbal content: "& þerfor sche cryed, 'Good Lord, make it wel & sende down sum reyn er sum wedyr þat may thorw þe mercy qwenchyn þis fyer" (163). These "cryings" are "appeals" in the root sense of this term as it is applied to criminal actions (as *appellum* is derived from *appellare,* which generally meant "to entreat, implore, beseech, invoke"); they are calques of legal speaking that, like that speaking, turn injury into the occasion for rightful demand.[60] This is not to say that the *Book of Margery Kempe* draws upon the law, but it is to say that a referent for Kempe's book, like Julian's, is the same struggle to speak and have that speaking written that was the referent for the criminal records. Those records, the *Revelation,* and the *Book* are homologous textual issue because they record identical forms of the female life: they deploy similar arguments because those arguments are the form that women's speaking took as it registered and thereby recruited the institutional restraints that determined it.

Probably the best summary of the importance of such representation is given in the capaciously sensitive account of the medieval English social world offered by the "father of English poetry" himself. In fact, a good concluding summary of the general importance of female speaking in medieval English women's lives can be found in the way Chaucer's most sustained attempt to represent the complexities of such lives curves inexorably toward exactly the representational issues I have been exploring. I am referring here, of course, to Criseyde in *Troilus and Criseyde* and, in particular, to the narrative and textual circumstances of the *Litera Criseydis* at the end of that poem, where Criseyde is given her opportunity to offer her own "space to speke," to present the case, as it were, in her own words.[61] It is significant in itself that Chaucer sees the necessity of including in the story of a woman that, as David Aers puts it, takes that woman's "social situation seriously," an attempt by that woman to tell her own story.[62] And it is equally significant that he makes part of that representation the resistance Criseyde's story meets. When E. Talbot Donaldson famously described the letter as "one of the most poisonously hypocritical letters in the annals of literature," he was in careful sympathy with the narrative's placement of Criseyde's text:[63] Troilus "wel understod that she / Nas nought so kynde as that hire oughte be" (5.1642–43), and Pandarus proclaims, as a result of the letter's report, "I hate, ywys, Cryseyde; / And, God woot, I wol hate hire evermore!" (5.1732–33). The impossibility that Criseyde's version will find a sympathetic hearing among these men is taken by Chaucer to be a crucial aspect of her *self*-representation; the "impossibility" that her life may be represented in accurate terms is a feature that Criseyde's living is made to know. As Carolyn Dinshaw has pointed out, Troilus and Pandarus have wholly conspired in the "traffic in women" that makes Criseyde's defining "sly- dynge of corage" necessary: "Her act of infidelity can thus be analyzed more in terms of complicity in than disruption or betrayal of fundamental masculine social control. What she betrays is not the power structure of masculine control; she betrays, in truth, only an illusion of reciprocity between men and women, an illusion generated as a cover for the real workings of traffic in women."[64]

To read the *Litera Criseydis* from Criseyde's perspective, then, is to see both its fundamental accuracy—its withering honesty—and the ne- cessity of the Criseydan behavior it accurately describes. Chaucer allows Criseyde to extend the reader an invitation to give the letter just this reading when he has Criseyde notice, earlier on in book 5, how unlikely her version is to receive any sort of sympathetic hearing:

> "Allas, of me, unto the worldes ende,
> Shal neyther ben ywriten nor ysonge
> No good word, for thise bokes wol me shende.
> O, rolled shal I ben on many a tonge!
> Thorughout the world my bell shal be ronge!"
> (5.1058–62)

This concern frames Criseyde's letter, and its presence makes more sig- nificant than her version of the story the fact that her version emphati- cally fails. Chaucer is complicit in this failure by giving the condemna- tions of Troilus and Pandarus the last word in his poem—by portraying Criseyde, in sum, as a betrayer—and Chaucer acknowledges this in the *Legend of Good Women*. But the quarter Chaucer gives to Criseyde's at- tempt to voice her story is also a mark both of the plenitude of his rep- resentation of the life of a woman in his portrait and of the importance of representational struggles to all women's lives in the Middle Ages (and here I understand Criseyde to be anachronistically, but importantly, an English woman, in the same sense that Troilus is a "knight"). In this episode and its narrative framing Chaucer shows that the full represen- tation of a woman's life in a medieval English poem *entailed* represen- tation of women's struggle for "world," for "consciousness"; it was, in fact, precisely the representation of this struggle that made the repre- sented life of such a woman "full."

The rights of medieval English women to represent their lived lives at law matter because the struggle to speak and describe lived events and have them written was a condition of female living in medieval En- gland. As the law understands it in theory and practice, as Langland takes it as material for political allegory, as Julian and Kempe register it auto- biographically, as Chaucer makes it central to the narrative representation of a woman, this struggle so generally marked lives that it necessarily marked the process by which those lives left textual traces. The resulting texts show the difficult process of recording the life—fraught with resistance, hemmed in by strictures—*as* the difficult process of living. The evidence of the legal theory and case law of the thirteenth and fourteenth centuries helps us understand the specificities of this process: it gives abundant testimony to the thinking that both created and restricted the space in which women's lives took documentary form and the arguments women addressed to restrictive limits to enter textual spaces. The general story of circumstance women told from within this space is at times of historical interest, as it shows women transforming disadvantage into an opportunity. But it is most steadily interesting as it measures limitations by recording them, as it limns the restrictions of the medieval law and thereby discloses the extended account given in that record of medieval English women's existential possibilities.

Notes

In developing the ideas presented here I benefited greatly from the comments of all my interlocutors at the "Crime and Social Control" conference and, particularly, from the attentive advice offered by Barbara Hanawalt. Carolyn Dinshaw and Antoinette Burton gave extremely helpful readings of an earlier draft of this essay, and the acute editorial ministrations of David Wallace (at every level of argument and detail) helped me finalize my thoughts in their present form. This essay began in and developed through extended conversations with Elizabeth Fowler, and it therefore owes its greatest debt to her capacious and inspiring understanding of the medieval law.

1. Carolyn Dinshaw, *Chaucer's Sexual Poetics* (Madison: University of Wisconsin Press, 1989), 25.

2. George Duby, *Love and Marriage in the Middle Ages*, trans. Jane Dunnett (Cambridge: Polity Press, 1994), 100–101. Duby also describes the breadth of this screen in all genres of historical evidence: "I am not referring simply to artistic or literary works, but to all the normative rules, all the legal documents which reveal a formal exterior rather than that which it covers. I am also referring to stories, chronicles, even autobiographies, since the person who says 'I' remains a prisoner of the ideological system which dominates him or her" (100).

3. Frederick Pollock and William Maitland, *The History of English Law*, 2nd ed., 2 vols. (Cambridge: Cambridge University Press, 1952), 1:xxvii. All subsequent references to this history are to this edition, cited by page number in the text and notes.

4. I do not mean here to marshal an allegorical figure as evidence for legal practice. I discuss this relevance of Langland's representation of Lady Mede to the law in more detail later in the chapter, but, in general, I do not adduce her here as anything but an illustrative schematic for processes that must otherwise be substantiated in their iterative (and more complex) material forms.

5. *Piers Plowman: The B Version*, ed. George Kane and E. Talbot Donaldson (London: Athlone Press, 1975; rev. ed., 1988), II.191, II.185, III.171. All subsequent citations from *Piers Plowman* will be to this edition of the B-text, cited by passus and line number in the text.

6. See Rita Copeland, "William Thorpe and His Lollard Community: Intellectual Labor and the Representation of Dissent," in *Bodies and Disciplines: Intersections of Literature and History in Fifteenth-Century England*, ed. Barbara A. Hanawalt and David Wallace (Minneapolis: University of Minnesota Press, 1996), 199–222 (for particular discussion of

this phrase and its ramifications, see 210–17). For the quotation from Thorpe's "Testimony" in which this phrase occurs, see *Two Wycliffite Texts,* ed. Anne Hudson, EETS, o.s., 301 (Oxford: Oxford University Press, 1993), 39. Copeland's exploration of the dissenting identity Thorpe fashions in his "Testimony" is worth mentioning at the beginning of this chapter because her analysis, although of very different material, has much in common with my own. In particular, her claim that dissent may be defined "through scenes of violent confrontation between the official voice of accusatory interrogation and Thorpe's own violently reactive hermeneutics" (203) resembles my own claim that a confrontation between women and a coercive law offered them occasion to point out the law's defining resistance and to thwart it. Of equal relevance in the same volume is Seth Lerer's " 'Representyd now in yower syght': The Culture and Spectatorship in Late-Fifteenth-Century England," 29–62. The punitive spectacle Lerer finds in both legal and liturgical theatrics is different from the cultural connections between the law and other textual kinds I will find here, but our investigation is similar in spirit.

7. *Bracton: De legibus et consuetudinibus Angliae,* ed. George E. Woodbine, translated with revisions and notes by Samuel E. Thorne, vols. 1 and 2 (Cambridge, Mass.: Belknap Press, 1968), vols. 3 and 4 (Cambridge, Mass.: Belknap Press, 1977). Hereafter this treatise will be cited as *Bracton,* and all quotations will be taken from this edition and translation. The dating and authorship of *Bracton* is a complex matter. Work ceased on it in "1256 or 1257," but parts "go back to the 1220's and 1230's." Since Bracton was born "about 1210," it is clear that the work grew under the stewardship of several hands; *Bracton,* 3:v. For more specific discussion of dating and authorship of individual parts of the treatise, see *Bracton,* 3:xiii–lii.

8. "Est autem alia divisio hominum quod alii sunt masculi, alii sunt masculi, alii feminæ, alii hermaphroditi. Et differerunt feminae a masculis in multis, quia earum deterior est condicio quam masculorum"; *Bracton,* 2:31.

9. "Item quædam sunt sub virga, ut uxores etcetera"; *Bracton,* 2:36.

10. "[Vir et uxor] . . . sunt quasi unica persona, quia caro una et sanguis unus" (4:335).

11. William Blackstone, *Commentaries on the Laws of England,* 11th ed., 4 vols. (London: Strahan, 1791), 1:433–45. Hereafter all references to these *Commentaries* will be to this edition by page number in the text.

12. J. H. Baker, *An Introduction to English Legal History,* 2nd ed. (London: Butterworths, 1979), 395. Hereafter all references to this history will be by page number in the text.

13. This is Caroline Barron's claim in "The 'Golden Age' of Women in Medieval London," *Reading Medieval Studies* 15 (1989): 35–58. She emphasizes the grounds for independent legal action even within marriage that I have noted here and focuses on even greater freedoms accorded women in the custom of London. Joan Kelly offers a much broader argument for medieval women's abilities in *Women, History, and Theory: The Essays of Joan Kelly* (Chicago: University of Chicago Press, 1984): "[There was a] general restructuring of social relations that entailed for the Renaissance noblewoman a greater dependence upon men as feudal independence and reciprocity yielded to the state" (45).

14. See Michael M. Sheehan, "The Influence of Canon Law on the Property Rights of Married Women in England," *Mediaeval Studies* 25 (1963): 109–24. Sheehan shows how a woman's property rights in England during the late twelfth and the thirteenth centuries arrived at a "final statement" that was "almost exactly that which the canonists had sought for her seventy-five years before" (117). He also notes changes in provisions of these rights that "by Elizabeth's time . . . involved a serious set-back to the property rights of married women of England" (123–24). See also R. M. Smith, "Women's Property Rights under the Customary Law: Some Developments in the Thirteenth and Fourteenth Centuries," *Transactions of the Royal Historical Society,* 5th series, 36 (1986): 165–94.

15. Judith M. Bennett has offered a sustained critique of the master narrative that says "things were better for women in the Middle Ages, and they worsened during the early-modern centuries," in "Medieval Women, Modern Women: Across the Great Divide," in *Culture and History, 1350–1600: Essays on English Communities, Identities, and Writ-*

ing, ed. David Aers (London: Harvester Wheatsheaf, 1992), 149. Bennett's article provides a useful summary of past adherents to the narrative (see esp. 149–50, 151–52), an incisive critique of its more subtle rationale (by making the Middle Ages a "socio-cultural palin-drome of modern life," it offers medievalists "segregated protection" [147]), and an illumi-nating analysis of its relation to the politics of feminism ("women's history, revolutionary in its subject matter, and marginal in its institutional status, simply cannot afford to ques-tion the master narrative" [149]). She also marshals convincing evidence to show that women's work, so far from changing across the medieval/early modern divide actually "stood still," retaining, not advantage, but "dismal characteristics over...many centuries" (164).

16. T. E., *The Lawes Resolutions of Womens Rights* (1632; reprint, Amsterdam: The-atrum Orbis Terrarum, and Norwood, N.J.: Johnson, 1979). All subsequent references to this treatise are by page number in the text. (The reader should beware that pagination is extremely unreliable in this treatise and that the reprint makes no attempts to correct these difficulties. On one occasion p. 22 follows p. 17, p. 23 is followed by p. 20, and p. 21 is followed by a second p. 22. No such difficulties immediately surround my citations, however.)

17. The "Epistle" is not paginated in either the 1632 edition or the reprint, but I quote from its second page.

18. The phrase I quote is the subtitle of this treatise as given on its original title page.

19. "Est etiam alia causa adquirendi rerum dominia quæ dicitur causa successionis, et quæ competit singulis heredibus de omnibus de quibus antecessores eorum obierint seisiti ut de feodo, vel etiam seisiti aliquo tempore ut de feodo et iure hereditario, quod quidem descendere debet heredibus propinquioribus, masculis et feminis"; *Bracton*, 2:184. There is also discussion of *iura* inherited by women in *Fleta* (c. 1290), a treatise heavily depen-dent on *Bracton*; see *Fleta*, 3 vols. (published as vols. 2–4), ed. and trans. H. G. Richardson and G. O. Sayles, Selden Society, vols. 72, 89, 99 (London, 1953–84), 4:107–9. (Hereafter all citations from *Fleta* are taken from this edition and cited by page number in the notes.) The treatise called *Britton*, written some years after *Fleta*, also discusses the inherited "dreits" of women. See *Britton*, ed. and trans. Francis Morgan Nichols (Oxford: Clarendon Press, 1865), 2:310–20. (Hereafter all citations from *Britton* are taken from this edition and cited by page number in the notes.).

20. "Uno mesuagio, quator acris gardini, una acra parci et uno columbario"; *Select Cases in the Court of King's Bench*, ed. and trans. G. O. Sayles, 7 vols., Selden Society, vols. 55, 57, 58, 74, 76, 82, 88 (London, 1936–71), 1:161. Mention is made in this record of one William of Harringworth who accompanies Milisent in the disseisen of the warden of this land, but Milisent is not described as William's wife, daughter, or ward.

21. "Et super hoc venit Matillis uxor Iohannis de Waltham, dicendo quod predictum mesuagium fuit ius suum et perquisitum et quod defalta viri sui ei nocere non debuit desi-cut ipsa presens in curia ante iudicium redditum parata fuit ad statum suum defenden-dum"; Sayles, *Select Cases*, 2:33. An action of 1290 also concerning Milisent de Mohaut's "estate" (*statum suum*) suggests that Milisent is defending her inheritance, since part of that case turns on a "permission" given by "Milisent's ancestors" (*permissione antecesso-rum predicte Milisente*); Sayles, *Select Cases*, 2:8. The right Matilda asserts is deemed not to be valid in the case of 1286, not because she is a woman, but because "John, her hus-band, was alone vouched to warranty and alone made warranty and alone is party to the suit" (*Iohannes vir suus solus vocatus fuit ad warantium et solus warantizauit et solus est pars placiti*); Sayles, *Select Cases*, 2:34.

22. Sayles, *Select Cases*, 2:7.

23. "The rightful dower of every woman is the third part of each tenement, of all the lands and tenements her husband held in his demesne and so in fee that he could endow her on the day he married her" (*Rationalibis autem dos est cuiuslibet mulieris de quocumque tenemento tertia pars omnium terrarum et tenementorum quæ vir suus tenuit in do-minico suo, et ita in feodo quod eam inde dotare poterit die quo eam desponsavit*); *Brac-ton*, 2:265.

24. "Et omnes pertinentiæ ad ipsam pertinent in advocationibus et collationibus ecclesiarum, in custodibus et releviis et maritagiis et omnibus aliis rebus, cum inde nihil specialiter excipiatur.... Et cum uxor sic dotata fuerit nominatum de quacumque certa re in ipsa constitutione dotis, statim incipit habere ius in ipsa re nominata"; *Bracton*, 2:270. The disjunct relationship between the Latin and the translation results here from Thorne's substitution of the thing named in his translation for the cross-reference to that thing in the Latin (the "re nominata").

25. For a woman's remedy in default of her rightful dower, see *Bracton*, 2:270. The thinking of the treatise is, admittedly, less concerned with the possibility that the wife will be underendowed, but this is surely the force of the claim here that "if there is less [than a third of his property in her dower] let that deficiency be made up to her in some certain and suitable place" (*si autem ibi minus fuerit, id quod defuerit perficiatur ei in aliquo certo et competenti loco*).

26. See the section called "Of Dower (*De Dote*)," *Bracton*, 3:357–412. This section chiefly concerns the rights of widows to reclaim the endowed lands heirs and tenants have deprived them of. *Fleta* devotes a large section to discussion of rights in dower (4:72–96) as does *Britton* (2:235–96).

27. "Quid sit actio? Et sciendum quod actio nihil aliud est quam ius persequendi in iudicio quod alicui debetur"; *Bracton*, 2:282.

28. For the "right of possession" (*ius possessionis*) and its protection by forms of action, see *Fleta*, 3:46. For the "manere de pleder el dreit de la propreté," see *Britton*, 2:309.

29. "Bona et catalla sua... ad valenciam centum solidorum"; Sayles, *Select Cases*, 1:64. The suit does not come to any conclusion in this record.

30. "Cuilibet de populo propter pacem regis et communem utilitatem"; *Bracton*, 2:283.

31. "Est etiam eorum officium in raptu virginum quod si quis ab aliqua de raptu fuerit appellatus, et factum recens fuerit, secundum quod multotiens videri poeterit per indicia certa, ut si huthesium levatum fuerit et recenter secutum et ruptum vestimentum, et si non ruptum vestimentum, et si non ruptum, sanguine tamen intinctum, tunc attachietur appellatus"; *Bracton*, 2:344–45.

32. "In quibus casibus femina appellum habeat videndum. Et sciendum quod non nisi in duobus, per quod alicui lex apparens debeat adiudicari, scilicet non nisi de iniuria et violentia corporis sui illata, sicut de raptu ut prædictum est. Item et de morte viri sui interfecti inter brachia, et non alio modo"; *Bracton*, 2:419. *Fleta* repeats this discussion of women's appeals but extends it to one further instance of murder; it also generalizes the violence of rape to any form of assault on a woman's person: "A woman may bring an appeal for the death of her husband, slain within her arms and not otherwise, and for a quickened child in her womb wickedly crushed or wickedly killed by a blow, and also for rape and violence done to her body" (*Femina autem de morte viri sui inter brachia sua et non aliter interfecti, et de puero suo animato in ventre suo nequiter oppresso vel perictum nequiter occiso, et eciam de raptu et violencia corpori suo illata poeterit appellare*); *Fleta*, 2:88.

33. Sayles, *Select Cases*, 3:164.

34. Sayles, *Select Cases*, 1:85, 1:101–2, 2:68, and 6:100.

35. "Predicta Nicholaa fuit in eundo versus Westmonasterium ad prosequendum ius Theobaldi, fillii sui, tanquam eius custos versus predictum Iohannem et quosdam alios... de aduocacione ecclesie de Ofham.... Idem Iohannes et alii ignoti... vi et armis... ibidem ceperunt et manus et pedes eiusdem Nicholae ibidem legauerunt et in ipsam insultum fecerunt et ipsam verberauerunt, vulnauerunt et male tractauerunt ita quod de vita eius desperatur, et quandam cartam... commedere fecerunt"; Sayles, *Select Cases*, 6:118–19.

36. "Et quandam cartam in qua continebatur quod Iohannes de Chydak', chiualer, feoffauit Thomam Godechep' et Isabellam de Ofham et heredes ipsius Thome de corpore suo legitime procreatos de duabus partibus manerii de Ofham vna cum aduocacione ecclesie predicte, qui quidem Thomas postmodum duxit in vxorem predictam Nicholaam, de quibus

exiuit predictus Theobaldus vt filius et heres secundum formam doni in predicta carta contentem . . . commedere fecerunt"; Sayles, *Select Cases*, 6:119.

37. The now classic account of the fictionality that inheres in criminal proceedings is Natalie Zemon Davis, *Fiction in the Archives: Pardon Tales and Their Tellers in Six-teenth-Century France* (Cambridge: Polity Press, 1987). For an incisive account of that fictionality in the record of medieval England, see Paul Strohm, "False Fables and Historical Truth," in *Hochon's Arrow: The Social Imagination of Fourteenth-Century Texts* (Princeton, N.J.: Princeton University Press, 1992), 3–9.

38. Sayles, *Select Cases*, 7:257.

39. Sayles, *Select Cases*, 1:101–2. The man Rose appeals for her rape is fined £10 subsequently when he is found guilty by jury.

40. "Elena in propria persona sua instanter appellat predictos Ricardum et Willelmum de eo quod, vbi idem Iohannes fuit in pace Dei et domini regis nunc apud Farnbergh' in comitatu Kancie, nocte, et die venneris proxima post festum sancte Margarete Virginis anno regni domini regis nunc quadragesimo secundo noctanter"; Sayles, *Select Cases*, 6:155.

41. The nature of the scribal screen and the perils in store for the historian who fails to account for its influence and agendas is explored by Steven Justice in "Inquisition, Speech, and Writing: A Case from Late-Medieval Norwich," *Representations* 48 (1994): 1–29.

42. Justice uses the phrase "acts of assertive literacy" to characterize the rebel letters recorded in chronicle accounts of the rising of 1381: "Writing itself — both the activity and the product — was at issue in these letters: their composition and copying, recomposition and recopying were so many *acts of assertive literacy*"; Steven Justice, *Writing and Rebellion: England in 1381* (Berkeley: University of California Press, 1994), 24; emphasis in original.

43. "Continetur in magna carta domini regis quod nulla mulier appellare debeat aliquem nisi de morte viri sui, si debeant ad apellum suum respondere. Ideo consideratum est quod predicti Henricus et Gilbertus eant inde sine die quo ad appellum suum et predicta Agnes committatur gaole"; Sayles, *Select Cases*, 1:90–91. Afterward, Agnes's jail term is remitted "because she is poor."

44. Catharine MacKinnon, *Toward a Feminist Theory of the State* (Cambridge, Mass.: Harvard University Press, 1989), 39, and "Feminism, Marxism, Method, and the State: Toward Feminist Jurisprudence," *Signs* 8 (1983): 636.

45. MacKinnon, "Feminism, Marxism, Method," 636.

46. MacKinnon, *Toward a Feminist Theory of the State*, 115.

47. I would recur here to Helen Cooper's important discussion in "Gender and Personification in *Piers Plowman*," *Yearbook of Langland Studies* 5 (1991): 31–48, and her particular observation that "the genders [Langland] chooses for the characters that throng *Piers Plowman*, whether they are primarily literal or conceptual, are inseparable from the import of the poem" (38). Cooper is most interested to understand how so many traditionally female allegorical figures become male in Langland's hands, and although she does not consider the figure of "Mede" directly, I take it that the "cognitive restructuring of the allegorical world" (34) she so clearly shows Langland effecting as he rethinks the gender of his personifications must have as its result a set of positive decisions that make the animation of a female "Mede" as striking and meaningful as, say, the animation of a male "Reason."

48. "Et quia dictum appellum non fuit cassatum aut conuictum vt falsum et bene constat quod eadem Cecilia bonam causam et iustam habuit appellum predictum facere et illud prosequi racionibus supradictis, licet illud prosequi non poterit eo quod virum habet, que quedam caua pocius est quedam stulticia quam falsitas, concessum est de gracia curie"; Sayles, *Select Cases*, 3:164.

49. J. B. Post, "Ravishment of Women and the Statutes of Westminster," in *Legal Records and the Historian*, ed. J. H. Baker (London: Royal Historical Society, 1978), 162. Post offers texts of the relevant statutes in an appendix to his article (162–64). See also *Statutes of the Realm* (London: Dawsons, 1963), 1:29, 87.

50. J. B. Post, "Sir Thomas West and the Statute of Rapes, 1382," *Bulletin of the Institute of Historical Research* 53 (1980): 24–25, 27. For the statute, see *Statutes of the Realm*, 2:27.

51. This complex history has been traced carefully by Sue Sheridan Walker in a series of articles. See, for example, "Common Law Juries and Feudal Marriage Customs in Medieval England: The Pleas of Ravishment," *University of Illinois Law Review* 3 (1984): 705–18; "Punishing Convicted Ravishers: Statutory Strictures and Actual Practice in Thirteenth- and Fourteenth-Century England," *Journal of Medieval History* 13 (1987): 237–50; "Wrongdoing and Compensation: The Pleas of Wardship in Thirteenth- and Fourteenth-Century England," *Journal of Legal History* 9 (1988): 267–309.

52. See Walker, "Punishing Convicted Ravishers," 238. In her discussion of the potential for settling suits of rape through marriage, Walker follows J. A. Brundage, "Rape and Marriage in the Medieval Canon Law," *Revue de droit canonique* 28 (1978): 62–75.

53. Richard H. Helmholz, *Marriage Litigation in Medieval England* (Cambridge: Cambridge University Press, 1974), 119 n. 19.

54. "A Satyre on the Consistory Courts" in *The Political Songs of England*, ed. Thomas Wright, Camden Society 6 (London, 1839), 155–59. For these lines, see 158.

55. I take the dates I give for Julian's text from Nicholas Watson, "The Composition of Julian of Norwich's *Revelation of Love*," *Speculum* 68 (1993): 637–83. Watson offers convincing arguments for giving the shorter text of Julian's *Revelation* a *terminas a quo* in 1382 and a *terminus ad quem* in 1388 (657–72), with the strong probability that the text was composed in "the later part of this period, after 1385" (672). His arguments about the longer text are more tentative but establish 1393 as its earliest date of composition (677) and propose that Julian may have still been at work on this text as late as 1413 (681). Watson's dates supplant older claims that the shorter version was written c. 1373 and the longer text c. 1393. For these dates, see Julian of Norwich, *A Book of Showings to the Anchoress Julian of Norwich*, 2 vols., ed. Edmund Colledge and James Walsh (Toronto: Pontifical Institute of Mediaeval Studies, 1978), 1:33, 2:285 and 520. All subsequent citations to Julian's text are to the longer version of this text by volume and page number in this edition.

56. Lynn Staley describes ways that Julian "employs strategies that seem to authorize her pen as an instrument of the communal 'body of Christ' "; Staley, *Margery Kempe's Dissenting Fictions* (University Park: Pennsylvania State University Press, 1994), 30.

57. *The Book of Margery Kempe*, vol. 1, ed. Sanford Brown Meech, EETS 212 (London, 1940), 1–6. Hereafter citations will be from this edition by page number in the text and notes.

58. The "confessour" mentioned in this passage is the "Duche prest" encountered by Margery in Rome who "wolde supportyn hir a-ȝen hir enmys . . . whan alle hir cuntremen had forsakyn hir" (83). The episode described in the passage I have quoted occurs slightly later during Margery's stay in Rome when the pilgrims who traveled to Jerusalem with her have complained to an English priest that Margery has been improperly confessed because her confessor "cowde not undirstondyn hir langwage ne hir confessyown" (97).

59. For a searching discussion of Kempe's English, see Staley, *Dissenting Fictions*, 129–55. Throughout her study Staley makes the distinction I make here between Kempe (the author of the *Book*) and "Margery" (the figure posited by that author).

60. For this definition of *appellare*, see *A Latin Dictionary*, ed. Charles Short and Charlton Lewis (Oxford: Clarendon Press, 1879), s. v. "appello," II, A.1. For the more strictly legal use of this verb and its derived noun, *appellum*, see *Dictionary of Medieval Latin from British Sources*, ed. R. E. Latham et al. (London: Oxford University Press, 1975–), s. v. "appellare," 4, and "appellum."

61. *Troilus and Criseyde*, 5.1590–1631, in *The Riverside Chaucer*, ed. Larry D. Benson, 3rd ed. (Boston: Houghton Mifflin, 1987). All subsequent quotations from Chaucer are taken from this edition and are cited by line number in the text.

62. David Aers, *Chaucer, Langland, and the Creative Imagination* (London: Routledge and Kegan Paul, 1980), 119. Aers's whole chapter "Chaucer's Criseyde: Woman in Society, Woman in Love" (117–42) takes this social situation seriously and describes the more general relations between "individual action, consciousness and sexuality" and "the specific social and ideological structures" (118) in *Troilus and Criseyde* that are only instanced in the episode I rehearse here.

63. E. Talbot Donaldson, "Criseyde and Her Narrator," in *Speaking of Chaucer* (Durham, N.C.: Labyrinth Press, 1983), 65–83 (for the quoted phrase, see 82).

64. Dinshaw, *Chaucer's Sexual Poetics*, 58.

CHAPTER 8

❖

Violence against Women in Fifteenth-Century France and the Burgundian State

Walter Prevenier

In this essay, I discuss the existence of the *systems* behind violence against women, especially the ways in which systems of ideology, of belief, and of prejudice inform patterns of violent behavior, and how systems of social control enable repression or prevention of these violent crimes. The study of these systems can be elucidated through two approaches. First, I will look at the legal tools for prosecuting and judging crimes against women. Second, the interpretation of individual cases is enhanced by reading them with reference to the analysis of narrative proposed by Roland Barthes, Noam Chomsky, Jacques Derrida, and the poststructuralists. What we observe in the course of analysis of a number of cases from the legal records is a struggle to control the dialogue and the narrative so that judicial opinions or the negotiated outcomes of the cases conform to prevailing ideologies. The systems evolve from the underlying narratives of the cases.

The Variety of Crimes against Women: Moral and Physical Harm

To begin, it is useful to consider whether contemporaries in the Netherlands and in the Burgundian state (now partly in France) had well-articulated definitions for the various types of violence against women and precise sanctions for each of them.[1] I do not include in this analysis crimes that are not typically gender related, such as robbery and murder. Even when limiting the discussion to crimes against women or in which women participated, the application of the laws is confusing. While the legal *theory* is quite clear and consistent, the *practices* of enforcement, jurisdictions, and jurisprudence are much more complicated because a second level of social ideas and conceptions influenced the application of the law.

Crimes involving deviant sexual behavior by consenting partners, such as adultery, homosexuality, and concubinage, might not be classified as violent or as crime at all in the medieval and modern periods, but rather as personal amusements and pleasures. I must, however, consider them here for two reasons. First, the church certainly classified these activities as offenses and transgressions of moral boundaries. By the late Middle Ages, ecclesiastical courts had replaced spiritual penalties such as penances by fines, but they continued to regard these activities as sinful.[2] If the church exhibited any gender discrimination here, it favored women: married men paid double the fine of married women.[3] Male priests had to pay for keeping concubines, but the concubines did not pay.[4] Civil authorities, on the other hand, were not interested in adultery as long as no violence accompanied the sexual activity.[5] Nevertheless, some cities introduced fines when they classified adultery as social disorder and saw prosecution of this offense as a source of income.[6] Second, adultery and concubinage, of course, were often the first steps in a process that could end in a social drama involving physical harm or murder, which is why I have included this category in the context of violence.

Prostitution was another area of crime involving women. A cosmopolitan city such as Bruges, which had a large number of foreign merchants coming to trade in cloth, had many prostitutes but did not engage in a severe repression of the occupation.[7] The city required prostitutes and their pimps to pay fines when they broke city ordinances that restricted their business to a few well-defined streets.[8] Flemish civil authorities also took some action to repress pimps as such, but I have found no trace of repression of prostitutes' customers.[9] Apparently, the city had no desire to discourage businessmen who used their services.

A third type of violence was seduction of women. Again, the action would not be considered morally violent as long as the woman consented. In most of the cases the woman simply decided in favor of a partnership or a marriage with a young man for whom she felt affection or love. Civil authorities, nevertheless, considered seduction as an offense when the parents, the extended family, or the friends of the woman opposed the relationship. Urban laws punished it with a banishment of three years.[10] If a man seduced a married woman and if he and his beloved took part of the husband's patrimony with them when they fled, the exile was extended to ten years for both lovers.[11] But in many cases the bailiffs proposed that the offenders make financial recompense equal to one-half year of unskilled labor. Most of the legislation against seduction entered law at the behest of parties who felt responsible for the young women. Urban and committal ordinances regulated the consequences of seduction for people who felt they had a vested interest. Essentially, the laws permitted the city officials or the count to recover the woman's property by confiscating her actual goods and by excluding her from an inheritance. As soon as she left her lover, she was fully restored in both of her rights, which provided a strong economic incentive for the family to back up the moral pressure they were already putting on her.[12] The law penalized the woman in order to persuade her to act as her family wished.

A fourth area of crime was abduction and rape. Since illicit sex overlapped in these cases with violent actions, canon law did not handle these offenses; instead they came under lay legislation and jurisdiction. Abduction was punishable by death or, at least, by banishment for life.[13] The rapist was considered an outlaw for life, and his act was considered a crime not only against the woman, but also against her family and the public order.

Decoding the Discourse on Violence and on Repression of Crimes against Women

The fifteenth-century discourse on adultery and concubinage was complex. On the one hand, adultery was a common topic for ironical treatment in literature and theater; on the other hand, it was archetypical of a fatal attraction that could lead to extreme jealousy and to the lovers' murder by the cuckolded husband. The contradiction between the two discourses, however, is not as great as it seems. Each discourse forms part of the same reality, but is effective in its individual narrative. The literary narrative criticizes and makes fun of the naive behavior of ridiculous husbands. The narrative of the court and the pardon process justifies the anger of the duped husband, who finds an effective, albeit violent, way to fight back against the lover. A husband's violent outrage was a widely accepted excuse to justify murder and to obtain pardon. In a sense the literary treatment of the cuckolded husband sets up the alibi for a husband who murders his wife's lover.

The elites in fifteenth-century Burgundian society had no strong moral condemnations against the phenomenon of entertaining mistresses or producing bastard children.[14] In part, a man who maintained mistresses and had bastards about the house was part of a snobbish way of life that conferred high status.[15] Such a man imitated the duke himself. Only foreign visitors to the Netherlands, like the Czech Leo von Rosmital in 1465–67, showed indignation and disbelief in observing the comfortable position of bastards at the duke of Burgundy's court.[16] One Breton Carmelite in 1428 took considerable risk in criticizing Flemish clerics openly for their frivolous behavior, but his admonitions had no practical effect.[17]

In lower- and middle-class society, by contrast, adultery often turned into social drama because of the element of public scandal. If neighbors of the village or the urban parish openly observed the behavior of the adulterous partner, the betrayed husband (less frequently the wife) was pushed, because of shame, to violence or even to homicide. The victim was the wife's lover and the motive was jealousy, dishonor, or anger (*chaude colle*).[18] Natalie Davis and Claude Gauvard have shown that "hot anger" or fury was an argument that was frequently accepted as an exculpatory motivation for the grant of pardon by the French king. The fifteenth-century dukes of Burgundy followed the same practice.[19]

Public dishonor also appeared as a theme in socially mixed, extramarital relations. The disadvantage in these cases accrued to the poor mistress of a well-to-do, elite male, as can be seen in the play *Mirror of Love* (c. 1480) by the Brussels poet Colyn van Ryssele. Catherine, the main female character and a poor seamstress, is in love with the son of a rich merchant. She repeatedly complains that she cannot marry him because his family is socially superior to hers. When a friend suggests that she simply be his mistress for a while,[20] Catherine rejects the proposal on moral grounds and argues, fundamentally, that as a poor working girl she would lose her honor and destroy all her hopes for a proper marriage.[21] Her virginity is her only capital. Van Ryssele (a tender anarchist, as I have elsewhere called him) adds a social reflection: he has Catherine argue that dishonor is not the price of a fling for wealthy ladies because, although they lose their paradise of love, they retain a second capital, the family's patrimony. Only poor women suffer both physical loss and loss of honor in illicit sex.

The legal discourse on medieval prostitution shows the same ambiguity and double moral standard as today. On the one hand, prostitution was considered a forbidden activity and a sin; on the other, it was accepted and tolerated as a useful way to keep the sexual needs of young people under control within the framework of the *bien commun*. Rape of a prostitute was often not considered a crime.[22]

In the discourse on seduction, we might expect condemnation to come from ecclesiastical sources, since the act involves fornication. But the ecclesiastical authorities could fit seduction within an ideology of free will and the church's teaching that marriage was valid only between consenting partners, and would be so even if the liaison was against the will of the parents. Priests seem to have been quite helpful to couples seeking this type of matrimonial alliance. The only point at which the church objected was when seduction took the form of a clandestine marriage, that is, when no priest officiated. But from the Fourth Lateran Council of 1215 to the Council of Trent of 1563 clandestine marriage was accepted as a valid, although neither desirable nor legal, form of marriage.[23]

The real indignation against seduction came from parents and extended family, who regarded it as an infringement on parental authority and on the integrity of the patrimony. The Flemish bourgeoisie convinced the count of Flanders in 1297 to publish a charter by which a seduced girl lost all her possessions and inheritance, *as if she were dead*, in favor of the rest of the family.[24] In 1438 the discourse of the duke of Burgundy, inspired by the same burghers, represented seduction and clandestine marriages as a social plague. Adding force to his admonitions, he introduced sophisticated techniques for confiscating the seduced girl's goods and for offering attractive provisions to induce her to leave the unwanted lover and rejoin the family.[25] Parents frequently tried to eliminate a daughter's lover in a radical way by representing the sexual relationship to the court as a rape when, in fact, it was a seduction.[26] In England in the seventeenth century clandestine marriages also seem to have been a way to avoid social control by parents and extended family.[27]

The medieval prosecution of and discourse on rape and abduction raised many of the cultural attitudes toward women that characterize it today. Is the woman's complaint legitimate? Has the woman provoked her attacker's violent behavior or even consented to the sexual act? The woman's complaint is further undermined by lies from the aggressor and male chauvinism from the judge. Contemporary literature borrowed the misogynistic image of the eternal seductive Eve that generations of theologians had developed and articulated.[28] In courts sarcastic stories about "false" accusations by abducted women suggest that the theologians' misogyny permeated male society at large. Because an act of rape was not necessarily public, the victim often found it hard to supply evidence or witnesses, so that accusation and defense were reduced to her word against that of the accused man. The decisive factor was whether or not the woman cried at the time of the alleged rape.[29] But witnesses often lied about what had happened, as did the victim herself. In some cases an inquiry by *matrones* was organized to inspect the victim to determine if loss of virginity had occurred.[30] A final problem area in the prosecution of rape cases was the twilight zone between seduction and abduction. The actors and the outsiders often changed their accounts during the investigation or the trial, either out of self-interest or out of pressure from other parties to the case.

These three factors influenced, without any doubt, the discourse on fifteenth-century testimonies on rape, and they complicate our decoding of these texts. But in addition to these problems we struggle with another uncertainty: do the authors reflect the facts objectively or do they select and manipulate them according to their own ideology? Chomsky, Derrida, and the poststructuralists have shown that texts are often used as weapons in social battles and, as such, are sophisticated constructions, appropriate for analysis under a deconstructivist reading. We must not neglect the difference between the *competence* of the author and the *performance* in the use of the message, between the intentions of the witness and the effect on the audience.[31] Linguists tell us that readers decode texts in thousands of different ways, corresponding to thousands of realities. In other words, interpretation is totally free. But Umberto Eco has helped us to escape from this text-critical anarchy.[32] He suggests that the limit on interpretative freedom is the consensus of a few specialists, in this case scholars of the fifteenth century who are familiar with the semantics, the ideas, and the social mores of the time. We can easily apply here the idea of Pierre Bourdieu: "le discours juridique est une parole créatrice, qui fait exister ce qu'elle énonce" (the juridical discourse is a creative text, which brings into reality what it expresses); ideas creating reality.[33]

Why do we find in the sources of fifteenth-century jurisprudence so many contradictory meanings on the importance and the condemnation of the crime of rape and abduction? Why did judges and princes frequently make inconsistent decisions when they repressed this same category of offense — sometimes invoking the death sentence, sometimes reconciliation proceedings with a financial compensation, and sometimes pardon? Why does one rape story end in perpetual banishment and another in successful marriage? The technical handicaps discussed above help to explain the divergencies, but we need further analysis.

The first and most comprehensive explanation for the contradictions and inconsistencies is the changing social dynamic in the view of women and their victimization in crime. Françoise Autrand, Henriette Benveniste, and Claude Gauvard have demonstrated that the juridical and political discourse of the lawyers and judges of the Parlement of Paris at the end of the fourteenth century reflected the general public and royal ideology: to preserve the existing social relations by legitimizing the sexual act through marriage.[34] This ideology produced a cultural model in which the rapist could rely on considerable tolerance and comprehension if the victim finally consented to a marriage. This view changed in the beginning of the fifteenth century, when rapes started to become a plague, disturbing social peace by bringing about private wars between families. From then on the repression of rape became a more serious matter for the state, which focused more on the protection of families and the "chose publique" than on the concern about marriage and the position of women. An analogous change occurred in Flanders and in other parts of Europe in the same period.[35]

In the remainder of the essay I want to elaborate on two aspects of ideology about women and the law. The first is that we must not reduce the discourse of public authority to a single voice, because the notion of "public authority" is too abstract. We must distinguish at least three levels within the juridical system, each producing specific narratives of its own. I will leave aside for the time being the distinctions between individual medieval bailiffs and judges. As historians we are dependent on surviving written records and statements, composed personally by officials or decision makers or drafted by secretaries who represented more or less accurately the words and ideas of the actors. Do we look totally through the eyes of the notaries of the courts? Do we really hear the voices of the witnesses? Do we hear the female voice? I reserve these aspects of the problem for later research. I concentrate now on the different voices of judicial authority.

The first level of distinction within the judicial system is that of the police officers (bailiffs). Their duties included hearing the complaints of women and deciding to take them seriously or not, investigating the case, arresting the suspect, analyzing the facts, and suggesting sanctions and penalties.[36] Their ideology was a more or less rudimentary sense of law and order. The motivation for an obstinate inquiry might be ascribed to self-interest. For instance, in 1463 the bailiff of Hulst suspected a twenty-one-year-old *povre compaignon*, Guillaume de Waghenaere, of the rape of a woman of fifty-four. The bailiff tells us himself that he could not furnish conclusive evidence because of the lack of cries and witnesses. There was a reasonable chance that no rape had occurred and that the case rested solely on gossip and rumors. The rest of the bailiff's narrative tells the story of the man who has courted an older woman but regrets it after meeting a nice young girl. He is afraid that he will be made a fool because of his relationship with an older woman. The woman, on the other hand, tries to make him live up to the promised marriage and terrorizes him by unwanted visits. She is terrorized in turn by the young man, who beats her every day. Finally, the young man himself is terrorized by the police officers and flees the city for fear of being arrested. The story, however, has a happy ending: once the bailiff finds out that there has been a clandestine marriage between the young man and the older woman and that they are protected by well-to-do burghers in Hulst, Guillaume is allowed to come back into the city after having paid to the bailiff, or having persuaded his enlarged family and circle of friends to pay for him, a fine corresponding to a year's wages of an unskilled worker. Many different interests inform the action of this narrative, not the least of which is the bailiff's self-interest.[37] It is also a story of the effect of extended family protection.

The second level within this system is the lay court, the court of the city, and the court of the duke. Here we find the confrontation of many discourses in permanent and evident contradiction: the discourses of the statements of the two parties, defendant and complainant; the more sophisticated discourses of the prosecutor and of the advocates of the parties, which make use of a huge repertory of procedural tricks, and thereby leave the judge and the historian to verify the arguments and to struggle with their own personal opinions. One of the spectacular tricks of fifteenth-century lawyers was the claim that the defendant had clerical status and could not be judged by a lay court. In 1395 the archbishop of Reims used this argument to defend his protégé, Jean de Thuisy, in a case before the Parlement of Paris in order to rescue him from the clutches of the duke of Burgundy's officials. The technique was efficient, even though it could well be based on a false story of tonsure.[38]

The third level is located at the top of the state hierarchy, the ducal or royal court, and entails the grant of pardon by the ruler. The duke could intervene at the first level, before a conviction. But a real pardon came after the second phase, especially after a banishment. The remission document, the famous pardon tale, necessarily mixed up opinions on crime and social order with the discretionary power of the prince. As Natalie Zemon Davis explains, the pardon tale needs a specific narrative construction.[39] It starts with daily business and builds to a climactic out-burst, drama, or tragedy and, finally, to violence. Then begins a tale of circumstances ("daily business") that builds to the climax of a tragic event; the end is often a flight and always a conviction. The second part of the pardon tale deals with a discourse on innocence and unintentionality, suggesting the legitimacy of the actions. It mentions useful witnesses and details (what Barthes calls the "reality effect"), securing credibility and compassion for the defendant. I am afraid that in many of the stories the remission text suggests a narrative logic that has no genuine logic at all. But the ritual is effective.

A useful case to illustrate the three levels is that of Clais Boudinszoon, valet of a squire in the isle of Kruiningen in Zeeland in 1447, who wished to force a marriage with a rich widow he knew living in Hulst as a way of social promotion. The criminal facts were evident, and the local bailiff did his job. The committal court of Flanders made the correct judicial decision: banishment from Flanders for fifty years not only for the rapist Boudinszoon, but also for his friends and his squire, the lord of Kruinin-gen. Nevertheless, one year later the duke of Burgundy granted pardon, for which the squire had applied, because it would have been politically dangerous for the duke not to have done so. The squire was a member of one of the Zeeland families supporting the Zeeland nobility, who were struggling for independent status in opposition to Burgundianization of the area. These families also had control over the granting or refusing of the regional taxes to the central state. The duke reasoned that it was better to have the squire as an ally. In addition, the lord of Kruiningen had family ties with important judges in the Court of Flanders.

At the time of my research and article on Boudinszoon's case in 1987 I was forced to state that the pardon tale was not very convincing and showed a clear internal contradiction.[40] The first part, "daily business," is from the start a brutal story of violence, terror, explicit protest (*clamor*) of the widow attested by witnesses, and marriage under pressure.[41] The second part is a portrait of the "good" squire, who tries to prevent crime and violence without much success, and pleads pardon for himself and for his servants simply because they are the servants of an honorable man, because they enjoyed a good reputation until the crime, and because they will be kept under control by him in the future.[42] The pardon by the duke in 1449 was a decision of power, not of morality. But why did the duke *not* intervene during the first level (the bailiff's actions)? Why did the protection of the family of the powerful squire not work on the second level (the conviction in the court)? An intervention by the duke from the start would have allowed a more discreet management of the case, avoiding the incredibility of the pardon. I overlooked an important link in 1987: the identity of the victim. Research for the exhibition in 1994 of the paintings of Hans Memling demonstrated that the raped lady was represented on a panel of a Memling painting and was a member of high society in Flanders, mother of the influential abbot of Ten Duinen, and close to the court circles of the duke.[43] It is clear that the bailiff of Hulst and the judge of the Flemish court had to take her complaint seriously.

So much for the contradictions between different levels of the repression process. My second remark on Benveniste's stimulating analysis concerns contradictions, or rather changes, within the discourse of a single person who may be one of the actors as well as one of the authorities.

An actor's change of view of the circumstances of the case may be the result of a real psychological shift. In 1438 Jan Wouterszoon fled with sixteen-year-old Jakemien from Middelburg to a village in Brabant, where they declared before the local aldermen that Jakemien had freely accompanied her lover and that she intended to consent to marry him. Indeed, that is what happened a day later in a valid and legal marriage before a priest. Some months later the girl probably became homesick (my interpretation).[44] What the source explicitly tells us is that she contacted her family in Middelburg (or did they come to her?) and that they pressed her in such a way that she introduced a complaint for abduction against her husband before the Court of Holland. The court convicted the husband, but he appealed to the duke and got a pardon. A Romeo and Juliet story became an abduction tale for a while, and then reverted to the narrative of a marriage based on seduction once again. It is absolutely clear that Jakemien changed her opinion within a year. We have hard evidence for her successive opinions: her declaration of free flight (that is, seduction) before the aldermen in Brabant and her complaint of abduction before the Court of Holland. What we do not know and never will know is whether she changed her mind by free will because her affection for Jan came to an end or because of pressure from her family.[45]

A change could also occur in the mind of the public authority in the short term and within one case. The 1477 drama in Mechlen of the widow of the Lord of Humbercourt, one of the duke of Burgundy's top officials, is a case in point.[46] During a revolt of the Flemish cities, Lord Humbercourt, together with Hugonet, the prime minister of Duke Charles the Bold, died in Ghent on the scaffold in April 1477, as a symbol of the power of the central state. Eight months later a squire, Adriaan Vilain, eager for social promotion, abducted Humbercourt's wealthy widow and tried to convince her to consent freely to marry him.[47] Archduke Maximilian and his wife moved heaven and earth to rescue the widow, and their efforts were successful. Vilain was arrested, but escaped and fled to Calais, continuing on to different places in France. In 1481 he received remission from the same archduke, who had secured, four years earlier, so much police effort to arrest him.

The interesting point in the two cases of changing views is, of course, the explanation of the change. I propose in both cases to argue for the presence of a second, underlying discourse, explicit or implicit. In the case of Middelburg the pressure applied by the family on the married woman is explicitly mentioned. Let us be careful, however: the accusation of pressure is part of the pardon tale inspired by the husband and reflects his view. The interpretation must be close to reality: the grant of pardon was based not only on an inquiry that checked the actions of the family at the Court of Holland, but also on hard evidence, namely documents indicating free marriage. The underlying discourse was, therefore, the defense of the family patrimony against intruders.

In the Humbercourt case, as in many others, the plot is much more complex. In 1477 the protection of the widow so recently after the execution of her husband was for Archduke Maximilian a point of honor and a demonstration of the existence and the efficiency of the clan system of the Burgundian duke. Maximilian also showed that he could provide a social safety net for the widow and the children of a deceased loyal top official of the Crown.[48] Four years later the conditions changed completely. Indeed, when Adriaan flew from prison in 1488, he found a refuge in the clan of the count of Romont, an army officer so successful in the war against the French that the archduke made him a knight of the Golden Fleece. Via the clan of Romont, friend of the archduke, the former rapist Vilain was able to move into the clan of the duke. Four years later the widow of Humbercourt made no objections against pardon for her rapist. Although invited three times, she did not come to the court. The old story, the danger, and the importance of public punishment were over.

In this second case the underlying discourse is related to the demonstration of the continuous attractive power of networks and clans. It is part of what Barbara Hanawalt once called "fur collar crime."[49] I refer to typical cases in my area: that of the widow Ysablet des Champions in Paris in 1393–94, that of Jean Pastoure in Champagne in 1383, that of Jean de Thuisy in Rethel in 1395, that of squire Zweer van Kruiningen in Zeeland in 1449, that of Dirk van Langerode, patrician of Louvain in 1477, and many others.[50] Most of these networks include members of the various elites, as well as lower-class people, servants, and "underdogs" such as the servants of the squire of Kruiningen who got off with complicity in rape, and poor Guillaume de Waghenaere and his Berthele in Hulst who escaped prosecution for rape because of the intervention of richer members of their extended family and because of their connections to civil authorities.

One conclusion we may draw from this examination of rape cases suggests that rape and abduction are crimes, in most cases effectively liable to prosecution and conviction; that is, death sentence or exile for life. Some culprits escaped by fleeing abroad. Some rapists arranged, with the help of the bailiff, a compromise (*compositio*) with the family of the raped girl in an effort to integrate the offender into the family by way of marriage.[51] Others reached a compromise with the civil authority by paying a large fine.[52] Sometimes the family of a condemned man tried to obtain pardon from the prince before the wretch was executed, often without success.[53] The most effective technique was pardon after banishment or flight, on condition that the supplicant could be subsequently integrated into a protection network.

Social Control of Violence against Women

The regular juridical system for repression of crime seems to have worked for most of the complaints, at least for the initiation of the prosecution. But the follow-up of a case, as we have seen, could be interrupted or influenced by interventions of networks.

For the tracing of adultery, prostitution, seduction, and rape, two local or regional systems were effective for hunting down the perpetrators. For moral offenses (adultery, concubinage) a network of parochial priests and local synods (with lay inspectors) took care of the detection and punishment of the suspects. For violent offenses the efficiency of the bailiffs was encouraged through financial incentives, and the duke's repression of violence was also linked to his financial goals.[54] There must also have been a lot of local jealousy and gossip that brought cases into the courts.[55] But the apparent anarchy in the granting of remissions hides what was, in fact, a well-organized system of clan activity and counter-powers. During the late Middle Ages the dukes of the Burgundian Netherlands attempted to link, through the ritual of granting pardons, the urban solidarity systems and social networks to the well-developed clan of the dukes of Burgundy.

Notes

1. A marvelous introduction to the changing attitudes of society on sanctions for different crimes is Petrus Cornelis Spierenburg, *The Spectacle of Suffering: Executions and the Evolution of Repression: From a Pre-industrial Metropolis to the European Experience* (Cambridge: Cambridge University Press, 1984), a work essentially based on data from Amsterdam between 1650 and 1750.

2. Monique Vleeschouwers–Van Melkebeek, "Aspects du lien matrimonial dans le Liber Sentenciarum de Bruxelles (1448–1459)," *Tijdschrift voor Rechtsgeschiedenis* 53 (1985): 43–97.

3. Archives Départementales du Nord (ADN), Lille, 14 G 93, fol. 71r: "In Sancta Maria Brugensi: Philippus van Thilrode, conjugatus, et Katharina nunc uxor Juliani Hugout, quia invicem adulterium commiserunt. Solvit vir 12 lb., et mulier 6 lb., sunt 18 lb." (In [the parish of] Our Lady in Bruges: Philip van Thilrode, married, and Catherine now wife of Julianus Hogout, because they committed adultery with each other; the man pays 12 lb., the woman 6 lb., the total is 18 lb.) (account of the ecclesiastical court of Tournai). In an account of 1388, the bailiff of Assenede makes the following statement: "dont l'amende est 5 lb., pour cause que une femme ne doit que demi amende" (for this the fine is 5 lb., because a woman must pay only half of the fine); Algemeen Rijks Archief (ARA), Brussels, Rolrekeningen, 1389.

4. ADN, Lille, 14 G 93, fol. 75r: "In Arssebroucq: magister Johannes Maghelin, presbyter, curatus ibidem, quia diverses mulieres communes diversis vicibus per certum tem-

poris spatium in sua domo tenuit, solvit 6 lb." (In Assebroek: master John Maghelin, cleric, parish priest, because he kept several prostitutes from several neighborhoods in his house for a certain length of time, paid 6 lb.).

5. In 1517 a deal is made between the ecclesiastical and civil authorities in Flanders: "affin qu'il soit interdit au juge ecclesiastique de, a cause de fornications, deflorations et aultres delictz mixtifori, condemner les personnes layes...fors seulement pour adultere publique" (with the intention that the ecclesiastical judge would be prohibited from condemning lay persons for fornication, rape, and other offenses of the category "mixtifori"... with the only exception of public adultery); A. Dubois and L. De Hondt, *Coutume de la ville de Gand* (Brussels, 1887), 2:101.

6. For example, the city of Breda in 1454; see W. Bezemer, *Oude Rechtsbronnen der stad Breda* (Utrecht, 1892), 56–57.

7. Leah Otis, *Prostitution in Medieval Society: The History of an Urban Institution in Languedoc* (Chicago and London: Chicago University Press, 1985), 25–39. In the fourteenth and fifteenth centuries prostitutes in the cities of the south of France enjoyed real protection from the municipal and royal authorities; see also Jacques Rossiaud, *La prostitution médiévale* (Paris, 1988); translated by Lydia G. Cochrane under the title *Medieval Prostitution* (Oxford: Blackwell, 1988).

8. Archives of the city of Bruges, Hallegeboden, 1490–99, fol. 69: "Item dat gheene vrauen...van wilden...levene bij avonde achter strate te ghane ghelike ter Cranen, ter Buersen...up den ghuenen die bevonden zullen worden...ghebannen te zijne ter discrecien van scepenen" (Item that no prostitute is allowed to walk at night in streets such as ter Cranen, ter Buersen...; those found doing so will be banished at the discretion of the aldermen) (September 27, 1491). The motivation was to keep the commercial heart of the city safe. Otherwise there was no real segregation behavior for prostitutes in Bruges; Guy Dupont, *Maagdenverleidsters, hoeren en speculanten: Prostitutie in Brugge tijdens de Bourgondische periode (1385–1515)* (Bruges, 1996), 140.

9. ARA, Brussels, Rekenkamer, Reg. 14.460, fol. 13r (account of the bailiff of the Land van Waas, September 1433–September 1434): "De Henry Tac...lequel fut banny hors du pays de Flandres par la loy de Hulst III ans, et fu son title d'avoir vescu sur avantage de femmes communes, on le dyst en flamenc putierscap" (From Henry Tac...who has been banished from Flanders by the aldermen of Hulst for three years, and the cause was that he lived on the resources of prostitutes, which in Flemish is called *putierscap*). Cf. Dupont, *Maagdenverleidsters,* 115–27.

10. On the different sanctions in Flanders, see R. C. Van Caenegem, *Geschiedenis van het strafrecht in Vlaanderen van de XIe tot de XIVe eeuw* (Brussels: Verhandelingen Koninklijke Academie voor Wetenschappen, 1954), 104–5.

11. ARA, Brussels, Rekenkamer, Rolrekening 1389: "(part: Ce sont les banniz): Maes Bouters banni X ans...pour le grant mal et outrage qu'il a fait et a emmené la femme d'un preudhomme nommé Gillez le Baec et ont emporté son avoir. Item Margriete la Charatiere, femme du devant dit Gillez le Baec, banni X ans...pour ce qu'elle s'en est alé auvecque Maes Bouters" (These are the exiles: Maes Bouters, banished for 10 years,...because of the great harm and damage that he caused, by the abduction of the wife of a man of good name called Gillez le Baec; they also took the goods of this man. Item Margriete la Charatiere, wife of the aforenamed Gillez le Baec, banished for ten years,...because she ran off with Maes Bouters).

12. Charter of the count of Flanders (April 8, 1297) (translated from Dutch): "if a man seduces a woman having father or mother, with her will, or an orphan, and if he is doing this against the will of the father and the mother...all her goods will be confiscated, as well as her future inheritance. The goods are going to her heirs, as if she were dead. The man who is seducing her, will be banished for three years from Flanders"; A. E. Gheldolf, *Coutume de la ville de Gand* (Brussels, 1868), 1:450, art. 59.

13. On the various sanctions, see Van Caenegem, *Geschiedenis van het strafrecht,* 97–104.

14. See Françoise Autrand, "Naissance illégitime et service de l'état: Les enfants naturels dans le milieu de robe parisien, XIVe–XVe siècle," *Revue Historique* 514 (1982): 289–303; and Ludwig Schmugge, *Kirche, Kinder, Karrieren: Päpstliche Dispense von der unehelichen Geburt im Spätmittalter* (Zurich, 1995). On Flanders, see Myriam Carlier, "La politique des autorités envers les bâtards dans les Pays-Bas bourguignons," in *Public and Private Finances in the Late Middle Ages*, ed. Walter Prevenier and Marc Boone (Louvain and Apeldoorn: Garant, 1996).

15. For a contemporary view, see H. Beaune and J. d'Arbaumont, eds., *Olivier de la Marche, Memoires* (Paris, 1883–88), 1:55.

16. Leo von Rozmital, "Ritter-, Hof- and Pilger-Reise," *Bibliothek der Literarischen Vereins in Stuttgart* 7 (1844): 28: "Aderant tum tres Bastardi ejusdem (= Ducis Burgundiae), qui in nostri regione spurii appellantur. Ii in illis regionibus in nullo probro habentur, veluti apud nos. Namque itidem illis cibis et potus praegustatur, sicut filio Ducis legitimo" (Three bastards of the same [duke of Burgundy], who would be called children of a whore in our region, were present. But in these regions there was no disdain for them, as there would be at home. For them the victuals and the drinks were tasted beforehand, just as for the legitimate son of the duke).

17. "Qui publiquement tenoient femmes en leur compagnie et enfraignoient le voeu de chasteté" (those who publicly keep women with them, and break the vow of chastity); Walter Prevenier and W. P. Blockmans, *The Burgundian Netherlands* (Cambridge: Cambridge University Press, 1985), 149.

18. Cf. the Pardon letter of Duke Philip the Good for Jacot Barcueille from July 1455 (ADN, Lille, B 1686, fols. 39 v–40r): "Le suppliant eust deffendu audit Estevenin la hantise de son hostel... aussi qu'il se gardast de soy accointer a sa dicte femme;... retourné... de nuyt en son hostel... il trouva ledit Estevenin... en son dit hostel avec sa femme... et oy qu'ilz se acorderent ensemble de couchier l'ung avec l'autre... telement que le dit suppliant de chaude colle couru sus au dit Estevenin et le navra telement d'ung costel... que Estevenin termina vie par mort.... Ledit Estevenin estoit homme de mauvaiz gouvernement, vanteur de femmes.... il s'estoit par plusieurs fois vanté en divers lieux qu'il avoit eu habilitacion charnelle avec la femme d'icellui suppliant" ([It is said that] the supplicant forbade the aforenamed Estevenin from frequenting his house... and also from approaching his wife;... coming back home at night, he found the aforenamed Estevenin... in his house with his wife... and found out that they slept with each other... so that the aforenamed supplicant was seized by rage and assaulted the aforenamed Estevenin, and injured him with a knife, so thoroughly that Estevenin died. The aforenamed Estevenin was a man of bad behavior, who boasted about [his success with] women.... he bragged many times that he had had sexual intercourse with the wife of the supplicant).

19. Natalie Zemon Davis, *Fiction in the Archives: Pardon Tales and Their Tellers in Sixteenth-Century France* (Stanford, Calif.: Stanford University Press, 1987), 36–76; Claude Gauvard, *"De grâce especial," crime, état et société en France à la fin du Moyen Age*, 2 vols. (Paris: Publications de la Sorbonne, 1991), 705–52 (*l'honneur blessé*). On the argument of anger in the letters of remission of the dukes, see Marc Boone, "Want remitteren is princelijck: Vorstelijk genaderecht en sociale realiteiten in de Bourgondische periode," in *Liber Amicorum Achiel de Vos* (Evergem: Heemkundig Genootschap van het Meetjesland, 1989), 53–59; and Monique Pineau, "Les lettres de rémission lilloises fin du XVe., début du XVIe. siècle," *Revue du Nord* 55 (1973): 236–37. On remissions in France, see *La faute, la répression et le pardon: Actes du 107e. Congrès national des Sociétés Savantes, Brest 1982* (Paris, 1984).

20. Marc Boone, Thérèse de Hemptinne, and Walter Prevenier, "Fictie en historische realiteit: Colijn van Rijsseles De Spiegel der Minnen, ook een spiegel van sociale spanningen in de Nederlanden in de late middeleeuwen," *Jaarboek Koninklijke Soevereine Hoofdkamer van Retorica De Fonteine te Gent* 34 (1984): 9–33.

21. In M. W. Immink, ed., *De Spiegel der Minnen door Colijn van Rijssele* (Utrecht, 1913), 98, lines 2772–74, when her nephew suggests that Catherine become a mistress

("wildy dan heymelijcke brocxkens stelen in Venus boomgaert?" [Will you secretly steal morsels in Venus's orchard?]), Catherine answers that she cannot because it would be considered scandalous behavior ("Eylacen neen ick, tware vylonye" [Alack, not I, it would be villainy]).

22. In 1510 the Flemish jurist Filip Wielant proclaimed this theory; see Jos Monballyu, *Filips Wielant Versameld Werk* (Brussels, 1995), 1:88–89, 223. In France it has been a permanent point of discussion; see Otis, *Prostitution*, 68–69. The servants of the duke of Burgundy, aggressors of a widow at night in the streets of Paris in 1394, use the excuse that they thought the widow was a prostitute; when the widow asks the men to leave her in peace ("lessez moy aler, je suy mariee et femme de mesnage" [Let me go, I am married and a housewife]), they answer, "Vous y mentez, putain, ne scet l'en pas bien qui vous estez, je vous ay foutue passé a XII ans" (You lie, whore, I know exactly who you are, I fucked you twelve years ago) (ADN, Lille, B 1276–12.884 [January 2, 1394, n.s.]). I discuss this case in "Violence against Women in a Medieval Metropolis: Paris around 1400," in *Law, Custom, and the Social Fabric in Medieval Europe: Essays in Honor of Bryce Lyon*, ed. Bernard S. Bachrach and David Nicholas (Kalamazoo, Mich.: Medieval Institute, 1990), 264, 270.

23. See J. Bossy, *Christianity in the West, 1400–1700* (Oxford: Oxford University Press, 1985), 25; and J. Boulton, "Clandestine Marriages in London: An Examination of a Neglected Urban Variable," *Urban History* 20 (1993): 191–210.

24. Gheldolf, *Coutume*, 1:450.

25. Text from 1438: Frans De Potter, *Petit cartulaire de Gand* (Ghent, 1885), 66–69: "Comme puis aucun temps en ça pluseurs prinses, ravissemens, efforcemens et violences de pucelles et autres femmes aient esté soubz umbre de mariage faites...par aucuns... par convoitise d'avoir leurs chevances;...Et se ainsi avenoit que par le consentement delle mariage d'eulx deux se feist ou qu'ilz se tenissent...ensemble couvertement ou appartement...elle ne joyra delors en avant de ses biens, mais le droit hoir d'elle les cueillera... et en joyra comme de ces propres biens, ainsi que se elle feust morte. Et se ledit mariage ne se faisoit et qu'elle se absentast de luy, et que par justice ou autrement le facteur alast de vie à trespas ou qu'elle se mariast à autre, elle auroit lors la jouissance de sesdiz biens" (Since for some time many abductions, rapes, and violence against virgins and other women have occurred under the appearance of marriage...by some men, eager for the patrimony [of these women];...And if the two of them consented to marriage, or started to live together, openly or secretly...the girl will no longer enjoy the possession of her goods... but her heir will inherit...and this person will enjoy these as if they were his own goods, and as if she were dead. And if the marriage is not consummated, and the girl leaves the man, and that by justice or otherwise the rapist dies, or if she marries another man, she will enjoy her own goods).

26. ARA, Brussels, Rekenkamer, Rolrekeningen, 1293, bailiff of Ghent châtellenie (January 1424–January 1425), in the village of Lembeke: "Pieter de Wulf avoit emmené la fille de Alard Stouten oultre le gré et volenté dudit Alard;...et tant que il (= le bailli) parla a la dicte fille, laquelle lui (= bailli) dist que tout ce que ledit Pierre de Wulf avoit fait, estoit de son gré et consentement....Et lesquels Wulf et la fille prinrent l'un l'autre a mariage;... le dit bailli le laissa composer pour la somme de 36 lb." (Pieter de Wulf had abducted the daughter of Alard Stouten against Alard's will;...and as long as the bailiff talked to the girl, she told him that everything that Pierre de Wulf did with her was done with her consent....And the aforenamed Wulf and the girl took each other as man and wife;...the aforenamed bailiff let them settle for a sum of 36 lb.).

27. John Gillis, *For Better, for Worse: British Marriages, 1600 to the Present* (Oxford, 1985), 96; on the same topic in the Low Countries, see A. G. Weiler, "De ontwikkeling van de middeleeuwse kerkelijke rechtspraak in het bisdom Utrecht inzake excommunicatie belopen vanwege clandestiene huwelijken, tot aan het Concilie van Trente," *Archief voor de geschiedenis van de katholieke kerkj in Nederland* 29 (1987): 149–65.

28. Marie-Thérèse d'Alverny, "Comment les théologiens et les philosophes voient la femme," *Cahiers de Civilisation médiévale* 20 (1977): 105–29; Chiara Frugoni, "La femme

imaginée," in *Histoire des Femmes en Occident,* vol. 2: *Le moyen âge,* ed. Georges Duby and Michelle Perrot (Paris: Plon, 1990), 357–437.

29. On this element in the Low Countries, see Jan Buntinx, "Verkrachting en hulpgeroep in het Oud-Vlaams recht," *Handelingen Zuidnederlandse Maatschappij voor Taal-, Letterkunde, en Geschiedenis* 9 (1955): 15–21.

30. For examples of the "research" of hard evidence in the trial of Jehan de Thuisy, see Archives Nationales (AN), Paris, X 2a 12, fols. 259r–260r). Thuisy, accused of rape of a girl, makes the following statement: "et fut admenee la dicte fille par devant le dit gouverneur et interroguee se le dit de Thuisy ne l'avoit pas baisiee et efforciee, et elle respondi que non;...et apres le dit gouverneur parla a elle; et le dimanche ensuivant...fist on dire a la fillette qu'elle requeist que on lui feist justice du dit de Thuisy;...pour ce qu'il ne confessoit le fait...le mistrent a question par six fois...et ne volt riens confesser;...le dit Thuisy dist qu'il ameroit mieulx confesser qu'il en eust efforcié XX que estre plus questionné" (the aforenamed girl was brought before the governor, and was interrogated to see if the aforenamed de Thuisy had had sexual intercourse with her, and she said no:...then the governor talked to her; the next Sunday...they made the girl say she wanted justice to be done to de Thuisy;...because he did not confess the facts, they tortured him six times...and he did not confess;...the aforenamed de Thuisy said that he preferred to confess that he raped 20 women, than to be questioned further under torture). The bailiff claimed that "la fillette...dist que le dit...l'avoit...efforciee et avoit esté pour ce bien malade;...il fist visiter la dicte fillette et fut trouvee violee par le rapport des matrones" (the girl said that [Thuisy] did rape her and that she had been awfully sick by this;...he asked to have the aforenamed girl inspected, and she was found to have been raped by a report of the matrones [= midwives]). On the method of the inquiry by *matrones,* see Vleeschouwers–Van Melkebeek, "Aspects du lien," 82, 88.

31. Noam Chomsky, *Aspects of the Theory of Syntax* (Cambridge: Cambridge University Press, 1965); Jacques Derrida, *Of Grammatology,* trans. Gayatri Chakravorty Spivak (Baltimore, Md.: Johns Hopkins University Press, 1976); Roland Barthes, "The Discourse of History," in *The Rustle of Language,* trans. Richard Howard (New York: Hill and Wang, 1986), 127–48; Hans Robert Jauss, *Pour une esthétique de la réception* (Paris, 1978); published in English as *Toward an Aesthetic of Reception,* trans. Timothy Bahti (Minneapolis: University of Minnesota Press, 1982).

32. Umberto Eco, *Les limites de l'interpretation* (Paris: Grasset, 1992), 23–47.

33. Pierre Bourdieu, *Ce que parler veut dire: L'économie des échanges linguistiques* (Paris, 1982), 21.

34. Françoise Autrand, *Naissance d'un grand corps de l'Etat: Les gens du Parlement de Paris (1345–1454)* (Paris: Publications de la Sorbonne, 1981); Henriette Benveniste, "Les enlèvements: Stratégies matrimoniales...en France à la fin du moyen âge," *Revue Historique* 283, no. 1 (1990): 13–35; Claude Gauvard, "Paroles de femme: Le témoignage de la grande criminalité en France pendant le règne de Charles VI," in *La femme au moyen âge* (Maubeuge, 1990), 327–40.

35. Myriam Greilsammer, *L'envers du tableau: Mariage et maternité en Flandre mediévale* (Paris: Colin, 1990), 70–73; Barbara Hanawalt, *Crime and Conflict in English Communities, 1300–1348* (Cambridge, Mass.: Harvard University Press, 1979), 106; Guido Ruggiero, *The Boundaries of Eros: Sex Crime and Sexuality in Renaissance Venice* (New York: Oxford University Press, 1985), 12, 96.

36. On the investigation function of the Flemish bailiffs, see Jan Van Rompaey, *Het grafelijk baljuwsambt in Vlaanderen tijdens de Boergondische periode* (Brussels: Verhandelingen Koninklijke Academie voor Wetenschappen, 1967), 269–99.

37. ARA, Brussels, Rekenkamer, Reg. 14.116, bailiff of Hulst: "De Guillaume de Waghenaere...povre compaignon eagié de XXI ans...la somme de soixante livres par... pour ce qu'il estoit accusé d'avoir environ a III ans violé et enforchié Berthele fille Jehan Sceppers eagié de LIIII ans...dont le dit bailli n'a nullement sceu trouver qu'il y eust aucuns criz, noyses, ne autres forches publiques" (From Guillaume de Waghenaere...poor com-

panion 21 years old...a fine of 60 lb. *parisis*...because he was accused of the abduction and rape, three years ago, of Berthele, daughter of Jehan Scepper, 54 years old....the bailiff was unable to discover if there had been public protest or breach of the peace).

38. AN, Paris, X 2a 12, fols. 259r–260r. During the trial the archbishop of Reims claims that "[d]it l'arcevesque de Reins que il a requis le dit de Thusy comme son clerc a lui estre rendu" (The archbishop of Reims said that he claimed the aforenamed de Thuisy as his clergyman and that as such he should be released). Later on, Girart Alart, provost of Rethel, one of the defendants, reacts: "lors dit le dit de Thusi qu'il estoit clerc, combien que par inspection lui qui parle (= le prevost) ne apperceust aucune tonsure sur sa teste" (then the aforenamed de Thuisy said that he was a clergyman, although the provost inspected him, and could not find any tonsure on his head).

39. Davis, *Fiction*, 43–48; Roland Barthes, "The Reality Effect," in *French Literary Theory Today*, ed. Tzvetan Todorov (Cambridge: Cambridge University Press, 1982), 11–17.

40. Walter Prevenier, "Vrouwenroof als middel tot sociale mobiliteit in het 15e-eeuwse Zeeland," in *De Nederlanden in de late middeleeuwen*, ed. Dick De Boer and J. W. Marsilje (Utrecht: Aula, Het Spectrum, 1987), 410–24.

41. ADN, Lille, B 1684, fol. 10r–13r.

42. ADN, Lille, B 1684, fol. 10r–13r.

43. The analysis is by Dirk De Vos, *Catalogus Hans Memling* (Antwerp, Bruges: Ludion, 1994), 42–45, of the triptych of Jan Crabbe, abbot of the abbey of Ten Duinen in Koksijde in Flanders (the three parts are now located at Vicenza, Pierpont Morgan in New York, and Bruges) identifies the left panel as a portrait of Ann, mother of the abbot, backed by Saint Ann. At a Memling colloquium in Bruges, on November 12, 1994, the Bruges archivist Noël Geirnaert identified the mother of the abbot on the Memling panel with the abducted widow of the Boudinszoon story. At that time Ann Willemszoon was a widow for the second time; her first husband, Hugo Crabbe, is the father of the abbot. She next married Christophe de Winter, whose wealthy family was politically active in Hulst. We may suppose that at the time of the rape this widow was indeed well-to-do and socially and politically well protected, as well locally (in Hulst) as at the court of the duke. The information on the age of the widow in the pardon document allows Geirnaert to change the date of the Memling triptych from 1479–80 to 1467–70 because it provides more solid evidence than the hypothetical chronology of the catalog of 1994; Noël Geirnaert, "Le Triptyque de la Crucifixion de Hans Memling pour Jean Crabbe, abbé de l'abbaye des Dunes (1457–1488)," in *Memling Studies*, ed. Hélène Verougstraete and Roger van Schoute (Louvain: Peeters, 1997), 25–30.

44. ADN, Lille, B 1682, fol. 1v (pardon document of May 7, 1438): "ung an...le dit suppliant (Gauthier filz Jehan) s'estot racointie d'une josne fille, de l'eaige de XVI ans ou environ, nommee Jaquemine fille de Guillaume...et telement que icelle fille s'en ala avec le dit suppliant au pais de Brabant au lieu que l'en dit tSerboudens Polre. Auquel lieu la dite fille confessa pardevant les eschevins illec estre venue de son gré, et telement que par la main du curé du dit lieu espouserent l'un l'autre, comme par lettres sur ce faites peut apparoir plusaplain. Et apres ce que le dit suppliant et elle orent esté ensi par l'espace de III mois ou environ, elle se tray devers ses amis pour trouver traictié et accort avec son dit pere et amis. Toutesvoies aucuns d'iceulx ses amis l'ont depuis telment advertie qu'elle s'en est alee avec iceulx par devers les gens de notre conseil en Hollande lui applaindre du dit suppliant, disant qu'elle a esté emmenee par le dit suppliant contre son gré et voulenté, combien que paravant aucuns amis d'elle avoient par le sergeant de la Vere, notre rentmeester de Zellande, et aucuns de noz hommes de fief fait enquerir se la chose avoit esté faite du gré de la dite fille ou non, lesquelz trouvairent aussi qu'il estoit avenu du consentement d'elle comme dit est" (The aforenamed supplicant, Gauthier filz Jehan, met a young girl, about 16 years old, named Jaquemine daughter of Guillaume...; and this happened in such a way that the girl left with the supplicant for the country of Brabant to a place called tSerboudens Polre. In this place the girl declared before the aldermen that she came to the spot of her own free will, and by the hand of the parish priest they married each

other, as is made more clear by letters on this. After the supplicant and the girl had been together for about three months, she went back to her friends, in order to make a deal and an agreement with her father and her friends. Nevertheless some of these friends convinced her in such a way that she approached the people of our Council in Holland to formulate a complaint against the supplicant, saying that she was abducted by the supplicant against her will, although some of her friends requested the sergeant of Veere, our receiver of Zeeland, and some of our vassals to find out if the abduction happened with the consent of the girl or not. They concluded that everything had occurred with her consent, as has been said). Pardon is granted by the duke, so the marriage remains valid and legal, as it was before.

45. Walter Prevenier, "Quelques réflexions sur la situation de l'individu face au pouvoir dans les Pays-Bas de l'ancien régime," *Recueils de la société Jean Bodin pour l'histoire comparative des institutions* 48 (1989): 358.

46. Walter Prevenier, "Geforceerde huwelijken en politieke clans in de Nederlanden: De ontvoering van de weduwe van Guy van Humbercourt door Adriaan Vilain in 1477," *Liber Amicorum prof. dr. Michel Baelde* (Ghent: Vakgroep Nieuwe Geschiedenis, UG, 1993), 299–307.

47. ADN, Lille, B 1703, fols. 24v–25r (remission of August 1481).

48. Archives of the City of Malines, Lettres Missives, 308: letter of the archduke to the aldermen of Malines (December 14, 1477): "nous donnons merveilles de la petite dilligence par vous faite de rescourre la dite dame et prendre les criminelz facteurs contre nous et notre seigneurie; . . . idem, 309" (We are astonished by the lack of diligence shown by you to help the aforenamed lady and arrest those who have offended against us and against our lordship); letter of the archduchess Marguerite (December 15, 1477): "nous sommes advertie que depuis le rapt commis en la personne de la dame de Humbercourt par un nommé Adrien de Lyekerke . . . vous avez commis au gouvernement des biens des enffans de la dite dame gens qui sont parens et adfius du malfacteur, dont nous donnons grandes merveilles, consideré le grant oultraige qu'on a fait a la dite dame et a ses dits enffans qui n'est pas a tollerer. . . . Y commettez gens resseans, non favorables. . . . En quoy faisant vous ferez ce que par bonne justice faire se doit" (we have been informed that, since the rape committed on the person of the lady of Humbercourt by a man named Adrien de Lyekerke . . . you placed the goods of the children of the lady in the hands of people who are related to the criminal, and we are astonished by this, considering the great and unbearable damage imposed on the lady and her children. . . . appoint for this purpose people who are not prejudiced. . . . In so doing, you will give good justice).

49. Barbara A. Hanawalt, "Fur Collar Crime: The Pattern of Crime among the Fourteenth Century English Nobility," *Journal of Social History* 8 (1975): 1–17.

50. Prevenier, "Violence," 263–84; Prevenier, "Vrouwenroof," 410–24; Walter Prevenier, "Huwelijk en cliëntèle als sociale vangnetten: Leuven in de vijftiende eeuw," in *Van blauwe Stoep tot Citadel. Varia Historica Brabantica L. Pirenne dedicata* ('s Hertogenbosch: Stichting Brabantse Regionale Geschiedboefening, 1988), 83–91.

51. On the technique of the *compositio*, see Jan Van Rompaey, "Het compositierecht in Vlaanderen van de veertiende tot de achttiende eeuw," *Tijdschrift voor Rechtsgeschiedenis* 29 (1961): 43–79.

52. Typical is the case of Heinrik Tolvin. There is no doubt that it started with a rape: "It must be known to everybody that Heinrik Tolvin violated damsel Kateline van Libercha; . . . Tolvin was received in the mercy and pardon of Jan, father of Kateline; . . . Kateline is restored in the possession of her goods and inheritance"; Archives of the City of Ghent, Reg. 301.10, fol. 41r; March 25, 1385, n.s. In 1390 a source mentions that Tolvin and Libercha married: "Heinrich Tolvine als wettelik man van joncvrouwe Katheline Jans dochter van Lipersa" (Heinrik Tolvine as legal husband of Lady Kateline daughter of Jan Lipersa); ibid., 301.10, fol. 30r. In 1424 part of a famous house in the Onderstraat in Ghent, owned at least since 1410 by Heinrik Tolvin, who was deceased by 1424, is sold for a sum of 18.240d. gr.; ibid., 301.28, fol. 70r.

53. ARA, Brussels, Rekenkamer, reg. 14.461 (account of the bailiff of the Land van Waas, May 1480–July 1480), fol. 41v: "Aussy de ce qu'il prinst prisonnier et mena audit chasteau de Rupplemonde ung nommé Jacop de Pottere, accusé d'efforcement de josnes filles, lequel fut ou chastel prisonnier XL jours a 3 s. par. pour jour. Dont les parens dudit Jacques payerent mesmes les XXVI jours pour ce que ledit bailli fist ung peu de delay a lui fere justice en esperant de obtenir grace, ce que faire ne se povoit.... Item pour les despens des hommes de fief pour estre presens a examiner ledit Jacop et a sa sentence par laquelle fut condempné a morir" (Furthermore because he took a man called Jacop de Pottere as a prisoner and brought him to the castle of Rupelmonde; this man was accused of the rape of several young girls; he was prisoner in the castle for 40 days, at 3 shillings *parisis* a day. The parents of the aforenamed Jacop even paid for 26 days, in order to give some delay to the bailiff before the judgment, hoping to obtain pardon, but that did not help.... Item for the expenditures of the vassals to be present for the examination [= torture] of the aforenamed Jacop, and to be present at the handing down of his death sentence). Later on (May 1481) the family, by solidarity, pays 12 lb. to the ecclesiastical court "pro gratia sepeliendi in terra sancta cadaver Jacobi de Pottere publice per laicales justiciarios propter sua demerita morte puniti" (for the grant to bury the corpse of Jacobus de Pottere in sacred ground publicly, after he had been condemned by lay judges to death for his indecent behavior); sources quoted from Monique Vleeschouwers–Van Melkebeek, "Het parochiale leven in het oude bisdom Doornik tijdens de late middeleeuwen," in *Ter overwinning ... Iuris scripta historica,* ed. Serge Dauchy (Brussels: Koninklijke Academie voor Wetenschappen, 1994), 7:50.

54. In the case of the widow of Humbercourt, the enthusiasm of Duke Maximilian in his efforts to free the widow from her rapist cannot only be explained by the clientelism argument. Indeed a huge sum (3,100 lions d'or) has been transferred from the widow's patrimony to the duke's receiver in 1480; ADN, Lille, B 2121, fols. 258v–259r (information from Marc Boone).

55. Account of the bailiff of the castellany of Ghent, 1469–70 (ARA, Brussels, Rekenkamer, Reg. 14.159, fol. 2v): "certains tesmoings qui savoyent a parler du dit Jehan et de son dit fait (= de sodomie); il fu mis a torture et examinacion ... neantmoins riens ne confessa" (A certain number of witnesses who were able to speak about this Jan and his deeds; he was tortured and examined, but did not confess). Ibid., fol. 1v: "mis en paine de ... et rudesse sur une femme pour avoir sa volenté de la dite femme ... selon murmure" (he made some efforts ... and used violence on a woman in order to have sex with her ... as rumor has it).

CHAPTER 9

The Host, the Law, and the Ambiguous Space of Medieval London Taverns

Barbara A. Hanawalt

The most notable depiction in Middle English of an innkeeper-taverner appears in *The Canterbury Tales* in the character of the Host. Harry Bailly's Tabard Inn, where the pilgrims gather, suggests an institution that is replete with ambiguity and contradictory images. In the *Prologue* the Tabard is described as a "gentyle tavern" rather than one of the sordid establishments that were common in London and South-wark. Its clientele is a varied one that represents regular and secular clergy, nuns, rural laity ranging in social degree from knight to plowman, and a large contingent of Londoners of different ranks and occupations. Not only the variety of social classes represented but also the gender mix are somewhat surprising for medieval society: a woman (the Wife of Bath) traveling alone and a Prioress, who is appropriately accompanied but suspect because she is staying at an inn rather than one of the well-endowed nunneries of London. The Monk, likewise, could have found lodging in a monastery. Were they all eager for an early start, or was Harry's place recommended for its fine wines, ales, and cuisine? The Tabard was certainly well known for its food, both historically and in the *Tales*.[1] The space within the inn also defies the conventional ordering of society in that Harry's wife, Harry eventually confesses, dominates the domestic power relations and challenges his manhood. His position as guide and the acceptance of his role by his social superiors among the pilgrims is also of interest: no one, except the Cook, disagrees with his self-designation as "judge," "governor," "referee," and punisher of "rebels" against his rule. I argue in this chapter that Harry Bailly's character and that of his inn may be understood more fully when seen in the context of London inns, their regulation, and the power invested in inn and tavern keepers.[2] While modern readers often see the Host only as a buffoon, a medieval audience would certainly have known the official role of innkeepers and would have understood that encouraging mirth is but one technique for diffusing the hostilities and fights that arise in a drinking establishment and, by extension, on a pilgrimage. Certainly, a personal knowledge of innkeepers and taverners had considerable bearing on the language Chaucer used to describe Harry Bailly.

Taverns and inns were among the most complex institutions of medieval social life and social regulation because they occupied contradictory roles both in reality and in the mentality of the age. Their very interior spaces were ambiguous territories. On the one hand, guests were invited to share domestic and primarily female space—the main living area or hall, where food and drink were served, and the bedchambers. On the other hand, the men and women who congregated in breweries, alehouses, taverns, and inns were held in general suspicion as potentially disorderly. Another ambiguity was that inns and taverns were the resort of ordinary villagers, citizens, and servants, as well as of foreigners from other countries, transient English, unspeakable Scots, and a general rabble of rootless people. Within both the local and foreign categories were honest peasants and artisans, respectable merchants and their factors, pilgrims, clerics of various sorts, royal officials, nobles, knights, robbers, prostitutes, and con men. Mingling with all these people were authors such as Geoffrey Chaucer, William Langland, and Thomas Hoccleve, who recorded their impressions of taverns and inns. Over all this tumult of people—a hall full of folk—reigned the taverner or innkeeper.

To speak of a drinking establishment as domestic, female space requires an explanation. In preindustrial England, as in most of Europe at the time, the sexual division of labor was pronounced, with men doing field work, construction, and production of manufactured goods and women rearing and training children, managing houses, and supplementing the household economy with a number of by-occupations such as brewing, spinning, and tending domestic animals.[3] The division of labor also implied a division of the physical space that the sexes occupied in daylight hours. Women's work centered around the home, village, or city quarter while men's centered on fields, streets, and public work space.[4] Given the gendered division of labor and space, the production and consumption of alcohol stands out as an economic and social site at which traditional distinctions were blurred. In the countryside, brewing and running a tavern were extensions of domestic labor and domestic space, with women making and buying ale for home consumption. But the brewer's house was also a social gathering place that both women and men frequented. In cities, where brewing was more professional and more male dominated, taverns were, like their nineteenth-century descendants, a recreation area away from the cramped rooming quarters of a town or city and a resting place for travelers and foreigners. Taverns and inns retained many features of the home atmosphere, but women associated with them had a very bad reputation—that of offering sex as well as other domestic comforts. The domestic space of the tavern or inn tainted the women who worked or routinely visited there.

Presiding over the ambiguous space was the taverner or innkeeper (male or female), who was empowered by statute law and London ordinances to act as paterfamilias or materfamilias over both the household and the guests (*familia* was still defined in the Roman sense of comprising the servants and guests as well as kin in a domestic environment). He or she was thereby required to assume legal responsibility for the good and honest behavior of guests, employees, and kin. The position was both quasi-legal and quasi-familial in that it required both discipline and nurturing protection. In the London records taverners and innkeepers are the only people who are *consistently* referred to by the title paterfamilias and the corresponding materfamilias. But the host's position required a difficult balance. Guests had different needs and different relationships to the law, and the taverner or innkeeper wanted to make the most profit he could by accommodating them all. Some otherwise respectable travelers or citizens encouraged the taverner to act illegally as procurers of prostitutes. Others wanted him to arrange for fencing stolen goods.

Finally, within the limited space of the tavern or inn (within its hall, drinking area, and chambers), the taverner or innkeeper had to maintain the medieval social hierarchy, serving each guest according to his or her degree. Seating at the table followed the social status of the guests, and terms of address mirrored these people's places in society. The small domain of the inn or tavern maintained a semblance of the external world order even though society generally perceived it as potentially chaotic. Respectability, compliance with the law, and suitable service to customers rested with the owner of the establishment. Harry Bailly's role was as complex as the space over which he presided.[5]

The Permeable Domestic Space in Inns and Taverns

An understanding of the structure of inns and taverns and the role of women in them will help to explain the gender ambiguity of these spaces. Although large quantities of wine were imported and drunk in both private homes and taverns, ale and later beer were the most common drinks and women the usual brewers. While most housewives had the equipment to make ale—pots, ladles, and straining cloths—the process was time-consuming and required careful attention. Malt was easily ruined by mold or heat, and ale soured and went off quickly, so that brewing had to be done frequently and usually in large enough quantities to make the laborious process worth the effort. Many households, therefore, purchased ale or beer either from neighbors who specialized in its production, from regraters who purchased beer for resale in the urban streets, or from taverns.[6] In the countryside, some peasant families invested in larger, leaden vats so that their wives could supplement their agricultural income by selling ale or beer. The homes of these brewsters became both taverns and shops and were thus extensions of domestic space and female production.[7]

In market towns such as York, Norwich, and Exeter married women also predominated as brewers through the middle of the fifteenth century. Even after losing their dominance of production, they still acted as retailers of ale and beer.[8]

In London, brewing was already a large-scale industry in the late thirteenth and early fourteenth centuries because its population (in excess of sixty thousand) was too large for extensive domestic brewing, and the housing did not permit home brewing for many people. The sheer problem of supplying the malt and water for the operation required more than household production. In-home brewing continued in larger establishments with the wife or servants brewing for a household. A servant woman, for instance, was hired in a large household to do the brewing for the family, servants, and apprentices.[9] London women also engaged in brewing as wholesale traders. Indeed, the *Liber Albus,* an early-fifteenth-century compilation of the laws and ordinances of London, refers to brewers as "she" throughout the ordinance on brewing.[10] About 10 percent of the members enrolled in the London Brewer's company were women paying their dues alone. Most of these were widows, but a few were single women. The number of women engaged in brewing, however, was much higher, since couples paid dues together. In all, perhaps a third of the members of the Brewers Guild in London were women.[11]

Taverns and inns not only sold drink, but also served meals and offered sleeping accommodations.[12] While these establishments might have brewed their own ale, many did not and most sold wine as well. The domestic nature of the business meant that the presence of women was desired and needed. Married couples ran most inns and taverns because the division of labor that typified an ordinary household translated well into serving strangers. The wife oversaw the running of the house and management of household servants, while the husband supervised the guests and provisioned the establishment.

Innkeeping was rarely a female-only business. In 1384 only ten women were listed as innkeepers, compared with 183 men.[13] Women acquired inns either by taking over their former husband's business or through inheritance and managed the premises themselves.

The official tallies of inn and tavern keepers, however, underrepresent women's actual participation in the lodging and victualing business.[14] Taking in lodgers and boarders has been a time-honored by-occupation for women. In medieval London the frequency of such arrangements might well have been greater than it is today. Two factors contributed to both the supply and the demand for lodging. London women, when they married, contracted to contribute a dowry and were awarded a dower in rents and real estate should they outlive their husbands. At the very least, a widow would receive the principal dwelling as her home for life use. Many London widows, therefore, had rooms to rent and had a need for the extra income.[15] On the demand side, London, like other medieval European cities, did not replace its own population. It relied on immigrants from the countryside and, as a major trading and administrative center, it also had to house a number of foreign merchants, fortune seekers, suitors at court, and delegations to the Crown. Widows had a ready market for their rooms and meals, but they were not registered as innkeepers.

Despite the fact that some women owned breweries, taverns, and inns, most of the women who worked in these spaces served in other capacities, such as wife of the proprietor, tapster, or domestic servant. A London hostelry could be a large establishment. It included buildings for horses, draught animals, and fodder; a large courtyard with a well and latrines; and a house with a large hall for dining, drinking, and games, a kitchen, and chambers for sleeping. Such establishments employed a number of servants who were part of the innkeeper's *familia*. Taverns and breweries were simpler establishments that might consist of a place to drink and assemble, and a shop window for selling ale, beer, and wine as "take out." Both male and female help was employed in this important service industry.

Every female role associated with taverns and inns turned the domestic nature of the association on end and implied tainted womanhood. The disparaging term "alewife" was not the only insult directed at women associated with brewing and drink. For a materfamilias of a tavern, the titles of "procurer" or "bawd" were ready to the tongue and, for the tapster, the association with prostitution was all too much of a stereotype. In a mid-fourteenth-century London ordinance, brewsters were lumped with nurses, other servants, and "women of disreputable character" in a prohibition against adorning themselves with hoods furred with finer furs "after the manner of reputable women."[16]

Women who worked in the service occupations in taverns were at risk of being pimped by their masters and mistresses for the sexual satisfaction of male customers. Thus Thomesina Newton was said, in the London Consistory Court, to have worked for William Basseloy, the paterfamilias of a tavern who acted as her pimp. The owner of the Busche tavern was accused of pimping for his two servants, Mandeleyn and Alice. Others were accused of adultery with members of their establishment, as was the proprietor of the Lodyn Proche with his tapster, Mariota, and William le Hostler of Le Crown, who was said to have fathered the daughter of his servant, Matrosa.[17] The materfamilias was no better than her male counterpart. The one who kept "le tavern near the church" was accused of adultery with her servant, and the one running Le Schippe procured her tapster as a prostitute.[18] The tapsters themselves acquired a neighborhood reputation. Elizabeth Machyn, tapster of the Red Lyon, was accused of adultery and of the same at Le Cok in Woodstreet, while Mariona, who was the sometime tapster at the Vine in the parish of Saint Helen and at the Choker in the high street, was accused of being "a common scandalizer [*scandilizatrix*], especially with Thomas, one of the deacons of Saint Paul."[19]

A 1516 case demonstrates the role of the taverner or innkeeper as a go-between. Elizabeth Tomlins was in an alehouse next to the Bell Inn and sent for the hostler inquiring if Gregory Kyton, a priest, was there. The innkeeper told Kryton that there was a woman waiting for him. It was arranged that the priest would have her in his chamber, and the innkeeper then suggested that the priest go to the George in Lombard street and that Elizabeth would come to him there. The hostler took her into a chamber at the George and the priest came and joined them. The hostler's pay was a meal shared with them at the priest's expense.[20]

Taverns provided opportunities for pimps and prostitutes that apparently went unregulated by the proprietors. John Mande and his wife pimped his sister at a tavern and others made contacts with prostitutes at taverns.[21] The Pye in Quenhithe had a reputation as a place "which is a good shadowing for thieves and many evil bargains have been made there, and many strumpets and pimps have their covert there, and leisure to make their false covenants." The neighbors wanted it closed at night.[22]

Suspicion fell on ordinary female patrons of taverns as well as on servants and known prostitutes. The popular poetry suggested that female patrons of taverns were of easy virtue, so the presence of the Prioress along with the Wife of Bath at the Tabard casts some doubt on their good sense. One of the few advice poems directed toward women specifically has been edited as "How the Good Wife Taught Her Daughter." Although probably not written by a woman, it reflects popular concepts of appropriate behavior for them. The "Good Wife" cautions her daughter that she should not spend all the money she makes selling her cloth in the city on taverns because "they that taverns haunt / From thrift soon come to want." The first warning, then, is that taverns are places to throw away money. The second warning is about the effects of drunkenness on reputation:

> And if thou be in any place where good ale is aloft,
> Whether that thou serve thereof or that thou sit soft,
> Measurably thou take thereof, that thou fall in no blame
> For if thou be often drunk, it falleth to thy shame.
> For those that be often drunk —
> Thrift is from them sunk,
> My lief child.

The poem presumes that the young woman might either be a tapster or a patron. The other warnings about the temptations of the city urge her to avoid going to wrestling matches or cock shooting for fear of being mistaken for a strumpet.[23]

The second type of literature that speaks about women frequenting taverns is the drinking song. In one such song, the gossips—Elinore, Joan,

Margery, Margaret, Alice, and Cecily—come together at a place where they can get the best wine and strong ale. Bringing cold dishes to enjoy with their drink, they come in twos so as to conceal their drinking from their husbands. At the taverns they drink, eat, and complain about men, particularly husbands who beat their wives:

> Whatsoever any man thynk,
> We com for nawght but for good drynk;
> Now let us go home and wynke,
> For it may be seen
> Where we have been
> Good Gossips myn, a!

The poem concludes that some women come once a week for wine but others "be at the tavern thrise in the weke" or even every day until they are sick: "For thyngis used / Will not be refused."[24] The latter indictment of women was also applied to their sexual appetites once they had lost their virginity.

The space of inns and taverns, being domestic, facilitated not only sexual contacts but also violence between men and women. For instance, five men with accomplices were indicted for being present with arms at the inn of John Fodard, a hostler, in Cornhill. The charge was that they broke into Katherine de Brewes's chamber and dragged her along the floor by her arms and clothing so that she was naked upward to the waist and her hair was hanging over her bosom. She was only saved when the servants and neighbors rescued her.[25]

In 1325 Walter de Benygtone with seventeen companions came to the brewhouse of Gilbert de Mordone with stones in their hoods, swords, knives, and other weapons. They sat in the tavern drinking four gallons of ale. Their objective was to seize Emma, daughter of the late Robert Pourte and a ward of Gilbert. Mabel, Gilbert's wife, and Geoffrey, his brewer, asked them to leave. They refused to do so, saying that it was a public tavern and that they had the right to stay and drink. Mabel took Emma to an upper chamber while the men dealt with the ruffians. A fight ensued and spilled into the streets, where the neighbors came to the rescue and one of the thugs was killed. In another brawl, two men were quietly playing checkers in a tavern when some rowdies came in and laid a woman across the checkerboard.[26]

The ambiguous space of the tavern and the battles between the sexes for control over it appear without a previous hint in Harry Bailly's reaction to the *Tale of Melibee.* Paterfamilias and materfamilias Bailly are in contention over the inn, its employees, and the sexual symbols of office. He explains that when he undertakes to beat the knaves who serve in the tavern, she complains that he is inadequate in his discipline—he has yet to break their backs or bones.[27] When she is in church and the neighbors fail to show respect for her social station by taking precedence at the pews, she returns home in a rage crying, "False coward, wrek thy wyf! / By corpus bones, I wol have thy knyf, / And thou shalt have my distaf and go spynne!" (VII.1905–7). The symbolism of their disputed roles and control of the inn could not be more explicit. She proposes to give him the universal symbol of womanhood, the distaff, and take the phallic symbol of the knife for her own. His impotence, in her words, takes on a childish symbolism when she describes him as a "milksop or a coward ape" (VII.1910). He goes on to lament that he can carry the knife only outside the disputed space of the inn, where he is a dangerous man: not a cowardly ape but a foolhardy "wilde leoun," apt to kill "som neighbor" (VII.1913–23). She has demonstrated that she can take over the inn's ambiguous domestic space very effectively and even drive him out of it. He is willing to leave it in her hands while he goes to Canterbury. Becoming a guide to pilgrims en route, a role not open to a materfamilias, is his way out of his embattled space. If his busman's holiday has some foolhardy bravado mixed with better sense and appropriate discourse, the reader can appreciate his sense of release as well as his professionalism as a host.[28]

Disorderly Spaces

London was famous for its many places to drink. One of the few complaints that William FitzStephen made about thirteenth-century London was "the immoderate quaffing among the foolish sort."[29] By 1309 there were 354 taverns and 1,334 brewhouses in the city. The smallest measure in which ale was sold was a quart.[30] The disorder of taverns and inns centered not only on the gender mix within its space, but also on the other types of business and recreation that took place there. The vices available in inns and taverns were stock targets for sermons and homilies,[31] and also appear in *Piers Plowman* and *The Canterbury Tales*.[32] Official opinion about the potential for disorder in these places of resort was clearly stated in the Statutes for the City of London promulgated by Edward I in 1285. Complaining about those who wandered the streets at night with arms, the statute goes on to say that,

> whereas such offenders as aforesaid going about by night, do commonly resort and have their meetings and hold their evil talk in taverns more than elsewhere, and there do seek for shelter, lying in wait, and watching their time to do mischief; it is enjoined that none do keep a tavern open for wine or ale, after the tolling of the aforesaid curfew; but they shall keep their tavern shut after that hour and none therein drinking or resorting.[33]

The *Liber Albus* copied the statute in the early fifteenth century, but it had been invoked and enforced from the time it was issued and long after.[34]

Court cases leave little doubt about taverns and inns encouraging concentrations of disorderly behavior, which took the form of noisy pranks, brawling, homicide, prostitution, rape, and insurrection. The king, the London magistrates, the taverners themselves, and the neighbors all had a stake in keeping such behavior under control, if not entirely eliminated.

The disorderly nature of inn and tavern appears in a 1276 coroner's inquest from a ward near the Tower and close to Fenchurch. The case was brought ten years before Edward I's statute and indicates the type of problem the statute addressed. Agnes de Essex ran a lodging house and rented to knights of the household of Robert de Munceny and his son. After curfew had rung, one Richard Moys came to the house next door, banged on the door, and shouted to be let in. Robert's men told him to "cease making noise," but he persisted. This roused Robert de Munceny, his son, and others of the household, who pursued the noisemaker into the nearby drinking establishment of Alice le Official. A number of people were drinking there and the door was open. One can sympathize with Alice: the location attracted the soldiers who assembled near or in the Tower, and business was brisk on that Saturday, the Eve of All Hallows. The noisemaker, Richard Moys, was able to hide among the barrels, but a patron Richard de Parys, challenged the hotheads and cried out, "Who are these people?" He was stabbed through the body by Robert de Munceny's impetuous young son and died. Robert de Munceny watched from the doorstep of his lodging, but did not move to stop the action. The youth fled, but his possessions and those of his father were confiscated. Agnes de Essex, her maidservant Alice, and all those connected to the house of Alice le Official were attached in connection with the homicide.[35]

Violence is often perpetrated by young males, and fourteenth-century London had its share of problems from this group. As Thomas Hoccleve observed, "willful youthe" is tempted by taverns; Venus can always catch him in her snares; and he likes a good fight.[36] One such group of young servants had filled an empty cask with stones on a Monday at midnight and "set it rolling through graschirchestrate to London Bridge to the terror of the neighborhood."[37] Other rowdy behavior starting in taverns ended in homicide. The apprentices of the Bench who lived in and around the Inns of Court were responsible for some of the major riots in medieval London's west end. On one occasion it was the taverner who was the object of an old argument. When the taverner was attacked, he raised the hue and cry, which was joined by apprentices of the Bench and other taverners. An apprentice was killed in the resulting riot.[38]

The noise and disturbance from the less established drinking places were also disruptive. Agnes de Louthe, who was described as a common and notorious prostitute, kept a house in Paternoster Row beside the gate of the Lord Bishop of London:

On account of her remaining there quarrels and contentions frequently arise between the neighbors, so that the neighbors dwelling near her can have no peace or rest in their houses at nighttime, nor dare they ofttimes leave their homes for fear of death by the attack of diverse men unknown coming by night to the said Agnes with drawn swords and stones to throw through the windows of the neighbors.

Some of the neighbor women were cited for spending their "filthy lucre" in her house on drink.[39]

Taverns were also places for games, and although most games, we must assume, went on in an orderly fashion, those we know about often ended in homicide or accusations of cheating. Michael le Gaugenour and John Faukes had been playing a game called "hasard" in a brewhouse after curfew. John was apparently a sore loser and, when he left the brewhouse, he lay in wait for Michael, killing him with a sword. Stephen de Lenn, a taverner himself, was killed after winning a game at tables in another tavern where he was playing after curfew. The loser ran him through with a sword in the streets.[40]

The connection between dramatic homicide cases and taverns suggests the conclusion that drinking houses were very dangerous places, but drink was mentioned in only 6.2 percent of the 130 London homicides involving men. Taverns and brewhouses were the location of just 7.6 percent of all 144 homicides. In rural Northamptonshire only 4.3 percent of the 347 homicides mentioned drinking as a cause, and taverns figured as the place of homicide in 7 percent of the cases.[41]

All sorts of deals, both shady and legitimate, took place in taverns. They were places to draw up contracts, to arrange service and apprenticeship agreements, to share drink sealing a deal or a successful arbitration, to discuss business, and to plot. But, again, the deals that led to disorder were more likely to be reported than the thousands of peaceful transactions. Richard and William met at the Horn in Milk Street and were having a drink of wine together. Apparently William wanted to settle his debts to Richard and wanted Richard to turn over his bonds. Being illiterate, he asked Richard to read the bonds that he had in a box. Richard took them to read, but refused to give them back, saying that William had diverse writings and muniments pertaining to his property. William became furious and said that "Richard should deliver them to him in his clenched teeth" and took up a pewter pot standing between them, intending to strike Richard. Richard disarmed him and went off carrying the bonds.[42]

Other cases were much more sinister than taking advantage of a poor illiterate. Nicholas le Barbour; Agnes de Houdan, his mistress; and John Joye, a webber, met in a tavern to lure a client to Agnes's house, where they killed and robbed him instead of entertaining him.[43]

Fear of disorder in taverns permeated all official ranks. The king's chief concern, however, was that taverns were places where people could meet to form "congregations, unions [*alligaciones*], and covins." Thus in 1368 a group of skinners was attached to stand trial because they had met in a tavern and other places and formed a coven.[44] The church was concerned about taverns as places to talk heresy and to slander the church.[45] The mayor and aldermen were concerned about keeping order in their city and continually prodded the taverners and innkeepers to take legal responsibility for their clients and for enforcing curfew and other city ordinances.

Mandate for Social Control

Expectations for the peacekeeping role of taverners and innkeepers were high and, as such, turned them into officers of the peace. In medieval England many people played such semiofficial roles with no payment for executing them. In the case of London's purveyors of drink and lodging, their official stature came from statute law and London ordinances. In the absence of licensing, the presumption that an innkeeper or taverner would carry out the mandates rested on the force of the king's law; the necessary city, neighborhood, and client approval; and the honesty of the proprietors. Edward I's 1285 statute sought a solution to the problem of nightwalkers and plotters in closing down taverns after curfew:

> It is enjoined that none do keep a tavern open for wine or ale, after the tolling of the aforesaid curfew; but they shall keep their tavern shut after that hour, and none neither shall any man admit others in his house except in common taverns, for therein drinking nor resorting; whom he will not be answerable unto the king's peace. And if any taverner be found doing the contrary, the first time he shall be put in pledge by his tavern drinking cup, or by other good pledge there found, and be amerced 40d.; and if he be found a second time offending, he shall be amerced half a mark; and the third time ten shillings; and the fourth time he shall pay the whole penalty double, that is to say, twenty shillings; and the fifth time he shall be forsworn of his trade for ever.[46]

Penalties were gradual but severe, and presumed that the proprietors were both well informed and answerable to the king for their tavern hours and their clientele.[47]

Control over foreigners, always a worry of governments that witness large influxes of aliens, was a second concern of the statute. The language has a modern ring in complaining that

> some from parts beyond the sea, and others of this land, ... do there [in London] seek shelter and refuge, by reason of banishment out of

their own country, or who for great offense or other misdeed have fled from their own country; and of these some do become brokers, hostelers, and innkeepers within the City, for denizens and strangers, as freely as though they were good and lawful men of the franchise of the City; and some nothing do but run up and down through the streets, more by night than by day and are well attired in clothing and array, and have their food of delicate meats and costly.

The solution the statute offered was to allow only citizens or those who had become citizens and sworn their oaths to the mayor and aldermen to become innkeepers. Aspiring foreign innkeepers had to provide testimony from their home residence as to their good character, as well as arrange for Londoners to stand surety for their willingness to enforce the law.[48]

The *Liber Albus*, in repeating the 1285 statute, added that no foreigner could have an inn or lodging house on the waterside of the Thames because of the fear that foreigners lodging with foreign hosts were likely to form covens.[49] Zenobius Martyn, for instance, was indicted in Langbourne Ward as a common bawd and associate of prostitutes. He admitted to this charge and also confessed that he ran a "lodging house for aliens and had acted as a broker against the ordinances of the City." He suffered the prescribed penalty of being put into prison.[50]

The distinction between denizen or local person and stranger or foreigner was very important to the medieval concept of order and peace. The *Liber Albus* begins its section on taverns, breweries, and inns with an injunction: "In the first place, that the peace of God and the peace of our Lord the King shall be well kept and maintained among denizens and strangers."[51] Local people's reputations were well known in their communities, where they were described as of either good or ill repute. Since Anglo-Saxon times the society had been organized into tithing groups (frankpledge, after the Norman Conquest), which all freemen were required to enter when they reached the age of twelve. Women were in the charge of their husbands or fathers, and clergy were answerable to their bishop or abbot. The purpose of the tithing group was to ensure the good behavior and lawfulness of its members and to agree to reveal those within their group who broke the law. When a crime was committed, the tithing group was responsible for identifying the perpetrator. The English legal system in the Middle Ages was built on the concept of community responsibility for policing its neighbors and neighborhood.

But what did one do to ensure the good behavior of numerous people who wandered into communities: migrant workers, minstrels, knights errant, foreign merchants, craftsmen, and pilgrims? The terms *stranger* and *foreigner* were applied to English men and women from another village or town as well as to those who came from Italy, Germany, or Flanders. Anglo-Saxon law specified that the first night a person lodged in a house he was considered a visitor, the second night a guest, and the third night a member of the household. If no one took responsibility, the person was considered a vagabond.[52]

The 1285 statute and the *Liber Albus* echoed the Anglo-Saxon customs, but put the innkeeper in charge:

> And that no one in the City shall harbor any man beyond a day and a night, if he be not willing to produce such person to stand trial. In case such person shall commit an offense and absent himself, the host shall make answer for him. And no one shall be resident in the Ward of an Alderman beyond a day and a night, if he be not in view of frankpledge, or if his host be not willing to produce him to stand trial.[53]

Essentially, the law held the host responsible for the good behavior of his clients and forced him to stand surety for them if they committed an offense and did not appear for trial.

The repeated appeals to innkeepers indicate on-going scandals. In 1384, Nicholas Brembre, mayor, again appealed for order, complaining that "larcenies and diverse evil deeds" were committed openly because innkeepers were not careful about those they harbored or how long they allowed them to stay. Innkeepers were to abide by the statute and not allow "travaillyngmen" and other strangers at their tables on pain of paying a £100 fine. At that time, Brembre had 197 innkeepers swear to obey the law and to report innkeepers who did not do so.[54]

Further ordinances made taverners and innkeepers responsible for informing guests about the laws regarding bearing arms, keeping curfew, holding guests' goods in safekeeping, and so on. Aldermen and wardmoots were to keep a close watch on guests to see that they complied with the laws.[55] The officials and citizens duly carried out their responsibilities so that in 1372, for instance, Adam Grymmesby was committed to prison for not warning his lodger to leave his knife indoors after curfew. The watch confiscated the knife and Adam was instructed to redeem it for his guest.[56]

Innkeepers were also responsible for protecting the property of their guests. William Beaubek of Kent claimed remedy against John de Waltham, innkeeper, on these grounds in 1345, and John Sappy, knight, did so against Thomas Hostiller of Le Swerd in 1380. William Beaubek stated that he rented a room for 1 1/2 d. a week and that the innkeeper gave him a key to the room, claiming that his goods would be secure. William relied on the help of the innkeeper to collect a debt and deposited the money in a box in his room. Later, not only was the money missing, but so too were gold and silver ornaments and plate that were in the box. The innkeeper claimed that his brewer had entered the chamber by a garden door, but William held the innkeeper responsible for recovery of the value of the goods stolen. The court upheld him and the law. Sir John Sappy was also successful in his suit.[57]

On the whole, innkeepers and taverners appear more often as breakers of the law than as enforcers. By far the most common complaint was that they did not use the correct measures for their beer and ale, or that they were mixing bad wine with good, or that they did not let customers see their wine drawn.[58] In addition to charges of prostitution, which have already been mentioned, charges of assault against taverners and innkeepers were also brought.[59]

It is the nature of court records and ordinances, our chief sources for information on taverns and inns, to record the negative rather than the positive side of the picture. Reissuing of regulations for taverners, suits against them for noncompliance with laws, complaints from the neighbors about noise, loose women, prostitution, and undesirable characters all appear with great regularity. Only occasionally does one find a case such as that of Margaret Rumbold, who was arrested for theft by John Grove, a taverner.[60]

Harry Bailly, Host of the Tabard

Harry Bailly's character has a clear job description, as laid down in law, custom, and practice. Any traveler, such as Chaucer, could remind a host of his legal responsibilities, and any denizen of London knew them well because he had to enforce them. That the Tabard was located in Southwark rather than in London did not exempt it from most of the laws and customs that would have been typical of "gentil hostelrye" (I.718), nor did it significantly alter Harry Bailly's responsibilities as an innkeeper.[61] Many of the statutes applied to England as a whole, such as the assize of ale and the ordinances regarding wine, while others, such as the responsibility of the innkeeper for his guests and their goods, applied to all who made or sold alcoholic beverages or ran inns for respectable travelers. Sir John Sappy, mentioned above, made his claim against Thomas Hostiller "in accordance with the common custom of the realm that the keeper of a hostelry was responsible for the goods and chattels brought by lodgers to his hostelry." Richard Waldegrave, a knight, complained on the basis of the custom in 1384, and John Prene also appealed to the encumbrance of "every common innkeeper...bound by law and custom to guard his inn."[62] Chaucer's knowledge of inns and taverns would have been informed by his experience with a variety of London establishments rather than any specific innkeeper in one tavern. Too much can also be made of the location of the tavern in Southwark, the sexual suburb of London and location of stews, brothels, breweries, gambling, and animal shows. The juxtaposition of respectable housing and brothels was a problem about which many proper London citizens complained. Aldermen lived side by side with strumpets, bawds, and regraters.[63]

Although the ordinances and statutes do not specify the appearance or manners of innkeepers and taverners, certain physical and psychological types made for a successful trade:

> A semely man Oure Hooste was withalle
> For to been a marchal in an halle.
> A large man he was with eyen stepe —
> A fairer burgeys was ther noon in Chepe —
> Boold of his speche, and wys, and wel ytaught,
> And of manhod hym lakkede right naught.
>
> (I.751–56)

Success as an innkeeper, therefore, lay in a ready wit heightened by some education, sharp eyes, a physical appearance and strength adequate to act as a bouncer, and a certain presence and seeming gentility of manner. But he only *resembled* an exalted marshal serving in a lord's hall or one of the extravagantly wealthy merchants living and trading on Cheapside. He was neither a gentleman servant nor a goldsmith. Indeed, innkeepers did not hold such high status in society. Chaucer's Host has the pilgrims pay their bills before proposing to accompany them (I.760).

A smooth businessman knew how to address his diverse clientele while maintaining the appropriate social distance. Thus on the day they depart, the Host immediately singles out the two highest-status pilgrims: "Sire Knyght, . . . my mayster and my lord" and "my lady Prioresse" (I.837, 839). Polite address, however, is not always successful in managing customers. Peacekeepers have often found that assuming a jocular manner or even the role of buffoon is an effective way of dealing with potentially violent people. If he jollies along the drunken miller or cook, allowing them to stew in their own juices, that, too, was acceptable within the medieval social hierarchy as long as it was effective in minimizing conflict. Direct physical contact with a burly drunk was dangerous. But his general form of address, "Lordynges," was an all-inclusive compliment.

The quasi-legal side of a host's job also appears in Chaucer's description of Harry Bailly, often in the same language used in statute and ordinance. In a sense, Harry Bailly has a doubly ascribed legal role because his name implies that he is a bailiff and that his occupation is that of enforcer of laws over his guests. The *Liber Albus*, in its section on "rebellious persons," enjoins that the bailiff is to have control over them, just as the hostelers or herbergeour shall not "harbour any man beyond a day and a night, if he be not willing to produce such person to stand trial." Furthermore, "the host has to make answer" for the person who commits an offense and absents himself.[64] These legal roles and those discussed in previous sections appear again in the role the Host undertakes in the fellowship, offering to "be youre gyde" with a proviso: "And whoso wole my juggement withseye / Shal paye al that we spenden by the weye" (I.804–6). The party agrees to the extension of his role: "he wolde been oure governour," "oure tales juge and reportour" (I.813–14).[65] They seal the agreement with another drink of his good wine. This symbolic drink also had its judicial place, for it was used commonly in London and elsewhere to conclude contracts or to seal an arbitration. (The shared drink is similar to the kiss of peace that the Pardoner and the Host exchange after the Pardoner's challenge to Harry's authority [VI.962–67].) Host Bailly reminds the pilgrims of his powers the next morning by outlining the punishment of "Whoso be rebel to my juggement" (I.833). By the *Parson's Tale*, the Host announces that his "ordinaunce" has been fulfilled, an echoing of the municipal rules for taverns and inns (X.19).

The arrogant exercise of his powers at times seems to overtake the Host's judgment. For example, he addresses the Reeve "as lordly as a kyng" (I.3900), but the Cook (the natural enemy of the innkeeper as a rival for the victualing trade or as an employee) soon draws him back to reality. Running an "herbergage," the Cook points out, means that the hostler is responsible for the behavior of those he harbors at night who may be very dangerous sorts (I.4329–34). Bailly responds that the Cook has endangered the lives of many pilgrims by reheating meat pies and by overlooking the flies that abound in his shop (I.4346–52). It is, perhaps, because of his professional worries about having to produce his clientele before the law that the Host is so concerned about people straying from the party. Still, when a real scoundrel joins the party, the alchemist Canon, Harry advises the Yeoman to let his master leave—a prudent move for a responsible host (VII.697–98).

Whether he takes the role of a clown or a mock courtier, the Host does have the signal triumph of keeping the party together, keeping them from coming to blows, maintaining the social hierarchy, and earning their respect for *his* rules of the game. Most of the storytellers refer to the peacekeeping role that he occupies and accept his authority.[66] Only Harry Bailly's wife successfully challenges his abilities as a peacekeeper within the ambiguous space of the tavern.

Notes

This chapter has been previously published as chapter 7 by Barbara Hanawalt in *"Of Good and Ill Repute": Gender and Social Control in Medieval England* (New York: Oxford University Press, 1998), 104–23. The editors thank the publisher and author for permission to reproduce this essay.

1. For a discussion of the historic Tabard Inn and the historical Harry Bailly, see George R. Corner, "On Some of the Ancient Inns of Southwark," *Surrey Archaeological Collections* 2 (1864): 50–81; W. H. Hart, "Further Remarks on Some of the Ancient Inns of Southwark," *Surrey Archaeological Collections* 3 (1865): 193–207; Philip Norman, "The Tabard Inn, Southwark, The Queen's Head, William Rutter, and St. Margaret's Church," *Surrey Archaeological Collections* 13 (1897): 28–38.

2. John Matthews Manly, *Some New Light on Chaucer: Lectures Delivered at the Lowell Institute* (New York: Henry Holt, 1926), 78–82. It is not the purpose of this chapter

to add further to the discussion of the real Harry Bailly. Nonetheless, a discussion of London inns and taverns has considerable bearing on the language Chaucer used to describe Harry Bailly and his character development as framer of the tales.

3. Martine Segalen, *Mari et femme dans la société paysanne* (Paris: Flammarion, 1980). In her *Historical Anthropology of the Family*, trans. J. C. Whitehouse and Sarah Matthews (Cambridge: Cambridge University Press, 1986), 205–12, 218–19, she extended the observation of a sexual and spatial division of labor to other preindustrial classes. See also Barbara A. Hanawalt, introduction to *Women and Work in Preindustrial Europe* (Bloomington: Indiana University Press, 1986), xiv–xvi, for a survey of other literature dealing with the sexual division of labor in traditional Europe.

4. Barbara A. Hanawalt, "At the Margins of Women's Space in Medieval Europe," in *Matrons and Marginal Women in Medieval Society*, ed. Robert R. Edwards and Vickie Ziegler (Woodbridge, England: Boydell Press, 1995), 1–17.

5. A brief and unsystematic literature survey of the character of Harry Bailly has turned up many explanations for his behavior except the obvious one of his training and occupation in the demanding role of innkeeper. Kemp Malone, *Chapters on Chaucer* (Baltimore, Md.: Johns Hopkins Press, 1951), 193, found a comic inversion in the innkeeper telling his customers what to do and yet performing thereby exactly the role expected by statutes. He has been portrayed as a Christ figure, and the prize banquet as the Eucharist, by Rodney Delasanta, "The Theme of Judgment in *The Canterbury Tales*," *Modern Language Quarterly* 31 (1970): 298–307, and as embodying Chaucer's concept of the monarchy by David R. Pichaski and Laura Sweetland, "Chaucer on the Medieval Monarch: Harry Bailly in the Canterbury Tales," *Chaucer Review* 11 (1977): 179–200. Cynthia C. Richardson, "The Function of the Host in the *Canterbury Tales*," *Texas Studies in Literature and Language* 12 (1970): 327, portrayed him as "the middlest of the middle class," perhaps because she took literally that he was the fairest burgess in Cheapside (325). But she also asked the shrewd question, "Why an innkeeper?" (326) and answered it equally well by saying that only in an inn would one find the combination of social classes that one finds on the pilgrimage.

6. See Judith M. Bennett, "The Village Ale-Wife: Women and Brewing in Fourteenth-Century England," in *Women and Work in Preindustrial Europe*, ed. Hanawalt, 20–22, for the production of beer in villages.

7. Ibid., 23–30. In Brigstock (Northamptonshire) Bennett found that about a fourth of the adult women brewed beer, but most engaged in only minor commercial ventures. Only 11.5 percent of the brewers could be called real "alewives" who routinely produced beer for sale. These alewives usually came from families who had long been resident in their communities and often came from the wealthier families or had married into them. Their brewing was intermittent, undertaken as time and opportunity permitted. All were married women (not widows) who seemed to have used family labor or to hire village girls and women to help with brewing.

8. P. J. P. Goldberg, "Women in Fifteenth-Century Town Life," in *Towns and Townspeople in the Fifteenth Century*, ed. John A. F. Thompson (Gloucester: Alan Sutton, 1988), 116–17.

9. Public Record Office (PRO), Chancery Petitions C1/142/18.

10. *Liber Albus: The White Book of the City of London*, ed. and trans. Henry Thomas Riley (London: Richard Griffin, 1861), 238.

11. Judith M. Bennett, "Working Together: Women and Men in the Brewer's Gild of London, c. 1420," in *The Salt of Common Life: Individuality and Choice in the Medieval Town, Countryside, and Church*, ed. Edwin DeWindt (Kalamazoo, Mich.: Medieval Institute, 1996), 181–232. In contrast to the brewers, women in the wine trade were rare. Widows could inherit the vintner trade, but carrying it on by themselves was difficult. Widows do appear collecting the debts of their vintner husbands. For instance, one wife sued to collect a debt of £40 because her husband was abroad (PRO C1/46/341). The trade required either travel or the use of agents and apprentices to do the traveling for them. A fe-

male vintner would not travel to Bordeaux and could have difficulty managing factors and apprentices. It was not a trade that was easy to practice as an extension of other domestic occupations. See Margery Kirkbridge James, *Studies in the Medieval Wine Trade* (Oxford: Oxford University Press, 1971), 160–171, for a description of the trade requirements.

12. Peter Clark, *The English Alehouse: A Social History, 1200–1830* (London: Longman, 1983), 5. The distinctions between alehouses, taverns, and inns was not made until a statute in the sixteenth century, which described alehouses as the lower end of the social scale (existing primarily for drink and perhaps some lodging), taverns as selling wine, and inns as being at the upper end of the scale, providing respectable wine, ale, beer, food, and chambers. In the Middle Ages, taverns sold both ale and wine, while alehouses sold only ale.

13. Bennett, "Working Together"; Henry Thomas Riley, *Memorials of London and London Life in the Thirteenth, Fourteenth, and Fifteenth Centuries* (London: Longmans, Green, 1868), 182. Only two women were among the twenty-nine taverners who shut their shops and would not sell wine in defiance of a city ordinance (1331) that all wine be sold from taverns with doors and windows open to the daylight.

14. Gervase Rosser, "London and Westminster: The Suburb in the Urban Economy in the Later Middle Ages," in *Towns and Townspeople in the Fifteenth Century,* ed. John A. F. Thomson (Gloucester: Alan Sutton, 1988), 53, observes that women in Westminster ran rooming houses.

15. Barbara A. Hanawalt, "The Widow's Mite: Provisions for Medieval London Widows," in *Upon My Husband's Death: Widows in the Literature and Histories of Medieval Europe,* ed. Louise Mirrer (Ann Arbor: University of Michigan Press, 1992), 21–45.

16. *Calendar of Letter Books of the City of London, A* (1275–1497), ed. R. Sharpe (London: John Edward Francis, 1899), 220.

17. Guildhall, Consistory Court 9064/1 ms. 5, 5v, 6, 26v, 30, 31, 64v, 65, 66, 81v, 114, 116, 116v, 119, 119v, 122v, 155v. John Godwynn and Agnes his wife were accused in the wardmote of Billingsgate of keeping misrule in an inn called "the Mermaid" held on lease from the Chamberlain of London; PRO C1/136/79.

18. Guildhall, Consistory Court, 9064/1, ms. 68, 83, 84, 91v.

19. Ibid., ms. 110v, 114v.

20. Corporation of London Record Office, Repertory 5, fol. 52r–v.

21. Guildhall, Consistory Court 9064/1 143, 43, 32.

22. A. H. Thomas, ed., *Calendar of Plea and Memoranda Rolls of the City of London, 1323–1482,* (Cambridge: Cambridge University Press, 1943), 4:138.

23. Edith Rickert, ed., *The Babees' Book: Medieval Manners for the Young* (New York: Cooper Square, 1966), 34–35.

24. H. S. Bennett, ed., *England from Chaucer to Caxton* (New York: Harcourt, Brace, 1928), 134–38.

25. A. H. Thomas, ed., *Plea and Memoranda Rolls, 1323–1482* (Cambridge: Cambridge University Press, 1929), 2:184 (1374).

26. Reginald Sharpe, ed., *Calendar of Coroners' Rolls of the City of London* (London: Richard Clay and Sons, 1913), 17–18, 114–16.

27. *The Riverside Chaucer,* ed. Larry D. Benson, 3rd ed. (Boston: Houghton Mifflin, 1987), VII.1897–1900. All subsequent references to Chaucer's poetry will be from this edition, and hereafter fragment and line numbers will appear in text. The Host's treatment of the women on the pilgrimage, the Prioress and even the Wife of Bath, is courteous. His general reactions to women and wives fall within the traditional misogynistic tradition of the period. In the epilogue to the *Merchant's Tale* (IV.2419–2440), he returns to his complaints about his wife, but they are in more generalized terms than those pertaining to their struggle for control of the inn.

28. The ambiguity of who controls public taverns came out in a case in 1395 in which a brewer complained against William Rothewell, chaplain, that he had entered his house at night against his will and carried off his goods, worth 100 marks, and that he also "suspected relations with his wife." He had, therefore, denied him entrance to his house. The

defendant claimed that the house was a "common inn," that he had entered as a lodger, and that the plaintiff was an innkeeper; *Calendar of Plea and Memoranda Rolls*, vol. 3 (1359), 218–19.

29. Quoted by John Stow, *The Survey of London* (Oxford: Oxford University Press, 1908), 74. Taken from the 1603 edition of Stow's *Survey*.

30. Gwyn Williams, *Medieval London from Commune to Capital* (London: Athlone, 1963), 21–22.

31. Gerald R. Owst, *Literature and the Pulpit in Medieval England*, 2nd ed. (Oxford: Blackwell, 1961), 435–41.

32. See William Langland, *Piers Plowman: An Edition of the C-Text*, ed. Derek Pearsall (Berkeley: University of California Press, 1987), VI.350–441, in which Glutton stops at a tavern on the way to Mass. In *The Canterbury Tales*, the *Pardoner's Tale* has an excellent description of the games, drink, and vices one finds in a medieval tavern and the appropriate condemnation of them (VI.463–73).

33. *Statutes of the Realm: Printed by the Command of George III* (1810), 13 Edward I, 102.

34. *Liber Albus: The White Book of the City of London*, ed. and trans. Henry Thomas Riley (London: Richard Griffin, 1861), 240–41. This collection of London's laws, ordinances, and customs was compiled in 1419 by John Carpenter, the common clerk, and Richard Whittington, mayor. The book drew on a number of sources and was compiled for the convenience of city officials.

35. Riley, *Memorials of London and London Life*, 9–11.

36. Thomas Hoccleve, *La Male Regle*, in *England from Chaucer to Caxton*, ed. Bennett, 138–41.

37. *Calendar of Early Mayor's Court Rolls Preserved among the Archives of the Corporation of the City of London, 1298–1307*, ed. A. H. Thomas (London, 1924), 124 (1302).

38. *Calendar of Coroners' Rolls*, 134–35.

39. Corporation of London Record Office (CLRO), MC1/1/153.

40. *Calendar of Coroners' Rolls*, 38–39, 77–78.

41. Barbara A. Hanawalt, "Violent Death in Fourteenth and Fifteenth Century England," *Journal of Comparative Studies in Society and History* 18 (1976): 297–320.

42. *Select Cases of Trespass from the King's Courts, 1307–1399*, ed. Morris S. Arnold (London: Selden Society, 1985), 28.

43. *Calendar of Coroners' Rolls*, 143–44. See also Just.2/94a ms. 1, 1d. for other plots ending in homicide.

44. *Calendar of Plea and Memoranda Rolls*, 2:88. For a larger suspected rebellion, see *Calendar of Plea and Memoranda Rolls*, 3:278 (1406).

45. Guildhall, Consistory Court, 9064/1 m. 133 (1470–73).

46. *Statutes of the Realm*, 1:102.

47. *Calendar of Plea and Memoranda Rolls*, 2:218–19. The churches that rang curfew were Saint Mary le Bow, Kerkyngcherche, Saint Bride, and Saint Giles without Cripplegate. The hours of curfew were nine or ten o'clock to prime.

48. *Statutes of the Realm*, 1:104.

49. Ibid., 234–35.

50. *Calendar of Plea and Memoranda Rolls*, 2:151.

51. *Liber Albus*, 228.

52. Felicity Heal, *Hospitality in Early Modern England* (Oxford: Clarendon Press, 1990), 1–22, discusses the shifting attitude toward foreigners and extending them hospitality. As early as the London Eyre of 1244 the Anglo-Saxon law was reiterated: "Be it known also, that the mayor and citizens say that no one may be in the City as a citizen, and stay there and enjoy the law of the City for more than three nights, unless he finds two pledges and thus is in frankpledge; and if he stays longer in the City in the manner aforesaid, and does not stand his trial, the alderman in whose ward he was, ought to be in mercy for harboring him

in his ward when he is not in frankpledge"; *The London Eyre of 1244*, ed. Helena M. Chew and Martin Weinbaum, London Record Society, 6 (London: Chatham, MacKay, 1970), 25.

53. *Liber Albus*, 234.

54. *Calendar of Plea and Memoranda Rolls*, 3:78–79. Because this ordinance is contemporary to both Chaucer and the Revolt of 1381, a quote is in order: "Whereas larcenies and divers evil deeds are commonly perpetrated more openly, notoriously and frequently in this present than in past times in the city of London, its suburbs and neighbourhood, which would not have been possible, if the thieves and evildoers had not been maintained and harboured by persons dwelling in the city and suburbs and residing with innkeepers, who cared little what kind of men they received, to the great damage of the citizens of the city and those repairing there to the great disgrace and scandal of the same, and in order to prevent such damage and scandal of the same, it was agreed that Sir Nicholas Brembre, Mayor, and the Aldermen [should see] that the innkeepers within the liberty should be sworn to harbour no one longer than a day and a night unless he were willing to answer for them and their acts, nor to receive to their tables any strangers called 'travaillyngmen' or others, unless they had good and sufficient surety from them for their good and loyal behavior, under penalty."

55. *Letter Book A*, 127; *Calendar of Plea and Memoranda Rolls*, 1:18, 45, 154, 156, 163; *Letter Book G*, 294.

56. *Calendar of Plea and Memoranda Rolls*, 3:146. The proclamation was repeated in 1376 (218–219): "No one shall carry arms within the city except the 'valet' of great lords of the land carrying their masters' swords in their presence, the serjeants-at-arms of the King and the Prince and the King's children, and the officers of the City and their companies."

57. *Calendar of Plea and Memoranda Rolls*, 1:220–21; 2:260–61. Sappy claimed loss of £18 6s. 8d. from two chests when the door of his room was broken open. The innkeeper tried to blame Sappy's servants, but the mayor and aldermen viewed the evidence of the broken door and sided with Sappy, making Hostiller responsible under "the common custom of the realm that the keeper of a hostelry was responsible for the goods and chattels brought by lodgers to his hostelry."

58. *Calendar of Plea and Memoranda Rolls*, 1:45, 235; 4:119, 121, 125, 131, 135–36, 139–40, 145, 159; *Letter Book F*, 19, 77.

59. See *Calendar of Plea and Memoranda Rolls*, 2:30, in which Isabel de Chepsted complained that William Dyne, taverner, had beaten and wounded her in 1365 to her damage of 40s. He confessed to the assault and was mainprised [the fine was paid] by John Chaucer (probably the poet's father).

60. CLRO, Journals I, m. 6.

61. Frederick B. Johassen, "The Inn, the Cathedral, and the Pilgrimage of *The Canterbury Tales*," in *Rebels and Rivals: The Contestive Spirit in* The Canterbury Tales, ed. Susanna Greer Fein, David Raybin, and Peter C. Braeger (Kalamazoo, Mich.: Medieval Institute, 1991), 12–13, has made a great deal of the exemptions of Edward III to Southwark from London laws and the general reputation of the borough, but this interpretation is forced by his argument of going from sin to salvation or inn to cathedral.

62. *Calendar of Plea and Memoranda Rolls*, 3:11 (1382) and 172–74 (1390).

63. *Calendar of Plea and Memoranda Rolls*, 4:1551–54.

64. *Liber Albus*, 231, 234.

65. For a discussion of the terms applied to the Host, see David Wallace, *Chaucerian Polity: Absolutist Lineages and Associational Forms in England and Italy* (Stanford, Calif.: Stanford University Press, 1997), chap. 2.

66. The Clerk defers by saying "Hooste, . . . I am under your yerde; / Ye han of us as now the governance, / Ane therefore wol I do yow obeisance" (IV.22–24). The Squire also defers to the host and will not be a rebel, and the Nun's Priest promises the host to be merry (V.3–4; VII.2816–17). The Franklin also agrees to obey when receiving a reprimand that he must tell a tale or pay up (V.700–706).

CHAPTER 10

⁜

Slaughter and Romance
Hunting Reserves in Late Medieval England
William Perry Marvin

A mong discursively defined and contested spaces in medieval rural England, hunting reserves long figured as foci of significant material and ideological investment. William of Normandy must be credited with having imported this once Frankish institution into England in the form of royal forests, a policy that was to have a significant impact on English constitutional history.[1] Of comparable cultural moment was how this institution of reserves set a precedent for varied imitation. The next centuries saw a gradual proliferation of privately chartered hunting grounds (parks and zones defined by free chase and free warren), to the extent that by the fourteenth century hunting reserves had become a ubiquitous and characteristic feature of the English countryside.[2] Requiring specialized personnel and maintenance, hunting reserves were costly. The cull of venison produced a highly esteemed supplement to table fare, but this alone did not balance the economic investment. Subsidiary material gains came from timber, grazing, and some agricultural use, whereas it was elite sport that afforded the cultural advantages. A potent symbol of the high social status of those who owned them, these reserved spaces figured as wooded arenas in which the high and low nobility might stage their pursuit of the rigorous delights of medieval hunting. The ability to exercise ritual violence in the scope of exclusive franchise, and chiefly for purposes of entertainment, became a significant matter of honor. In the words of Thorstein Veblen, this honor was tantamount to a "high office of slaughter, [which] as an expression of the slayer's prepotence, casts a glamour of worth over every act of slaughter and over all the tools and accessories of the act."[3] Because of the premium placed on symbolic violence in these sporting sanctuaries, medieval hunting reserves were notoriously vulnerable to trespass.[4] This essay addresses representations of violence in these spaces by examining how medieval hunting was textualized in discourses of law and romance.

We can visualize a broad spectrum of factors relating to problems of "social control" in hunting reserves. The secular ritual of the hunt, whose historical development was closely associated with the formal segregation of hunting space,[5] required a self-reflexive discipline in the hunter to accommodate its elaborate regimen. Careful attention to speech and gesture showed the hunter's knowledge of the complex codification of the "art of hunting."[6] This art constituted a privileged discourse whose exclusivity was challenged by the practices of a disprivileged other (the poacher). The hunting sanctuary was watched over by warreners, parkers, woodwards, or other appointees in order to keep poaching in check, for trespasses threatened more than just the wild game. Poachers had to be ejected from the hunting grounds or prosecuted in order for the rightful owner to maintain the liberty of the reserve, which would be forfeited if the private hunting in effect became common.[7] Chartered hunters, who had rights upon the bodies of animals and men in their private hunting grounds, understood poaching trespasses to be something significantly greater than just the tenants' or neighbors' desire to eat well. As studies by James C. Scott and more recently Roger B. Manning have shown, poaching may articulate a complex social response to privileged control, a control that lords enforced by lawfully abrogating hunting rights from local inhabitants and neighboring gentry alike.[8] Furthermore, as Barbara Hanawalt has argued, poaching appears to have been chiefly men's sport, something of a game complex enough in its signs and combinations to have constituted a pervasive "expression of male gender identity," adding to a licit hunt numerous "elements of stealth, danger, violence, sexuality, and assertion of independence."[9] To reserve hunting rights in a patriarchal world was an act bound to generate, indeed invite, resistance; for hunting is evocative of the deeds of ancestors, and therewith also of ancestral liberties.

In this essay I shall examine how issues of class and gender relate to the spatial context of control in the hunting reserve. The circumstances of physical or legal enclosure were crucial factors in medieval hunting culture not only because they were in Veblen's sense "accessories of the act," contrived to facilitate success in the hunt as much as was any technique of "craft" that masters described in their technical treatises. One of the most intriguing textual loci for examining spatial ideologies at work is the game law of 1390, which radically redrew the lines of exclusion in English hunting culture. An explication of the statute lets issues surrounding the control of reserves fall sharply into relief. I will track this law back to what I believe to be its origins in the Northern Rebellion of the Beckwiths in the 1380s, where the sequence of events will elucidate the stakes involved in men's control of hunting reserves in the late fourteenth century. The discussion will then turn to the contemporaneous romance of *Sir Degrevant*, which functions within and as part of the variously discursive "textual environment" (as Paul Strohm has defined this concept)[10] of medieval English hunting culture. The hunting violence in this romance illustrates how forested hunting reserves in medieval England were hardly intelligible as free or liminal spaces disposed marginally to the world of social regulation.[11] Where forest and game law revoked the general freedom to "occupy" (in the legal sense) nondomestic animals in the wild, it reproduced ideologies already obtaining in domestic realms. The discourses of social control we find textualized in game law and hunting treatises could undergo retextualization in English romance, in whose aesthetic organization the violent class and gender rivalries of the hunting elite may appear culturally productive.

Reserving the "Disport of Gentilmen"

The ratification of the first "game law" brought a sudden and enduring alteration in the way sporting rights were apportioned in England. Introduced as a plea of the Commons in the Westminster Parliament of January 17 to March 2, 1390, about one-half year after King Richard had reassumed his regality, it became law in the first of three statutes issued by that assembly.[12] Much attention has been paid to the fact that this law spawned generations of oppressive legislation up until the reforms of 1831, but little if any discussion has been devoted to the circumstances of its conception.[13] In contradistinction to regulations passed in the same statute with respect to fishing, the original game law cannot be said to have stemmed from any concern for wildlife management.[14] Rather, the game law was a part of the broader discursive net at that time being cast over problems of public disorder pursuant to the creeping "bastardization" of feudal relationships.

The control of varying and, in the Commons' view, unethical uses of liveries was close to the heart of parliamentary politics in Ricardian England not only because these were perceived to be cutting the ideological ligaments of the feudal order; the livery issue had also become a factor determining how the rule of the Lords Appellant would weather the period following their coup against King Richard's administrative clique in the Merciless Parliament of 1388. The nobility was thoroughly implicated in prolonging the livery "abuses" that the parliamentary Commons sought to curtail, for it was chiefly through their own high-power rivalries, increasing their households and aggravating conflicts of loyalty among their retainers, that lawlessness was widely abetted. As the Monk of Westminster viewed it, the Appellants' policy of advocating the correction of individual abuses judicially, while resisting any legislative action to abolish the use of liveries, amounted eventually to a mismanagement of the issue.[15] This was to have a twofold consequence. First, the Appellants eventually lost the popular confidence in their will and, compounded with their diplomatic failures, in their ability to govern for the peace of the realm. And second, the Appellants thereby opened a window of opportunity for Richard to reinstate his authority beginning in May 1389. "In 1389–90," explains Anthony Tuck, "the king may have been looking for a new power base among the knightly class. His policies towards both taxation and retaining were calculated to appeal to that social group. By implementing a programme which was attractive to them, he hoped to prevent their alliance with the nobility, which had led to disaster in 1386 and 1388."[16]

Fundamental for Richard's approach to the Commons was the policy on public order that he pursued between May 1389 and May 1390. As Strohm has described it, Richard's policy entailed his adopting an array of performative stances, first as a mediator between the Appellants and the Commons, then as an enemy of the associative forms so widely capitalized upon by the nobility, then as an exponent of reform.[17] The Westminster Parliament of 1390, falling midway in the course of the king's conciliatory efforts, offered a moment propitious for setting forth grievances and wishes dear to the body of the esquire landholders who constituted its Commons. Besides reaching a compromise on liveries in the third statute to be issued, their petition for confirmation and procedural clarification of the statute of 12 Richard II (providing for the fixing of rates paid to artificers and laborers) was ratified into law, as was their plea newly to regulate the measures and weights for wool and cloth.[18]

Thus enters the game law. In the short term it was a part of the king's package of conciliatory boons held out to the Commons; in the long term, it became a landmark in the history of hunting legislation and the advancing fortunes of the gentry:

> Item, Forasmuch as divers artificers, labourers, and servants, and grooms, keep greyhounds and other dogs, and on the holydays, when good Christian people be at church, hearing divine service, they go hunting in parks, warrens, and connigries of lords and others, to the very great destruction of the same, and sometime under such colour they make their assemblies, conferences, and conspiracies for to rise and disobey their allegiance. It is ordained and assented, that no manner of artificer, labourer nor any other layman, which hath not lands or tenements to the value of 40s. by year, nor any priest nor other clerk, if he be not advanced to the value of £10 by year, shall have or keep from henceforth any greyhound, hound, nor other dog to hunt; nor shall they use fyrets, heys, nets, harepipes, nor cords, nor other engines for to take or destroy deer, hares, nor conies, nor other gentlemen's game, upon pain of one year's imprisonment; and that the justices of peace have power to enquire, and shall enquire of the offenders in this behalf, and punish them by the pain aforesaid.[19]

The clause presents itself as a law-and-order measure conceived to protect hunting reserves from trespass and to preclude outbreaks of riot. Its method is to establish property qualifications that must be met before one may legally hunt or possess dogs with which to hunt wild animals. Such a method, however, even at the time, must have seemed intrinsically ill-devised to safeguard such reserves from trespass, since poaching was a kind of encroachment highly valued by men of all estates as a sport unto itself.[20] A more obviously appreciable aim would be a reduction of competition in the hunting field. At any rate, it is against the liberty of rural laborers and the artisan-workers of guilds not only to hunt, but also to associate freely, that the weight of the law most heavily bears. The drafters are careful to exploit widely shared presumptions about unlawful association and to deploy the terms of covinage in order to array their language with the discourse used to problematize bastard forms of retaining and indenture.[21]

The preamble of the law consists of a narrative of laboring-class misbehavior and violation of upper-class status symbols sufficient to generate anxiety over fissures in the social order. The desire to regulate the manifest signs and attributes of social estate, revoking the rights of "subgentry" lay and clerical classes to keep greyhounds and take venison, is in spirit as in action reminiscent of the sumptuary legislation passed and then repealed under 37–38 Edward III, which targeted both apparel and diet.[22] The "lawing" of dogs (mutilating their paws) had long been a notorious draconian rule of forest law, but the game law's prohibition is now absolute, denying insufficiently propertied men the stylish accompaniment of hounds. The notion that deer, hare, and other wild animals are not beasts *ferae naturae* or beasts of warren as in the forest law[23] but (in the words of the fifteenth-century translation of this statute) the "disport of gentilmen" seems to be added finally as so obvious an observation that it evokes no gesture to qualify it. Indeed it assumes a legitimating task itself, presenting as matter of fact what in no way follows from the law's own argument about the threat of laboring-class conspiracy. Such a notion is not novel at this time, to be sure. It was originally not part of the Commons' petition, but of the king's response, his addendum to the plea's rationale.[24] In point of fact, however, it frames the crucial ideological element of the text, and the consequences of its entry into legal discourse are nothing short of radical.

While a threshold of forty shillings is too low to outline anything like the lower rank of the gentry, the point lies in who, exactly, shall be given access to the *desduit des gentils*.[25] The bottom line of the new law is that insufficiently propertied subjects are henceforth disqualified from hunting and are to be excluded everywhere from the right to take wild game. The time-honored and conventional means hitherto used to suspend common hunting rights and to invest them in individuals to the exclusion of others had been (and still was) to charter hunting reserves in the form of forest, chase, park, or free warren. These reserves were defined topographically with varying degrees of clarity in their demarcation, but they were all constituted by an essentially spatial dimension that could be imagined and effectively imposed over the contours of the land. They were tangible and integral spaces within which the hunt, not the animals, could be privatized; outside them, the common chase obtained wherein hunting was regulated by custom, not by law.[26] Hence these were spaces that in effect criminalized outsiders, redefining unwelcome hunters as poachers who encroached.

By contrast with laws protecting hunting reserves, then, the radical novelty of the "game law" lies first in how suddenly it defines wild animals as *desduit* (here, "game"), and second in how it redraws the boundaries of exclusion. Whereas hunting reserves delineated the difference between licit and criminal activity according to real topographical criteria, the game law draws a boundary at points contrived to mark a cleavage in the social hierarchy, demarcating a level of nominal or performative gentility below which a large part of the hunting public was at best to be disenfranchised and at worst criminalized.[27] Such, in short, is the force of a logic that grounds its sanctions not in the acts of riot narrated in its pretext, but in a formula that tacitly consecrates the bodies of wild animals to the propertied as exclusive objects of desire.

Most earlier law, such as that set in place by the Forest Charter (1217) or the Statutes of Westminster I (1275), had benefited primarily magnates and the nobility, either by limiting the forest rights of the king with respect to his barons or by protecting individual hunting grounds.[28] To guard against the violation of these spaces, a statute of 21 Edward I even gave foresters, parkers, and warreners license to use lethal force with impunity.[29] Of itself, however, the law could not ideologically tie the semantic of hunting to social estate absolutely. For, even while it was continually shrinking in real terms, the ancient common chase had presumably always obtained outside reserved spaces.[30] But the game law, in that it revoked the individual right to hunt from persons who did not meet the property qualifications it established, in effect legally closed the common chase to the majority of the population. In broad historical terms, it was perfecting a development that had begun with the Normans' institution of the forests, and hence finally channeled the same discourse of exclusion—inventing the concept of privatized hunting space for the rich—into the lately empowered voice of property owners more modestly endowed. This, in the words of Sir William Blackstone, was the "bastard slip" that sprang from the root of forest law, the game law waxing as an illegitimate offshoot of a waning royal prerogative. As with a bastardization of the feudal idea at work in associational forms, land and money were now undergoing revaluation as resources of both material and symbolic capital in the hunting field, reflecting seemingly inexorable shifts in configurations of social power. Thus Blackstone later declared with notable insight that, whereas of old "the forest law established only one mighty hunter throughout the land, *the game laws have raised a little* Nimrod *in every manor.*"[31]

William Perry Marvin

The Forester and His Horn

The game law's preamble observes with evident annoyance that laboring-class hunters were undermining gentlemen's privileges; its tone suggests alarm, however, when it states that people assembling under "such color" threaten revolt. Was the law calculated to excite wary memories of the uprising of 1381?[32] There the specter of riot loomed large with an oft-iterated call for liberty and hunting rights. A notable example was the violence that befell Saint Albans, a monastery of ancient endowment and lucrative exemption, handsomely appointed with woods, fishponds, warren and deerfold, together with the chartered liberties reserving the fruits of these. Thomas Walsingham, a monk of Saint Albans, relates how the tenants' list of long-standing grievances (or as Scott would say, "hidden transcript")[33] was aired publicly in the context of the June rebellion, as the tenants treated in London with respect to "the aims they had long secretly desired: namely to have newly defined boundaries around their town within which they might pasture their animals freely; to enjoy fishing rights in various places without dispute; to possess hunting and fowling rights in certain places and to be able to erect hand-mills where they pleased and as they wished."[34]

At the monastery the people's uprising evolved into "impious assembly" and oath-taking, the burning of buildings, and a wild hunt in the warren that saw the quarry hoisted on a staff over the pillory in the vill "to signify the liberty of the warren thus seized."[35] The desire to perpetuate this liberty issued in its subsequent translation into the language and scribal medium of Latin charters, "violently extorted" from the abbot and ceding to the tenants the use of their hunting dogs and coils.[36]

The most dramatic confrontation on this theme was, of course, alleged to have occurred at Smithfield in the face-off between King Richard and the rebels headed by Wat Tyler. "The rebels petitioned the king," recounts Henry Knighton, "that all preserves of water, parks and woods should be made common to all: so that throughout the kingdom the poor as well as the rich should be free to take game in water, fish ponds, woods and forests, as well as to hunt hares in the fields — and to do these and many other things without impediment."[37]

Knighton's account has the notorious foible of conflating the persons of Tyler and Jack Straw, and his failure to ascribe a clear motive to Tyler's abrupt yank at the bridle of the king's horse invites question. But his introduction of a recurring element of insurgent discourse at this crisis point of the rebellion in London may testify to some, perhaps popular, belief that the restrictions on hunting and fishing were an ideological front where the line was to be drawn. The *Anonimalle Chronicle* reports the rebels' last demand as a call to raze the social hierarchy, "that there should be no more villeins in England, and no serfdom or villeinage, but that all men should be free and of one condition."[38] Knighton's account reifies this desire for free condition in its palpable form as the liberty to exploit natural resources, qualifying all to "be free to take game."

But was it the memory of Smithfield and Saint Albans, of a potential revisitation of similar violence to person, privilege, and the social order, that the game law of 1390 sought to evoke? Perhaps. Traumatic though this memory remained to some, however, it does not account for the timing of the law's enactment nearly a decade after the uprising.

The complaints of the law's preamble suggest contemporary events that gave cause for alarm and that reflected similar violations of holy days' peace, laboring-class allegiance, and hunting reserves. All these factors were relevant to a conflict of major proportions that was then indeed embroiling Lancastrian officials and countrymen of the West Riding of Yorkshire. The so-called Northern Rebellion of Sir William Beckwith, which had been in progress since September 1387, evoked a commission of *oyer et terminer* only one week after the close of the Westminster parliament, "touching treasons, felonies, murders, homicides, robberies, insurrections and other offenses in John, Duke of Lancaster's lordship and liberty of Knaresburgh and in the forest and chase thereof."[39] A further commission of *trailbaston* was to follow in the summer.[40] As J. G. Bellamy has described it, this unrest was neither a reverberation of 1381 nor a matter of Lollard dissent, but a "feud of the old sort" conducted by Lancastrian ministers and allowed to persist during John of Gaunt's absence in Spain.[41] According to the *Westminster Chronicle*, Beckwith had laid claim to a bailiwick or wardenship in the chase of Knaresborough "hitherto held by his ancestors."[42] It happened, however, that Sir Robert Rokely, constable of Knaresborough castle and master forester of the chase, awarded the office to a man not of that locality; and Beckwith, thus embittered, retaliated with private war on the authors of his disparagement.[43] Any further narrative of Beckwith's exploits must be reconstructed chiefly from pardons later granted to a few of his associates, documents no longer extant but calendared with the letters patent.

First, a word must be said about the actors involved here. The conflict grew to such magnitude as to polarize most of the county. As it seems to have drawn landlords of West Yorkshire into one faction allied with Lancastrian authority, and the rural tenantry into another faction, the polarization took shape along class lines. Bellamy concludes that Beckwith's sympathizers were local men from around Knaresborough, none having committed significant offenses before the feud or after it, and that Beckwith's force derived "almost entirely from the lower classes of society, menials, tradesmen, land holders of the poorer type with a leavening of clergy and a single manorial official."[44] The records give no overt indication of what was at stake for these persons in their support of Beckwith, be it material reward, defiance of landlords, outlaw fraternity, or militant sport. Some regional gentry long countenanced the uproar, although it is hard to say whether for reasons of sympathy or trepida-

231

tion.[45] At stake for Beckwith himself, as for several of his kinfolk who aided him, seems to have been the material and honorific proceeds deriving from the title of underforester or parker. In the course of the struggle the stakes surely changed as legal acquisition of the office became irrevocably foreclosed to him and he became enmeshed in the blow-for-blow economy of the feud. But as the private issue grew into concerted defiance, how did Beckwith's interests correlate with those of the community that supported him?

Directed first against the Lancastrian steward, then against the rival in office, Sir Robert Doufbygging, Beckwith's attacks seem to have been organized through "unlawful appointments and alliances" ordained at a certain recurring "parliament called 'Dodelowe.'"[46] On Sunday, October 4, 1388, Beckwith drew with his people before the castle of Knaresborough and began sniping at Sir Robert Rokely, the master forester. There they maimed Edmund Doufbygging, son of the rival forester. In November Beckwith's people laid siege to Haywrocastell (Haverah), a lodge in the Chase of Knaresborough, where Robert the forester was holed up to save his life. Probably it was at this time that they first havocked the park.[47] On Palm Sunday, 1389, they ambushed Robert Doufbygging in the metes of the chase as he was on his way to church "to hear divine service."[48] While the forester escaped, at least two of his company were chased down and murdered, and the Beckwiths crowned this coup with a staggering waste of timber and slaughter of venison. In the following July they broke into the forester's house at Redshaw, smashed twenty marks worth of housewares, and took a ceremonial silver-mounted dagger. In the course of this raid they advanced to the common pasture of Knaresborough Chase, hunted up and slaughtered the forester's domestic stock—six oxen, seventeen steers, four cows, and fifteen bullocks in toto. In August 1389, again on a Sunday, they revisited the lodge of Haverah and penetrated its chambers, destroying ten marks worth of the forester's household effects and seizing his silver-mounted horn together with his bows and arrows.[49] By the Sunday after Michaelmas, 1389, master forester Rokely's son Edmund was killed, the park of Haverah was for all intents and purposes destroyed, and its parkers were driven out and their dogs slain. Other parks in the chase were also broken and havocked, and besides further occasional murders and kidnappings, there continued an almost incessant massacre of oxen, cattle, horses, and wild animals.[50] The return of the duke, John of Gaunt, however, signaled the beginning of Beckwith's end. A commission of *oyer et terminer* in 1391 finally drove him and five hundred of his people into forest outlawry. By late winter 1392, Beckwith had been slain for blood money.[51]

As the specifics of most events here narrated figure in letters of pardon, they are framed entirely within the discourse supervising the suppression of the revolt and therefore touch only on the aggressive involvement of the grantees. Any counterstrokes the foresters undertook are omitted, but it is difficult to imagine that they stood idly by under the brunt of such punishment. This omission notwithstanding, Beckwith's campaign can be discerned to have established a pattern of raids growing out of the deliberations of subversive "parliaments," raids that were recurring chiefly on Sundays, that complemented their assaults on men with a wholesale killing of animals, and that insistently violated the private domain of the rival forester just as they brought forth an escalation of violence. From sniping outside the castle, ambushing in the park, and raiding of hunting reserves to the eventual entry into house and lodge, the Beckwiths carried their war into the inner spaces wherein the person of Forester Doufbygging merged vulnerably with his office.

The action continually defined the field of contestation in and around the most elite form of hunting reserve to be found in private hands, a park inholding within a free chase.[52] This encircled area, buffered by what formerly had been a royal forest, had had its administration reformed in the 1370s better to serve the pleasure of Gaunt. As part of the "finest collection of hunting preserves in England," Knaresborough Chase ideally reserved the recreation of martial disport for the duke and venison for his table.[53] If we conceptualize the chase as a hunting ground in such dimensions as Pierre Bourdieu ascribes to the "social topology" of a given institutional field, various positions emerge relative to the kinds of capital circulating within it and to the transitive trajectories of its defining practice, namely the hunt.[54] Viewed schematically, the administration of this space nominates foresters in powerful subject positions as wardens and hunters, situating deer and poachers as the authorized objects of foresters' controlling actions. The foresters facilitated the lord's hunt when he visited the chase, and they aided his huntsmen when these came for their regular cull of deer. They drew their own perquisites of hare hunting and venison as part of their fee. Charged also to suppress poaching, the foresters safeguarded the duke's exclusive right to delegate hunting privileges.[55] Beckwith, deprived of the title of forester, was evidently bent on forcibly converting the economic capital of venison to the symbolic capital of defiant possession, appropriating the perquisites and symbols of official forestry. Stalking the forester just as he hunted the deer in the man's charge, Beckwith penetrated deeper through the circles of official and personal authority manifested in park and lodge until he had finally laid hands on the phallic emblems of his rival's power, notably the knife and hunting weapons, and especially the horn. Symbolism, of course, is chiefly what Beckwith had to settle for. He had to reckon his achievements, if one can call them that, in the austere and bloody profits of vengeance. He could for a time play havoc and, as it were, administer the "high office of slaughter," but he still failed to oust the forester from the institutional field.

The records do not state that Doufbygging's horn was comparable to a forest warden's horn of office, but Beckwith's capture of it made it so.

The horn is not only a sign of animal potency but also an instrument for the production of signs, the "motes," by which the hunt's progress is signaled, hounds directed, the hunting party more or less held together, and the ritual moments of kill and presentation declared. In the institutional field, the horn is a manifest sign for the social capital represented by the formal relationship between the holder of the forest or chase (in this case the duke) and any hunter authorized to hunt at the lord's pleasure (here, the underforester entitled to fee deer). Whatever bond may be said to have existed between hunting lord and hunter rested on an agreement to share the deer, which remained technically wild no matter how enclosed. It is into this triangle—deer mediating a legal connection between two men—that Beckwith forcefully interposed himself. By rendering bodies passive, slaughtering beasts, and symbolically emasculating the forester with the theft of his horn, Beckwith at least temporarily set himself in the ascendancy among hierarchically ordered hunters in the reserve. To what extent this personal appropriation may have been gratifying to Beckwith's partisans is difficult to estimate; available to them at any rate was the satisfaction to be derived from paralyzing the duke's hunting administration and enjoying his sport. These numerous partisans were of great importance in the long run, for they were the ones more likely to alarm Parliament—the "divers artificers, labourers, and servants, and grooms"—not the Beckwiths themselves.

It appears to have been Gaunt's absence until 1390, a temporary key absence in the symbolic order of the hunting grounds, that opened an interval in which the Beckwiths' feud could develop into open rebellion, unchecked by the mechanisms of the law.[56] With the overlord's surveillance withdrawn, self-help seems to have become the order of the day. This is not to say, however, that all had devolved into anarchy. James C. Scott has articulated a conceptual model by which poaching in its clandestine form may be interpreted as an "infrapolitical" practice of subordinate groups, a means of rationally pushing against the constraints imposed by the contingencies of living a public life of subjection.[57] As such, poaching would constitute part of a "hidden transcript," or the covert discourses taking shape in opposition to the public forms of material appropriation and ideologies of dominant elites, by definition a function of counterbalancing a pragmatically ordained performance of obedience required in the "public transcript." Scott is careful to define the hidden transcript not as a substitute for real action; it is not to be understood as a "relief valve" that vents aggression without directing it into real force, and so would act to forestall rebellion. Such a model would recover any covert discourse into a pattern of those actions sanctioned by elites. Rather, with Foucault, Scott identifies the hidden transcript as a *"condition of practical resistance rather than a substitute for it."*[58] It is of itself a political domain with its own dynamic of establishing norms and enforcing conformity with them, albeit always in relation to the publicly operative norms of the dominant. These concepts make it possible to speculate on the environment of opposition that, kindled by personal antagonism and given opportunity by weaknesses in the chase's administrative mechanism, issued in the Beckwith faction's hidden transcript exploding into public discourse.

Crucial here is the problem of overlapping authorities and the fact that the master forester of Knaresborough Chase, out of prudence or animosity or both, had recruited Forester Doufbygging from Lancastrian domains.[59] The Yorkshire people of Knaresborough forest, laboring-class tenantry and lower clergy alike, were presumably confronted by a forester with whom they could claim no connection or affinity whatever. Indeed, his very appointment must have seemed designed to countervail existing tendencies, responding against the kinds of "appointments and alliances" later endorsed at the Dodelowe parliaments. The results of studies on medieval poaching and on poaching rebellions in later centuries make it reasonable to assume that poaching was occurring on some level in Knaresborough Chase long before the rebellion.[60] Noting Bellamy's remark that previous trespasses had been insignificant at most, it is plausible to conclude that poaching had been tolerated in its clandestine form by foresters who had been positioned in the network between the Yorkshire communities of their origin and their lords of foreign (i.e., Lancastrian) domain.

In this context, hunting will have figured as a preeminent political *factum* in daily life. Hunting was an integral part of compensating imbalances of power in the chase, justified as it was by a popular ideology that wild animals were the possession of no one (a notion that had underpinned demands of the rebels of 1381) and tolerated by a cadre of low-level ministers bound to the local community not only by covert exchanges of venison, but also by long-existing ties of cooperation, affinity, or kinship. In the public transcript, the venison of Knaresborough was reserved for the duke and his administrators. For the commons to live without harassment, a public performance of submission was required in which the people desisted from hunting and rendered their customary dues, repairing the park pales, providing for winter fodder, acting as beaters in the drive, and so on.[61] On the other hand, the hidden transcript counteracted this performative submission by secretly exacting compensation in the form of wild-animal bodies, covertly taking from the duke and his ministers the very objects of their sporting desire. The Beckwith rebellion did not present laymen and clergy with an opportunity to riot merely "under color" of hunting, as the language of the game law of 1390 would phrase such actions. It appears rather that the rebellion channeled the same infrapolitical transactions of daily life into an economy of vengeance, which compounded the personal motives of the Beckwiths with the community's apprehension that an era of tacit cooperation with the chase officials had reached its end.

A fundamental given in this scenario is the field of material domination that the hunting reserves imposed on the land. Both the stratagems of the rebels and the pretext of the 1390 game law present reserves as sites immanently disposed to stage the violence issuing from a conflict of class interests.[62] Within this field, the culture of medieval hunting invests its energy and signification in the bodies of deer, wild and not legally ownable, but nevertheless guarded for the sake of lawfully being killed by the members of a select community. The conflict takes shape through appropriations both real and symbolic in which asserting the right to kill is a function of status. For the game law, hunting reserves represent not only privatized hunting, but also the disprivilege of laborers, artisans, and most clergy to own dogs and hunt, much less even to assemble. The Yorkshire rebels temporarily annulled such disprivilege by desecrating this same status symbol through armed incursion and slaughter, laming the surveillance system, and seizing the emblems of the forester's title. But the question of the game law's relation to this conflict is probably not one of basic stimulus and response. As I said above, its measures simply did not address the facts of upper-class poaching in England. Certainly the association of popular hunting with the violence of 1381 remained vivid. When the moment for a demonstrative but relatively moderate point of alliance between landholders and the Crown was propitious, the reports of the Dodelowe "parliaments" and large-scale subversive poaching of the Beckwith rebellion gave an opportunity for certain long-desired legislation. By translating beasts *ferae naturae* to *desduit des gentils,* the "disport of gentilmen," the law seeks to construct a hunting subculture that is implicated with sedition. It may then attempt to suppress this subculture throughout the land by making all of England one great hunting reserve for the propertied.

Yet poaching was manifestly not a crime specific to lower social classes. Nor did medieval writers always imagine it as such. By turning the discussion to a text roughly contemporaneous with the events of Beckwith's poaching feud, we may examine how a similar pattern of incursion and slaughter for purposes of desecration could be retextualized in English romance, where the social scenario is imaginatively reconfigured around noblemen at odds over deer and a woman.

"To Brynge þe Dere to þe Grounde Was His Maste Glewe"

The tail-rhyme romance *Sir Degrevant* treats of a baron's efforts to restore his reputation following an unprovoked attack on his property, an undertaking that leads to a courtship with his enemy's daughter.[63] The narrator assumes the persona of a minstrel who is eager to attribute to his own profession the renown enjoyed by protagonists such as Degrevant and to sympathize with them in matters of love. Not surprisingly, then, the second segment of the plot takes up genre conventions of bride-winning, replete with Degrevant vying for his beloved's favor via her chambermaid, his repulse of a magnate suitor, a secret affair, his marriage to her (which entails for him entry into a higher social sphere), and, ultimately, the acquisition of his former enemy's estates. The poet may have conceived the protagonist as an English reflex of Agravain from French Arthurian narrative[64] and thereby single-handedly recovered a personage from the genealogy of classic Arthuriana for service in English romance. Nonetheless, the Arthurian milieu has little or no direct bearing on the events. Degrevant's character reveals a desideratum that romance regards as a fundamental problem in any courtly setting: his formal accomplishments in music and hunting satisfy his desires so fully that he has no need for a woman (33–64). To awaken this need, the bipartite plot devotes its first segment to problems arising from the protagonist's *Jagdlust*. In lieu of an episodic treatment in which the hunt figures as a device stressing the unforeseen and fortuitous nature of knightly adventure, the poet has opted for stricter causality and social realism, letting the action develop in a scenario very familiar to rural England.

The opening field of conflict here, as with the feud and rebellion discussed thus far, is a baronial hunting reserve, Degrevant's huge park, which the earl, his neighbor, attacks and havocks in its owner's absence. Not only do the earl and his people break through the park, slaughtering sixty fat deer; they also despoil the ponds of fish, kill game keepers, and menace Degrevant's tenants by destroying their traction animals and wagons (97–114). Degrevant, not unlike John of Gaunt, is summoned from his war on "heathen folk" in Spain, where he is engaged in conquering Granada (131). He at first attempts to "work by þe lawe," which for him means sending a messenger to the earl with a letter inquiring into the motives for the trespass (rather than engaging any shrieval mechanisms of remedy). His messenger is haughtily rebuffed, and Degrevant resolves to confront the earl with force, summoning ten score of knights and three hundred archers (153–240).

The minstrel does not spell out the earl's deeper motivation beyond mention of the "grete spyt" (101) he had of his younger neighbor, a term that it seems by the fourteenth century would overlap with the "odium" said by the Monk of Westminster to have imbued the atmosphere among Beckwith and his supporters. Rational economic or political motives for the earl's action are left to the imagination. With his emotion seemingly grounded in his "mechell pryd" (98), we are left to observe what appears to be the efforts of a "little Nimrod" to expand his verge. Indeed the tradition of understanding tyrannical behavior as an outgrowth of hunting lust is running strong; having achieved notable elaboration in John of Salisbury's influential *Policraticus* (1.4), it is still vital in Chaucer's *Clerk's Tale*. But there inheres in *spyt* a more conservative sense of injury and humiliation,[65] besides contempt, which directs our attention to the public transcript of reputations and honor-discourse in which the minstrel claims for himself and his craft significant agency.

From the broadly defined arena of the Knaresborough fight we are transported into the microcosm of a social elite where the competition for status is intense, notwithstanding the fact that both opponents possess such immense material resources in the form of land, rent, and hunting reserves as to make real differences between them seem negligible. Degrevant, besides being a nephew of King Arthur and a knight of the Round Table, is accorded high acclaim for his personal bearing. The narrator shows Degrevant's public persona to be informed by the possessions and practices of his high estate, that is, his hunting zeal, his deeds of arms, his largesse and hospitality and pious works, and his great repute, celebrated by minstrels, for his management of all of the above (33–96). The earl, in spite of his greater estate, is not so celebrated, and in such a competitive environment where the "social estimation of honor" with its effect of public authority must continually be negotiated with the community, we may infer that his policy is gauged on a hypersensitive balance of publicly spoken words.[66] The chief indication of what is at stake for the earl lies in how the narrator catalogs Degrevant's accomplishments, for which the minstrelsy "hade halowed hys name / wyth gret nobulle" (91–92). This institution of public acclaim, like the discourse of heralds and kings of arms, thus advanced Degrevant's rank symbolically while yet leaving the earl unheralded. So presumably unsteady has the status quo become that the magnate's project to "degrade" Degrevant (L 104) in absentia must be predicated upon a hierarchy of status in which honor capital has been felt to exceed official rank.[67]

The minstrel's exposition of Degrevant's character draws a fundamental connection between social franchise and the hunter persona. The baron is a "fayre man and free" (33) whose devotion to music gives way only to the greater pleasure he has in rising every day before dawn for Mass and in hawking and hunting in his reserves.

> Oþer gammnes he louede mare:
> Grewhundes for buk and bare,
> For hert, hynde, and for hare....
> To brynge þe dere to þe grounde
> Was his maste glewe.
>   (L 41–43, 59–60)

For, like the hunting lord Walter in Chaucer's *Clerk's Tale*, Degrevant is conspicuously uninterested in women, no matter the variety:

> Certis, wyfe wolde he nane,
> Wenche ne no lemman,

> Bot als an ankyre in a stane
> He lyued here trewe.
> (L 61–64)

The exuberant mirth of hunting *glewe* that keeps him unwomaned is no mean part of the anchoritic discipline that keeps Degrevant "true" to his world of men. By forcibly entering Degrevant's property and havocking all about, the earl is obviously precipitating a crisis in which his rival could lose face through inaction. Such is clearly entailed in an unprovoked act of destruction that calls out to be settled fairly or requited in kind. The important thing about social control in this context is that by killing, nay massacring, Degrevant's deer, the earl violates objects of his rival's desire that have complexly personal and public dimensions. To be sure, Degrevant, too, would have killed them eventually. But the fact that the earl can project his enmity upon the bodies of animals that Degrevant had reserved for himself and his yeomen to exercise their chief desire upon, in the *glewe*-some anticipation of chasing them, is no less a crass violation of his franchise than it is a kind of love-killing. Insofar as the younger man's public persona is defined through a presentation of himself as a rigorous, freeborn lover of the hunt, a massacre of his deer must cut his honor to the quick.

Late medieval audiences would have appreciated that the events thus narrated were typical of land wars fought between rural households supported by their ("bastard") retinues. These private wars, which generally resulted from complexities surrounding the transmission of property in trust, often took the form of forcibly entering into land, ousting servants, terrorizing tenants and vandalizing or distraining their goods.[68] The earl's riotous poaching, however, could scarcely be construed as a bona fide project of land recovery, for it is simply too felonious. But it does accord with tactics designed to humiliate a landlord, to harass his subjects and intimidate them into questioning their loyalties. The earl's poaching reflects what Bellamy calls "misbehavior ancillary to the main purpose of entry and ouster," the point being to "embarrass the party currently seised and cause him to lose face by his failure to protect" his tenants.[69] Particularly vulnerable, therefore, is the reputation of protector that property holders enjoyed; the efficacy of any incursion will be determined by how successfully the entrant-distrainor can impose his own habitus of lordship upon the field of contestation. In the world of *Sir Degrevant*, as for many a landlord in medieval England, one practice integral to the *habitus* of lordship was hunting.

Hunting constituted a conspicuous and sanguinary performance of physical mastery. When it was elaborated through "symbolic discourses" such as ritual, idiom, costume, and legal privilege, hunting became a performance of social mastery, as well.[70] Perhaps more than any particular technique, it was the hunting reserve that so greatly facilitated the chore-

ography of this performance, for parks and chases delimited the space in
which rights were abrogated from the commons and in which the spectacle of force merged perfectly with the facts of real and ideological domination. Much of the legitimation invented to support the creation and
maintenance of hunting reserves, from the royal forest to any lord's right
of free warren, derived from notions of recreation and protection. Dominant elites promoted the burden of rule as an entitlement to rights of
recreation that were as exclusive as their responsibilities, and blood
sport was found to be preeminently suited to the warrior fraternity, or
to those who thought of themselves as belonging to it.[71] When lords took
it upon themselves to kill the deer and wild boar that menaced their
tenants' crops, the notions of hunter and protector (even Langland would
agree) could be conflated most effectively.[72] Partly for this reason the
earl can strike at Degrevant's lordly persona by laying such a bloodthirsty
assault on his hunting parks, drawing attention to the latter's absence,
much as Beckwith had done with Gaunt. Nor may the baron too lightly
assess the damage, for his first action upon returning from abroad is to
secure the breached enclosures. The husbandmen's relief (146) is a realistic response to the disruption of manorial order we can imagine to be
embodied in the remaining deer grazing through their fields. For all the
narrative focus on the chief actors, the latent presence of the manorial
dependents becomes for a moment distinctly apprehensible in the prin-
cipals' fear of losing face.

As in the Beckwith raids, the strategies of hunting culture seek to in-
flict maximum harm obliquely. Force and discourse gravitate to the
bodies of deer as a symbolic substitution, vulnerably embodying rival
hunters' desire. The earl follows up his rejection of Degrevant's letter with
a second raid. Both parties amass their manpower in the hunting reserve, one hiding in the woods in ambush. The earl uncouples his braches
and greyhounds "withinne the knyghtus boundus, / bothe the grene and
þe groundus" (250–51), and these impel the harts before them until they
are dragged down or slain at bay. The narrator then sets the stage for Degrevant's retaliation at a high moment in the ritual sequence of the earl's
hunt. The passive bodies of sixty fat deer are laid out upon the laund before the "chief chieftain" that he may examine and receive the kill as
lord of the hunt (257–60), a dignity rightfully owing to Degrevant as owner
of the imparked reserve.[73] Whether or not the animals' bodies have been
broken and opened, the earl's possession of them is as yet imperfect:

> þane seys þe Eorl on þe land,
> "Wher ys now Sir Degreuuand?
> Why wol not com þis gyant
>   To rescow his dere?
> Hys proud hertes of grese
> Bereth no chartur of pes.

> We schall haue som ar we sese,
> Y wold he wer here."
>   (261–68)

This remark underscoring Degrevant's absence (it refers to the message Degrevant's squire bore earlier) ironically but revealingly ascribes a kind of textual agency to the deer. The remark clarifies the stakes of the poaching by troping the deer as members of the rival household; by blurring the distinction between servants and cervines; the earl plays with the idea that Degrevant's people can be forcibly subdued and butchered (and of course eaten) with an air of relative legitimacy. The poaching feud thereby shows its evil genius in the way it imagines the violent symbolic *in-corporation* of one household into another. This may give some indication of just how twistedly the earl subverts the moment. Since the early accounts of the great Carolingian hunts staged in forest reserves, the ceremonial act of presentation and the subsequent distribution of spoils had the effect of a "charter of peace" for all who engaged in the hunt.[74] It is the constitutional act of the hunting community, or fraternity, binding the body politic with a distribution of parts of the bodies of game. As the chief expression here is scorn, and the proper lord of the hunt is excluded from the exchange, it is but one head-of-household feeding off the status of another. When Degrevant breaks forth with his men from the covert of woods and comes on amain to "rescue," as the earl puts it (in the strict sense, forcibly recover), his deer, it is clear that more than just venison is at stake. His people turn the poachers in a rout, driving them through the fenland "as the deer in the den, / to dethe he tham denges" (339–40), turning the trope perforce upon them and ousting them from the hunter position they had acted in before.

The previously interrupted distribution of spoils begins to assume the function of a major motif, for its recurrence marks the critical juncture of the feud and bride-winning patterns. When the next day Degrevant challenges the earl's household to "three courses of war," he is answered by the countess, who appears on the wall with her daughter, Melidor, to attempt an arbitration of the men's dispute. In the very moment of insisting on restitution, Degrevant becomes infatuated with the comely and noble sight of Melidor. She, in turn, begins to harbor a secret affection for him. Retribution nonetheless takes its course, and Degrevant repairs with his people to the woods in order to hunt the earl's reserve. His party hauls down sixty deer with buckhounds; they also draw up pike from the stews and hunt the swans. Then Degrevant punctuates the moment with a gesture striking in its unexpectedness—he tenders to the earl an unspecified number of fee deer of the choicest bucks (L 514–15).[75] The deed is fair, although awkward given the context, and its complexity gives cause for thought. Technically speaking, it is a trespass, but the hunting culture grants it legitimacy as a countering transaction in the economy of the feud. Degrevant's gesture is a noteworthy use of hunting ritual as a means of social control, rendering to the lord of the hunt his due while also violating his authority. In a sense, the act may balance out to the positive, for within the violence of the feud exchange it would force an opposite exchange between hunting men—the bodies of deer as a "charter of peace"—to harness the conflict with a customary act of binding. (The earl, alas, later shows no signs of reading the gesture this way. His actions have already inscribed the bodies of deer with a capacity to mediate attack, and Degrevant's attempt to reconfigure this mediation through an act of exchange goes, on this level at least, without issue.)

During this retributive hunt, the earl's hunting reserve provides a scenario for a nexus of exchange that, in stanza 33 (lines 513–28), heralds a turning point for plot and character. Degrevant is so enamored of Melidor as to find gratification neither in the great slaughter of game nor in perfecting his vengeance on the earl in the terms of the conflict thus far. His deer-killing mirth goes frigid from incipient love agony:

> Bot now hym lyste noght playe,
> To hunt ne to ryvaye,
> For Maydyn Myldor þat may
>   His caris are calde.
> Als he hunted in the chase
> He tolde his sqwyere þe case:
> þat he luffed in a place
>   This frely to falde.
>
>   (L 521–28)

[Now, however, he takes no pleasure in sport either hunting or hawking; because of virgin young Melidor his grief disheartens him. He told his squire of his plight as he hunted in the chase, that somewhere he would like fondly to embrace this lovely woman.]

It is not only in the rhyme scheme that the minstrel is poised to extend the "pley" of hunting to the "may," or to communicate the pleasure of the "chas" to the "place" of love. Degrevant's exchange of deer with the earl coincides with an exchange of his love objects; likewise, the pragmatic logic of hunting and war yields to the erotic ambitions of romance "adventure."[76] In other words, the young protagonist's deer cathexis is exchanged via the violence of honor transactions for a woman of very agreeable estate, rich, beautiful, and ensconced in her father's fortress. Henceforth, hunting proper may disappear from the action, but the paradigm of male desire that the poem has established in the feud may still bear upon the lovers' courtship. As long as we entertain the terms of the men's unresolved quarrel, it appears possible for Degrevant to force an exchange of respective wards and objects of paternal protection—of deer for the daughter—through a long sequence of secret negotiations, a public duel, a clandestine liaison, the eventual destruction of the father's military resources, and finally a marriage. Not that all this can occur against the will of the daughter, for Degrevant's achievements become possible only through Melidor's defiance of her father. But Degrevant's secret entry through the castle wall, into the orchard, and ultimately into Melidor's bedchamber (beginning in stanza 40 and culminating in 86) is a trespass calculated to undermine the paternal authority of the earl in a manner that structurally parallels and thematically develops the trespasses of the first plot sequence.

Hunting reserves lent themselves to association with domestic sanctuaries by virtue of their being imagined as spaces under congruent modes of control. The classic example has its phrasing from the heyday of the royal forests. When Richard fitz Nigel, treasurer of the Exchequer under Henry II, sought to legitimate the arbitrary nature of the king's juridical authority in his hunting reserves, his strategy was to extend the lord's paternal household authority. "The forest has its own laws," he explains in the *Dialogue of the Exchequer,*

> based, it is said, not on the Common Law of the realm, but on the arbitrary legislation of the King; so that what is done in accordance with forest law is not called "just" without qualification, but "just, according to forest law." It is in the forests too that Kings' chambers [*penetralia regum*] are, and their chief delights. For they come there, laying aside their cares now and then, to hunt, as a rest and recreation. It is there that they can put from them the anxious turmoil native to a court, and take a little breath in the free air of nature. And that is why forest offenders are punished only at the King's pleasure.[77]

Obviously much had happened since fitz Nigel's day to mitigate forest law, and private parks and warrens were not protected by it, anyway. Nevertheless, the point of this passage lies in how one dominant discourse could fix the ideological underpinnings of the hunter's authority in the hunting reserve by likening this space of disport to the inner sanctum of the *domus*. By troping blood sport as recreation, the paterfamilias holds sway over both spaces—the hunting reserve and the household—as zones subject to his pleasure. Fitz Nigel's wording also carries a strong connotation of violability. Figuring in epic and biblical contexts, the *penetralia regum* allude to the awesome halls of Priam as these were defiled by the Greeks (*Aeneid* 2.484), as well as to the house of Pharaoh as it was penetrated by the plague of frogs (Psalm 104:30).[78] In fitz Nigel's conception of the law of the hunting reserve, then, poachers are a scourge violating the integrity of spaces ruled by the paterfamilias. The romance plot of *Sir Degrevant* retextualizes this political homology between the daughter's bedchamber and the hunting reserves by rendering them both preeminent targets of trespass. By postponing the composition of the feud in this case beyond the gesture of a venison exchange, the poet exploits a patriarchal logic that includes Melidor's *appartement* within the compass of spaces in which the two men are vying to assert control—the same logic namely that *Sir Gawain and the Green Knight* so shrewdly engages in its parallel of hunt and bedchamber. The environs of Melidor's chamber are in fact surveyed by a forester, who eventually will observe Degrevant's clandestine entry through the wall and report it to the steward (1575–84).[79]

This translocation of action from hunting to bride-winning also carries over to and reconfigures the mediating function of bodies and the distribution of spoils. Soon it is not with deer but with the squire's person that Degrevant tries to "bond" and "charter" a new alliance. He betroths his man with a chartered fee of land to the chambermaid, ostensibly to thank her for a dinner of wild fowl (she has just told him his rank is not high enough to contend with Melidor's suitor), but also to recruit her aid in disarming Melidor's resistance (881–912, 965–76). Her transaction with Degrevant becomes ceremoniously "feudal"—land and marriage in exchange for loyalty—but her answer shows a ready acceptance of "bastard" pragmatism when she overlooks his lavish gesture of thanks and responds, "I take on hand / Þat I shal do þyn errand" (913–14). Nor is the baron now likely to forgo violence in order to connect with his beloved. Melidor remains *daungerous* until Degrevant puts the rival duke of Gerle to acute shame at her father's tournament. Not until Gerle lies "swound" and "stonyd" at the receiving end of Degrevant's prowess does she come forward, and the rebuke she utters over the magnate's belabored body modulates in the next breath to a stunning declaration of succor to her *lemman* (1313–44). We see here, then, how aristocratic desire produces a homology between the bodies of deer and the pacified body of the rival, a body that the rigor of the bride-winning pursuit now invests with the potential to mediate an incipient bond between Degrevant and Melidor. Physical degradation of the duke on the tournament field— veritable "ground for blood to show its quality"[80]—correlatively exalts Degrevant's status and so positions him in a symmetrical relationship with the daughter of an earl. This symmetry then enables Degrevant to enter that same night with welcome into the *penetrale* of her ladyship.[81]

The spoils-of-the-hunt motif recurs when Melidor secretly admits her lover into her once taboo "chaumber of loue" (1439; cf. 797–99). She devotedly feasts him with a shoulder of wild boar, haslet, rabbit, and pheasant (1409–24), diverse fruits of the reserve served up as if to endorse the original violent enterprise that led Degrevant to this sanctuary; as if to say that from killing deer with "glewe," the pursuit comes around to "murþus" with which together "þei sleye care" (1438, 1440). The rich venison here is more than mere food. Melidor's offering of it in this space is a sign of her grace, and thus this fragmentary carnality (pieces of game) can intimate a specific coherence between power and courtly Eros. In one sense the venison figures metonymically for the earl's franchise, for the surplus embodied in lordly hunting reserves that Melidor serves as a reward. This reward, moreover, is just a beginning; her grace converts hunting spoils to signifiers of "fair welcoming," an eroticism to which Degrevant has violently sought access. Suddenly our eyes turn from the repast to explore Melidor's sanctuary, an exquisite tabernacle of her aristocratic imagination. We behold a vaulted interior resplendently inset with icons of biblical and patristic ancients, architectonically reproducing a cosmic hierarchy of heavenly beings and *auctores*, replete with a clock. Our view continues down along the walls showing the carved Worthies of Europe toward the azure canopied bed itself, adorned with parrots, figures of perfect lovers, and choice escutcheons (1441–1520). Thus wanders the gaze of the minstrel-narrator, weaving these images surrounding Melidor's silken bed into a text densely embodying associations of cultural authority with the young noblewoman's own exotic aesthetic of heritage and rank—until man the hunter wants to know when they will make love (1521–28).

The homology between the hunting field and the bedchamber takes narrative shape in this romance through the problems of male desire and control that interlink the poem's plot segments. Without the prospect of erotic interaction, the protagonist's love of hunting promises to thwart his maturation. But the lovers experience their courtship in such an adversarial posture to the earl that their union in a sense sublimates the open violence of poaching and retribution of the feud, so long as that feud goes uncomposed. The narrative strategy of postponing the men's reconciliation increases the daring of Degrevant, builds suspense, and highlights Melidor's autonomy, but it also accentuates her vulnerability. Degrevant's politic question "When wylt þou bryng me to rest?" (1526) expresses a desire for *satisfactio* relevant to both his love agony and the unsettled feud. What if she denies him consummate satisfaction?[82] For the moment this tension is resolved by appealing to the rigor of knightly discipline. Melidor promises Degrevant her body only upon their marriage; in the meantime, she accepts him into her bed to assay his commitment and self-restraint. If anything, the baron's sense of discipline and decorum when he sent the fee deer to the earl prefigures the self-control he must exercise in bed with Melidor. We are left to observe the two lovers bundling together secretly for about a year in a kind of chaste transgression, and postponement begins to assume positive value. The deferred consummation of their love thus validates the spirituality of the chamber, denying a satiation of the flesh that might have followed from a union inaugurated by giving out flesh. If Melidor's embrace of Degrevant in her *penetrale* abets a grievous trespass and so in that sense bears ambivalent regard for the "law of the father," her will to preserve her physical integrity still acknowledges the earl's honor no less than her own. Ultimately, *Sir Degrevant* shares with other medieval romance the narrative fact that, as Susan Crane has pointed out, "courtship appears a secondary formation, a palimpsest text which overwrites masculine relations without fully obscuring them."[83] Melidor promises Degrevant her body, indeed, but not without redirecting her lover's efforts toward winning "my fadirs wyll" (L 1550).

In one sense it would seem that Degrevant's ascendancy is sanctioned by virtue of what the poet evokes as his self-discipline and his rigorous observance of decorum in matters of love as well as of hunting. But it is also in this very ascendancy that the paradigm of the hunt reasserts itself through the way in which the controlling of bodies translates to more or less subtle modes of social control. Melidor, insistently chaste, finally forces the issue between Degrevant and her father the earl by threatening to starve herself—which self-abnegating mediation namely results in a successful reconciliation between the men, a bestowal of the daughter, and hence a massive augmentation of Degrevant's symbolic capital in terms of lordship. The subsequent pomp and transmission of wealth to Degrevant, which the minstrel describes without mention of Melidor, is well addressed by Eve Kosofsky Sedgwick's characterization of the homosocial bond, notably with respect to the schismatic experience of women both as objects of exchange and also as means for the realization of male *couenaunt* (as the poem would phrase it). Poaching and "bride-winning" therefore have much in common, for if homosocial disport in the world of *Sir Degrevant* is "embodied in its heterosexuality," as Sedgwick observes regarding cuckoldry, "its shape is not that of brotherhood, but of extreme, compulsory, and intensely volatile mastery and subordination."[84] The men's truculent feud, for which Degrevant made his rival pay a price high in blood, may seemingly be forgotten as "the ȝorle and he hade keste, / And to chaumber þei wende" (1819–20). Melidor, like the deer, becomes in her transactional agency more and more nondescript. But Degrevant, like the hunter whose project of rational dismemberment is aimed at the productive incorporation of the animal into his own body, inherits the earl's domains upon the latter's timely death, magnifying his own wealth and power as heir such that there "was neuer peres myȝth hym peyr" (1903).

Not unlike the Yorkshire rebellion, therefore, feud-style poaching in *Sir Degrevant* first materializes as acutely violent masculine disport within an institutional space where the symbolic order is attenuated by the absenteeism of the hunting lord. Beyond what could be considered a normative expectation of bloodshed in this space, men assay the limits of legitimate violence, intimidating their rivals (or their rivals' agents) through direct force and through modes of social control such as are available in the discursive constraints of hunting custom. In the case of Knaresborough Chase, the havoc wrought "under color" of hunting could assume violently homosocial dimensions as Beckwith symbolically emasculated his rival in order to interpose himself in a hierarchy of hunters. The most salient feature of the rebellion at the time, however, was counterparliamentary association and the formidable social cohesion occurring among Beckwith's partisans. The game law of 1390 (which I read as cognizant of this conflict and as motivated by an opportunistic desire to determine the social signification of blood sport) comprehends such poaching as a class conflict between two presumably easily distinguishable hunting communities. It ranks the two communities, constructing a broad subculture of laboring-class hunters by imputing to them an inclination to riotous assembly and by stigmatizing their traditional technology (snares and traps). It reinscribes wild animals as the "disport of gentlemen" in order to mediate an alliance between "gentry" property holders and the Crown, and suppresses this subculture by effectively turning all England into one huge hunting reserve. In *Sir Degrevant,* the minstrel-poet imagines poaching to be no less riotous, and yet the elaborate discursive imbrication of sporting privilege, feud law, and honor makes this same violent hunting appear a prime function of high "estate." Deer as the "disport of gentilmen" (a notion that authorized the criminalization of subculture hunting in the game law) become especially multivalent in *Sir Degrevant*: the *furor* of the disport acts as an index of the hunters' gentility, as these men "of quality" vie to determine what is game. People of the household are troped as animals and (perhaps more easily) hunted down like animals in order to serve the vital cultural work of holding the tenants beyond the pale, compassing the women and the deer, and firming up an ambivalent gender and class cohesion in a disport that the fraternity celebrates for its cultural "prepotence."

Notes

I would like to express my thanks to David Wallace, Rita Copeland, and Barbara A. Hanawalt for the generous criticism they have offered me in connection with this project. My thanks are due also to one anonymous reader for the Press.

1. When referring to "forest" throughout this essay, I mean it in the technical sense of a royal hunting reserve (as opposed to woodland or romance wilderness); see Charles R. Young, *The Royal Forests of Medieval England* (Leicester, England: Leicester University Press, 1979); Raymond Grant, *The Royal Forests of England* (Phoenix Mill, England: Alan Sutton, 1991), 3–20. Some type of hunting reserve, evidently restricted to demesne land, is attested for the reign of Canute; see Felix Liebermann, *Die Gesetze der Angelsachsen* (Halle: Niemeyer, 1903), 1:366. Yet, the rights claimed by Canute conform with Scandinavian custom, which is not demonstrably appurtenant to English (or to Roman) law, which had evidently favored the free capture of wild animals ("den freien Tierfang") throughout the country; see Kurt Lindner, *Die Geschichte des deutschen Weidwerks,* vol. 2: *Die Jagd im frühen Mittelalter* (Berlin: Walter de Gruyter, 1940), 150–52, 220–25.

2. Hunting reserves proliferated especially in less arable parts of England; see Leonard Cantor, "Forests, Chases, Parks, and Warrens," in *The English Medieval Landscape,* ed. L. Cantor (Philadelphia: University of Pennsylvania Press, 1982), 56–85, esp. 76–77, 82; and G. J. Turner, ed., *Select Pleas of the Forest* (London: Selden Society, 1901), cix–cxxxiv.

3. Thorstein Veblen, *The Theory of the Leisure Class* (1899; Harmondsworth, England: Penguin, 1994), 18.

4. In medieval England, poaching as an actionable offense chiefly concerned trespass against a franchise of reserved hunting, by which I mean any zone ruled by the principle of hunting *ratione privilegii* as this applied to the royal forests or to private hunting reserves of free chase, free warren, and parks; see Sir William Holdsworth, *A History of English Law,* 3rd ed., 13 vols. (London: Methuen, 1922–32), 7:490–92. If today we recognize many diverse criteria for poaching offenses, this is because changing environmental sensibilities have shaped legislation to accommodate such factors as culturally specific sporting ethics, rationales of game management, or modern proprietary notions of wildlife. Hunting becomes poaching when, for instance, people scorn closed seasons, disregard bag quotas, encroach upon public or private sanctuaries, kill by night, or seize endangered species in order to market parts of their bodies as (like any trophy) a fetishization of wilderness. Medieval criteria for poaching offenses outside of reserves first multiplied with the introduction of "game laws."

5. See Lindner, *Die Jagd im frühen Mittelalter,* 241, 445, and "Zur Sprache der Jäger," *Zeitschrift für deutsche Philologie* 85, no. 3 (1966): 407–31, esp. 429–30.

6. For recent critical work on medieval hunters and their *artes venandi,* see especially John Cummins, *The Hound and the Hawk: The Art of Medieval Hunting* (New York: St. Martin's Press, 1988); and Nicholas Orme, "Medieval Hunting: Fact and Fancy," in *Chaucer's England: Literature in Historical Context,* ed. Barbara Hanawalt (Minneapolis: University of Minnesota Press, 1992), 133–53. For a primary description of the skills required in woodcraft, see George Gascoigne, *Turbervile's Booke of Hunting: The Noble Arte of Venerie or Hunting* (Oxford: Clarendon Press, 1908), 132–35.

7. Cf. for instance the note of Chief Justice Scrope on a quo warranto proceeding against a franchise holder who had no official warrener: "If one neglects his [free] warren and lets it remain without any keeping so that men hunt there without his permission as well as in other lands that are not in warren, and he does not take his greyhounds nor attack them nor bring his actions of trespass against them so that the king can have of them the forfeitures to which he is entitled, that warren will be taken into the king's hand etc."; see Donald W. Sutherland, ed. and trans., *The Eyre of Northamptonshire, 3–4 Edward III, A.D. 1329–30* (London: Selden Society, 1983), 1:125–26. See also Turner, *Select Pleas of the Forest,* cxxv.

8. See James C. Scott, *Domination and the Arts of Resistance: Hidden Transcripts* (New Haven, Conn.: Yale University Press, 1990), 189. See also the excellent study by Roger B. Manning, *Hunters and Poachers: A Social and Cultural History of Unlawful Hunting in England, 1485–1640* (Oxford: Clarendon Press, 1993).

9. Barbara Hanawalt, "Men's Games, King's Deer: Poaching in Medieval England," *Journal of Medieval and Renaissance Studies* 18, no. 2 (1988): 177, 192. Manning's study generally confirms that these tendencies of male violence continued through postmedieval England.

10. Paul Strohm, *Hochon's Arrow: The Social Imagination of Fourteenth-Century Texts* (Princeton, N.J.: Princeton University Press, 1992), 6–8.

11. Cf. Ad Putter, *"Sir Gawain and the Green Knight" and French Arthurian Romance* (Oxford: Clarendon Press, 1995), 48–49.

12. 13 Richard II, stat. 1, c. 58, *Rotuli parliamentorum ut et petitiones, et placita in parliamento* (London, 1767–77), 3:273.

13. For discussions of the game law and its legacy, see Holdsworth, *A History of English Law,* 1:108; 9:543–45; Sir James Fitzjames Stephen, *A History of the Criminal Law in England* (1883; New York: Franklin, 1964), 3:275–77; Ch. Petit-Dutaillis, *Studies and Notes Supplementary to Stubb's Constitutional History* (Manchester: Manchester University Press, 1930), 247–48; Young, *Royal Forests of Medieval England,* 169; and Manning, *Hunters and Poachers,* 57–66.

14. 13 Richard II, stat. 1, c. 19; *Statutes of the Realm* 2:67.

15. See *The Westminster Chronicle, 1381–1394*, ed. and trans. L. C. Hector and Barbara F. Harvey (Oxford: Clarendon Press, 1982), 354–56.

16. Anthony Tuck, *Richard II and the English Nobility* (London: Edward Arnold, 1973), 148.

17. Strohm, *Hochon's Arrow*, 58–65.

18. 13 Richard II, stat. 1, cc. 8–9; *Statutes of the Realm* 2:63.

19. 13 Richard II, stat. 1, c. 13; trans. *Statutes of the Realm* 2:65.

20. See Hanawalt, "Men's Games," 175–93; Jean Birrel, "Who Poached the King's Deer? A Study in Thirteenth-Century Crime," *Midland History* 7 (1982): 19; and Manning, *Hunters and Poachers*, 4–56, 196–232.

21. A battery of measures invented to delimit the freedom of laboring-class association already existed in those laws under Edward III designed to control wages, restrict the practice of multiple trades, and prohibit "alliances and covines," and so on, formed by apprentices to counter the will of their masters (see, e.g., 25 Edw. III, stat. 2, cc. 3–4; 37 Edw. III c. 6; 34 Edw. III c. 9). The controversies of the 1380s over riot, liveries, and guilds gave this discourse free reign. More recently bearing on the context here are the measures of 12 Richard II against the unmonitored passage of laborers and workers overland, prohibiting their carrying weapons, and forbidding them from playing games like tennis, football, coits, dice, and "suche other plaies uncovenable"; *Statutes of the Realm*, 2:57. See also Frances Elizabeth Baldwin, *Sumptuary Legislation and Personal Regulation in England* (Baltimore, Md.: Johns Hopkins Press, 1926), 56–58, 70 f.

22. See John Scattergood, "Fashion and Morality in the Late Middle Ages," in *England in the Fifteenth Century: Proceedings of the 1986 Harlaxton Symposium*, ed. Daniel Williams (Woodbridge, England: Boydell Press, 1987), 255–72, esp. 259–60; and Baldwin, *Sumptuary Legislation*, 47.

23. See Turner, *Select Pleas of the Forest*, ix-xiv.

24. "Le Roy le voet: Ajouste a ycelle, leeces et furettes, haies, rees, hare-pipes, cordes, et toutz autres engynes pur prendre ou destruire savagyne, leveres, ou conylles, ou autre desduit des gentils" (The king assents; and append to this: leash-snares and ferrets, hay-nets, drive-nets, hare-pipes, lines, and all other devices for capturing and killing wild beasts, hares, rabbits, and other game of the gentle); *Rot. parl.*, 3:273.

25. On the other hand, the prescription of a £10 minimum for the clergy is, as it were, on the money; see N. Denholm-Young, *The Country Gentry in the Fourteenth Century: With Special Reference to the Heraldic Rolls of Arms* (Oxford: Clarendon Press, 1969), 23; and Nigel Saul, *Knights and Esquires: The Gloucestershire Gentry in the Fourteenth Century* (Oxford: Clarendon Press, 1981), 225. On the point of class dichotomy with respect to the game law, see Manning, *Hunters and Poachers*, 60.

26. On animals *ferae naturae* considered *res nullius* in England, see Holdsworth, *A History of English Law*, 7:490–93. A problem of recognizing hunting rights reserved *ratione loci*, i.e., by virtue of land possession, arises from the logical implications of specific liberties and prohibitions inscribed in forest and game law; see (besides Lindner, *Die Jagd in frühen Mittelalter*) Richard Kaeuper, "Forest Law," in *A Dictionary of the Middle Ages*, Joseph R. Strayer, gen. ed. (New York: Scribner's, 1985), 5:127–31; and Manning, *Hunters and Poachers*, 61–62. The fact that fallow deer could be hunted in the country at large (outside of forests, chases, and parks, but within zones of free warren, as the buck was not a "beast of warren") is attested by a King's Bench case quoted by Turner, *Select Pleas of the Forest*, cxxvii–viii.

27. As Stephen puts it, the game laws underwrote "the privilege of a class at once artificial and ill defined"; *History of the Criminal Law*, 3:281.

28. See Petit-Dutaillis, *Studies and Notes*, 187–232; Young, *Royal Forests of Medieval England*, 60–73; and Grant, *Royal Forests of England*, 137–42, 150–9.

29. *Statutes of the Realm* 1:111–12.

30. Notwithstanding some monarchs' (and historiographers') untenable attempts to claim universally the country's wild game for the Crown; see Stephen, *History of Crimi-*

nal Law in England, 3:275–77. Attempts to write the common chase out of existence begin with Henry I and continue (ironically enough, given his investment in civil law) with the discourse of Bracton. Cf. Holdsworth, *History of English Law,* 7:490.

31. Sir William Blackstone, *Commentaries on the Laws of England* (1765–69), IV.v.408–9. The emphasis is Blackstone's.

32. Stephen traces the pretext of the game law to 1381 (*History of Criminal Law,* 3:277), as does Manning (*Hunters and Poachers,* 57).

33. Scott, *Domination and the Arts of Resistance,* xii–xiii, 202–3.

34. From the *Historia Anglicana,* in *The Peasants' Revolt of 1381,* ed. and trans. R. B. Dobson (London: Macmillan, 1970), 269–70.

35. "...in signum libertatis et warennae sic adeptae": Walsingham, *Gesta Abbatum Monasterii Sancti Albani,* ed. H. T. Riley, Rolls Series 28, 4 (London: Longmans, Green, 1869), 3:303.

36. Walsingham, *Gesta Abbatum,* 3:318–19, 325, 328.

37. From the *Chronicon Henrici Knighton,* in *Peasant's Revolt,* ed. Dobson, 186.

38. Cited and trans. by Charles Oman, *The Great Revolt of 1381* (Oxford: Clarendon Press, 1969), 75.

39. March 10, 1390; *Calendar of Patent Rolls,* Richard II, vol. 4, 1388–1392 (London, 1902), 270.

40. *Polychronicon Ranulphi Higden manachi Cestrensis,* ed. J. R. Lumby, *Rerum britannicarum medii aevi scriptores,* 41:9 (London: Longman, 1886), 239.

41. J. G. Bellamy, "The Northern Rebellions in the Later Years of Richard II," *Bulletin of the John Rylands Library* 47 (1964–65): 254–74, esp. 260–61.

42. *Westminster Chronicle,* 442–43. Bellamy, "Northern Rebellions," 255, states that perhaps Beckwith's claim concerned the chief office of Bilton Park.

43. *Westminster Chronicle,* 442; *Calendar of Patent Rolls, 1392–96* (London, 1905), 273; *Polychronicon Ranulphi Higden,* 239; Bellamy, "Northern Rebellions," 256.

44. Bellamy, "Northern Rebellions," 261; see also 256, 260.

45. See Anthony Goodman, *John of Gaunt: The Exercise of Princely Power in Fourteenth-Century Europe* (New York: Longman, 1992), 332.

46. This "parliament" was "held at divers times of the year, in subversion of the law and oppression of the people, disinherison of the said duke [of Lancaster] and loss of life of his ministers"; *Calendar of Patent Rolls, 1392–96,* 273.

47. Ibid., passim.

48. Ibid., 551.

49. Ibid. These together bore the value of 40s.

50. Ibid., 552.

51. Bellamy, "Northern Rebellions," 258.

52. The boundaries of a "free chase" were somewhat more abstract than a park, which was enclosed. A chase could be likened to a royal forest inasmuch as it tended to overlie lands not belonging to the owner of the chase, thus revoking the hunting rights of landholders on these lands. It could be defined as conceptually different from a forest, as, e.g., with respect to the holder's claims on the vert, or timber and fallwood (see the quo warranto writ in Sutherland, ed., *Eyre of Northamptonshire,* 142). But if, on the other hand, the chase derived from an alienated forest through disaforestment, it might maintain some of the old administrative elements under the control of its latter owner (see Holdsworth, *History of English Law,* 1:100; Grant, *Royal Forests,* 30–31; and Turner, *Select Pleas of the Forest,* cix–cxv).

53. Goodman, *John of Gaunt,* 332, 358.

54. Cf. Pierre Bourdieu, *Outline of a Theory of Practice,* trans. Richard Nice (Cambridge: Cambridge University Press, 1990); *Language and Symbolic Power,* ed. John B. Thompson, trans. Gino Raymond and Matthew Adamson (Cambridge, Mass.: Harvard University Press, 1991), esp. 230; L. D. Wacquant, "Towards a Reflexive Sociology: A Workshop with Pierre Bourdieu," *Sociological Theory* 7 (1989):37–41.

55. See R. Cunliffe Shaw, *The Royal Forest of Lancaster* (Preston, England: Guardian Press, 1956), 29–33, 187; and Paul Stamper, "Woods and Parks," in *The Countryside of Medieval England*, ed. Grenville Astill and Annie Grant (Oxford: Blackwell, 1988), 128–48, esp. 140–47.

56. Bellamy, "Northern Rebellions," 261.

57. See Scott, *Domination*, esp. 183–201.

58. Ibid., 191. The emphasis is Scott's.

59. *Westminster Chronicle*, 442.

60. See Birrel, "Who Poached the King's Deer?" and Hanawalt, "Men's Games"; see also E. P. Thompson, *Whigs and Hunters: The Origin of the Black Act* (New York: Pantheon, 1975); Douglas Hay, "Poaching and the Game Laws on Cannock Chase," in *Albion's Fatal Tree: Crime and Society in Eighteenth Century England*, ed. Douglas Hay et al. (New York: Pantheon, 1975); P. B. Munsche, *Gentlemen and Poachers: The English Game Laws, 1671–1831* (Cambridge: Cambridge University Press, 1981); and Manning, *Hunters and Poachers*.

61. See Leonard Cantor, "Forests, Chases, Parks, and Warrens," 77, and Manning, *Hunters and Poachers*, 123–24.

62. The following discussion is indebted to the basic schema offered by Scott, *Domination*, 198.

63. This section refers to the edition prepared by L. F. Casson, *The Romance of Sir Degrevant: A Parallel-Text Edition from Mss. Lincoln Cathedral A.5.2 and Cambridge University Ff.I.6* (EETS, o.s., 221, [1949] 1970); citations, unless otherwise noted by the prefix L (the Thornton MS, Lincoln Cathedral A.5.2), are from C (Cambridge MS Ff.i.6).

64. As a son of the Scottish King Lothian, he is thus brother of Gawain and nephew to Arthur and Guinevere through his mother Queen Belisant. For this identification, Casson (*Sir Degrevant*, 116) leads evidence in support of J. O. Halliwell, the poem's first editor.

65. See the *Middle English Dictionary*, s.v. "spit(e)," n (2a); *Oxford English Dictionary*, s.v. "Spite," 2. William I. Miller's discussion of the role of envy in heroic action is instructive in this context; see *Humiliation: And Other Essays on Honor, Social Discomfort, and Violence* (Ithaca, N.Y.: Cornell University Press, 1993), 124–27.

66. See Howard Kaminsky, "Estate, Nobility, and the Exhibition of Estate in the Later Middle Ages," *Speculum* 68, no. 3 (1993): 684–709 (689 and passim). The quotation "soziale Einschätzung der Ehre" is from Max Weber's definition of "estate" in *Wirtschaft und Gesellschaft*, quoted by Kaminsky, 688 n. 14.

67. The earl's methods are indicative of what Roger B. Manning has described as a praxis common to what he calls the "deer-hunting culture." This, in brief, is a sphere of cultural activity in which the chief actors are predominantly "of gentry status or higher" and much given to the posturing of the warrior, in that "violence [in the form of poaching] and the readiness to resort to it to defend a code of honour helped to define a person of noble or genteel status and indicates a continuing disposition to actions outside the law and independent of the state"; see *Hunters and Poachers*, 232.

68. Here I return to J. G. Bellamy, although at a different site: *Bastard Feudalism and the Law* (Portland, Ore.: Areopagitica Press, 1989), 34–56. While these acts were illegal by common law, they could be accepted in equity judgments (so long as they did not amount to felony) as qualified means of land recovery. The crucial factor, the one that English juries considered with favor in granting entitlement to land, was to what extent forced entry, occupation, and distraint conformed to time-honored practices of lordship. Proof of legal seisin could be established by having tenants surrender their rents to the entrant, holding the manor court, selling or burning the woods, taking fealty, letting farms, dismissing the bailiff, and freeing unfree tenants; Bellamy, *Bastard Feudalism*, 43.

69. Ibid., 51 and 47, respectively.

70. See Bruce Lincoln, *Discourse and the Construction of Society: Comparative Studies of Myth, Ritual, and Classification* (New York: Oxford University Press, 1989), 4–5.

71. See John M. MacKenzie, *The Empire of Nature: Hunting, Conservation and British Imperialism* (Manchester: Manchester University Press, 1988).

72. Cf. *Piers Plowman* (B.VI.30–33), where Piers exhorts the knight to protect Holy-church from wasters and to go hunt the deer and boar that wreck his hedges or the wild-fowl that crops his wheat.

73. On this point, cf. the Porter MS (English) text of Master William Twiti's hunting treatise, which gives a finely differentiated protocol for the distribution of rights issuing from a stable hunt in the forest, but then states that "in parke may no man aske no fee but al at þe will of þe lord"; William Triti, *The Art of Hunting, 1327*, ed. Bror Danielsson (Stockholm: Almqvist & Wiksell, 1977), 58. Whereas in the forest or a chase the lord's huntsman must claim the lord's fee of head and neck by winding his horn, in the park the lord has all discretionary rights to control the distribution of fees.

74. See Janet Nelson "The Lord's Anointed and the People's Choice: Carolingian Royal Ritual," in *Rituals of Royalty: Power and Ceremonial in Traditional Societies*, ed. David Cannadine and Simon Price (New York: Cambridge University Press, 1987), 169.

75. Thus the unambiguous reading of L: "He sent þe Erle of þe best" (515). The reading of C, "temede þe Eorl on þe beste," has given editors difficulty (see Casson, ed., *Sir Degrevant*, 126). In specifically legal and religious usage it is congruent with the sense of L, where *temede* could be read as "vouched" or "honored" (*MED*, s.v. "temen," v [1] 2), but records do not show a perfectly idiomatic match with use of the preposition *on*. C and L both use the third-person plural present indicative form of *temen* at line 1110 in the sense of "empty": þe temes sadel ful tyte (C) (*MED*, "temen," v [2]), but this is even less likely here. For lack of fuller documentation, the safest reading of C, although it is at odds with the sense of L, may be *temien*, "to tame, subdue (the pride of)" (*MED*).

76. As in the romances of Tristan, Erec, or Ipomedon, the transition from hunting to bride-winning underwrites a maturing process in which the training and vigor of the male youth enables his passage into a complex domain of more overtly erotic interaction; see Marcelle Thiébaux, *The Stag of Love: The Chase in Medieval Literature* (Ithaca, N.Y.: Cornell University Press, 1974), 109; and Rooney, *Hunting in Middle English Literature*, 93–96.

77. Richard fitz Nigel, *Dialogus de Scaccario* 1.2, 23, ed. and trans. Charles Johnson, 2nd ed. F. E. L. Carter and D. E. Greenway (Oxford: Oxford University Press, 1983), 59–60.

78. Johnson notes these references to Virgil and to the Vulgate Bible without interpretation in his first edition.

79. This correlation was long-lived in the minds of those holding hunting reserves. One anonymous eighteenth-century sportsman, for example, made a very similar connection, although on the grounds of sentiment, when he commented on the sporting liberties of the gentry: "To many gentlemen of property, I am persuaded that the affection to their paternal fields is next in degree to the love of their friends and family, or the partner of their bed. What man of sense or sensibility would form a contract of copartnery in the article of wives, or allow to every one of his neighbours all rights and privileges with his spouse, because he had the same with theirs?"; from *Considerations on the Game Laws in Answer to a Pamphlet Intitled, The Present State of the Game Law...* (Edinburgh, 1772), 35–36, quoted by Hay in "Poaching and the Game Laws," 216.

80. V. G. Kiernan, *The Duel in European History: Honour and the Reign of the Aristocracy* (Oxford: Oxford University Press, 1988), 154.

81. I adapt here Eve Kosofsky Sedgwick's notion of fictional symmetry as it bears on the mediation of triangular relationships, reading for the moment in terms of fictional class symmetry rather than gender; see Sedgwick, *Between Men: English Literature and Male Homosocial Desire* (New York: Columbia University Press, 1985), esp. 28–48.

82. On the threat of rape posed by "man the hunter," see Arthur Brittan, *Masculinity and Power* (Oxford: Blackwell, 1989), 102.

83. Susan Crane, *Gender and Romance in Chaucer's Canterbury Tales* (Princeton, N.J.: Princeton University Press, 1994), 39.

84. See Sedgwick, *Between Men*, 66.

Contributors

❖

Christopher Cannon is a Fellow of Saint Edmund Hall and lecturer in English at Oxford University. He is the author of *The Making of Chaucer's English* (forthcoming) and is currently at work on a book about early Middle English literature.

Elizabeth Fowler is assistant professor of English at Yale University. Her work on the category of the person has appeared in *Speculum, Spenser Studies,* and *Representations* and is forthcoming as a book, *The Arguments of Person.* Fowler is also the coeditor, with Roland Greene, of *The Project of Prose in Early Modern European and New World Writing.*

Louise O. Fradenburg is professor of English at the University of California, Santa Barbara. She is the author of *City, Marriage, Tournament: Arts of Rule in Late Medieval Scotland,* the editor of *Women and Sovereignty,* and the coeditor, with Carla Freccero, of *Premodern Sexualities.*

Claude Gauvard teaches medieval history and is the director of the School of Doctoral Studies in History at the Sorbonne (Paris-I). She is also a member of the University Institute of France. Among her many publications is *La France au Moyen Age, du Ve au XVe siècle.*

Barbara A. Hanawalt is professor of history at the University of Minnesota. Her many books include *Crime and Conflict in Medieval England, 1300–1348, The Ties That Bound: Peasant Families in Medieval England,* and *Growing Up in Medieval London: The Experience of Childhood in History.* Hanawalt is also the editor of numerous books, the most recent of which is *Bodies and Disciplines: Intersections of Literature and History in Fifteenth-Century England* (Minnesota, 1996).

James H. Landman teaches English at the University of North Texas. He is currently developing a book that will explore intersections between the legal and literary cultures of late medieval England.

William Perry Marvin teaches medieval literature in the Department of English at Colorado State University.

William Ian Miller teaches law at the University of Michigan. While his research once focused on saga Iceland, he has recently become interested in virtues, vices, and the emotions that attend moral and social failure. Miller is the author of *Bloodtaking and Peacemaking: Feud, Law and Society in Saga Iceland*, *Humiliation*, and *The Anatomy of Disgust*.

Louise Mirrer is vice-chancellor for academic affairs at the City University of New York and professor in Hispanic and Luso-Brazilian Literatures and Medieval Studies at the CUNY Graduate Center. She is the author of, among other works, *Women, Jews, and Muslims in the Texts of Reconquest Castile*, *The Language of Evaluation: A Sociolinguistic Approach to the Story of Pedro el Cruel in Ballad and Chronicle*, and the editor of *Upon My Husband's Death: Widows in the Literature and Histories of Medieval Europe*.

Walter Prevenier is professor at the University of Ghent (Belgium). He is also the president of the Commission Internationale de Diplomatique and a member of the Institute for Advanced Study at Princeton.

David Wallace is Judith Rodin Professor of English at the University of Pennsylvania. His most recent book is *Chaucerian Polity: Absolutist Lineages and Associational Forms in England and Italy*, and he is currently editing *The Cambridge History of Medieval English Literature*.

Index

⁜

Compiled by Jonathan Good

MEDIEVAL CULTURES